The Concise Animal Encyclopedia

KINGFISHER
a Houghton Mifflin Company imprint
222 Berkeley Street
Boston, Massachusetts 02116
www.houghtonmifflinbooks.com

First published as *The Kingfisher Illustrated Animal Encyclopedia*
by Kingfisher Publications Plc 2000

Reprinted in a revised format by Kingfisher Publications Plc 2003
4 6 8 10 9 7 5 3

3TR/0206/C&C/*RDSOT(RNB)/157MA

LIBRARY OF CONGRESS CATALOGING-IN-PUBLICATION DATA
has been applied for.

ISBN 0-7534-5590-0
ISBN 978-07534-5590-6

Printed in China

Cover design by Jo Brown

FOR BOOKWORK
Project editor Louise Pritchard
Assistant editor Annabel Blackledge
Art editor Jill Plank
Assistant designer Yolanda Belton
Picture researcher Alan Plank

FOR KINGFISHER
Project editor Katie Puckett
Managing editor Miranda Smith
Art editor Mike Davis
Artwork research Christopher Cowlin
Artwork archivists Wendy Allison, Steve Robinson
DTP coordinator Nicky Studdart
DTP operator Primrose Burton
Production controller Jacquie Horner
Indexer Sylvia Potter

THE CONCISE
ANIMAL
ENCYCLOPEDIA

WRITTEN BY DAVID BURNIE

KINGFISHER

BOSTON

CONTENTS

Bluebottle
(Calliphora vomitoria)

Red piranha
(Serrasalmus nattereri)

Oyster drill
*(Ocenebra
erinacea)*

Common
periwinkle
*(Littorina
littorea)*

Common frog
(Rana temporaria)

Fire salamander
(Salamandra salamandra)

REPTILES

Eurasian robin
(Erithacus rubecula)

Common iguana
(Iguana iguana)

MAMMALS

BIRDS

Giraffe
(Giraffa camelopardalis)

INTRODUCTION

OUR PLANET IS HOME TO A VAST AND VARIED COLLECTION
OF ANIMALS. THEY LIVE EVERYWHERE, FROM THE TOPS OF
MOUNTAINS TO THE DEPTHS OF THE SEA, AND THEY HAVE
ALL DEVELOPED THEIR OWN METHODS OF SURVIVAL.

A nimals are all around us, so it is easy to think that we know exactly what animals are. But the animal kingdom is amazingly varied. Some animals have fur or feathers; others have shells or scales; many have no hard body parts at all. Animals often have eyes, ears, and legs, but there are many creatures that survive perfectly well without them. Many small animals spend most of their lives fastened to one place, and some microscopic ones can even survive being dried out or frozen solid.

Despite their differences, all animals share three key features. First, unlike the simplest living things, which are only a single cell, animals' bodies are made of many cells. These cells work together to carry out the different functions necessary for survival. Second, unlike plants, animals need to eat. Food is their fuel, and many animals cannot survive for long if this fuel supply begins to run out.

Finally, animals are the only living things that have muscles and nerves. These enable animals to move their bodies and to sense their surroundings. Animals with more sophisticated nervous systems, such as mammals and birds, react more quickly than other living things. Using their well-developed brains, they can keep track of what is happening around them and make split-second decisions to catch food or escape from danger.

Shield bug
(Sehirus bicolor)

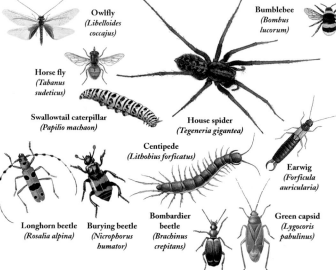

Owlfly
(Libelloides coccajus)

Horse fly
(Tabanus sudeticus)

Swallowtail caterpillar
(Papilio machaon)

Bumblebee
(Bombus lucorum)

House spider
(Tegeneria gigantea)

Centipede
(Lithobius forficatus)

Earwig
(Forficula auricularia)

Longhorn beetle
(Rosalia alpina)

Burying beetle
(Nicrophorus humator)

Bombardier beetle
(Brachinus crepitans)

Green capsid
(Lygocoris pabulinus)

HOW MANY ANIMALS?

When scientists first began to classify animals (see pages 8–11), they thought that there might be several thousand different kinds on earth. Since then, they have found that animal life is far richer than anyone had imagined. Already, more than two million types of animals have been discovered and classified. The true total will probably never be known, but some scientists think it could be 30 million, or even as high as 100 million.

Mammals and birds make up only a small proportion of this huge figure. Although they are spread all over the globe and are often large and conspicuous, they are outnumbered many times over by much smaller animals, such as insects, spiders, and worms. One bucketful of garden soil can contain more than a million minute roundworms; throughout the world, there are many trillions of these tiny creatures. However, because animals like these are small and difficult to see, we hardly notice them.

ABOVE *Chinchillas* (Chinchilla laniger) *live on rocky slopes on high mountains. Their thick fur helps keep them warm in the harsh climate.*

FITTING IN

Most animals are extremely particular about where they live. For example, brine shrimp always live in salty lakes, while blue morpho butterflies live in tropical rain forests. These homes are called habitats, and they provide everything that an animal needs to survive.

Like animals themselves, habitats are remarkably diverse. They include grasslands and forests, deserts and mountains, caves and the deep seabed. Some animals even live inside others—a living habitat that provides shelter and food.

In each habitat, animals have special features that help them survive. They may have strong legs for running or jumping, or poisonous stingers for defense or killing their prey. They behave in a particular way that is suitable for living in that habitat.

All these features develop through evolution, which works through a process called natural selection. This ensures that parents with the features most useful for survival produce the most young. As a result, the useful features become more common, and each species slowly changes, or evolves, over time. Evolution began over three and a half million years ago, at the dawn of life on earth, and is still continuing today.

ANIMALS IN DANGER

During earth's long history, evolution has produced many new types of animals. At the same time, many species have become extinct. In nature, extinction is a rare event, but in recent times, it has become much more common.

Some of the world's largest and most impressive animals, such as the tiger, the black rhinoceros, and the giant panda, are now so rare that they are endangered. In just 10 or 20 years' time, they may survive only in zoos. Many other animals will be seriously at risk if their numbers continue to fall.

Animals are in danger for many reasons, most of which are caused by humans. People collect animals as pets and hunt them for food and sport. People take over and destroy animals' habitats, leaving them with nowhere to live. We must protect the animals we have left, before it is too late.

ABOVE *Illegal hunting and a shrinking habitat have threatened the tiger* (Panthera tigris), *and the numbers left in the wild are diminishing rapidly.*
LEFT *Like many marsupials, the quokka* (Setonix brachyurus) *has been harmed by artificial changes to its habitat.*

CLASSIFICATION

WHEN STUDYING LIVING THINGS, SCIENTISTS ORGANIZE, OR CLASSIFY, THEM INTO GROUPS. THE GROUPS SHOW HOW LIVING THINGS ARE RELATED BY EVOLUTION AND WHERE THEY BELONG IN THE NATURAL WORLD.

On these two pages, you can see how scientists classify a single animal, the European green treefrog. The diagram below shows all the groups to which the frog belongs, from the most general to the most specific. The most general groups are called kingdoms, and the most specific are called species. Most biologists classify living things into five kingdoms, but classification can change as new discoveries are made.

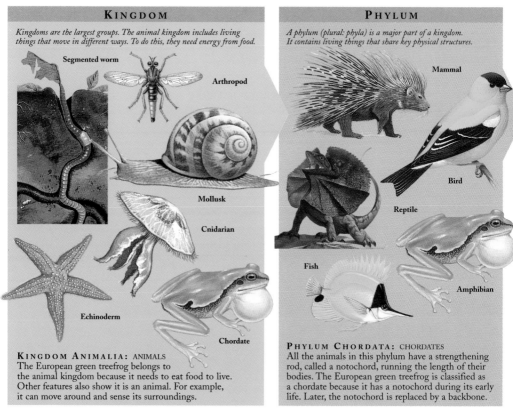

KINGDOM

Kingdoms are the largest groups. The animal kingdom includes living things that move in different ways. To do this, they need energy from food.

Segmented worm

Arthropod

Mollusk

Cnidarian

Echinoderm

Chordate

KINGDOM ANIMALIA: ANIMALS
The European green treefrog belongs to the animal kingdom because it needs to eat food to live. Other features also show it is an animal. For example, it can move around and sense its surroundings.

PHYLUM

A phylum (plural: phyla) is a major part of a kingdom. It contains living things that share key physical structures.

Mammal

Bird

Reptile

Fish

Amphibian

PHYLUM CHORDATA: CHORDATES
All the animals in this phylum have a strengthening rod, called a notochord, running the length of their bodies. The European green treefrog is classified as a chordate because it has a notochord during its early life. Later, the notochord is replaced by a backbone.

KINGDOMS OF THE LIVING WORLD

MONERANS

Monerans include bacteria and other kinds of microscopic life. They are the smallest living things, as well as the simplest and the toughest. Monerans were the first living things on earth.

PROTISTS

Like monerans, protists have just a single cell, but they are larger and more complicated. This kingdom includes protozoans—tiny creatures that behave like animals—and creatures that behave more like plants.

FUNGI

Fungi live on living things or their dead remains, growing tiny threads that spread through their food. Most fungi are microscopic, but some are easy to see because they grow mushrooms and toadstools when they reproduce.

PLANTS

Unlike monerans and protists, plants are made of many cells. Plants do not eat food to survive; instead, they use the energy they capture from sunlight to produce the substances they need. Plants are essential for animal life because they provide animals with food. If there were no plants, almost all the world's animals, including meat-eaters, would soon become extinct.

ANIMALS

The animal kingdom contains living things that have many cells and eat food. This kingdom is more varied than any of the other four, and it contains more species than all the others put together. Because animals do not need sunlight to survive, they can live in a great range of habitats, including caves, mountains, and the ocean depths.

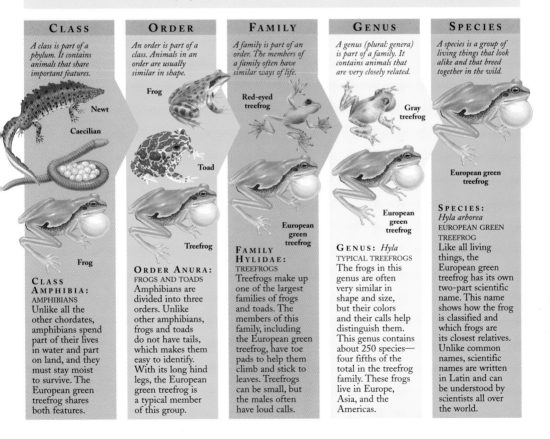

CLASS

A class is part of a phylum. It contains animals that share important features.

Newt

Caecilian

Frog

CLASS AMPHIBIA:
AMPHIBIANS
Unlike all the other chordates, amphibians spend part of their lives in water and part on land, and they must stay moist to survive. The European green treefrog shares both features.

ORDER

An order is part of a class. Animals in an order are usually similar in shape.

Frog

Toad

Treefrog

ORDER ANURA:
FROGS AND TOADS
Amphibians are divided into three orders. Unlike other amphibians, frogs and toads do not have tails, which makes them easy to identify. With its long hind legs, the European green treefrog is a typical member of this group.

FAMILY

A family is part of an order. The members of a family often have similar ways of life.

Red-eyed treefrog

European green treefrog

FAMILY HYLIDAE:
TREEFROGS
Treefrogs make up one of the largest families of frogs and toads. The members of this family, including the European green treefrog, have toe pads to help them climb and stick to leaves. Treefrogs can be small, but the males often have loud calls.

GENUS

A genus (plural: genera) is part of a family. It contains animals that are very closely related.

Gray treefrog

European green treefrog

GENUS: *Hyla*
TYPICAL TREEFROGS
The frogs in this genus are often very similar in shape and size, but their colors and their calls help distinguish them. This genus contains about 250 species— four fifths of the total in the treefrog family. These frogs live in Europe, Asia, and the Americas.

SPECIES

A species is a group of living things that look alike and that breed together in the wild.

European green treefrog

SPECIES:
Hyla arborea
EUROPEAN GREEN TREEFROG
Like all living things, the European green treefrog has its own two-part scientific name. This name shows how the frog is classified and which frogs are its closest relatives. Unlike common names, scientific names are written in Latin and can be understood by scientists all over the world.

THE ANIMAL KINGDOM

On these two pages you can see how all of the animals in this book fit into the animal kingdom. Each "folder" contains a distinct group of animals, and the folders are arranged to show which groups are most closely related. On this page, you can find out about invertebrates—animals that do not have backbones. On the opposite page are vertebrates and their relatives.

Subphylum

Class

Phylum

SIMPLE ANIMALS
(Several phyla)
Animals without heads or specialized sense organs, such as sponges, rotifers, and moss animals. Some are microscopic, while others are easily visible with the naked eye.

CNIDARIANS
(Phylum Cnidaria)
Animals with baglike or bell-shaped bodies and mouths that are surrounded by stinging tentacles. Most of them live in the ocean. They include jellyfish, sea anemones, and corals.

FLATWORMS
(Phylum Platyhelminthes)
Animals that have paper-thin, flat bodies with no legs. They move by sliding or swimming. Most flatworms live in water or damp places, but some live inside other animals.

ROUNDWORMS
(Phylum Nematoda)
Worms with cylindrical bodies covered by a hard outer "skin." Roundworms live in a wide variety of habitats, including in soil and inside other living things.

SEGMENTED WORMS
(Phylum Annelida)
Worms with bodies that are divided into rings, or segments. They include earthworms and many other species found in soil or in fresh or salt water.

MOLLUSKS
(Phylum Mollusca)
Animals with soft bodies, often with a shell. They include snails, scallops, and octopuses. Most live in water or damp places.

ECHINODERMS
(Phylum Echinodermata)
Sea animals with bodies that are divided into five identical parts. They include starfish, sea urchins, and sea cucumbers. They live in water, from the shallows to the greatest depths.

ARTHROPODS
(Phylum Arthropoda)
Animals that are covered by a body case, or exoskeleton, and that have several pairs of rigid, jointed legs. Arthropods live in almost every habitat on earth.

CRUSTACEANS
(Subphylum Crustacea)
Arthropods that have two pairs of antennae. Crustaceans include crabs, lobsters, shrimp, and wood lice. A few live on land, but most live in water.

CHELICERATES
(Subphylum Chelicerata)
Arthropods that have a body divided into two parts and that feed with mouthparts called chelicerae. Unlike other arthropods, they do not have antennae.

ARACHNIDS
(Class Arachnida)
Animals that have four pairs of walking legs. Arachnids include spiders, scorpions, ticks, and mites. Most of them live on land.

SEA SPIDERS
(Class Pycnogonida)
Animals with narrow bodies and slender legs that live in the ocean. Like true spiders, they have small mouths, and they usually have four pairs of legs.

HORSESHOE CRABS
(Class Merostomata)
Sea animals with horseshoe-shaped bodies and long tails. They live in shallow coastal water, often coming ashore to lay their eggs.

UNIRAMIANS
(Subphylum Uniramia)
Arthropods that have a single pair of antennae and pairs of unbranched legs. Most uniramians live on land, although some species live in fresh water.

CENTIPEDES AND MILLIPEDES
(Class Myriopoda)
Long-bodied arthropods with hard exoskeletons and many pairs of legs. Centipedes have one pair of legs per body segment; millipedes have two pairs.

INSECTS
(Class Insecta)
Animals that have three pairs of legs and often have two pairs of wings. This class of animals contains more species than any other.

CHORDATES
(Phylum Chordata)

Animals that have a reinforcing rod called a notochord running the length of their bodies. The notochord works as an internal support to anchor the muscles that make the body move. Like all the animals on the opposite page, the simplest chordates do not have backbones. However, most chordates have a backbone that forms part of a complete internal skeleton.

SIMPLE CHORDATES
(Subphyla Urochordata and Cephalochordata)

Chordates that have a notochord, but not a backbone. They include lancelets, sea squirts, and jellylike animals that drift in the ocean. They all live in water.

VERTEBRATES
(Subphylum Vertebrata)

Chordates with a backbone and a complete internal skeleton. Compared to most other animals, vertebrates are intelligent, with well-developed nervous systems and large brains.

JAWLESS FISH
(Class Agnatha)

Fish with eellike bodies, jawless, suckerlike mouths, and scaleless skin. They include lampreys, which often feed on living fish, and hagfish, which eat dead remains. Unlike cartilaginous and bony fish, jawless fish do not have paired fins.

CARTILAGINOUS FISH
(Class Chondroichthyes)

Fish with skeletons that are made of cartilage instead of bone. They have rough skin and stiff fins. They include sharks, skates, and rays. Most of them live in the sea.

BONY FISH
(Class Osteichthyes)

Fish that have bony skeletons and skin that is usually covered by thin, overlapping scales. Bony fish live in all kinds of watery places, from freshwater ponds to the deep sea, and they are the most numerous vertebrates on earth. They usually lay eggs that are fertilized in the water.

AMPHIBIANS
(Class Amphibia)

Animals that live partly in water and partly on land, and that change shape as they mature. Amphibians include frogs, toads, salamanders, newts, and caecilians. As adults, they are all predators, hunting other animals for food.

REPTILES
(Class Reptilia)

Animals with scaly skin that live on land or in water. They include lizards, crocodiles, and snakes. Most lay eggs, but some give birth to live young.

BIRDS
(Class Aves)

Warm-blooded animals that have wings, toothless beaks, and bodies covered with feathers. Most birds can fly, but several kinds are flightless. All birds lay eggs, and many feed their young.

MAMMALS
(Class Mammalia)

Warm-blooded animals with fur or hair that feed their young on milk. Most mammals develop inside their mothers' bodies or in a special pouch, but a small number hatch from eggs. Most mammals have legs, but some have flippers or wings, allowing them to swim or fly.

SIMPLE ANIMALS

THE FIRST ANIMALS EVOLVED FROM SINGLE-CELLED ORGANISMS CALLED PROTOZOANS ABOUT ONE BILLION YEARS AGO. TODAY'S ANIMALS ARE MADE UP OF MANY CELLS AND TAKE IN FOOD TO LIVE.

Amoeba

Cell nucleus

Cilia

Pseudopod

Cell nucleus

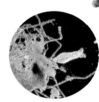

Rotifer

Above *A microscopic rotifer clings to strands of algae in a pond.*
Above center
A paramecium has just one cell, which is controlled by its nucleus.
Above right *An amoeba's cell changes shape to move. It flows forward, putting out lobes called pseudopods, or "false feet."*

Paramecium

Many kinds of protozoans still exist today, and almost all of them live in water. The simplest animals also dwell in water. Unlike protozoans, their bodies contain large numbers of cells. Many of them have complex body parts to help them move and catch their food. Most simple animals can be seen only under a microscope, but some, such as sponges, are large enough to be seen with the naked eye.

AMOEBA

Composed of only one cell, amoebas are protozoans with no fixed shape. Some build tiny shells, but many have no hard parts at all and look like microscopic blobs of jelly. An amoeba moves by making part of its cell flow in the direction it wants to travel. The rest of the cell slowly follows. To feed, an amoeba flows around other microorganisms and then engulfs them. To reproduce, it simply divides itself into two cells.

SCIENTIFIC NAME	*Amoeba* and other genera
DISTRIBUTION	Worldwide
SIZE	Up to 0.03 in. (0.8mm) long

PARAMECIUM

This tiny, slipper-shaped protozoan is common in lakes, ponds, and puddles. It moves constantly and speeds along by beating rows of microscopic hairs, called cilia, which work like miniature oars. *Paramecium* feeds on bacteria and other microorganisms, sweeping them into its groove-shaped mouth.

SCIENTIFIC NAME	*Paramecium* species
DISTRIBUTION	Worldwide
SIZE	About 0.006 in. (0.15mm) long

TRICHOPLAX

This is probably the simplest animal in the world. It lives in seawater and looks like a tiny pancake composed of many cells. It creeps over rocks, digesting any algae it finds on them. Although it is more complicated than a protozoan, *Trichoplax* does not have specialized organs. It was discovered in 1883 in an aquarium in Austria and was orginally thought to be an animal larva.

SCIENTIFIC NAME	*Trichoplax adhaerens*
DISTRIBUTION	Unknown
SIZE	About 0.1 in. (3mm) across

ROTIFER

Also known as wheel animals, rotifers are common in rivers, lakes, puddles, and gutters. They are among the smallest existing animals. Rotifers feed on protozoans and other tiny life-forms, which they catch by beating a crown of cilia to draw water into their mouths. In dry times, rotifers are dormant. Once in this state, they can stay inactive for many years.

SCIENTIFIC NAME	*Rotifera* and other genera
DISTRIBUTION	Worldwide
SIZE	About 0.01 in. (0.25mm) across

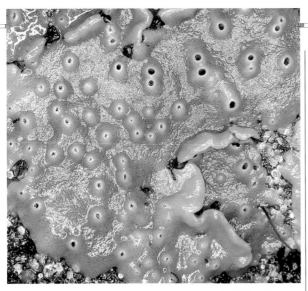

LEFT *The surface of a crumb of bread sponge looks like a volcano-studded landscape. Each of the "volcanoes" pumps out water that the sponge has filtered for food.*

CRUMB OF BREAD SPONGE

Most sponges have a skeleton made of tiny slivers of minerals and can grow into a variety of shapes. The crumb of bread sponge is an encrusting species, which means that it forms in flat mats over rocks. It gets its name because it crumbles into small pieces if touched. Like all sponges, it feeds by sucking water through small openings on its surface. After filtering the water for food, it then pumps it back out of larger openings.

SCIENTIFIC NAME	*Halichondria panicea*
DISTRIBUTION	Atlantic Ocean, Mediterranean Sea, Pacific Ocean
SIZE	Up to 8 in. (20cm) across

Sponge

INVERTEBRATES

More than 97 percent of animal species are invertebrates. An invertebrate is any animal that does not have a backbone. Some are soft-bodied, but others are protected by a shell or body case. Invertebrates were the first animals to appear on earth, and they live in habitats ranging from caves and the deep seafloor to the slopes of the highest mountains. There is a huge variety of invertebrates, some of which are shown here.

Jellyfish

SPONGES

Unlike other invertebrates, sponges have a skeleton made of microscopic slivers of minerals.

CNIDARIANS

Jellyfish and other cnidarians have bodies made of two layers of cells. All cnidarians live in water, and many can sting.

Earthworm

SEGMENTED WORMS

Like many invertebrates, earthworms and their relatives have a body divided into repeated units, or segments.

Beetle

ARTHROPODS

Insects, such as beetles, and other arthropods have an all-over body case made of hard plates that meet at flexible joints.

WATER BEAR

These minute animals live mainly in puddles and small freshwater pools. They have barrel-shaped bodies and clamber around on eight stubby legs, a little like a bear. Water bears, also called tardigrades, feed on the juices of mosses and other plants, and sometimes on other animals. They need moisture to stay active but can curl up and hibernate for up to 25 years if their habitat dries out. A water bear in this drought-resistant state is called a tun.

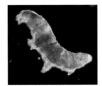

Water bear under a microscope

SCIENTIFIC NAME	*Macrobiotus* and other genera
DISTRIBUTION	Worldwide
SIZE	Up to 0.04 in. (1mm) long

MOSS ANIMAL

Also known as bryozoans, moss animals are found in both fresh and salt water. They use tiny tentacles to collect particles of food. Instead of moving around, moss animals live in clusters of boxlike cases. In some species, these cases form flat sheets that attach to shells and seaweed. The cases of other varieties look like plant leaves spreading out in the water. These clusters are sometimes washed up on beaches after storms.

SCIENTIFIC NAME	*Membranipora* and other genera
DISTRIBUTION	Worldwide
SIZE	Typical cluster about 4 in. (10cm) high

CNIDARIANS

THESE WATER-DWELLING ANIMALS HAVE
A HOLLOW OR BELL-SHAPED BODY AND A
MOUTH THAT IS RINGED BY TENTACLES. THEY
INCLUDE JELLYFISH, SEA ANEMONES, AND
CORALS, AS WELL AS LESS FAMILIAR ANIMALS
SUCH AS SIPHONOPHORES AND SEA PENS.

Common jellyfish

Sea pen

There are about 10,000 species of cnidarians. A few are found in fresh water, but most live in the sea. A cnidarian's tentacles are highly sensitive and are armed with a battery of stinging cells called nematocysts. If the tentacles brush against something edible, microscopic, poison-tipped threads explode out of the nematocysts and into the prey.

ABOVE *The exposed tip of a sea pen is crowded with stinging polyps along two sides of a central "stem."*
ABOVE RIGHT *A moon jellyfish has four violet reproductive organs in the center of its "bell."*
RIGHT *A Portuguese man-of-war preys on fish and other sea animals.*

SEA PEN

Portuguese man-of-war

The sea pen looks like an old-fashioned quill pen, which is how it got its name. A sea pen consists of many separate animals, called polyps, that live in a group. The lower part of a sea pen is anchored in sand or mud. The upper part contains feeding polyps, which use their tentacles to catch drifting food. Some sea pens are more than 5 ft. (1.5m) high, but most are smaller than this.

SCIENTIFIC NAME	*Pennatula* and other genera
DISTRIBUTION	Worldwide
SIZE	Typical colony 16 in. (40cm) high

PORTUGUESE MAN-OF-WAR

With its gas-filled float, the Portuguese man-of-war drifts great distances in the wind, like a miniature sailboat. Although it looks like a jellyfish, it is actually a siphonophore—a floating collection of cnidarians living together. One forms the float, while others sting, digest food, or reproduce. The man-of-war's poisonous tentacles trail beneath the float as it drifts along and can be up to 66 ft. (20m) in length. Their powerful stings can kill people who get tangled up in them.

SCIENTIFIC NAME	*Physalia physalis*
DISTRIBUTION	Warm seas worldwide
SIZE	Up to 12 in. (30cm) across

MOON JELLYFISH

Like most jellyfish, this blue species pushes itself through the water by contracting its bell-shaped body. Seawater is sucked into the "bell" and forced back out, propelling the jellyfish through the water. These jellyfish are weak swimmers and are often stranded on beaches by the tide. The moon jellyfish attacks small fish using

LEFT *Dwarfed by their much bigger parent, young beadlet anemones stretch out their tentacles to feed. If they get too crowded, beadlet anemones may fight. This helps them space themselves out in their rocky home.*

BY-THE-WIND SAILOR

Like the Portuguese man-of-war, this animal is blown along by the wind. It has short tentacles, a flat, air-filled float, and a single, upright "sail." By-the-wind sailors feed on small sea animals, and often drift in swarms that can be over 62 miles (100km) wide. In the tropics, they are often blown ashore, and millions can be seen on a single beach.

SCIENTIFIC NAME *Velella velella*

DISTRIBUTION Warm seas worldwide

SIZE Up to 3 in. (8cm) across

By-the-wind sailor floating on the water

SEA GOOSEBERRY

Although they are similar in appearance to jellyfish, sea gooseberries are not cnidarians. They belong to a group of animals called ctenophores. They have round, jellylike bodies and two long, slender tentacles, which they trail in the water to catch food. Sea gooseberries move by beating tiny hairs, or cilia, which are arranged in comblike rows along their bodies. If they are disturbed—by being touched or shaken, for example—they produce flashes of light that are visible several yards away.

SCIENTIFIC NAME *Pleurobrachia* and other genera

DISTRIBUTION Worldwide

SIZE Typical length 1 in. (2.5cm), excluding tentacles

Sea gooseberry flashing its light

TOP *This surface view of a by-the-wind sailor shows its vertical sail and cluster of hanging tentacles.*
ABOVE *Sea gooseberries look beautiful in the water, but when they are hauled out, they become shapeless blobs of jelly.*

stinging tentacles that trail from the edge of its "bell." It pulls the paralyzed prey into its mouth using larger, frilly tentacles. Its stings are painful, though not dangerous to humans.

SCIENTIFIC NAME *Aurelia aurita*

DISTRIBUTION Atlantic Ocean, Indian Ocean, Pacific Ocean, Mediterranean Sea

SIZE Up to 12 in. (30cm) across

AUSTRALIAN BOX JELLYFISH

Australian box jellyfish start life in shallow water near river mouths. During the rainy season, they are swept along the coast, often past places where people swim. This medium-sized jellyfish is so poisonous that swimmers can die within minutes of becoming entangled in its tentacles. Unfortunately, it is transparent, which makes it difficult to see. Box jellyfish got their name from the shape of their bodies, which are cubic rather than bell-shaped. When their tentacles are stretched out, they can measure up to 6 ft. (2m) in length.

SCIENTIFIC NAME *Chironex fleckeri*

DISTRIBUTION Indian Ocean, Pacific Ocean

SIZE Up to 10 in. (25cm) across

BEADLET ANEMONE

Many sea anemones look more like colorful plants than animals. Some anchor themselves in the sand, but most, like the beadlet anemone, spend their lives fastened to something solid—usually rock. They use their stinging tentacles to catch small animals swimming nearby. The beadlet anemone lives on the part of the shore that is often exposed at low tides, but it is expert at surviving out of the water. When the tide goes out, it pulls in its tentacles and fills its body cavities with water. This stops it from drying out when it is exposed to the air.

SCIENTIFIC NAME *Actinia equina*

DISTRIBUTION Atlantic Ocean, Mediterranean Sea

SIZE Up to 2.75 in. (7cm) high

Staghorn coral

ABOVE *This staghorn coral* (Acropora nasuta) *form dense underwater "forests" that shelter a wide variety of animals. Like the coral itself, many of these animals feed at night.*

STAGHORN CORAL

Corals consist of tiny, soft-bodied animals called polyps, which often live in large groups called colonies. In reef-building species, such as staghorn corals, the polyps make hard, chalky cases to protect themselves. These cases, cemented together, form a reef. New polyps can grow from buds, but corals also reproduce by shedding eggs into the sea. Coral polyps feed on drifting larvae and other tiny animals, which they catch with their stinging tentacles. They also get food from microscopic algae that live inside their cells. The shape of a coral colony depends on the way the polyps grow. Staghorn coral colonies branch repeatedly and look like a stag's antlers, which is how the corals got their name. Staghorn corals are fragile and usually grow in sheltered parts of a reef.

SCIENTIFIC NAME	*Acropora* species
DISTRIBUTION	Tropical seas worldwide
SIZE	Up to 3 ft. (1m) high

RED CORAL

Unlike most corals, which have brightly colored polyps set in a chalky-white skeleton, red coral has white polyps set in a black, pink, or red skeleton. It grows on the shady seafloor, in water up to 650 ft. (200m) deep.

SCIENTIFIC NAME	*Corallium rubrum*
DISTRIBUTION	Mediterranean Sea
SIZE	Up to 20 in. (50cm) high

BRAIN CORAL

With its round, deeply grooved surface, this slow-growing coral looks like a giant brain. It is formed by rows of polyps, with their tentacles arranged along the sides of the rows and their mouths forming a groove along the bottom. The coral's domed shape makes it strong enough to withstand pounding waves.

SCIENTIFIC NAME	*Symphyllia* and other genera
DISTRIBUTION	Tropical seas worldwide
SIZE	Up to 6 ft. (2m) across

MUSHROOM CORAL

This coral consists of a single polyp and lives in sandy places on the seabed. Its tentacles point upward to catch small animals that come within reach. Adult mushroom corals can move and, if upturned in a storm, can right themselves.

SCIENTIFIC NAME	*Fungia* species
DISTRIBUTION	Indian Ocean, Pacific Ocean
SIZE	Up to 10 in. (25cm) across

Orange sea fan coral (Synchiropus splendidus)

Tentacles extended

Tentacles withdrawn

Golden tubastrea coral (Tubastrea aurea)

CORAL REEFS

Some corals can live in cool, dark water, but reef-building species need water that is bright, warm, and clean. As these corals grow and die, their hard cases build into a pile that eventually forms a reef. The world's largest reef is the Great Barrier Reef off the coast of Queensland in Australia. It is about 1,250 miles (2,000km) long and is the largest object ever built by living things. Coral reefs support a wide variety of sea life, including sponges and certain fish that are immune to the corals' stings. The reefs provide food and some protection from predators.

FLATWORMS AND ROUNDWORMS

Tail sections full of eggs

A WORM IS ANY LONG, SOFT-BODIED ANIMAL WITHOUT LEGS. MANY WORMS SPEND THEIR LIVES IN WATER OR IN SOIL, BUT OTHER SPECIES ARE PARASITES THAT LIVE ON OR IN OTHER LIVING THINGS.

Flatworms are the simplest worms. They have a flat body, which can be paper thin. This group includes parasitic tapeworms and flukes as well as free-living species. Roundworms, or nematodes, have a cylindrical body. Many of them are parasites; they can live in a wide range of animal hosts.

DOG TAPEWORM

Tapeworms are highly specialized flatworms that live parasitically inside a variety of animals, including human beings. The dog tapeworm has a small, round head equipped with several rows of hooks. Its ribbon-shaped body is divided into as many as 150 sections, each one containing thousands of eggs. The tapeworm uses its hooks to fasten itself to the inside of a dog's intestines and lives by absorbing some of the food that the dog eats. As the tapeworm feeds, sections near the end of its body break away, carrying their eggs with them. New sections form behind the worm's head. Dog tapeworm eggs hatch if they are eaten by flea larvae. If a dog eats an infected flea, it becomes infected with tapeworms.

SCIENTIFIC NAME *Dipylidium caninum*
DISTRIBUTION Worldwide
SIZE Up to 20 in. (50cm) long

LIVER FLUKE

A fluke is a small, parasitic flatworm that feeds on the blood or body of its host. The sheep liver fluke attacks sheep and cattle and can also infect people, making them seriously ill. Sheep liver flukes spread when their eggs are eaten by a pond snail. The eggs hatch into larvae, which eventually leave the snail. If they are eaten by a sheep, they migrate to its liver, where they grow into adult flukes. Humans can catch liver flukes by eating the improperly cooked meat of an infected animal.

SCIENTIFIC NAME *Fasciola hepatica*
DISTRIBUTION Worldwide
SIZE About 0.8 in. (2cm) long

CAT ROUNDWORM

Roundworms are threadlike worms with a slender body and a pointed mouth. The largest parasitic species, which live in whales, are up to 30 ft. (9m) long, but most are much smaller. The cat roundworm lives in the intestines of cats. It passes from one cat to another when its eggs are eaten—usually in contaminated soil. Like its close relative the dog roundworm, it can hatch inside humans. This is dangerous, so hygiene is important around pet cats and dogs.

SCIENTIFIC NAME *Toxocara cati*
DISTRIBUTION Worldwide
SIZE Up to 6 in. (15cm) long

Tapeworm

Sheep liver fluke

Roundworms

TOP *Tapeworms do not have eyes or mouths. They absorb all their food through their skin.*
CENTER *Sheep liver flukes have a flattened body and a branching digestive system, which is clearly visible in their bodies.*
ABOVE *Adult cat roundworms live in a cat's intestines, but the young can live elsewhere in its body.*

SEGMENTED WORMS

WORMS WHOSE BODIES ARE DIVIDED INTO
RINGS OR SECTIONS ARE KNOWN AS
SEGMENTED WORMS, OR ANNELIDS. THEY
INCLUDE EARTHWORMS AND MANY SPECIES
THAT LIVE IN FRESH WATER OR IN THE OCEAN.

RIGHT
*These feather
dusters have
extended their
tentacles to collect
food from the water.*

Segmented worms usually have bristles along their bodies, but some also have flaps that look like small legs. They move by wriggling or by changing the shape of their segments. There are at least 13,000 species of segmented worms. Some roam in search of food, but many live in permanent tubes or burrows, collecting any edible thing that they find.

LEFT *Earthworms
have tiny bristles along
their bodies that help
them push their way
through the ground.*

COMMON EARTHWORM
Earthworms are some of the most useful animals on earth. As they tunnel into the ground, they swallow particles of soil and digest any dead remains that they contain. In damp weather, they drag dead leaves underground and feed on them. All this helps to aerate the soil and keep it fertile. Common earthworms are at their most active in warm, wet weather, when they crawl to the surface to mate. Each worm has both male and female reproductive organs.

SCIENTIFIC NAME	*Lumbricus terrestris*
DISTRIBUTION	Originally from Europe, but introduced into many other parts of the world
SIZE	Up to 12 in. (30cm) long

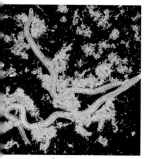

ABOVE *Sludge worms get
their bright red color from
hemoglobin, a substance
that helps them absorb
oxygen. Humans also have
hemoglobin in their blood.*

PALOLO WORM
The palolo worm lives in coral reefs and spends most of its life hidden in crevices. To reproduce, it grows a special tail section packed with sperm or eggs. On one night each year, the tail sections of all palolo worms break away and wriggle to the surface of the water. At dawn, the sections burst apart, the floating eggs are fertilized, and the worm's life cycle starts anew.

SCIENTIFIC NAME	*Eunice viridis*
DISTRIBUTION	Pacific Ocean
SIZE	Up to 16 in. (40cm) long

SLUDGE WORM
These worms live in clusters on the bottom of ponds and streams. They burrow into the mud and live upside down, waving their bodies in the water to collect oxygen. They are so efficient at collecting oxygen that they can thrive in polluted water, where oxygen levels are low.

SCIENTIFIC NAME	*Tubifex tubifex*
DISTRIBUTION	Europe, Asia, North America
SIZE	About 1.5 in. (4cm) long

MEDICINAL LEECH
Leeches are segmented worms that live in wet places and often feed on blood. Their bodies are flattened, with a sucker at each end, which they use to move and to cling to animals while they feed. A feeding leech produces a substance that keeps blood from clotting. At one time, doctors used medicinal leeches to "bleed" patients regularly, believing that blood loss could improve people's health.

SCIENTIFIC NAME	*Hirudo medicinalis*
DISTRIBUTION	Europe
SIZE	Up to 6 in. (15cm) long

FEATHER DUSTER

This animal looks more like a flower than a worm. It lives under water in a tube of mud and sand, which sticks up from the seabed. To feed, it extends delicate tentacles from the top of the tube, trapping any edible particles that drift within its reach. If the feather duster's feathery tentacles are touched, or if a shadow passes over it, it will vanish into the tube.

SCIENTIFIC NAME *Sabella pavonina*

DISTRIBUTION Atlantic Ocean, Mediterranean Sea

SIZE Up to 10 in. (25cm) long, including tube

Leaf being dragged into the soil

CLAM WORM

These worms live in seacoast mud. They wriggle along with the help of leglike flaps, searching for shrimp and other small animals to eat. Unlike earthworms, clam worms have powerful jaws, and large ones can bite through human skin. Like lugworms, these animals are important for birds such as curlews, which have long beaks adapted for probing the mud or sand for their food.

SCIENTIFIC NAME *Nereis diversicolor*

DISTRIBUTION Atlantic Ocean, Mediterranean Sea

SIZE Up to 5 in. (12cm) long

Clam worm

Common earthworm in underground tunnel

Iridescent hairs

SEA MOUSE

Despite its name, this animal is not a mouse but a worm with an unusual appearance. Its body is covered with long bristles that look like golden-green fur, and it has short, stumpy flaps that work like feet. The sea mouse lives in shallow seawater. It burrows its way through the sediment, feeding on small, soft-bodied animals, including other worms.

SCIENTIFIC NAME *Aphrodita aculeata*

DISTRIBUTION Atlantic Ocean, Mediterranean Sea

SIZE About 4 in. (10cm) long

LUGWORM

Like many other seacoast worms, the lugworm lives in muddy sand. It builds a U-shaped burrow, strengthened with a lining of mucus, with two openings at the surface. The worm draws sand into the burrow through one opening. It digests any food in the sand, then ejects it through the other opening. At low tide, piles of mud show where these worms have been at work.

SCIENTIFIC NAME *Arenicola marina*

DISTRIBUTION Atlantic Ocean

SIZE Up to 8 in. (20cm) long

Lugworm

LEFT *Clam worms and lugworms both live on muddy coasts, but only the lugworm burrows.*
BELOW *The sea mouse lives on coasts, near the low-tide mark.*

MOLLUSKS

AFTER ARTHROPODS, MOLLUSKS MAKE UP
THE SECOND LARGEST GROUP OF
INVERTEBRATES, WITH MORE THAN 50,000
SPECIES. ALL MOLLUSKS HAVE A SOFT
BODY, BUT MANY ARE PROTECTED
BY A HARD OUTER SHELL.

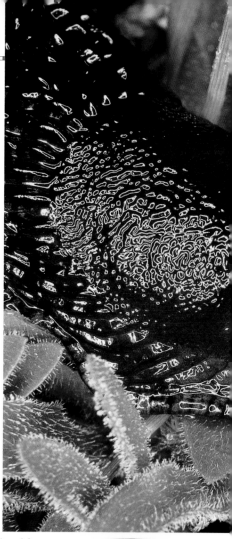

There are many varieties of mollusks. Some live on land, but the majority live in fresh water or in the ocean. Mollusks include many small and slow-moving species, as well as the largest, fastest, and most intelligent animals in the invertebrate world.

CHITONS AND TOOTH SHELLS

These two small groups of mollusks contain animals that live in very different ways. A chiton clings to rocks with a single, sucker-shaped foot and is the only mollusk with a shell made of eight separate plates. A tooth shell lives partly buried in the seabed, in deep or shallow water. Its pointed shell looks like a tiny elephant's tusk and has an opening at each end. There are about 800 species of chitons and 350 species of tooth shells.

PURPLE OR GREEN CHITON
Despite its colorful shell plates, this European chiton is well camouflaged for life on rocky coasts. It moves slowly, grazing algae from the surface of rocks. The chiton's muscular sucker usually keeps it firmly in place, but if it does fall off a rock, it can curl up to protect itself.

SCIENTIFIC NAME *Acanthochitona crinatus*

DISTRIBUTION Atlantic Ocean, Mediterranean Sea

SIZE Up to 0.5 in. (1.3cm) long

EUROPEAN TOOTH SHELL
Tooth shells are the only mollusks with a tubular shell. The European tooth shell makes its home in deep water, so living animals are rarely seen, but empty tooth shells are often found washed up on the shore. The tooth shell anchors itself to the ocean floor with a single, cone-shaped foot, which it can also use to pull itself into the sand to escape predators. Like other tooth shells, it feeds by probing the sand with 100 or more small tentacles. When a tentacle touches a particle of food, the animal uses it to pull the food toward its mouth.

SCIENTIFIC NAME *Dentalium entalis*

DISTRIBUTION Atlantic Ocean, Mediterranean Sea

SIZE About 1 in. (2.5cm) long

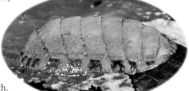

ABOVE
The green chiton is no bigger than a fingernail, but some of its relatives are more than 12 in. long.

SHELLS

Mollusks build their shells from the mineral calcium carbonate. The shell is produced by a soft organ called the mantle and grows throughout the mollusk's life. Gastropods have a one-piece shell. As the animals grow, they extend their shell outward to form, in many species, a spiral shape around a central pillar. Bivalves (pages 26–29) have a two-piece shell joined together by a hinge. In living mollusks, the outside of the shell may be covered by a thin, darker layer of material that protects it from acids in the surrounding water. In most species, the inside of the shell is smooth and shiny. It is made of a material called nacre, or mother-of-pearl.

Shell of a Roman snail (Helix pomatia)

Thick coating of slime

GASTROPODS

A gastropod is a mollusk with a single, suckerlike foot, and often a coiled or pointed shell. Four fifths of the world's mollusks are gastropods. They feed on plants and animals using a mouthpart called a radula, which is packed with rows of tiny teeth. As the teeth at the front are worn away, newer ones take their place. Gastropods begin life as eggs. When land-dwellers hatch, they look like small adults. Water-dwelling gastropods hatch as larvae and change as they grow.

Two pairs of tentacles

Garden snail on the move

GREAT BLACK SLUG

Most slugs do not have shells. They move over the ground on a layer of slippery mucus, leaving a shiny trail. The great black slug has a varied diet that includes rotting vegetation and the dead bodies of other slugs. It finds its food by touch and smell, using its sensitive tentacles.

SCIENTIFIC NAME *Arion ater*

DISTRIBUTION Europe

SIZE Up to 6 in. (15cm) long

ABOVE *Like other land slugs, the great black slug has a breathing hole on its side, just behind its head.*
BELOW *Sliding on a layer of mucus, the banana slug can reach a top speed of only 0.004 mph.*

BANANA SLUG

This yellow or green slug is the largest land mollusk in North America. It lives in coniferous rain forests and other damp, shady places, where it feeds on fungi and decaying plants. Banana slugs lay about 100 eggs each year and can live for five years.

SCIENTIFIC NAME *Ariolimax columbianus*

DISTRIBUTION Northwestern North America

SIZE Up to 8 in. (20cm) long

GARDEN SNAIL

Across Europe, and in places where it has been accidentally introduced, this snail is a serious pest. At night or after heavy rain, it rasps its way through soft-stemmed plants. During dry weather, it shuts itself up inside its shell, sealing off the opening with a "door" made of dried mucus. Like most slugs and snails, garden snails have both male and female reproductive organs, so any two snails can mate. They lay clusters of milky-colored eggs that are left to develop in the soil.

SCIENTIFIC NAME *Helix aspersa*

DISTRIBUTION Originally from Europe, but introduced to many other parts of the world

SIZE Body up to 3 in. (8cm) long

GIANT AFRICAN SNAIL

This mollusk is the world's largest land-dwelling snail. It can weigh more than 1.75 lb. (800g), and its shell may measure up to 8 in. (20cm) long. The giant African snail has been introduced to other warm countries, sometimes as a source of food. It has now become one of Southeast Asia's most destructive agricultural pests.

SCIENTIFIC NAME *Helix aspersa*

DISTRIBUTION Originally from Europe, but introduced to many other parts of the world

SIZE Body up to 3 in. (8cm) long

Common limpet shell

Common periwinkle shell

COMMON LIMPET

Limpets live on exposed coastal rocks, where they are battered by the full force of the waves. Their shells are conical instead of coiled, making them extremely strong. When the tide is out, limpets clamp their shells tightly to the rock, but at high tide they loosen their grip and wander over the surface of the rock to feed. Using their microscopic teeth, they scrape away tiny seaweeds and other algae, roving up to 3 ft. (1m) from their home. When the tide goes out, they return to the exact spot from which they started.

SCIENTIFIC NAME	*Patella vulgata*
DISTRIBUTION	Atlantic Ocean, Mediterranean Sea
SIZE	Shell up to 2 in. (5cm) across

RED ABALONE

Abalone shells coil in an unusual way. As the shell grows, it spirals outward very quickly, so most of the shell consists of a single shallow turn. It has a series of holes that the animal uses for breathing, and the inside surface is covered in a layer of shimmering mother-of-pearl. The red abalone is one of the largest species. It was once an important source of food for Native Americans living on the coast.

SCIENTIFIC NAME	*Haliotis rufescens*
DISTRIBUTION	West coast of North America
SIZE	Shell up to 10 in. (25cm) long

ABOVE *This abalone's head is hidden beneath the top edge of its shell.*
BELOW *Like many sea snails, the common whelk has a long tube, or siphon, through which it draws in water over its gills.*

COMMON PERIWINKLE

Periwinkles live on rocky shores, where they feed on seaweed and plant remains. At low tide, crowds of them shelter in rocky crevices. Like other water-dwelling gastropods, common periwinkles have a hard flap, called an operculum, at the back of their foot. When the periwinkle withdraws into its shell, the operculum fits over the entrance, sealing the creature inside.

SCIENTIFIC NAME	*Littorina littorea*
DISTRIBUTION	Atlantic Ocean, Mediterranean Sea
SIZE	Shell about 1 in. (2.5cm) high

COMMON WHELK

Whelks live on the ocean floor in water up to 330 ft. (100m) deep, feeding on the remains of dead animals. Common whelks lay large clusters of eggs, and their empty egg cases are often washed up onto the shore. Females can produce more than a million eggs, but only a few of them hatch. The rest are food for the developing young.

SCIENTIFIC NAME	*Buccinum undatum*
DISTRIBUTION	Atlantic Ocean
SIZE	Shell up to 5 in. (12cm) long

Ridged shell

Operculum seals the shell when the whelk is inside

Siphon

Suckerlike foot

Sensory tentacle

TURRET SNAIL

The turret snail has a shell that turns much more tightly than most. Its shape resembles a castle tower, which is how it got its name. It lives on the seabed, buried up to the tip of its shell in sand or mud, and feeds by filtering small particles of food from the water. Turret snails are abundant, and when they die, their empty shells are often washed up onto the shore. Different varieties live throughout the world's oceans, even in places where the water is very cold. *Turritella communis* lives as far north as Iceland, in the icy waters of the North Atlantic Ocean.

SCIENTIFIC NAME *Turritella communis*

DISTRIBUTION Atlantic Ocean, Mediterranean Sea

SIZE Shell up to 2 in. (5cm) high

Oyster drill shell   Turret snail shell

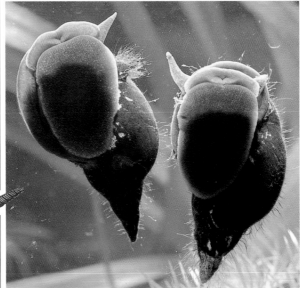

OYSTER DRILL

Although this rough-shelled mollusk looks harmless, it is a patient and very efficient predator. It attacks oysters, using its microscopic teeth to bore a small hole through their shells. This can take up to a week. After the oyster drill has broken through the tough shell of its victim, it feeds on the soft flesh inside. Unable to move, the oyster has no way of escaping or fighting back.

SCIENTIFIC NAME *Ocenebra erinacea*

DISTRIBUTION Atlantic Ocean, Mediterranean Sea

SIZE Shell about 2 in. (5cm) high

VIOLET SEA SNAIL

This remarkable mollusk is one of the world's great oceanic travelers. It lives in the tropics and drifts far out to sea, suspended upside down beneath a mass of bubbles made of mucus. Violet sea snails feed on other drifting animals, such as the by-the-wind sailor (page 15). Their empty shells are often thrown up onto beaches after they die, but because they are thin, they easily break.

SCIENTIFIC NAME *Ianthina ianthina*

DISTRIBUTION Warm seas worldwide

SIZE Shell up to 0.8 in. (2cm) high

GREAT POND SNAIL

Most water-dwelling mollusks get oxygen from the water using organs called gills. The great pond snail is an exception: it has a lung and breathes air. Great pond snails feed on microscopic algae and animal remains and are almost always found in still water. Like land snails, they have both male and female reproductive organs. Pond snails fasten their eggs to the leaves of underwater plants.

SCIENTIFIC NAME *Lymnaea stagnalis*

DISTRIBUTION Europe, Asia, North America

SIZE Shell up to 2 in. (5cm) high

ABOVE *Pond snails are useful in aquariums. They scrape algae from the glass, helping to keep it clean.*

LEFT *The violet sea snail is practically unsinkable because the bubbles of its "raft" harden soon after they form.*

QUEEN CONCH

When it is fully grown, a queen conch can weigh up to 4 lb. (2kg). Protected by its massive shell, it lives on the seabed in shallow water, feeding mainly on seaweed. Like all conchs, it has a hard plate that can seal it into its shell. It can also use this plate to pull itself across the ocean floor. Queen conchs were once common, but their numbers have been reduced by people who kill them to collect their shells.

SCIENTIFIC NAME *Strombus gigas*

DISTRIBUTION Caribbean Sea

SIZE Up to 9 in. (23cm) long

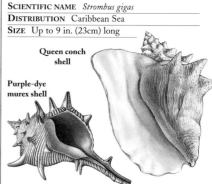

Queen conch shell

Purple-dye murex shell

PURPLE-DYE MUREX

There are many species of murex, some with spiny or branching shells. Most live close to the shore or on coral reefs, where they feed on animals, including other mollusks. The purple-dye murex gets its name from a dye that can be extracted from its body. During the days of the Roman Empire, the dye was used to stain clothes purple—a color reserved for the emperor and other high-ranking officials.

SCIENTIFIC NAME *Murex brandaris*

DISTRIBUTION Mediterranean Sea

SIZE Up to 2.75 in. (7cm) long

TEXTILE CONE SHELL

Most gastropod mollusks are harmless, but cone shells are a deadly exception. They feed on fish and other animals, stabbing them with poisonous, harpoonlike mouthparts. A hollow tooth at the tip of the harpoon injects the prey with venom and is replaced each time it is used. The textile cone shell's venom is poisonous enough to kill humans who are stung. There are more than 500 species of cone shells. Most live in coral reefs or in sand near the shore.

SCIENTIFIC NAME *Conus textile*

DISTRIBUTION Indian Ocean, Pacific Ocean

SIZE Up to 3.5 in. (9cm) long

ABOVE *A tiger cowrie crawls across submerged rocks close to the shore. Its frilly tentacles help it find algae and small animals to eat.*

TIGER COWRIE

Cowries live mainly in tropical seas. Their shells have a long, slit-shaped opening on the underside and a shiny upper surface with beautiful markings. The tiger cowrie is one of the largest species. Its milky-colored shell is dappled with brown spots. People have collected cowrie shells for centuries and, in the past, have used some species as a form of money. A cowrie's shiny surface is not always visible on the live animal because it is often hidden by the mantle—the thin body layer that encloses the shell.

SCIENTIFIC NAME *Cypraea tigris*

DISTRIBUTION Indian Ocean, Pacific Ocean

SIZE Up to 3.5 in. (9cm) long

SEA SLUG

Slow-moving sea slugs are among the most colorful animals in the sea. They do not have shells, but their bright colors warn other animals that they are dangerous to attack. One reason for this is that they eat cnidarians (pages 14–16), and their skin stores stinging cells from their prey. If an animal tries to eat a sea slug, the stinging cells fire into its body. Sea slugs are most common in the tropics. *Chromodoris quadricolor* is common on Red Sea coral reefs, where many other eye-catching species are found.

SCIENTIFIC NAME *Chromodoris quadricolor*

DISTRIBUTION Red Sea, Indian Ocean

SIZE About 2 in. (5cm) long

Sensory tentacles

Brightly colored gills

ABOVE *Unlike land slugs, sea slugs do not have lungs. Instead, they breathe through tuftlike gills on their backs.*

BELOW *Sea hares often form lines to breed, each animal fertilized by the one behind. The sea hare in front has laid a string of eggs on the rocky ocean floor.*

Egg strings up to 65 ft. long

SEA BUTTERFLY

These mollusks feed on algae or small animals. They live in the open ocean and often form huge swarms close to the surface that can stretch for many miles. Like other gastropod mollusks, sea butterflies have a single foot, but the foot has two winglike flaps that the animals beat to push themselves along. Some sea butterflies have shells, but many do not. *Clione limacina* is one of the most common species. Its body is almost transparent, with a yellow tinge.

SCIENTIFIC NAME *Clione limacina*

DISTRIBUTION Arctic Sea, northern Atlantic Ocean, northern Pacific Ocean

SIZE Up to 0.8 in. (2cm) long

SEA HARE

The sea hare has a thin, fragile shell that is hidden inside its humped body. It can move in two different ways. It can either creep along using its muscular foot or swim by moving the flaps that fold over its back. The sea hare eats algae, and substances from its food give it its color.

SCIENTIFIC NAME *Aplysia punctata*

DISTRIBUTION Atlantic Ocean

SIZE Up to 5.5 in. (14cm) long

Narrow flaps of skin along the back

BIVALVES

There are about 15,000 species of bivalves, including mussels, oysters, and clams. Almost all live in water. Unlike gastropods, their shells are made up of two halves, called valves, hinged with an elastic ligament. Most bivalves have strong muscles that can tighten to lock their valves, securing them inside. Many spend their adult lives fixed in one place, and breed by releasing reproductive cells into the water. They use gills to breathe and to filter food from the water around them.

RIGHT *This common mussel has opened its shell to feed. The mussel pumps water through two short, flattened siphons. One siphon sucks in the water, and the other squirts it out.*

COMMON MUSSEL

Like most bivalves, the common mussel starts life as a tiny larva drifting in the water. The larva eventually settles on a rock, where it slowly grows to adulthood. Once it is on a solid surface, the mussel produces a sticky liquid that turns hard in water. The hardened liquid produces a collection of tough threads, called a byssus, which fixes the mussel in place. When the tide is high, mussels filter food from the surrounding water. At low tide, when they are exposed to the air, they keep their shells tightly shut. Mussels usually live on rocks in exposed places where the currents bring plenty of food their way.

SCIENTIFIC NAME	*Mytilus edulis*
DISTRIBUTION	Worldwide
SIZE	Up to 3 in. (8cm) long

FILTER FEEDING

Bivalves are not the only animals that live by filtering their food from the water. Other filter-feeding invertebrates include rotifers, sponges, and many sea-dwelling worms. These animals all have body parts that work like sieves to collect small particles of food.

Blue whale (*Balaenoptera musculus*)

Some vertebrates feed in a similar way. Instead of teeth, many whales have long, fringed plates of baleen, a horny substance, along their upper jaws. These enable the whale to strain animals from the water. Flamingos use their tongues to strain water through comblike plates in their bills called lamellae.

Greater flamingo (*Phoenicopterus ruber*)

ZEBRA MUSSEL

This small, striped mussel lives in rivers, lakes, and canals, where it fastens itself to anything solid. At one time, zebra mussels were found only in Asia, but in the last 150 years they have spread westward across Europe. In the 1980s, a ship accidentally carried zebra mussels to North America, where they have multiplied with amazing speed. Along the shores of the Great Lakes, these mussels have clogged up water treatment plants and power plant pipes, and killed off water plants needed by other animals.

SCIENTIFIC NAME *Dreissena polymorpha*

DISTRIBUTION Asia, Europe, North America

SIZE About 1.5 in. (4cm) long

SWAN MUSSEL

This pale brown mussel lives in muddy rivers, partly buried in mud or silt. It feeds by sucking water in through a short, fleshy tube, or siphon.

Swan mussels on a riverbed

After filtering out any food, it pumps the water out through a second siphon. Swan mussel larvae do not drift in the water like the larvae of most mussel species. They fasten onto fish and feed on them for several weeks before dropping off to start their adult life on the riverbed.

SCIENTIFIC NAME *Anodonta cygnaea*

DISTRIBUTION Europe, Asia

SIZE Up to 9 in. (23cm) long

COMMON FAN MUSSEL

Muddy sands below the low-tide mark provide a home for the fan mussel. Instead of lying on its side, like most mussels, the fan mussel stands on the pointed end of its shell, where the hinge is. It anchors itself to stones and is partly buried in sand. The shell gapes open to let the mussel collect food particles from the water. Large fan mussels can be 17.5 in. (45cm) high.

SCIENTIFIC NAME *Pinna fragilis*

DISTRIBUTION Atlantic Ocean

SIZE Up to 12 in. (30cm) high

ABOVE *This edge-on view of a great scallop clearly shows the animal's tentacles and the numerous small eyes along its shell.*

Great scallop

GREAT SCALLOP

The great scallop is one of the few bivalves that can swim by opening and shutting its valves. If it is threatened, it snaps its shell shut and squirts out a jet of water that makes it shoot backward. It has a fringe of tentacles, and rows of more than 100 tiny blue eyes along the edge of its shell.

SCIENTIFIC NAME *Pecten maximus*

DISTRIBUTION Atlantic Ocean, Mediterranean Sea

SIZE Up to 5 in. (13cm) long

EDIBLE OYSTER

This bivalve lives on the muddy shores of river estuaries. It has a rough, uneven shell with one flat valve and one curved valve. The flat valve faces upward, with the curved one fixed firmly to a rock or to another oyster.

Edible oyster shell

SCIENTIFIC NAME *Ostraea edulis*

DISTRIBUTION Atlantic Ocean, Mediterranean Sea

SIZE Up to 4 in. (10cm) long

HAMMER OYSTER

The T-shaped shell of this oyster makes it look like a hammer. The "handle" is made of two valves that open when the oyster feeds. It lives in the sand of the ocean floor in the tropics.

SCIENTIFIC NAME *Malleus malleus*

DISTRIBUTION Indian Ocean, Pacific Ocean

SIZE Up to 6 in. (15cm) long

COMMON COCKLE

Frilly siphons used for feeding and breathing

Rounded, ridged shell

Common cockle

Huge numbers of common cockles live along low-lying shores but, because they bury themselves in sand or mud, living animals are rarely seen. Their empty shells are often found on beaches where birds such as oystercatchers and seagulls have dropped them while feeding. Cockles feed by pumping water in and out through two frilly siphons. If a cockle is touched, it draws in its siphons and shuts its shell.

SCIENTIFIC NAME *Cerastoderma edule*

DISTRIBUTION Atlantic Ocean, Mediterranean Sea

SIZE About 1.5 in. (4cm) long

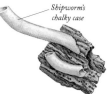

Shipworm's chalky case

TOP *The shell of a cockle can be white to mid-brown. It is deeply ridged with more than 20 ribs.*
ABOVE *When shipworms die, their chalky shells are left behind in the wood.*

HEART SHELL

This bivalve is unlike any other. Each of its valves has a coiled base, bulging outward near the hinge. Together, the valves give the animal a heartlike shape. Heart shells live in sand or mud in water at least 33 ft. (10m) deep. Complete shells rarely turn up on the shore because the two valves break apart so easily.

SCIENTIFIC NAME *Glossus humanus*

DISTRIBUTION Atlantic Ocean, Mediterranean Sea

SIZE About 3.5 in. (9cm) long

SOFT-SHELLED CLAM

This clam's shell has a soft, rubbery edge, which is actually part of the animal's body. Found in sand and mud, soft-shelled clams live up to 12 in. (30cm) beneath the surface. To breathe and feed, they use a pair of long siphons wrapped in a leathery sheath. One of the tubes sucks water into the clam's body. Once anything edible has been filtered out, the other pumps it back up to the surface of the sand. In North America, these clams are often dug up and eaten.

SCIENTIFIC NAME *Mya arenaria*

DISTRIBUTION Atlantic Ocean

SIZE Shell up to 4 in. (10cm) long

GIANT CLAM

The giant clam is the world's largest bivalve. Large specimens can weigh as much as 650 lb. (300kg). Over 95 percent of this weight is made up by the shell. These huge mollusks live in shallow water on coral reefs. Like many other bivalves, they filter food from the water around them using two siphons. Giant clams also feed in another way. Their fleshy, brightly colored lips contain microscopic algae that make their own food using the energy in sunlight. A giant clam gets a share of this food and, in return, provides the algae with a safe place to live.

SCIENTIFIC NAME *Tridacna gigas*

DISTRIBUTION Indian Ocean, Pacific Ocean

SIZE Up to 3 ft. (1m) across

SHIPWORM

With a long, fleshy body and only a tiny shell fixed to the end of it, this animal looks more like a worm than a mollusk. The two halves of its shell have razor-sharp edges, which the shipworm uses to bore through submerged timber. As it burrows, it swallows and digests particles of wood, seriously weakening anything through which it bores. In the days when most ships were made of wood, constant repairs were needed to keep shipworms at bay.

SCIENTIFIC NAME *Teredo navalis*

DISTRIBUTION Worldwide

SIZE Up to 8 in. (20cm) long

Common piddock buried in rock

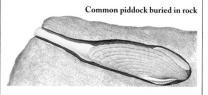

COMMON PIDDOCK

Piddocks live by filtering particles of food from seawater. They protect themselves by boring into rock, so that only the tips of their siphons are left outside in the water. As a piddock grows, it widens its burrow, but the entrance stays the same size. This means that the animal is trapped, and it is almost impossible for a predator to extract it. These creatures often produce a green light. It is not known why they do this, since they spend their lives entombed in rock.

SCIENTIFIC NAME *Pholas dactylus*

DISTRIBUTION Atlantic Ocean, Mediterranean Sea

SIZE Shell up to 6 in. (15cm) long

LEFT *Brilliant blue lips line the edges of a giant clam's shell. As they grow, giant clams become wedged in coral crevices, protecting them from the waves.*

Razor clam using its powerful foot to pull itself into the sand

ABOVE AND BELOW *Razor clams normally come to the surface of the sand only when the tide is in. There are several species of razor clams. Some are straight, while others are more curved.*

Large razor clam

Small razor clam (*Ensis ensis*)

LARGE RAZOR CLAM

Shaped like an old-fashioned razor, these bivalves have a long, narrow, square-ended shell. They live in sand near the low-tide mark, filtering food from the seawater above. Razor clams have a short foot that they use to move around and to dig into the sand. The foot grips the walls of the burrow and contracts, pulling the shell downward. When razor clams feed, they are always alert for signs of danger. The slightest vibration makes them dig their way into the sand, and they disappear with amazing speed.

SCIENTIFIC NAME *Ensis siliqua*

DISTRIBUTION Atlantic Ocean, Mediterranean Sea

SIZE Up to 6 in. (15cm) long

CEPHALOPODS

Octopuses, squid, cuttlefish, and nautiluses are members of a group of mollusks called cephalopods. Cephalopods have a large head, well-developed eyes, and a beaklike mouth ringed by sucker-tipped arms. They grab their prey with their arms and kill it with a poisonous bite. To move, cephalopods suck water into their mantle cavity—the space between the mantle and the body—and squirt it backward, sending themselves speeding forward, trailing their arms behind. There are about 650 species of cephalopods, all living in the sea.

ABOVE *A cuttlefish grabs a shrimp by shooting out a pair of extra-long tentacles.*

CUTTLEFISH

With their flattened bodies, cuttlefish are well suited to life on the seabed, where they hunt for other mollusks and small fish. They have a chalky internal shell called a cuttlebone. These cuttlebones are often washed up onto the shore. Cuttlefish can change color to match their background and hide from predators. They do this by adjusting the size of pigment sacs in their skin.

SCIENTIFIC NAME	*Sepia officinalis*
DISTRIBUTION	Atlantic Ocean, Mediterranean Sea
SIZE	Up to 12 in. (30cm) long

Common squid

Giant squid

CENTER *The common squid feeds on fish and other animals.*
ABOVE *A giant squid could easily catch a diver in its tentacles.*

COMMON SQUID

Squid have a streamlined shape for life in open water. They have a slender internal shell called a pen, which is covered by a muscular mantle. They use jet propulsion to move quickly, but they can also swim slowly by rippling finlike flaps on their sides. Like cuttlefish, squid have eight arms and two longer tentacles with sucker-tipped pads at the ends. They shoot out their tentacles to catch food. Common squid hunt in groups and rarely come near the shore.

SCIENTIFIC NAME	*Loligo vulgaris*
DISTRIBUTION	Atlantic Ocean
SIZE	Up to 20 in. (50cm) long

ATLANTIC GIANT SQUID

The giant squid is the largest invertebrate in the world, weighing as much as two tons. Its eyes, the largest of any animal, can be up to 1.5 ft. (50cm) in diameter. Its suckers can be over 3 in. (8cm) across. It lives at great depths and feeds on fish, catching them in total darkness. No one has yet seen a giant squid in its natural habitat. Our knowledge of it comes mainly from dead or injured animals that have risen to the surface or have been washed ashore.

SCIENTIFIC NAME	*Architeuthis dux*
DISTRIBUTION	Atlantic Ocean
SIZE	Up to 52.5 ft. (16m) long

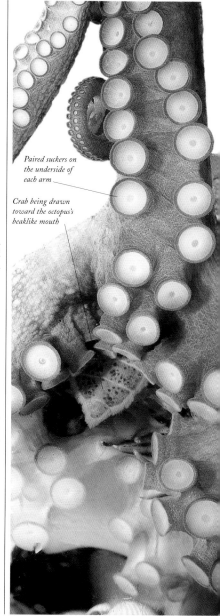

Paired suckers on the underside of each arm

Crab being drawn toward the octopus's beaklike mouth

ABOVE AND LEFT *The common octopus does most of its hunting at night. During the day it hides in a lair among the rocks.*

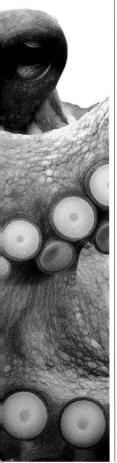

VAMPIRE SQUID

First seen in 1903, this jet black animal is not a true squid, but the only known survivor of an ancient group of cephalopods that is otherwise extinct. It has luminous eyes, and arms that work like the spokes of an umbrella, holding open a funnel that leads toward the animal's mouth. Vampire squid live in the darkness of the deep sea, and no one has ever seen how they feed. Their eyes probably attract fish toward the funnel, and into the animal's mouth.

SCIENTIFIC NAME	*Vampiroteuthis infernalis*
DISTRIBUTION	Worldwide
SIZE	Up to 12 in. (30cm) long

COMMON OCTOPUS

The common octopus is one of the most intelligent invertebrates. It lives among rocks on the seabed. Unlike squid and cuttlefish, octopuses do not have a pair of long tentacles or an internal shell. They use their eight arms to search for crabs and other small animals, reaching into crevices in the rocks to pull them out. The female common octopus is much smaller than the male. Octopuses breed by laying eggs, which the female guards in an underwater lair. In the six weeks before the eggs hatch, she has nothing to eat. Once hatching is complete, she dies.

SCIENTIFIC NAME	*Octopus vulgaris*
DISTRIBUTION	Atlantic Ocean, Mediterranean Sea, Caribbean Sea
SIZE	Up to 3 ft. (1m) long

BLUE-RINGED OCTOPUS

This Australian octopus is the only cephalopod whose bite can kill a human. The bite itself is almost painless, and it can take more than an hour for the poison to take effect. Fortunately, blue-ringed octopuses are not aggressive animals, so fatalities are rare. The species often lives near the shore and is named for the bright blue rings around its body.

SCIENTIFIC NAME	*Hapalochlaena maculosa*
DISTRIBUTION	Australia
SIZE	About 8 in. (20cm) long

ARGONAUT

This unusual octopus spends most of its life in open water. The female is up to 20 times bigger than the male, and she has a paper-thin, spiral shell. Unlike other mollusks, the argonaut's shell is not attached to its body—the female holds it in place with her arms. She uses her shell to protect her eggs, and once they have hatched, she will often discard it.

SCIENTIFIC NAME	*Argonauta argo*
DISTRIBUTION	Warm seas worldwide
SIZE	Females up to 8 in. (20cm) long, males from 0.4 in. (1cm) long

CHAMBERED NAUTILUS

Nautiluses are the only cephalopods with a permanent external shell. Millions of years ago, they were among the most numerous invertebrates in the sea, but today only a handful of species survive. A nautilus's shell contains a series of gas-filled chambers that work together as a float. The animal itself lives in the biggest chamber and is protected by a fleshy hood. It can have as many as 90 arms, but they are short and do not have suckers.

SCIENTIFIC NAME	*Nautilus pompilius*
DISTRIBUTION	Indian Ocean, Pacific Ocean
SIZE	About 6 in. (15cm) across

LEFT *When feeding, the chambered nautilus holds its prey with its arms.*

ARACHNIDS

THERE ARE ABOUT 70,000 SPECIES OF ARACHNIDS, INCLUDING
SPIDERS, SCORPIONS, MITES, AND TICKS. AFTER INSECTS,
ARACHNIDS MAKE UP THE SECOND LARGEST GROUP
OF ARTHROPODS. MANY ARE PREDATORS AND
HAVE A POISONOUS BITE.

Arachnids have four pairs of legs and a body that is divided into two parts. Most live on land. Many arachnids have sharp fangs, which they use to hunt small animals. These fangs inject their prey with digestive juices. Once the juices have broken down the tissue, the arachnid sucks up its meal. Most arachnids lay eggs, but a few give birth to live young.

A long-legged cellar spider showing how it got its name

SPIDERS

These are the best-known arachnids because many of them live in our homes and backyards. All 35,000 species are carnivorous, which means that they eat other animals, and all of them kill their prey with poisonous fangs. Most spiders have four pairs of eyes, although they usually hunt by touch. They make silk, which they use to protect their eggs, to travel, and to trap their food.

Garden spider with prey

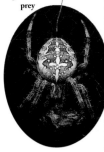

LONG-LEGGED CELLAR SPIDER

This slender spider is most often seen indoors, where it hangs upside down from its untidy web. If the web is touched, the spider vibrates up and down to fend off possible attack. Unlike some webs, the ones built by this spider are not sticky. If an insect lands on the web, the spider immobilizes it by quickly wrapping it up in silk. Long-legged cellar spiders do not always wait for food to come their way. They may wander onto other spiders' webs, stealing food and even eating the owners.

SCIENTIFIC NAME	*Pholcus phalangioides*
DISTRIBUTION	Worldwide
SIZE	Legspan about 2.75 in. (7cm)

GARDEN SPIDER

The garden spider is an orb weaver, a species that catches insects by building a round, sticky web. The spider spins its web at night and spends the day waiting on or near the web,

ready to pounce on anything that gets caught. When something is trapped, the web may be damaged. Instead of repairing it, garden spiders often eat the web and make a completely new one to replace it.

SCIENTIFIC NAME	*Araneus diadematus*
DISTRIBUTION	Europe, Asia, North America
SIZE	Legspan up to 0.8 in. (2cm)

TRAPDOOR SPIDER

There are many species of trapdoor spiders. They hide in underground burrows, which can be over 10 in. (25cm) deep and 1 in. (2.5cm) wide. The burrows are sealed with hinged doors made of silk and mud. To feed, the spiders ambush their victims from below, lifting the door and dragging passing insects under ground.

SCIENTIFIC NAME	*Bothriocyrtum* and other genera
DISTRIBUTION	Worldwide
SIZE	Legspan up to 2 in. (5cm)

ABOVE *Bird spiders and their relatives have jaws that bite downward, impaling their victims against branches or the ground. This spider has caught a mouse and is about to start eating.*

BIRD SPIDER
Often called tarantulas, hairy bird spiders are the largest spiders in the world. They live in tropical rain forests, where they spend the day in burrows and emerge at night to hunt. Although they have eight eyes, their sight is poor, and they find their prey mainly by feeling for it with their feet. Bird spiders, as the name suggests, can eat small birds. They can drag young birds straight from their nests, or catch adult birds that are roosting during the night. These spiders also feed on lizards, frogs, large insects, and small mammals.

SCIENTIFIC NAME	*Theraphosa* species
DISTRIBUTION	Tropical South America
SIZE	Legspan up to 11 in. (28cm)

BLACK WIDOW SPIDER
Although this spider has tiny fangs, the female's bite can be deadly to humans. Fortunately, black widows are not aggressive, so few people are bitten. In the wild, black widows live under fallen branches and in other dry places, where they catch insects in untidy webs. Some live in gardens and near houses in built-up areas.

SCIENTIFIC NAME	*Latrodectus mactans*
DISTRIBUTION	North America
SIZE	Legspan up to 1.5 in. (4cm)

AUSTRALIAN FUNNEL-WEB SPIDER
This spider is one of the most poisonous species in the world. It catches insects using silken trip-lines that spread out from the entrance of its burrow. The males sometimes bite people during the breeding season, when they wander in search of a mate.

SCIENTIFIC NAME	*Atrax robustus*
DISTRIBUTION	Eastern Australia
SIZE	Legspan up to 2 in. (5cm)

Black widow spider

Australian funnel-web spider

TOP *The female black widow spends most of its time motionless on its web.*
ABOVE *Male Australian funnel-web spiders do not hesitate to bite, using their large, powerful fangs.*

ARTHROPODS

Arthropods are animals that have an external body case, or exoskeleton, and several pairs of legs. The exoskeleton is made from hard plates that meet at flexible joints. It forms all the outer parts of the body, including the jaws, claws, pincers, stings, and wings. Exoskeletons protect arthropods from attack and also stop them from drying out. Arthropods outnumber all the other animal species put together. They include arachnids, crustaceans, insects, centipedes, and millipedes.

Scorpion

SCORPION
A scorpion's exoskeleton seals in moisture, acting like a waterproof suit of armor.

Crustacean

CRUSTACEAN
Crustaceans, the largest arthropods, live in water. They can grow larger than land-dwelling arthropods because the water helps support their bodies.

Centipede

CENTIPEDE
In centipedes and millipedes it is easy to see the segments that divide an arthropod's body.

Insect

INSECT
Insects are the most numerous arthropods and the only ones that can fly. Most species have two pairs of wings.

Body divided into
two main segments—
the head section, or
cephalothorax, and
the abdomen

Eight legs, all
attached to the
head section

RIGHT *Hiding in a flower,
this crab spider has ambushed
a moth. Once it has finished
feeding, it will drop the moth's
body to the ground.*

RIGHT *The house spider
is found outdoors as well
as inside houses and
other buildings.*
FAR RIGHT *A zebra
spider can leap many
times its own length.*

Four pairs
of eyes

Large, forward-
facing eyes

House spider

Two pedipalps
for grasping prey

Zebra spider

Fang

Female
carrying eggs

TOP AND ABOVE *The wolf
spider has two large fangs
with which it injects
venom into its prey.*

HOUSE SPIDER

This hairy, long-legged spider often lives
indoors. It hides in dark corners, where
it spins a silk tube that opens out into a
sheet-shaped web. The spider waits in the
tube and rushes out to catch insects that
settle on the web. Sometimes male house
spiders come out of hiding and can be seen
at night, running across the floor. These males
are likely to be in search of a mate. During
their wanderings, they occasionally fall into
bathtubs and sinks. Unable to climb up the
slippery sides, the spiders cannot escape.

SCIENTIFIC NAME *Tegeneria gigantea*

DISTRIBUTION Europe, North America, Australia

SIZE Legspan up to 2.75 in. (7cm)

WOLF SPIDER

These large-bodied hunters rarely make webs.
Instead, wolf spiders wander over the ground,
often at night, using their large eyes to spot
their prey. Like most spiders, wolf spiders wrap
up their eggs in silk cocoons. The female
fastens the cocoon to her spinnerets, nozzles on her
abdomen that produce silk. This allows her
to carry her eggs while she hunts. There are
many species of wolf spiders. *Lycosa narbonensis*
used to be called the tarantula, but the name
is now used for bird spiders (page 33).

SCIENTIFIC NAME *Lycosa narbonensis*

DISTRIBUTION Europe

SIZE Legspan about 1.5 in. (4cm)

ZEBRA SPIDER

The small, striped zebra spider is one of the
acrobats of the spider world. Like its many
relatives, known as jumping spiders, it leaps
through the air to catch small animals to eat.
Compared to other spiders, jumping spiders
have very good eyesight, which they use when
hunting. One extra-large pair of eyes helps
them judge distances before they leap. The
zebra spider is frequently seen on sunny walls,
even in busy urban areas. Other jumping spiders
live in a variety of habitats, from arid deserts
to tropical rain forests.

SCIENTIFIC NAME *Salticus scenicus*

DISTRIBUTION Europe, North America

SIZE Legspan up to 0.4 in. (1cm)

DWARF SPIDER

Dwarf spiders are certainly worthy of their
name—a typical legspan is less than one tenth
of an inch (2mm). Despite their small size,
they are probably the most numerous spiders
on earth. They are usually found in grassy fields,
where they spin sheetlike webs to trap small
insects near the ground. Dwarf spiders are tiny
and cannot go far on their legs, but they have an
unusual way of traveling. On breezy days, they
let out a long strand of silk. These catch the
wind, carrying the spiders off into the air.

SCIENTIFIC NAME *Dismodicus* and other genera

DISTRIBUTION Mainly Northern Hemisphere

SIZE Typical legspan 0.08 in. (2mm)

SPITTING SPIDER

Spitting spiders catch their prey by spraying it with jets of glue. The glue squirts from the spider's fangs and sets rapidly, pinning the victim to the ground. The spider wraps its prey in silk and then moves in to feed.

SCIENTIFIC NAME *Scytodes thoracica*

DISTRIBUTION Worldwide

SIZE Legspan about 0.6 in. (1.5cm)

FISHING SPIDER

This spider hunts on the surface of the water. It rests on a floating object, with its front legs touching the surface. When it feels vibrations made by an animal, it lunges forward to bite its prey. Some species are large enough to catch tiny fish.

SCIENTIFIC NAME *Dolomedes* species

DISTRIBUTION Europe

SIZE Legspan up to 2 in. (5cm)

Fishing spider catching a fish

Extra-long front legs

CRAB SPIDER

With their crablike shape and their habit of walking sideways, it is easy to see how these spiders got their name. Many have brightly colored camouflage. They often lurk in flowers to catch their food, where their bright colors help conceal them among the petals. A crab spider will wait for hours with its front legs held wide apart. As soon as a suitable insect lands on the flower, the spider seizes it and starts to feed.

Crab spider

SCIENTIFIC NAME *Diaea* and other genera

DISTRIBUTION Worldwide

SIZE Typical legspan 0.6 in. (1.5cm)

WATER SPIDER

One of the few species of spiders to spend its life under water, the water spider lives in ponds and ditches. It feeds on water animals, including recently hatched fish. Although it hunts, feeds, and breeds below the surface and can swim and dive, the water spider breathes air like all other spiders. It can live under water because it builds a bell-shaped air chamber out of silk, which it anchors to underwater plants. It stocks the chamber by bringing air bubbles down from the surface, trapped in the fine hairs that cover its body.

SCIENTIFIC NAME *Argyroneta aquatica*

DISTRIBUTION Europe, Asia

SIZE Legspan about 0.8 in. (2cm)

RIGHT *The water spider holds its prey, a dragonfly nymph, in its fangs.*

SCORPIONS, TICKS, AND MITES

In addition to spiders, arachnids include several other groups of animals, ranging from giant scorpions to microscopic mites. These animals all have four pairs of legs, although some use the front pair as feelers instead of for walking. Some are hunters, but others eat a variety of things, from plant and animal remains to stored food, blood, and even flakes of human skin.

SCORPION

Scorpions are the heavyweights of the arachnid world, with bodies as long as 9 in. (23cm). They are armed with a pair of pincers and a long tail that carries a stinger. They hunt small animals after dark, usually catching their prey with only their pincers. A scorpion's sting is normally reserved for self-defense, though its effect varies from one species to another. The largest scorpions often have mild stings, but a few of the smallest ones are very dangerous. Like other species, the one shown to the right, *Urodacus novae-hollandiae*, carries its young on its back.

SCIENTIFIC NAME	*Urodacus* and other genera
DISTRIBUTION	Warm places worldwide
SIZE	Typical species about 2.75 in. (7cm) long

BELOW *This giant whipscorpion has swiveled its tail forward, ready to spray acid over an enemy.*

GIANT WHIPSCORPION

This sinister-looking animal does not have a stinger, but it does have strong pincers. It hunts for small insects after dark, using its whiplike front legs as feelers. When threatened, the whipscorpion can spray a jet of acidic liquid from the end of its body, though it is not dangerous to humans. The liquid smells like vinegar, which is why this animal is also known as a vinegarone.

Pincers for seizing prey

SCIENTIFIC NAME	*Mastigoproctus giganteus*
DISTRIBUTION	North America
SIZE	Up to 3 in. (8cm) long

PSEUDOSCORPION

These scorpion-like animals are common all around the world, but few people ever get to see one. This is because the largest are less than 0.3 in. (8mm) long. Pseudoscorpions, or false scorpions, live in soil, on rocks, and among fallen leaves, where they feed on animals smaller than themselves.

Pseudoscorpion on a leaf

BELOW *Scorpions have tiny eyes and find their prey mainly by touch. Most of them hunt at night.*

Four pairs of walking legs

Pseudoscorpions do not have stingers, but nip with their poisonous pincers. They often travel by clinging to spiders' legs.

SCIENTIFIC NAME	*Chelifer* and other genera
DISTRIBUTION	Worldwide
SIZE	Typical species about 0.08 in. (2mm) long

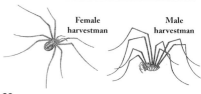

Female harvestman

Male harvestman

HARVESTMAN

Although harvestmen are frequently mistaken for spiders, they differ from them in several ways. They have an oval-shaped body that, unlike a spider's, is not divided into two parts. Their legs are extremely slender, they do not have fangs, and they have just two eyes set in a turret on their back. Harvestmen feed on small animals, as well as on dead remains. Often called daddy longlegs, most harvestman species are active at night.

SCIENTIFIC NAME	*Phalangium* and other genera
DISTRIBUTION	Worldwide
SIZE	Typical legspan 2 in. (5cm)

SEA SPIDERS AND HORSESHOE CRABS

Despite their names, sea spiders are not spiders, and horseshoe crabs are not crabs. They belong to two separate groups of invertebrates that are related to arachnids. Like arachnids, they do not have antennae, and their bodies are divided into two parts, although with sea spiders this is not always easy to see. There are at least 1,000 species of sea spiders worldwide, but only four species of horseshoe crabs, off the east coasts of North America and Asia.

SEA SPIDER OR PYCNOGONID

Members of this group have four to six pairs of spindly legs, a slender body, and a tiny head. Many sea spiders live in deep water. They crawl over the seabed, clinging to anything within reach with their legs. Sea spiders eat small animals, such as bryozoans, harvesting them with their pincers. They pierce their prey with their jaws and suck out the body fluids. Some sea spiders measure as much as 16 in. (40cm) across with their legs stretched out, but most are much smaller than this. They live throughout the world's oceans and can be brightly colored.

SCIENTIFIC NAME	*Pycnogonum* and other genera
DISTRIBUTION	Worldwide
SIZE	Typical species about 0.8 in. (2cm) long

TICK

These flat-bodied parasites live by sucking blood. To find a host animal, a tick waits on grass or trees, sometimes for weeks or months. When a suitable animal walks past, it climbs aboard using its sharp claws and begins to feed. Its body swells up with blood, and when it is full, it drops off. Ticks attack many mammals, including cattle, sheep, and humans. Their bite can transmit many diseases, some of which can be fatal.

SCIENTIFIC NAME	*Ixodes* and other genera
DISTRIBUTION	Worldwide
SIZE	Up to 0.6 in. (1.5cm) long after feeding

DUST MITE

Mites are the smallest arachnids. Most are so tiny that they are invisible to the naked eye. Some live in water, some on animals. There is even a mite that lives on human eyelashes. Many mites clamber around in or on their food. The dust mite lives in household dust and feeds on microscopic flakes of skin. It does no direct harm, but its droppings can cause allergies such as asthma.

SCIENTIFIC NAME	*Dermatophagoides farinae*
DISTRIBUTION	Worldwide
SIZE	About 0.008 in. (0.2mm) long

HORSESHOE CRAB

With their domed bodies and spiny tails, horseshoe crabs look more like pieces of armor than living things. They live in shallow coastal seawater, where they burrow into the sand to eat worms and other animals. Horseshoe crabs have five pairs of legs and a small pair of pincers, which they use to pick up their food. These are hidden by a shield called a carapace and are visible only if the animal is turned upside down. Each year, female horseshoe crabs come ashore and lay their eggs near the high-tide line. The larvae are washed out to sea with the tide.

SCIENTIFIC NAME	*Limulus polyphemus*
DISTRIBUTION	Atlantic coast of North America, Gulf of Mexico
SIZE	Up to 23.5 in. (60cm) long

ABOVE *A group of horseshoe crabs gather on a sandy beach to breed. While they are out of the water, many are attacked by birds.*

CRUSTACEANS

THESE CREATURES GET THEIR NAME FROM THEIR EXOSKELETONS, WHICH FORM CHALKY CRUSTS AROUND THEIR BODIES. LIKE OTHER ARTHROPODS, THEY SHED THEIR EXOSKELETONS AS THEY GROW, BECAUSE THE EXOSKELETONS DO NOT GROW WITH THEM. MOST CRUSTACEANS HAVE MANY PAIRS OF LEGS AND TWO PAIRS OF ANTENNAE.

This varied group of invertebrates contains about 38,000 species and includes animals as diverse as water fleas, barnacles, lobsters, and wood lice. A few crustaceans live on land, but most live either in fresh water or in the ocean. Crustaceans eat a range of things. Many sift their food from the water, while others hunt or scavenge for dead remains. Some are parasites, living on or inside other animals.

Water flea

Brine shrimp

ABOVE LEFT *A water flea usually swims with its body upright. Its thin body case is almost transparent, revealing its internal organs.* **ABOVE RIGHT** *A brine shrimp uses its legs to collect food from the water.*

WATER FLEA
Despite their name, water fleas are not true fleas, but tiny crustaceans that live in lakes and ponds. They have microscopic legs and large, feathery antennae. They flick these antennae to swim jerkily through the water. Water fleas feed on bacteria and other minute life-forms. During the fall, they scatter their eggs, which settle in the mud and hatch the following spring. Water fleas' eggs are often carried to new areas on birds' feet. In warm weather, the adults multiply rapidly, and many of them are eaten by fish.

SCIENTIFIC NAME	*Daphnia* species
DISTRIBUTION	Worldwide
SIZE	Up to 0.1 in. (2.5mm) long

BRINE SHRIMP
These small crustaceans live in salty lakes, which often dry out for long periods. To survive these droughts, brine shrimp lay tough eggs that can remain out of water for five years or more. Once wet, they hatch within a few hours.

SCIENTIFIC NAME	*Artemia* species
DISTRIBUTION	Worldwide
SIZE	About 0.6 in. (1.5cm) long

PLANKTON

Many crustaceans start life as microscopic larvae. They drift near the surface of the water with many other tiny life-forms. This teeming mass of life is called plankton. Many small crustaceans remain in the plankton all their lives, but others grow and move to different habitats, such as the shore.

Plankton also includes microscopic algae that absorb energy from sunlight. These are eaten by tiny animals that, in turn, are eaten by larger animals. Eventually, the

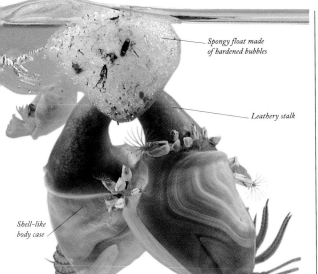

Spongy float made
of hardened bubbles

Leathery stalk

Shell-like
body case

Feathery legs
extended when feeding

LEFT AND ABOVE *These
goose barnacles hang in
the water from floats of
gas-filled bubbles. Other
species hang beneath
floating wood.*

**Plankton seen under
a microscope**

energy from the
sun is passed on to
all the animals in the
ocean, from predators,
such as sharks, to
deep-sea sponges that
filter the sea for food.
Without plankton,
most sea life would
not exist.

FAIRY SHRIMP

Well-adapted to living in
temporary pools of water, fairy
shrimp can be found in shallow
ponds and puddles on muddy roads.
Although their life span is short, they breed
quickly, often laying eggs when they are only
two weeks old. Once their home has dried out,
the adults die, but their eggs survive to be spread
far and wide by the wind. Fairy shrimp have
few natural enemies.

SCIENTIFIC NAME	*Eubranchipus* and other genera
DISTRIBUTION	Worldwide
SIZE	Typical species 1 in. (2.5cm) long

TADPOLE SHRIMP

From a distance, this shrimp looks like a tadpole,
with its large head and wriggling, swimming
motion. The front of its body is protected by
a carapace, and it has up to 70 pairs of legs.
Tadpole shrimp live in puddles of water.
In desert areas, they appear suddenly after
storms, disappearing again during dry
times, but leaving their eggs behind.

SCIENTIFIC NAME	*Triops* and other genera
DISTRIBUTION	Worldwide
SIZE	Typical species 1.5 in. (4cm) long

ROCK BARNACLE

Surrounded by what looks like a shell, barnacles
were once mistaken for mollusks. The shell is
actually a specialized body case with a volcano-
like shape. It is always fastened to something
solid. Most barnacles fasten themselves to rocks,
but some live on animals, such as crabs or
whales. They keep their cases closed at low tide
to avoid dehydration. At high tide, barnacles
extend their feathery legs from the top of the
case and strain particles of food from the water.
There are many different species. *Balanus
balanoides* is common along Atlantic shores.

SCIENTIFIC NAME	*Balanus balanoides*
DISTRIBUTION	Atlantic Ocean
SIZE	Up to 0.4 in. (1cm) wide

GOOSE BARNACLE

These barnacles have a long, leathery stalk
and a case made of five shiny, white plates.
They attach themselves to pieces of driftwood
or to rafts of bubbles that they make themselves.
Goose barnacles can drift thousands of miles
across the oceans and are frequently thrown up
onto beaches after storms. Many centuries ago,
they were thought to develop into geese,
which is how they got their name.

SCIENTIFIC NAME	*Lepas fascicularis*
DISTRIBUTION	Worldwide
SIZE	Up to 2 in. (5cm) long

SEED SHRIMP OR OSTRACOD

When swimming, a seed shrimp looks like
a tiny seed speeding through the water. Its
body is enclosed by a hinged carapace, which
the animal can shut to protect itself. It swims
by flicking its antennae and can use its legs to
crawl in mud. Seed shrimp are found in ponds
and lakes, where they feed mainly on algae.

SCIENTIFIC NAME	*Cypris* and other genera
DISTRIBUTION	Worldwide
SIZE	Typical species 0.08 in. (2mm)

**Tadpole shrimp in
a puddle**

NORTHERN LOBSTER

Lobsters are the heaviest crustaceans. Some Northern lobsters can weigh 45 lb. (20kg), but because they are caught for food, few survive to grow to this size. Lobsters belong to a large group of crustaceans called decapods, all of which have ten legs. They are hunters and scavengers, using their powerful claws to crack open shells and to slice up the bodies of their prey, such as crabs, small fish, and even other lobsters. They live on the seabed and in rocky crevices, and reproduce by laying thousands of eggs, which the female carries until they hatch.

Northern lobster

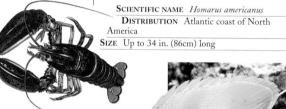

SCIENTIFIC NAME	*Homarus americanus*
DISTRIBUTION	Atlantic coast of North America
SIZE	Up to 34 in. (86cm) long

ABOVE
The Northern lobster is the heaviest of all lobsters.
RIGHT *The bright colors of a cleaning shrimp help it attract the attention of fish that need to be cleaned.*

WEST INDIES SPINY LOBSTER

Spiny lobsters have only small pincers, but are protected with sharp spines. They feed on worms and dead remains on the seabed. They usually move by walking, but they can swim backward by flicking their tail. West Indies spiny lobsters spend the summer on reefs near the coast, migrating to deeper water in the fall. They travel in groups of fifty or more, scuttling along in a line.

SCIENTIFIC NAME	*Panulirus argus*
DISTRIBUTION	Caribbean Sea
SIZE	About 23.5 in. (60cm) long

CRAYFISH

These small relatives of the lobster live in lakes, rivers, streams, and swamps. They hide by day, usually in underwater holes, and emerge at night to hunt for snails, small fish, and other water animals. Like lobsters, female crayfish carry their eggs with them. When the eggs hatch, the young crayfish cling to their mother's body for several days until they are able to fend for themselves.

SCIENTIFIC NAME	*Astacus* and other genera
DISTRIBUTION	Europe
SIZE	About 4 in. (10cm) long

CLEANING SHRIMP

Brightly colored cleaning shrimp feed by picking dead skin and parasites off the bodies of fish. This is a useful service to the fish, so cleaning shrimp are allowed to clamber over their "clients" without being chased away. *Lysmata grabhami* comes from the Caribbean, but other species are found throughout the tropics.

SCIENTIFIC NAME	*Lysmata grabhami*
DISTRIBUTION	Caribbean Sea
SIZE	About 2 in. (5cm) long

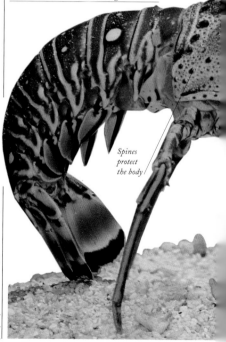

Spines protect the body

MANTIS SHRIMP

The front legs of the mantis shrimp work like the legs of a praying mantis (page 54). Each leg ends in a long claw with a set of six spines along one edge. The claw can snap back against the rest of the leg in a fraction of a second, stabbing and gripping at the same time. Mantis shrimp live on coral reefs and on the seabed in shallow water. They feed on worms, fish, and other animals. Large species, like this one, can slice a fish in half and could easily stab through a person's finger.

SCIENTIFIC NAME *Squilla empusa*

DISTRIBUTION Atlantic Ocean, Caribbean Sea

SIZE About 10 in. (25cm) long

Eyes are on short stalks

Second pair of antennae are longer than the rest of the body

LEFT *The West Indies spiny lobster is famous for its long migrations across the seabed. It moves to deep water to escape being buffeted by winter storms.*

Ten slender legs

RIGHT *Freshwater shrimp are sometimes found under ground in streams that run through caves.*
BELOW *Beach fleas are common along the high-tide mark.*

Freshwater shrimp

Beach flea

FRESHWATER SHRIMP

Instead of swimming upright, freshwater shrimp often move along on one side, flicking and wriggling their way through shallow water. They can also jump. Freshwater shrimp are not true shrimp. They are amphipods, crustaceans with seven pairs of legs and a flattened body. They can survive out of water as long as they stay damp. Freshwater shrimp eat decaying leaves and the remains of small animals. They have long antennae that help them find food.

SCIENTIFIC NAME *Gammarus* species

DISTRIBUTION Worldwide

SIZE About 1 in. (2.5cm) long

BEACH FLEA

There are many species of beach fleas. They are relatives of freshwater shrimp and live on the shore. The easiest way to see beach fleas is to lift up a piece of seaweed. If any beach fleas are feeding on it, they will jump away quickly. They jump by flicking their tail backward against the ground, catapulting themselves into the air.

SCIENTIFIC NAME *Orchestia* and other genera

DISTRIBUTION Worldwide

SIZE Up to 0.8 in. (2cm) long

KRILL

Found in the cold seas around Antarctica, these shrimplike animals have a bright red body. They feed on planktonic algae, which they collect using legs covered with fine hairs. Krill live in vast swarms that are preyed on by fish, seabirds, seals, and whales.

SCIENTIFIC NAME *Euphausia superba*

DISTRIBUTION Southern Ocean

SIZE About 2 in. (5cm) long

CRABS

Despite their different shape and way of moving, crabs are closely related to lobsters. A crab's body looks as if it has been stretched sideways and, in most species, is covered by a hard, chalky shell. There are more than 4,000 species of crabs, including both the world's largest crustaceans and some animals not much bigger than a pea. Most crabs live in or close to water, though some only return to the water to breed. Crabs usually swim well, but many shore-dwelling species can also scuttle sideways away from danger at high speed.

Crab's underside is protected by its claws

RIGHT *When it holds its claws close to its body, the box crab is difficult to attack. This one is carrying a sea anemone for extra protection.*

Edible crab

Blue crab

TOP *Edible crabs are often caught for food by luring them into special pots.*
ABOVE *The blue crab has flattened back legs, which it uses like a pair of paddles when swimming.*

EDIBLE CRAB

This crab has a heavy, domed shell, or carapace, with a crimped edge. As in other crabs, the carapace protects the animal's internal organs. The edible crab feeds on living animals and dead remains, using its powerful pincers to crack open shells. The adult crab lives in deep water, but its thick case makes it too heavy to swim. Instead, it sidles across the seabed, finding food mainly by touch and smell. Edible crabs lay up to three million eggs a year. Like most crabs, their larvae start life drifting in the plankton near the sea's surface.

SCIENTIFIC NAME *Cancer pagurus*

DISTRIBUTION European coasts, including the Mediterranean Sea

SIZE Up to 8 in. (20cm) across

SPONGE CRAB

A sponge crab camouflages itself by fastening living sponges to its back. The sponges continue to grow on the crab's back, and the crab holds them in place using its two back legs. This works well until the sponge crab outgrows its shell and the time comes for it to molt. Just before it molts, the crab removes the sponges. Once its new shell has hardened, it puts the sponges back again, or replaces them with others.

SCIENTIFIC NAME *Dromia* and other genera

DISTRIBUTION Worldwide

SIZE Typical species 3 in. (8cm) across

BOX CRAB

This brightly colored crab has pincers that fold away, giving its body a boxlike shape. With its pincers stowed flat, there is less chance that it might be injured by another animal. Many species of box crabs carry sea anemones (page 15) on their shells. The sea anemones' stinging tentacles protect the crab from predators. The anemones benefit from this partnership too, because they have more food to choose from when they are being carried on the crab's back.

SCIENTIFIC NAME *Calappa granulata*

DISTRIBUTION Eastern Atlantic Ocean, Mediterranean Sea

SIZE Up to 4 in. (10cm) long

BLUE CRAB

Found in shallow waters close to the shore, blue crabs have a spiked edge to the front of their shells, and long spines that stick out on either side of their bodies. They walk along the seabed to find worms and other small animals to eat, but they are also good swimmers. Like other swimming crabs, they push themselves through the water with their back legs. Blue crabs are common and are often caught for food.

SCIENTIFIC NAME *Callinectes sapidus*

DISTRIBUTION Atlantic coast of North and South America, Caribbean Sea

SIZE Up to 9 in. (23cm) across

JAPANESE SPIDER CRAB

Spider crabs have a pear-shaped body with slender legs and pincers. The Japanese spider crab lives in water at least 100 ft. (30m) deep and feeds mainly on mollusks. Its legspan can exceed 10 ft. (3m), making it both the largest crustacean and the largest arthropod. It moves by walking over the seabed, but its legs are so long that it has difficulty moving on land.

SCIENTIFIC NAME *Macrocheira kaempferi*

DISTRIBUTION Pacific Ocean off Japan

SIZE Legspan about 12 ft. (3.6m)

DECORATOR CRAB

The decorator crab is a type of spider crab. Many spider crabs camouflage themselves by draping seaweed and sponges over their bodies; the decorator crab is an expert at this form of self-defense. It keeps still during the day and is very difficult to spot among weed-covered rocks. Like other camouflage-carrying spider crabs, it fastens its camouflage in place with the hundreds of tiny hooks that cover its body.

SCIENTIFIC NAME *Oregonia gracilis*

DISTRIBUTION Pacific coast of North America

SIZE Legspan up to 10 in. (25cm)

MASKED CRAB

This nocturnal animal has an oval body with a thin shell and a pair of long antennae. The shell has facelike markings, from which the masked crab got its name. It spends the day buried in the sand, with only the tips of its antennae showing above the surface. On its inner edge, each antenna has a fringe of hairs which lock together to form a tube. The tube takes water to the buried crab so that it can breathe.

SCIENTIFIC NAME
Corystes cassivelaunus

DISTRIBUTION
Atlantic Ocean

SIZE Shell up to
1.5 in. (4cm) long

Tube formed by antennae

The male masked crab's claws are twice as long as its body

ABOVE *Decorator crabs lose their camouflage when they molt, so they must build up a new covering each time.*
RIGHT *Masked crabs live buried in sand in shallow water. At night, they clamber out onto the sand to feed.*

Only the protected front part of the body sticks out of the shell

LEFT A red hermit crab (Dardanus megistos) *peers out from the shell that has become its home.*

HERMIT CRAB

Unlike most crabs, a hermit crab has a narrow body and a long, soft abdomen. Only the front part of the body is covered by a hard exoskeleton. To protect itself from attack, it backs into empty mollusk shells. Its abdomen is coiled to enable it to fit, and its legs and claws are shaped so that they can block the entrance to the shell if anything tries to get in. As the crab grows, it periodically has to move to a new home. It begins by carefully investigating empty shells with its claws and, if it finds a suitable one, quickly makes its move. For hermit crabs, finding a shell is a matter of life and death, and fights often break out among them when shells are in short supply.

SCIENTIFIC NAME *Dardanus* and other genera

DISTRIBUTION Worldwide

SIZE Typical species 1 in. (2.5cm) across

MITTEN CRAB

Many crabs have hairy legs, and some even have a hairy body. The hairs help the crab swim or help keep camouflage in place. The mitten crab has a tuft of hair behind each pincer, making it look as if it is wearing a pair of furry mittens. It lives in estuaries and in fresh water close to the coast.

SCIENTIFIC NAME *Eriocheir sinensis*

DISTRIBUTION Southern Asia, Europe

SIZE About 4 in. (10cm) across

COMMENSAL CRAB

Instead of living out in the open, tiny commensal crabs shelter inside the bodies or homes of other animals. They do little or no harm to their hosts and survive on leftover scraps of food. Some live inside worm burrows or on shrimp, but *Pinnotheres pisum* tucks itself away inside the shell of bivalve mollusks, such as mussels and oysters.

SCIENTIFIC NAME *Pinnotheres pisum*

DISTRIBUTION Atlantic Ocean, Mediterranean Sea

SIZE Up to 0.4 in. (1cm) across

ABOVE *This commensal crab lives inside the shell of a mussel. Adult commensal crabs have to leave their hosts to breed.*

GHOST CRAB

These crabs live on sandy beaches in warm parts of the world. They spend the daytime hidden in burrows beneath the surface, emerging at night to pick through the sand for scraps of food. They feed on fruit and dead animals that are left when the tide goes out. Ghost crabs are very pale, which helps them blend in against the sand. Despite this camouflage, they are always on the lookout for danger. If anything comes too close, they break into a high-speed run, shooting sideways across the sand and into their burrow.

SCIENTIFIC NAME *Ocypode* species

DISTRIBUTION Tropical shores worldwide

SIZE Typical species 2 in. (5cm) across

Its huge legspan enables the robber crab to grasp the trunk of a coconut tree as it climbs

LAND CRAB

Adult land crabs spend their lives out of water, the females returning to it only to lay eggs. They survive by spending the day in burrows and feeding at night when there is less danger of drying out. Land crabs are found only in the tropics and subtropics, but in some areas they are so common that they pick over every inch of the ground for food. Most feed on fallen leaves and fruit, but they are also attracted by dead fish and other animal remains.

SCIENTIFIC NAME *Gecarcinus* and other genera

DISTRIBUTION Warm coastal regions worldwide

SIZE Typical species 4 in. (10cm) across

ROBBER CRAB

These are the largest and heaviest land-dwelling crustaceans. They weigh as much as 9 lb. (4kg) and have massive, strong claws. Despite their menacing appearance, robber crabs feed almost entirely on fruit, particularly young coconuts that have fallen before they are ripe. If they cannot find enough food on the ground, robber crabs will clamber up trees to eat. The males spend all their adult lives on land, but females return to the sea to lay eggs.

SCIENTIFIC NAME *Birgus latro*

DISTRIBUTION Islands in the Indian and Pacific Oceans

SIZE Legspan up to 3 ft. (1m)

FIDDLER CRAB

Fiddler crabs live on muddy coasts, mainly in warm parts of the world. During high tide they hide in burrows, but when the water level drops, they crawl out on the mud to feed. Fiddler crabs eat tiny specks of food that are mixed with the mud. They collect the mud with their pincers and then discard it as pellets when they have eaten whatever it contains. Female fiddler crabs have two small pincers, but males have one small pincer and one giant one, which can be as heavy as the rest of the body put together. The males use their oversized pincers during courtship displays, when they wave them at other fiddler crabs across the mud. They do this to warn away rival males and to attract females to mate.

SCIENTIFIC NAME *Uca* species

DISTRIBUTION Tropical and subtropical shores worldwide

SIZE Typical width 0.8 in. (2cm)

Giant pincer of male fiddler crab

Female fiddler crab

ABOVE *Male and female fiddler crabs on the mud at low tide.*
BELOW *Two robber crabs tussle over a coconut washed up on the shore.*

Seven pairs of legs

Wood lice

WOOD LOUSE

Apart from land crabs (page 45), wood lice are the only widespread crustaceans that have successfully taken up life on land. They can be found under logs and in damp crevices, where they feed on plant remains. Wood lice do not live in water, but they have gills and need to stay damp to breathe. If they find their way into a house, they often die of dehydration. Female wood lice lay eggs, which they keep in a pouch beneath their body. The eggs hatch as fully-formed young that are soon able to take up life on their own.

SCIENTIFIC NAME	*Oniscus* and other genera
DISTRIBUTION	Worldwide
SIZE	Typically 0.6 in. (1.5cm) long

SEA ROACH

This animal looks like a large wood louse, but it moves about much more quickly. It lives on rocks and piers near the high-tide mark. It scavenges for food washed in by the ocean, using its long antennae to track down anything edible. The sea roach is nocturnal, sheltering in crevices during the day. Occasionally it does venture out in daylight. If it finds itself out in the open, the sea roach will quickly dash for cover.

SCIENTIFIC NAME	*Ligia oceanica*
DISTRIBUTION	Worldwide
SIZE	Up to 1 in. (2.5cm) long

WATER SLATER

Compared to most water animals, water slaters are poor swimmers, preferring to crawl on their seven pairs of legs. They feed on fallen leaves and the dead remains of plants, and can survive in stagnant water that contains little oxygen. *Asellus aquaticus* lives in slow-flowing rivers, streams, and ponds, but some of its relatives live in caves. These cave dwellers are blind and colorless, unlike the drab brown slaters that live above ground.

SCIENTIFIC NAME	*Asellus aquaticus*
DISTRIBUTION	Europe
SIZE	Up to 0.6 in. (1.5cm) long

RIGHT *The water slater absorbs oxygen through gills tucked away near the base of its legs.*

ABOVE *Sea roaches have large eyes at the sides of their heads. Their bodies can change color and are usually darker during the day than at night.*

SELF-DEFENSE

For wild animals, life is a dangerous business. Whenever they feed or travel, they risk being attacked and eaten. They have to be experts in self-defense to survive this constant threat.

The simplest method of self-defense is to make a fast escape. Crabs run for cover at high speed, but when cornered, they switch to another kind of self-defense: they fight back with their pincers. Many other animals also defend themselves with weapons, such as sharp teeth, claws, or stings.

Wood lice cannot move fast, and they have no weapons. They rely on their unpleasant taste to deter predators. Many millipedes use a similar kind of self-defense. Some animals, such as arrow poison frogs, taste bad and are also highly poisonous. If a wood louse's chemical defenses fail, it relies on its body case, which acts like a suit of armor. Some wood lice can roll up into a ball if they are threatened. The same technique is used by other animals, including armadillos and pill millipedes.

Pill millipede in open and defense positions

CENTIPEDES AND MILLIPEDES

THESE LONG-BODIED ARTHROPODS HAVE MANY PAIRS OF LEGS. CENTIPEDES ARE PREDATORS, KILLING PREY WITH POISONOUS CLAWS AT THE SIDES OF THEIR HEAD. MILLIPEDES EAT FRESH AND DECAYING PLANTS AND HAVE SMALL JAWS.

Centipedes and millipedes are closely related, but it is easy to tell them apart. Centipedes have a flat body with a single pair of legs on each segment. Millipedes have a cylindrical body, and each of their body segments carries two pairs of legs. Centipedes can have up to 170 pairs of legs, while millipedes may have 375 pairs. There are about 2,800 species of centipedes and 8,000 species of millipedes. They are most common in warm countries.

GIANT CENTIPEDE
The name centipede means "one hundred feet"—although some species have just thirty. The giant centipede has boldly colored legs, signaling that it is dangerous to touch. Its poisonous claws can kill small mammals and reptiles, and are strong enough to pierce human skin. Like other centipedes, this species spends the daytime in dark crevices and emerges to hunt at night. Centipedes reproduce by laying eggs, and many of them, including the giant centipede, are careful parents. The female lays eggs in an underground burrow and wraps herself around them. She licks them to keep them clean and guards them for several weeks until they hatch.

SCIENTIFIC NAME	*Scolopendra morsitans*
DISTRIBUTION	Warm places worldwide
SIZE	Up to 12 in. (30cm) long

LONG-LEGGED CENTIPEDE
This is the fastest centipede. It can sprint in short bursts at nearly 1.25 mph (2km/h). It frequently lives in houses, where it can be seen running across walls after its prey.

SCIENTIFIC NAME	*Scutigera coleoptrata*
DISTRIBUTION	Europe
SIZE	Up to 1 in. (2.5cm) long, excluding legs

GIANT MILLIPEDE
Giant millipedes live in the tropics, where there is a year-round supply of decaying leaves. They are largely harmless, although some species can squirt a poisonous spray if they are threatened. A millipede has a blunt head to help it push through fallen leaves. Its body is reinforced with a chalky substance for extra strength.

SCIENTIFIC NAME	*Scaphistostreptus seychellarum*
DISTRIBUTION	Seychelle Islands
SIZE	Up to 11 in. (28cm) long

PILL MILLIPEDE
With a maximum of 19 pairs of legs, pill millipedes are shorter than most of their relatives. They can roll up into a ball to protect themselves, just as many wood lice do. Pill millipedes live among dead leaves, helping break them down so their nutrients can be recycled.

SCIENTIFIC NAME	*Glomeris marginata*
DISTRIBUTION	Europe
SIZE	About 0.5 in. (1.2cm) long

TOP *The giant centipede has been accidentally introduced from Southeast Asia to many warm parts of the world, including the southern United States.*
ABOVE *The long-legged centipede hunts at night for small insects.*

INSECTS

INSECTS ARE AMONG THE MOST SUCCESSFUL ANIMALS ON EARTH. NEARLY ONE MILLION SPECIES HAVE BEEN IDENTIFIED, RANGING FROM FLIES SMALLER THAN THE PERIOD AT THE END OF THIS SENTENCE TO BEETLES BIGGER THAN A HUMAN HAND.

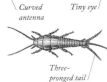

Curved antenna — Tiny eye

Three-pronged tail

TOP *This springtail (Tomocerus longicornis) is one of more than 1,500 species found throughout the world. Most springtails live in grass or leaf litter, but some float in clusters on pools and puddles.*
ABOVE *Silverfish keep growing after they have reached maturity.*

Insects are arthropods with an external skeleton and jointed legs. An adult's body is divided into three parts: the head, the thorax, and the abdomen. The head includes the eyes, antennae, and several sets of mouthparts. Some insects crush or chew solid food, but most suck up liquids. The thorax usually has three pairs of legs and one or two pairs of wings. The abdomen contains the insect's reproductive organs and most of its digestive system. Most insects start life as eggs. When they hatch, they may look different from their parents, but change shape as they mature. Many insects can fly, so they easily spread from place to place. They live on land, in fresh water, and in the air, but they cannot survive in the ocean.

WINGLESS INSECTS

These small, primitive animals live mainly among fallen leaves or in the soil. There are about 3,000 species worldwide, found as far apart as the Amazon rain forest and Antarctica. Some species are numerous, but because they are mostly tiny and drab, few are ever noticed. As well as being wingless, these animals differ from most insects in other ways. Not all of them have to mate to reproduce, and they alter in shape only slightly as they grow to adulthood.

SPRINGTAIL

Few people would recognize a springtail, but they are among the most common animals on earth. In lush grassland, there can be more than 250 million in each acre, feeding on plants and their decaying remains. Springtails get their name from a peg organ tucked under the rear of the body. If a springtail is disturbed, it reacts by releasing the peg, which flicks it through the air. Most springtails are harmless, but some are serious farmland pests.

SCIENTIFIC NAME	*Tomocerus* and other genera
DISTRIBUTION	Worldwide
SIZE	Typical length 0.2 in. (5mm)

SILVERFISH

The silver scales that cover this creature's body give it its name. The silverfish often lives in houses, where it can be spotted scuttling away from the light when doors or drawers are opened. It feeds on starchy substances, such as paper, flour, breadcrumbs, and some kinds of glue. Female silverfish lay pearly-white eggs in crevices and on floors. The young are white and turn silver as they get older.

SCIENTIFIC NAME	*Lepisma saccharina*
DISTRIBUTION	Worldwide
SIZE	About 0.6 in. (1.5cm) long

FIREBRAT

Although its body is brown, the firebrat is similar to the silverfish. It is also found indoors, but it chooses places that are hot and damp, including bakeries, factories, and heating ducts. The firebrat continues to molt throughout its life. Each time it molts, it replaces any legs that have been lost in accidents.

SCIENTIFIC NAME	*Thermobia domestica*
DISTRIBUTION	Worldwide
SIZE	About 0.6 in. (1.5cm) long

LICE, THRIPS, AND WEBSPINNERS

These unrelated groups of insects are all small and easily overlooked, but some can be serious pests. Thrips feed on plants and their decaying remains, and can cause widespread damage to crops. Webspinners eat plants or tiny animals. Lice live in two very different ways—booklice eat molds or plants, but some parasitic lice feed on blood, feathers, or skin. These biting and sucking species cause discomfort to animals and people and spread disease. There are about 10,000 species of lice, webspinners, and thrips all over the world.

HUMAN HEAD LOUSE

This parasitic insect lives in human hair, where it feeds by sucking blood. It is found only on the head, although its relatives—the body louse and the crab louse—live on other parts of the human body. Its short legs end in a single claw, which can grip hairs so tightly that the insect is almost impossible to dislodge. It lays eggs that it fastens to hair. When they are ready to hatch, the tops pop off, and the young lice crawl out. The head louse cannot fly; it is spread by physical contact. It can be killed with insecticidal shampoos.

SCIENTIFIC NAME *Pediculus humanus capitis*

DISTRIBUTION Worldwide

SIZE About 0.1 in. (2.5mm) long

BOOKLOUSE

If you see something move in an old book, it is probably a booklouse. These insects eat molds that grow on paper and plants. Female booklice can often reproduce without having to mate. Most lay their eggs one by one in webs of silk.

SCIENTIFIC NAME *Liposcelis* and other genera

DISTRIBUTION Worldwide

SIZE Typical length 0.08 in. (2mm)

Long antennae

THRIPS

These tiny, black insects fill the air on warm, stormy days, often settling on clothes and skin. Thrips hibernate in crevices. Indoors, they squeeze into all kinds of objects, from clocks to computer keyboards—but rarely manage to escape.

SCIENTIFIC NAME *Thrips* and other genera

DISTRIBUTION Worldwide

SIZE Typical length 0.08 in. (2mm)

WEBSPINNER

Found among fallen leaves, webspinners live in a tangled network of silk tunnels. They produce the silk from glands on the tip of their front legs. They forage in and around their tunnels and quickly disappear if disturbed.

SCIENTIFIC NAME *Embia* and other genera

DISTRIBUTION Worldwide

SIZE Typical length 0.4 in. (1cm)

Feathery wings

TOP *Booklice that live indoors, such as the common booklouse (Liposcelis terricolis), are almost all wingless.*
CENTER *Thrips feed on plant juices. These are grain thrips (Limothrips cerealium) on a convolvulus flower.*
ABOVE *Like all thrips, onion thrips (Thrips tabaci) have featherlike wings.*

Abdomen swells up as the louse feeds

RIGHT *Head lice have a flattened body, a small head, and very strong legs. Their color varies, helping camouflage them in hair.*

Mouthparts are stowed away when not in use

Short, spiky legs

DRAGONFLIES, MAYFLIES, AND STONEFLIES

There are about 5,000 species of dragonflies, 2,000 species of mayflies, and 1,600 species of stoneflies. They all start life as underwater nymphs. Nymphs look similar to their parents, although they do not have wings. Dragonfly nymphs are fierce predators and use a hinged mouthpart, called a mask, to attack small animals. Stonefly nymphs are also carnivorous, but mayfly nymphs eat microscopic plants. As adults, mayflies and most stoneflies eat nothing at all, but adult dragonflies are skilled hunters, catching other insects in midair.

Gauzy wings are outstretched when the dragonfly rests

Front and back wings similar in shape and size

Large thorax houses the dragonfly's wing muscles

GREEN DARNER

This North American dragonfly has a bright green abdomen shaped like a darning needle. It is one of the largest dragonfly species and is commonly seen over ponds in North America. Darners hunt by sight, using their huge compound eyes to spot any movement that might be a meal. Their eyes are so big that they meet in the middle of the head, giving them an all-around view of their surroundings. Green darner nymphs feed on tadpoles and small fish and take two years to turn into adults.

SCIENTIFIC NAME	*Anax junius*
DISTRIBUTION	North America
SIZE	Up to 3 in. (8cm) long

BELOW *Dragonflies have the biggest eyes in the insect world. In this species (Hemianax papuensis) from western Australia, they occupy most of the insect's head. Each eye is divided into about 25,000 compartments.*

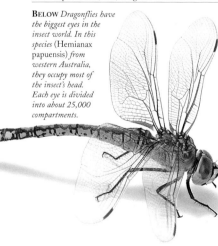

EMPEROR DRAGONFLY

With a wingspan of nearly 5.5 in. (14cm), this impressive insect is one of Europe's biggest and fastest dragonflies. It is a "hawker" dragonfly, which means that it spends most of its time on the wing, patrolling over water and marshland for food. Emperor dragonflies chase other dragonflies out of their feeding territories and sometimes catch and eat smaller species. During their life under water, emperor dragonfly nymphs are well camouflaged. This is essential for their survival because, if they are spotted by older nymphs, they are likely to be eaten.

SCIENTIFIC NAME	*Anax imperator*
DISTRIBUTION	Europe, Africa, Asia
SIZE	Up to 4 in. (10cm) long

BROAD-BODIED LIBELLULA

This thickset insect is a "darter" dragonfly. Darters spend most of the time resting on a perch, darting into the air only when they spot likely prey. The broad-bodied libellula feeds over slow-flowing water and often perches on dead twigs. It holds its body horizontally with its wings swept forward, ready to take off at a moment's notice. Both the male and female are brown in the first few days of life. After that, however, the male's abdomen turns bright blue.

SCIENTIFIC NAME	*Libellula depressa*
DISTRIBUTION	Europe, Central Asia
SIZE	Up to 3 in. (8cm) long

ABOVE *This emperor dragonfly's bright blue abdomen and clear wings show that it is a male. Dragonflies can beat their two pairs of wings independently, which allows them to hover and move forward and backward.*

Four dark wing spots

Bright blue body of male

TOP *The four-spotted libellula (Libellula quadrimaculata) gets its name from the dark marks on its wings.*

ABOVE *The broad-bodied libellula takes one to two years to turn into an adult.*

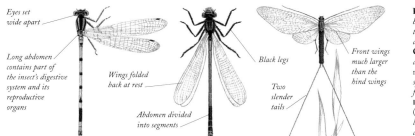

Eyes set
wide apart

Long abdomen
contains part of
the insect's digestive
system and its
reproductive
organs

Wings folded
back at rest

Abdomen divided
into segments

Black legs

Two
slender
tails

Front wings
much larger
than the
hind wings

FAR LEFT *The common
blue damselfly is one of
the most widespread
damselflies in the world.*
CENTER *The large red
damselfly* (Pyrrhosoma
nymphula) *is a European
species that often flies over
fields and meadows.*
LEFT *This species of mayfly*
(Isonychia ignota) *lives by
lakes and rivers in southern
and central Europe.*

COMMON BLUE DAMSELFLY

Damselflies are related to dragonflies. They are smaller and thinner, often with wings that fold over their backs when they rest. Damselflies seem delicate, but they are tougher than they look. The common blue damselfly can survive in the Arctic tundra, where temperatures fall to -35°F (-30°C). Adults feed on small insects that they pick off plants. They lay their eggs in the stems of water plants, and their nymphs usually live under water for a year.

SCIENTIFIC NAME *Enallagma cyatherium*

DISTRIBUTION	Europe, Asia, North America
SIZE	Up to 1.5 in. (4cm) long

HELICOPTER DAMSELFLY

This rain-forest damselfly has record-breaking wings, which measure up to 7.5 in. (19cm) from tip to tip. The damselfly hunts by flying slowly through the forest in search of spiders. It hovers in front of a spider's web like a helicopter, then makes a lightning-fast lunge. It eats the spider's abdomen but cuts off the head and legs, letting them fall to the ground. Spiders do not seem to notice the damselfly's approach, probably because its body is slender and its wings transparent.

SCIENTIFIC NAME *Megaloprepus caeruleata*

DISTRIBUTION	Central and South America
SIZE	Up to 5 in. (12cm) long

STONEFLY

The life of a stonefly begins in a cool stream or lake, where it feeds on small animals and plants. At between one and three years old, the nymph clambers out of the water and turns into a dark-brown adult that only lives for about a month. Stoneflies are not good fliers and often scuttle around on rocks at the water's edge.

SCIENTIFIC NAME *Perlodes and other genera*

DISTRIBUTION	Worldwide
SIZE	Typical length 1 in. (2.5cm)

MAYFLY

These insects have one of the strangest life cycles in the insect world. They spend up to three years as underwater nymphs, feeding on algae and tiny plants. Once they leave the water and become winged adults, they have no digestive system—they cannot eat and often die within hours. Adult mayflies appear in early summer, when they flutter over rivers and lakes in dense swarms. After mating, the females scatter their eggs on the water.

SCIENTIFIC NAME *Ephemera and other genera*

DISTRIBUTION	Worldwide
SIZE	Typical length 2 in. (5cm), including tails

ABOVE *Stoneflies, such
as this European* Perlodes
microcephala, *have much
shorter tails than mayflies.*
BELOW *This adult stonefly*
(Leuctra fusca) *is resting
on a waterside flower.*

GRASSHOPPERS, KATYDIDS, AND CRICKETS

There are at least 20,000 species of grasshoppers, katydids, and crickets, found most commonly in warm parts of the world. They have powerful back legs that they often use to jump away from danger, instead of flying. Many of these insects do not have wings, but those that do have two quite different pairs. The forewings are tough and leathery; they protect the delicate hind wings. Many crickets are hunters or scavengers, but most grasshoppers and katydids feed on plants. During the breeding season, all these insects communicate by sound. Each species has its own distinctive "song," enabling males to attract the right mate. After mating, the females lay their eggs on plants or in the ground. The young, called hoppers, look like tiny versions of their parents, although they do not have fully formed wings.

Feet have hooked claws

Abdomen expands like a telescope for laying eggs in the ground

ABOVE *Meadow grasshoppers have very small hind wings and cannot fly.*

RIGHT *The great green bushcricket (Tettigonia viridissima) is a European relative of the true katydid. It hunts other insects after dark, using its oversized antennae to track them down.*

BELOW *This green katydid (Horatosphaga leggei) comes from Namibia in southwest Africa. Many katydids are green, making them difficult to see among plants.*

MEADOW GRASSHOPPER

This widespread insect lives in all kinds of rough grassland, where its "song" can be heard throughout the summer. As with most grasshoppers, the males do almost all the singing, rubbing their back legs against their front wings. Each back leg has a line of tiny pegs on the side facing the grasshopper's body. When the legs move up and down, the pegs scrape against hard ridges on the wings, creating a short burst of sound.

SCIENTIFIC NAME	*Chorthippus parallelus*
DISTRIBUTION	Europe
SIZE	Up to 1 in. (2.5cm) long

DESERT LOCUST

A locust is any kind of grasshopper that moves in swarms, attacking and destroying crops. There are many species, but the desert locust is by far the most famous. It lives like other grasshoppers, but in some weather conditions, locusts gather together. When their food runs out, they take off in a swarm that can contain 50 billion individuals. The swarm can do tremendous damage, and once the locusts settle on crops, little can be done to move them on.

SCIENTIFIC NAME	*Schistocerca migratoria*
DISTRIBUTION	Africa, Asia
SIZE	About 3.5 in. (9cm) long

Powerful back legs

Spiny forelegs grip prey

Slender hind legs

TRUE KATYDID

Katydids are flattened from side to side, and camouflaged to look like bright green leaves. They have very long antennae, and their ears are on their front legs. They live in trees and bushes, where their camouflage is so convincing that they are hard to spot until they move. Katydids feed mainly at night; this is also when they sing. True katydids have a two-part song that sounds like "katy-did, katy-did." There are many other species of katydids, particularly in the tropics, whose calls can be very different.

SCIENTIFIC NAME	*Pterophylla camellifolia*
DISTRIBUTION	Eastern North America
SIZE	Up to 2 in. (5cm) long

CAMOUFLAGE

Grasshoppers, katydids, and crickets have few defenses against attack from other animals. To survive, many of them rely on being difficult for predators to see. This is called being camouflaged. Many insects use camouflage because they are small and easily disguised.

In the simplest kind of camouflage, an animal blends in with its background. Many grasshoppers are green or brown, which helps hide them among leaves. Blending in is especially important in habitats where there are few places to hide from predators. In deserts, insects and lizards are camouflaged so that they blend in with stones. In polar regions, hares and foxes have a white coat and owls have white feathers to blend in with the snow. Some of these animals change color with the seasons, so that they do not stand out when the snow melts in spring.

Another kind of camouflage, called mimicry, uses shape for disguise. For example, some caterpillars look like bird droppings, while many moths resemble twigs. By resembling things that are inedible, they stand a much better chance of being left alone by predators. Some animals boost their chances of survival by imitating other animals that are poisonous or that bite or sting. Even though they are harmless, predators think that they are dangerous and leave them alone.

RIGHT
*This
gum leaf
grasshopper*
(Goniaea
australasiae)
*from Australia is
well camouflaged to
hide on a eucalyptus leaf.
Even its eyes are brown.*

TOP *Even though it lives under ground, the mole cricket can fly.*
CENTER *The house cricket is also a good flier.*
ABOVE *The European field cricket* (Gryllus campestris) *cannot fly.*

HOUSE CRICKET

At one time, the chirping of house crickets was a common sound in many homes. Today, people are not so welcoming to these insects, but the house cricket is still widespread in homes and garbage dumps throughout the world. Crickets have short forewings, and hind wings that roll up. They sing mainly at night by lifting up their forewings and rubbing one against the other. Crickets eat a wide variety of food. The house cricket survives on all kinds of kitchen scraps, from breadcrumbs to old vegetables.

SCIENTIFIC NAME *Acheta domestica*

DISTRIBUTION Originally from Africa and the Middle East, but introduced worldwide

SIZE About 0.8 in. (2cm) long

EUROPEAN MOLE CRICKET

Unlike other crickets, mole crickets spend most of their life under ground. They have small wings, a blunt, armored head, and powerful front legs that they use for tunneling through the soil. Mole crickets eat plant roots and can be a pest in some places. They are some of the noisiest insects in the world. During the breeding season, the males broadcast their song from a funnel-shaped chamber that acts as an amplifier. On a calm night, the song can be heard up to a mile (1.6km) away.

SCIENTIFIC NAME *Gryllotalpa* species

DISTRIBUTION Worldwide, particularly in warm regions

SIZE Typical length 2 in. (5cm)

GIANT WETA

Weighing up to 3 oz. (85g)—about three times as much as a mouse—this wingless cricket from New Zealand is one of the world's heaviest insects. Giant wetas spend the day hidden away and emerge at night to feed on leaves and seeds. Like many crickets, the female has a sword-shaped egg-laying tube, or ovipositor, that is easily mistaken for a dangerous sting. Wetas have existed in New Zealand for millions of years and, for most of that time, have had few natural enemies. Today, rats and other introduced mammals have hunted them almost to extinction.

SCIENTIFIC NAME *Deinacrida heteracantha*

DISTRIBUTION New Zealand

SIZE Up to 3 in. (8cm) long

STICK INSECTS, MANTISES, AND COCKROACHES

There are approximately 2,000 species of stick insects, 1,800 mantises, and about 5,000 cockroaches. They all have wings, but they often seem reluctant to use them. Stick insects and mantises spend most of their life on plants and are often superbly camouflaged. Cockroaches generally live on the ground. As well as living in different habitats, these insects eat different things. Stick insects are vegetarians, while mantises are stealthy hunters, stabbing other insects with their barbed front legs. Cockroaches are not fussy about what they eat. They nibble at any edible thing they can find. All these insects reproduce by laying eggs. Cockroaches lay theirs in a hard case that they sometimes carry around.

Praying mantis about to strike

BELOW *This American cockroach has recently shed its skin. It takes several hours for its new skin to harden.*
BOTTOM *Oriental cockroaches crowd together to nibble on a sandwich.*

STICK INSECT

Stick insects live in trees and bushes, where they feed on leaves. Most species are green or brown, and although they can be more than 6 in. (15cm) long, their slender bodies make them very difficult to spot. They move slowly and normally feed at night. Some stick insects can fly, but their wings are almost invisible when they are folded. Female stick insects often reproduce without mating. They scatter their eggs as they feed, letting them fall to the ground. When the young hatch, they look like small, wingless adults.

SCIENTIFIC NAME	*Carausius* and other genera
DISTRIBUTION	Worldwide
SIZE	Up to 12 in. (30cm) long

PRAYING MANTIS

A mantis holds its front legs together when poised to attack, so that it looks as if it is praying. If an insect lands nearby, the mantis keeps watch, then suddenly strikes. Its front legs snap around its victim and it begins to feed immediately, even though its prey may still be struggling to escape. Female mantises are larger than males, which can cause problems when they mate. The female may eat her partner, starting with the head. Except for flower mantises, which are brightly colored and have large, petallike flaps on their legs, most mantises are green or brown. They lay their eggs in foamy masses that they fasten to twigs. The foam soon hardens, protecting the eggs until they hatch.

SCIENTIFIC NAME	*Mantis* and other genera
DISTRIBUTION	Worldwide, usually in warm places
SIZE	Typical length 3 in. (8cm)

AMERICAN COCKROACH

Although it can fly, this unwelcome visitor usually scuttles around houses on its long, bristly legs. It is one of the fastest runners in the insect world, dashing into crevices as soon as it is disturbed. American cockroaches are active at night and will eat leftover food, paper, and even soap. Cockroaches rarely spread disease, but they contaminate food and leave an unpleasant smell. In warm conditions, they breed rapidly.

SCIENTIFIC NAME	*Periplaneta americana*
DISTRIBUTION	Worldwide
SIZE	Up to 2 in. (5cm) long

ORIENTAL COCKROACH

This cockroach is a poor flier—the male has short wings and the female is wingless. It eats a wide range of food and leaves a particularly strong smell where it has been foraging.

SCIENTIFIC NAME	*Blatta orientalis*
DISTRIBUTION	Worldwide
SIZE	Up to 1 in. (2.5cm) long

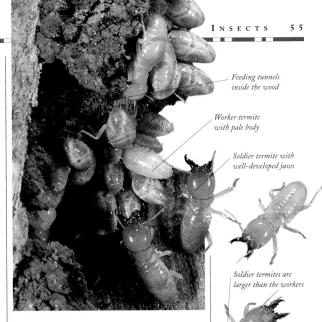

Feeding tunnels
inside the wood

Worker termite
with pale body

Soldier termite with
well-developed jaws

Soldier termites are
larger than the workers

TERMITES AND EARWIGS

There are about 1,900 species of termites, found only in warm parts of the world. Apart from ants, bees, and wasps, termites are the only insects that live in permanent family groups. These groups, called colonies, can be over two million animals strong. In each colony, only the queen lays eggs. Other members of the colony, called workers and soldiers, maintain the nest, forage for food, look after the young, and keep predators at bay. Termites are normally wingless, but during the breeding season, winged forms develop. These leave the nest to begin new colonies of their own. Some termites eat leaves and wood, but many use these to grow edible fungi that they cultivate under ground. There are about 1,200 species of earwigs throughout the world. They are not related to termites and do not live in colonies. They eat a wide variety of food and, like termites, are active mainly at night.

AFRICAN SAVANNA TERMITE

This termite builds giant nests up to 20 ft. (6m) high. Workers make the nest by mixing soil particles with their saliva, then letting the mixture harden in the sun. The interior of the nest contains the colony's fungus "gardens," together with chambers for the queen and the developing young. The queen is so large that she cannot leave her cell. She is tended by workers—they feed her and carry away her eggs. She can lay up to 30,000 eggs a day and may live for 25 years.

SCIENTIFIC NAME	*Macrotermes natalensis*
DISTRIBUTION	Tropical Africa
SIZE	Queen up to 5.5 in. (14cm) long; workers about 0.3 in. (8mm) long

COMPASS TERMITE

These Australian termites build nests in grassland and open woodland. Their nests are flattened from side to side, and the narrow ridge at the top always points in a north–south direction. This helps control the temperature inside. At dawn and dusk, when the air is cool, the east or west face of the nest soaks up the warmth of the rising or setting sun. At midday, when the air is hot, the nest is edge-on to the sun, so it does not absorb too much heat.

SCIENTIFIC NAME	*Amitermes meridionalis*
DISTRIBUTION	Australia
SIZE	Up to 0.3 in. (8mm) long

TREE TERMITE

Not all termites nest on the ground. Some species spend much of their lives in trees, where they build spherical nests high above the ground. They often make these nests from chewed-up wood fibers. Tree termites live throughout the tropics. Like ground-dwelling termites, the soldiers protect the colony fiercely. The soldiers of the species *Nasutitermes arboreus* have a head like a nozzle and can squirt a toxic liquid at anything that attacks the nest.

SCIENTIFIC NAME	*Nasutitermes* and other genera
DISTRIBUTION	Worldwide
SIZE	Typical length 0.25 in. (6mm)

COMMON EARWIG

Despite their name, earwigs have no interest in climbing into human ears! Instead, they hide among flower petals and in dark crevices by day, emerging after dark to feed on plants and small animals. They have pincers at the end of their body that they sometimes use to catch their prey. Although the pincers look dangerous, they are far too weak to pierce human skin. Female earwigs are careful parents, guarding their eggs until they hatch.

SCIENTIFIC NAME	*Forficula auricularia*
DISTRIBUTION	Originally from Europe, but introduced to North America, Australia, and New Zealand
SIZE	Up to 0.6 in. (1.5cm) long

ABOVE *Termites feed after dark and shy away from daylight. Here, a piece of rotting wood has been broken open to show an Australian species of termite* (Mastotermes darwinensis) *feeding inside. While the soldiers stand guard, the workers run for cover.*
BELOW *Earwigs have wings, but they are packed away under small wing covers and folded up many times.*

Common earwig

TRUE BUGS

There are at least 70,000 species of bugs, and they are found all over the world. The word "bug" is often used to mean any kind of insect, but true bugs are insects of a particular kind. They have mouthparts shaped like a beak, and they eat by piercing things and then sucking up liquid food. A bug's beak hinges where it joins its head and can be stowed under the body when not in use. Many bugs live on plants and feed on sap. Others attack animals, feeding on blood and other fluids. Some bugs are wingless. Those that do have wings hold them in different ways. Some fold them flat on their backs like a pair of crossed hands, while others fit them together to make a shape like a roof. Bugs reproduce by laying eggs. The young look similar to their parents and change shape gradually as they mature.

ROSE APHID

Aphids are tiny, sap-sucking bugs with a complicated life cycle. They can reproduce with amazing speed because the females often do not need to mate. They give birth to live young and can do so several times a day. As a result, they are soon surrounded by their growing families, all clustering together as they feed. They can be found in almost any garden, and they often attack crops, sometimes with serious results. The rose aphid is a common garden pest. It appears on roses in spring and damages leaves and buds.

SCIENTIFIC NAME	*Macrosiphum rosae*
DISTRIBUTION	Worldwide
SIZE	About 0.08 in. (2mm) long

TOP
These black bean aphids (Aphis fabae) *are crowded together on a broad bean plant. These aphids feed on many garden plants and spend the winter on shrubs.*
ABOVE *This orange-banded cicada* (Melampsalta melete) *is from Australia. There are more than 2,000 species of cicadas, each with its own song.*

CICADA

These noisy insects live in trees and shrubs. The males call by clicking hard plates on their abdomen. Each plate pops in and out like the lid of a can, making a high-pitched screech. Cicadas live in warm places and spend their early lives under ground.

SCIENTIFIC NAME	*Tibicen* and other genera
DISTRIBUTION	Worldwide
SIZE	Typical length 3 in. (8cm), including wings

THORN TREEHOPPER

Many bugs are protected from attack because they taste or smell unpleasant, but the thorn treehopper has a different protection. Its thorax is covered by a large, bright green shield that spreads backward over its wings. The shield has a sharp, upward-facing spine, making the insect look like a plant thorn. If a bird does try to eat the bug, the spine makes it difficult to swallow.

SCIENTIFIC NAME	*Umbonia spinosa*
DISTRIBUTION	South America
SIZE	About 0.4 in. (1cm) long

LANTERN BUG
OR PEANUT BUG

This tropical bug has two pairs of mothlike wings and a head ending in a big, bulbous "nose." The nose is the size and shape of a peanut and is almost half the length of the body. No one knows why lantern bugs have this nose. One suggestion is that it may deter predators, but there is no evidence that this is true.

SCIENTIFIC NAME	*Lanternaria lanternaria*
DISTRIBUTION	Central and South America
SIZE	About 2 in. (5cm) long

ASSASSIN BUG

These bugs feed on other animals, either by killing them outright or by feeding on their blood. Most assassin bugs have slender bodies and long legs, and although many species can fly, they often approach their victims on foot. In the tropics, assassin bugs sometimes live in houses. They hide by day and come out after dark to suck blood from people while they sleep. *Rhodnius prolixus* is one of several assassin bugs that can spread dangerous diseases as it feeds.

SCIENTIFIC NAME	*Rhodnius prolixus*
DISTRIBUTION	South America
SIZE	About 0.4 in. (1cm) long

Water strider catching prey

WATER STRIDER

Water striders can walk on water because their legs are tipped with water-repelling hairs. They feed on other insects that have crash-landed on the water's surface. When the insects struggle, ripples spread out from them. The water striders feel the ripples and move in to feed.

SCIENTIFIC NAME	*Gerris* and other genera
DISTRIBUTION	Worldwide
SIZE	Typical length 0.4 in. (1cm)

BACKSWIMMER

These common freshwater bugs swim
through water upside down. They use their
long, flattened hind legs like a pair of oars
to push themselves along. Backswimmers are
aggressive predators with a powerful bite. They
feed on tadpoles and small fish and often live in
garden ponds and cattle troughs. Backswimmers
have to surface to breathe, but they trap a thin
film of air around their body, which allows
them to stay under water for several minutes
at a time. They are good fliers.

SCIENTIFIC NAME *Notonecta* species

DISTRIBUTION Worldwide

SIZE About 0.6 in. (1.5cm) long

GIANT WATER BUG

This fearsome-looking insect is one of the
largest water bugs in North America. It feeds
on tadpoles, salamanders, and small fish, and
can stab its beak through human skin. An
animal this size needs a good supply of oxygen.
The giant water bug gets oxygen through a pair
of telescopic breathing tubes that stick out from
the end of its abdomen. It lays batches of about
100 eggs on underwater plants. The young are
cannibalistic—which means that they eat each
other—so only a few grow to adulthood.

SCIENTIFIC NAME *Lethocerus americanus*

DISTRIBUTION North America

SIZE Up to 2 in. (5cm) long

ABOVE *A backswimmer*
(Notonecta glauca) *lurks
at the surface of the water,
waiting for its prey. It is
covered by a bubble of air.*
BELOW *The giant water
bug clutches animals with
its front legs, then stabs
them with its
mouthparts.*

LACEWINGS, CADDISFLIES, AND FLEAS

There are about 5,000 species each of lacewings and caddisflies, and about 1,800 species of fleas. Caddisflies are most common where there is cool, flowing water, but lacewings and fleas are found everywhere. Adult lacewings and caddisflies all have long, narrow wings, but apart from this, the two groups look different and live in different ways. They do have one important feature in common—they start life as grubs, or larvae, and change shape abruptly as they mature. This process is called "complete metamorphosis." Lacewings usually spend their whole lives on land. Their wings are thin and transparent, with a complicated network of veins. Caddisflies start life in fresh water. As adults they have wings covered in fine hairs. Fleas do not have wings. When they become adults, they live on the skin of mammals and birds, where they feed by sucking blood.

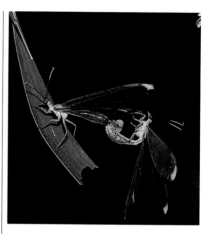

ABOVE *This is an Australian owlfly* (Nymphes melionides). **LEFT** *The owlfly* Libelloides coccajus *lives in southern and central Europe.*

Lacewings fly well and can take off vertically

Densely netted wings

ABOVE
A green lacewing (Chrysopa septempunctata) *takes off from a flower bud, using its wings like propellers.*

LACEWING

During early autumn, lacewings often come into houses in search of somewhere to hibernate. These insects are easily recognized by their lacy wings, but another striking feature is their eyes, which have a metallic, golden sheen. The adults lay eggs on stalks of mucus that quickly dry out in the air. The stalks are long and slender, and probably help keep the eggs out of the reach of hungry animals. Lacewing larvae have powerful jaws and often feed on aphids. Many camouflage themselves by wearing their victims' empty skin.

SCIENTIFIC NAME	*Chrysopa* and other genera
DISTRIBUTION	Worldwide
SIZE	About 0.7 in. (1.8cm), including wings

**Adult ant lion
(Palpares libelluloides)**

ANT LION

Ant lions are insect larvae that grow up to look like lacewings. In warm, dry parts of the world, sandy ground is often covered by small pits with sloping sides. Each one is made by an ant lion in search of food. They lurk at the bottoms of their pits with only their powerful jaws exposed. If an ant walks near the edge of the pit, the ant lion flicks sand at it until the ant falls in. Then it sucks its prey dry and throws the lifeless body back out of the pit.

SCIENTIFIC NAME	*Palpares* and other genera
DISTRIBUTION	Worldwide
SIZE	Typical adult about 4 in. (10cm) long, including wings; larva about 0.5 in. (1.2cm) long

OWLFLY

With two pairs of long, filmy wings, owlflies resemble dragonflies, and like dragonflies, they hunt other insects on the wing. Unlike dragonflies, however, they have short abdomens and long antennae. Owlflies actually belong to the same group of insects as lacewings. They spend all their lives on land. Owlfly larvae look like ant lions, but their bodies are flatter. They do not dig pits as ant lions do, but hide on the ground and under stones, grabbing any small insects that come within reach.

SCIENTIFIC NAME	*Libelloides* and other genera
DISTRIBUTION	Worldwide
SIZE	Typical length 2 in. (5cm)

MANTIDFLY

With its slender body and stabbing front legs, a mantidfly looks just like a small praying mantis (page 54). It is actually a relative of the lacewing, with similar delicate wings. Mantidflies use their front legs like praying mantises to catch prey, but they tackle much smaller insects. The European species *Mantispa styriaca* eats midges and other small flies, and its larvae feed on spiders' eggs.

SCIENTIFIC NAME	*Mantispa styriaca*
DISTRIBUTION	Europe
SIZE	About 0.7 in. (1.8cm) long, including wings

SNAKEFLY

A snakefly's head is on a long "neck," which is actually part of its thorax. The neck is usually raised above the rest of the body, making the fly look like a snake about to strike. Snakeflies live in trees and are fierce predators of aphids and beetles. They lay their eggs in crevices in bark. Their larvae feed underneath the bark, hunting out the grubs of wood-boring insects.

SCIENTIFIC NAME *Raphidia* and other genera

DISTRIBUTION Worldwide

SIZE Typical length 1 in. (2.5cm)

CADDISFLY

All caddisflies lay their eggs on water plants or on the surface of ponds and streams. When the larvae hatch, they are vulnerable to attack. Their first task is to make themselves a case from grains of sand, tiny shells, and parts of plants, binding them together with silk. Each species always uses its distinctive design. When the case is finished, only the larva's head remains outside, allowing it to collect small scraps of food.

SCIENTIFIC NAME *Phryganea* and other genera

DISTRIBUTION Worldwide

SIZE Typical length of adult 1.5 in. (4cm)

ABOVE *The case of the caddisfly larva* Phryganea grandis *is made of small pieces of leaf arranged in a spiral.*

At rest, the wings fold over the body to form a roof

Egg-laying tube, or ovipositor

Powerful jaws

Small, buttonlike eyes

Long antennae

Transparent, heavily veined wings

Snakefly with open wings

CAT FLEA

Fleas are specially shaped for life aboard other animals. They have sharp mouthparts and powerful back legs, and their bodies are flattened from side to side to help them slip through feathers or fur. They feed on their host's blood. Cat fleas are the most common species inside homes, where they bite people and dogs as well as cats. They start life as legless larvae, growing up in places where cats sleep. After a few weeks, each larva spins a tiny cocoon and changes into an adult flea. If a person or a pet walks past, the flea senses the vibrations. Within seconds, it breaks out of its cocoon and jumps on its host.

SCIENTIFIC NAME *Ctenocephalides felis*

DISTRIBUTION Worldwide

SIZE About 0.08 in. (2mm) long

ABOVE *Sitting at the tip of a twig, a snakefly (*Raphidia notata*) waits for a chance to feed.*
LEFT *A cat flea scuttles through its host's fur. Fleas are very tough, which makes it difficult to kill them.*

BEETLES

With about 300,000 species, beetles make up about one third of all the insects that scientists have identified. Found all over the world, they include tropical heavyweights more than 5 in. (12cm) long, as well as tiny animals barely visible to the naked eye. All beetles have hard forewings, called elytra. When the elytra are closed, they fit together over a beetle's abdomen, covering its hind wings like a case. The beetles can then crawl around without damaging their hind wings, which they use to fly. Beetles live on land and in fresh water. They eat all kinds of food, from pollen and leaves to wool and animal remains. They start life as larvae, or grubs, with strong jaws and tiny legs—or in some cases, no legs at all. Many beetle larvae are active hunters, but others tunnel their way through their food, keeping safely out of sight. After a time, a beetle larva turns into a pupa; after weeks, or sometimes months, an adult beetle emerges.

Streamlined body for fast swimming

Large eyes can see under water

Fringed legs work like paddles

Mouthparts used for tasting prey

ABOVE *A green tiger beetle* (Cicindela campestris) *makes a meal of a caterpillar, slicing it up with its jaws.*

Antennae can detect animals moving under water

Front legs used for grasping prey

TIGER BEETLE

Tiger beetles rival cockroaches for the title of the fastest-running insects in the world. They spend most of their lives on the ground, chasing small insects in daylight and snatching them up in their long, powerful jaws. Their larvae dig burrows in the ground. They use their head to plug the burrow, then ambush creatures that pass nearby. Adult tiger beetles have very good eyesight, and most of them are good fliers. Many species have bright metallic colors.

Green tiger beetle on the ground

SCIENTIFIC NAME	*Cicindela* and other genera
DISTRIBUTION	Worldwide
SIZE	Typical length 0.6 in. (1.5cm)

GREAT DIVING BEETLE

Although they are good fliers, diving beetles spend almost all of their lives under water. They live in ponds and lakes and breathe air that they store under their elytra. This air supply makes them very buoyant, and they have to swim hard to stay submerged. Adult diving beetles are ferocious predators, eating tadpoles and even small fish. At their largest stage, the larvae are even longer than the adults. They are just as aggressive as their parents and catch their prey with huge curved jaws. The great diving beetle is one of the largest species—many others are found throughout the world.

SCIENTIFIC NAME	*Dytiscus marginalis*
DISTRIBUTION	Europe, Asia, North America
SIZE	Up to 1.5 in. (4cm) long

ABOVE *A great diving beetle refills its air reserves. It replaces the bubble of air under its elytra by breaking through the surface of the water with its abdomen.*

Air stored beneath elytra

Whirligig beetle from above

BOMBARDIER BEETLE

The bombardier beetle has a unique and startling way of defending itself. If threatened, it squirts a flammable gas that explodes as it sprays into the air. The explosion produces a sharp crack and a puff of smoke, and is often enough to deter the beetle's enemies. The gas is made in the beetle's abdomen and streams out of a nozzle that can be pointed at the attacker. Sometimes, however, the bombardier is the attacker—both the adults and larvae are carnivorous.

SCIENTIFIC NAME *Brachinus crepitans*
DISTRIBUTION Europe
SIZE Up to 0.4 in. (1cm) long

BURYING BEETLE

Found all over the world, burying beetles are nature's undertakers. They use their keen sense of smell to find the dead bodies of small birds and mammals after dark. When they discover one, they dig away the soil beneath it until the body is buried. Once the remains are under ground, the female makes a nest chamber near the body and lays her eggs on a ball of decaying flesh. She feeds the larvae for a few days after they hatch, but after this they feed on the carcass itself. Some burying beetles are black all over, others are black and red.

SCIENTIFIC NAME *Nicrophorus* and other genera
DISTRIBUTION Worldwide
SIZE Typical length 1 in. (2.5cm)

ROVE BEETLE

With its long, black body and powerful jaws, this nocturnal beetle has a menacing appearance. If anything does try to attack it, it opens its jaws and raises its abdomen like a sting. Rove beetles have short elytra but well-developed hind wings folded up many times. Most of them are

carnivorous. There are many species of rove beetles, but they are not often seen because they hide during the day.

SCIENTIFIC NAME *Staphylinus olens*
DISTRIBUTION Europe
SIZE About 1 in. (2.5cm) long

Whirligig beetle on water

WHIRLIGIG BEETLE

These small, oval beetles live on ponds and slow-flowing streams, where they speed along on the surface of the water. Their legs are short and covered with water-repellent hairs, which prevent them sinking through the surface. Whirligigs feed on small water animals and on insects that have fallen into the water. Their eyes are divided into two parts, so that they can see above and below the surface of the water at the same time.

SCIENTIFIC NAME *Gyrinus* species
DISTRIBUTION Worldwide
SIZE Typical length 0.3 in. (8mm)

VIOLET GROUND BEETLE

Unlike tiger beetles, ground beetles hunt mainly at night and do not need to be brightly colored. The violet ground beetle is a somber purple-blue color, with an iridescent sheen. Ground beetles' legs are strong and powerful, enabling them to sprint after their prey. Their larvae are also efficient hunters. They actively search out caterpillars and other small insects, helping to control species that are garden pests. There are thousands of species of these useful insects. The violet ground beetle is common in gardens.

SCIENTIFIC NAME *Carabus violaceus*
DISTRIBUTION Europe
SIZE Up to 1 in. (2.5cm) long

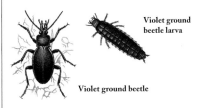

Violet ground beetle larva

Violet ground beetle

Bombardier beetle squirting gas

Bombardier beetle

Burying beetle

Rove beetle

ABOVE *The bombardier beetle, burying beetle, and rove beetle spend most of their lives on the ground. They can fly if they have to.*

DWARF BEETLE

As well as being the smallest beetles in the world, dwarf beetles are among the smallest of all insects. The smallest species, *Nanosella fungi*, looks like little more than a speck. These beetles feed on the decaying remains of plants and fungi. Their feathery hind wings fold when not in use.

SCIENTIFIC NAME	*Nanosella fungi*
DISTRIBUTION	Central and South America
SIZE	.01 in. (0.25mm) long

STAG BEETLE

Tough elytra

Male stag beetles have elongated jaws shaped like a pair of antlers. During the breeding season, they use their jaws to grapple with rival males, sometimes lifting them off their feet. The fights are not dangerous because the jaws cannot fully close. After the battle, the loser walks away. Adult stag beetles feed on tree sap, and their larvae grow up in decaying wood. There are nearly 1,000 species of stag beetles worldwide. Most are black or chestnut brown.

SCIENTIFIC NAME	*Lucanus* and other genera
DISTRIBUTION	Worldwide
SIZE	Males typically about 2 in. (5cm) long including jaws; females smaller

ABOVE *Despite its fearsome appearance, the male European stag beetle (Lucanus cervus) is a harmless vegetarian.*
BELOW *Stag beetles mate only after a lengthy courtship. The female lays her eggs in the rotting wood of old trees.*

DUNG BEETLE

As their name suggests, dung beetles eat animal dung. They shape it into balls, rolling it away and burying it as food for their young. Their broad front legs and shovel-shaped heads are ideal tools for dealing with their food. Dung beetles are very useful animals because they get rid of dung and help to fertilize the soil. They are found in all warm parts of the world, but are particularly common in Africa. In the 1960s, thousands of African dung beetles were introduced to Australia to get rid of cattle dung.

SCIENTIFIC NAME	*Scarabaeus* and other genera
DISTRIBUTION	Worldwide
SIZE	Typical length 1 in. (2.5cm)

JAPANESE BEETLE

This small beetle feeds on leaves and fruit, and can seriously damage crops. Its larvae live under ground, where they also cause damage when they feed. Originally from Japan, this beetle reached North America in 1916, stowing away inside a cargo of plants. It has now spread throughout the eastern United States. The Japanese beetle and its relatives often fly into brightly lit windows after dark.

SCIENTIFIC NAME	*Popilla japonica*
DISTRIBUTION	Japan, North America
SIZE	Up to 0.5 in. (1.2cm) long

Japanese beetle—a relative of the cockchafer

COCKCHAFER

This large beetle usually flies after dark and sometimes causes alarm when it zooms noisily through an open window in spring. Despite its size, the cockchafer is harmless to people, though it can be a serious pest on farms and in gardens. Adult cockchafers feed on the leaves of trees. Their larvae live under ground, where they chew their way through roots and often attack cereals and other crops. They take up to four years to mature.

SCIENTIFIC NAME
Melolontha melolontha

DISTRIBUTION Europe

SIZE Up to 1 in. (2.5cm) long

Fan-shaped antennae

Hind wings unfolded, ready for flight

LEFT *Like all beetles, cockchafers flap only their hind wings when they fly. Their forewings stay still, sticking out at right angles to the body.*

HERCULES BEETLE

The male Hercules beetle is the world's longest beetle. Half of its length comes from a pair of gigantic "horns." The horns are arranged one above the other—the lower one is attached to the beetle's head, the upper one to its thorax. The horns are not used as weapons, but help the males attract females. The females are much smaller than the males and have much shorter horns. Hercules beetles feed on fruit and are found only in the American tropics.

SCIENTIFIC NAME *Dynastes hercules*

DISTRIBUTION Central and South America, Caribbean islands

SIZE Males up to 7.5 in. (19cm) long including horns; females about 2 in. (5cm) long

GOLIATH BEETLE

This beetle, the heaviest insect alive today, weighs up to 3.5 oz. (100g). Despite its weight, it is a good flier. The Goliath beetle lives in tropical forests, where the adult eats flowers high above the ground. Its larvae develop in rotting wood.

SCIENTIFIC NAME *Goliathus giganteus*

DISTRIBUTION Central and West Africa

SIZE Up to 4 in. (10cm)

Elytra lifted away from the body

CLICK BEETLE

These beetles have an unusual way of getting out of danger. If click beetles are threatened, they drop to the ground on their back, with their legs held closely by their sides. Then, with a sudden click, they flip themselves into the air. Click beetles can do this because they have a special joint in their thorax. It is normally locked by a peg, but if the beetle arches its back, the joint suddenly bends, throwing the beetle upward. Click beetles feed on plants. Their larvae, called wireworms, live under ground and can cause damage to plants by eating their roots.

SCIENTIFIC NAME *Athous* and other genera

DISTRIBUTION Worldwide

SIZE Typical length 0.6 in. (1.5cm)

Adult
cockchafer

Cockchafer
larva

Click beetle
larva

Male click beetle
(*Athous haemorrhoidalis*)

TOP *Cockchafer larvae have powerful jaws and well-developed legs. They curl up in the shape of the letter C.*
ABOVE *Click beetle larvae have a slender body and small legs, which is why they are called wireworms.*

GLOWWORM

On warm summer nights, female glowworms climb up blades of grass and produce a light to attract males flying overhead. They generate the light in a special organ on the underside of their abdomen. If disturbed, they turn off their light immediately. The females look more like wood lice than beetles, with stubby legs and no wings. Glowworms eat small snails. They paralyze them with a digestive fluid that turns the snail's body into liquid, then suck up their meal.

SCIENTIFIC NAME	*Lampyris noctiluca*
DISTRIBUTION	Europe
SIZE	Up to 0.6 in. (1.5cm) long

FIREFLY

Fireflies are related to glowworms, but unlike glowworms, both males and females produce a light as a way of finding a mate. Male fireflies flash their light as they fly a few yards above the ground. The females flash back from the ground or from trees, guiding the males toward them. Each firefly species has its own flashing sequence, to ensure that they find the right mate.

SCIENTIFIC NAME	*Photinus* and other genera
DISTRIBUTION	Worldwide
SIZE	Typical length 0.6 in. (1.5cm)

Two-spotted ladybug (*Adalia bipunctata*) eating an aphid

Aphids can produce enough young to cover a rose bush in only a few days

Ladybug holds its prey in its strong jaws

Seven-spotted ladybug (*Coccinella 7-punctata*)

LADYBUG

Few insects are as well-known as ladybugs, or as useful. These brightly colored beetles spend their lives on plants, feeding on aphids and other garden pests—which is why they are welcome in gardens. The two-spotted ladybug (*Adalia bipunctata*) is one of the most common and widespread ladybugs. Young ladybugs do not look much like their parents, with a narrow body and stubby legs, but they usually eat the same kind of food. During the fall, ladybugs often gather together to hibernate under loose bark or among fallen leaves. Their bold colors warn birds and other animals of their unpleasant taste.

SCIENTIFIC NAME	*Adalia* and other genera
DISTRIBUTION	Worldwide
SIZE	Typical length 0.2 in. (5mm)

TOP LEFT *Clinging to the top of a blade of grass, a female glowworm waves her luminous abdomen to attract winged males.*
TOP RIGHT *Ladybugs can eat up to 50 aphids a day.*
ABOVE *Many ladybugs are named after their spots. Some species have more than 20 spots, which can be difficult to count.*

MUSEUM BEETLE

This small insect belongs to a family of beetles that often damage fabrics, fur, and stored food. It gets its name because it attacks stuffed animals, ruining many museum displays. The adult beetles, which are small and oval, do little harm. Most of the damage is done by their furry larvae, which are known as woolly bears. Museum beetles and their many relatives do not need to drink because they get all the water they need from their food. They can survive for years locked in closets or cabinets, slowly eating their way through the contents.

SCIENTIFIC NAME	*Anthrenus museorum*
DISTRIBUTION	Worldwide
SIZE	About 0.2 in. (5mm) long

FURNITURE BEETLE

More commonly known as a woodworm, this beetle bores its way through all kinds of dead wood. The larvae do most of the damage, and given enough time, they can reduce timber and furniture to dust. Adult furniture beetles tunnel out of the wood to breed, leaving the circular holes that are a sure sign of woodworm damage. Like many other wood-boring beetles, these insects have a cylindrical body and a small head tucked away beneath the thorax. Because wood is not very nutritious, they can take a long time to reach maturity.

SCIENTIFIC NAME	*Anobium punctatum*
DISTRIBUTION	Worldwide
SIZE	About 0.2 in. (5mm) long

DEATHWATCH BEETLE

This small, brown beetle feeds on wood, especially old trees and decaying trunks. If it gets inside a building, it can attack large timbers, sometimes causing them to collapse. Adult deathwatch beetles attract each other by tapping their jaws on the wood. This gives the beetles their name—the eerie sound was often heard in the middle of the night, and was particularly noticeable to those who sat silently watching over a person on their deathbed.

SCIENTIFIC NAME	
	Xestobium rufovillosum
DISTRIBUTION	Worldwide
SIZE	About 0.3 in. (8mm) long

LONGHORN BEETLE

There are about 25,000 species of longhorn beetles. They are wood-boring insects that attack trees all over the world. They have long front legs and even longer antennae, or "horns," and many are beautifully colored. The harlequin longhorn (*Acrocinus longimanus*) is one of the most spectacular of all. It has brilliant black, red, and yellow markings, and its antennae can be over 5 in. (12cm) long—longer than the rest of its body. Harlequin longhorns live in tropical forests. They are active by day, but often crash into lights after dark.

SCIENTIFIC NAME	*Acrocinus* and other genera
DISTRIBUTION	Worldwide
SIZE	Up to 3 in. (8cm) long, excluding antennae

WASP BEETLE

This European longhorn beetle is vividly colored yellow and black. Many people mistake it for a wasp—as do birds and other animals. They see its wasp-like colors, think it has a dangerous sting, and leave it alone. The colors are only part of the beetle's strategy—it also moves in a jerky, wasp-like way.

SCIENTIFIC NAME	*Clytus arietis*
DISTRIBUTION	Europe
SIZE	Up to 0.7 in. (1.8cm) long

Furniture beetle

Deathwatch beetle

TOP *When furniture beetles become adults, they bite their way out of wood, making tiny, round holes.*
ABOVE *Deathwatch beetles tap on wood during their breeding season in spring and early summer.*
BELOW *Wasp beetles are good fliers. This one is opening its brightly colored forewings, ready to take off.*

Adult hazelnut weevil

Hazelnut weevil larva emerging from a hazelnut

FLEA BEETLE

If a flea beetle is touched, it escapes by jumping like a flea. Flea beetles can do this because they have a small, light body and specially thickened hind legs. These tiny beetles nibble the surface of leaves and can be numerous enough to cause problems in gardens and on farms. Each kind of flea beetle has its own favorite plants. Some species feed on turnips, cabbages, and cauliflowers. Other common species eat the leaves of potatoes, grapevines, and beans.

SCIENTIFIC NAME	*Phyllotreta* and other genera
DISTRIBUTION	Worldwide
SIZE	Typical length 0.1 in. (2.5mm)

OIL BEETLE

These lumbering insects have a large abdomen and no hind wings. If they are touched, they can produce an oily liquid that blisters human skin, so they are sometimes called blister beetles. Adult oil beetles feed on plants, but their larvae are parasites of other insects. When the larvae hatch, they cling to other insects with their long legs and sharp claws and feed on the insects' eggs or young. Later, they become more like maggots, losing their legs before finally turning into adults. Some oil beetles attack bees, but many others target grasshoppers.

SCIENTIFIC NAME	*Meloe* and other genera
DISTRIBUTION	Worldwide
SIZE	Typical length 1 in. (2.5cm)

TORTOISE BEETLE

Tortoise beetles have a humped back formed by their thorax and elytra. The hump covers their legs and head, just like a tortoise's shell. These beetles feed on plants. They are often brightly colored, sometimes with a metallic sheen. Some species are brilliant green, which makes them difficult to see on leaves.

SCIENTIFIC NAME	*Cassida* and other genera
DISTRIBUTION	Worldwide
SIZE	Typical length 0.4 in. (1cm)

COLORADO POTATO BEETLE

This beetle is one of the world's most damaging agricultural pests. Adult Colorado potato beetles and their larvae thrive on potato leaves and can soon reduce an entire field to little more than stalks. An inhabitant of North America, it originally fed on wild mountain plants. When potato farming spread across the continent in the mid-1800s, the beetle spread too. During the 1920s, it was accidentally introduced into Europe, and it is still spreading in other parts of the world.

SCIENTIFIC NAME	*Leptinotarsa decemlineata*
DISTRIBUTION	North America, Europe, and other parts of the world
SIZE	Up to 0.5 in. (1.2cm)

HAZELNUT WEEVIL

There are about 40,000 species of weevils, making them the largest family in the insect world. Most of them have a long, curving snout, with antennae halfway down and mouthparts at the end. The female hazelnut weevil uses its snout to gnaw holes in young hazelnuts. It lays an egg in each hole, and the larva uses the nut as a home and as food. When the nut drops off the tree, the larva climbs out and grows to adulthood in the soil.

SCIENTIFIC NAME	*Curculio nucum*
DISTRIBUTION	Europe
SIZE	Female about 0.3 in. (8mm) long, including snout; male slightly smaller

BOLL WEEVIL

In the 1890s, the boll weevil spread from Mexico to the United States, where it has been a problem ever since. The adult weevils feed on the seedpods, or bolls, of cotton plants, and lay their eggs inside them. Cotton bolls normally produce cotton fibers, but when they are attacked by weevils they fall off the plants, ruining much of the crop. Boll weevils breed quickly, cramming

LEFT *A hazelnut weevil larva emerges from a nut, ready to turn into an adult.*
BELOW AND RIGHT *Green tortoise beetles* (Cassida viridis) *keep their heads tucked under their "shells."*

ABOVE LEFT *The Colorado potato beetle has five black stripes on each elytron.*
ABOVE RIGHT *Oil beetles cannot fly. This is a male beetle; females are slightly larger.*

Narrow gap between thorax and elytra

TOP AND ABOVE *Adult elm bark beetles emerge from trees in late spring and early summer. They spread a fungal disease through elm trees, preventing them from moving water from their roots to their leaves. The leaves turn yellow and fall early, and after a few years, the diseased trees die.*

Neck hinges where the head and thorax join

ABOVE *The giraffe beetle's neck is made up of a very long thorax and a stretched-out head.*

up to ten generations into a single year. This makes them very difficult to control.

SCIENTIFIC NAME *Anthonomus grandis*

DISTRIBUTION North and South America

SIZE Up to 0.3 in. (8mm) long

GIRAFFE BEETLE

This weevil has a hinged "neck" that is over twice as long as its body. Its antennae are just behind its mouthparts and look like whiskers at the end of its nose. The giraffe beetle lives on trees, and its neck helps it to reach its food.

SCIENTIFIC NAME *Tribus attelabini*

DISTRIBUTION Madagascar

SIZE About 1 in. (2.5cm) long

ELM BARK BEETLE

Bark beetles live beneath tree bark, where the larvae feed by tunneling through the surface of the wood. As they feed, they create a branching pattern of tunnels, called a gallery, which is easy to see when the dead bark falls away. When a larva becomes an adult, it stops feeding, chews its way through the bark, and flies away to breed. As their name suggests, elm bark beetles attack elm trees. They do not kill elm trees themselves, but they spread Dutch elm disease as they feed. This disease originally came from Asia, but it has spread all over the Northern Hemisphere, killing millions of trees in Europe and North America.

SCIENTIFIC NAME *Scolytus scolytus*

DISTRIBUTION Europe, Asia, North America

SIZE About 0.2 in. (5mm) long

FLIES

Unlike most other insects, flies have just one pair of wings. Instead of hind wings, they have small, pin-shaped organs called halteres, which help them balance during flight. Most flies are extremely nimble in the air. They can hover and land upside down, and they can dodge out of the way very quickly, which makes them difficult to catch. Adult flies almost always feed on fluids, including nectar and blood. Some have mouthparts that pierce and suck, but others have a pad that dissolves their food and soaks it up like a sponge. Fly larvae, or maggots, eat a wide range of different foods. Unlike adult flies, they have no legs, and they often burrow through what they eat. Nearly 90,000 species of flies have been identified from all over the world. Many other insects, such as dragonflies (page 50) and butterflies (pages 72–79), have the word "fly" in their name, but they do not belong to this group.

Midge

Mosquito

Bee fly

TOP *A male chironomid midge. This type of midge is harmless because neither the male nor female bites.*
CENTER *Mosquitoes live wherever there are pools of water in which to lay their eggs. This is a male of the species* Culex pipiens.
BOTTOM *Unlike a real bee, the bee fly has only one pair of wings.*

CRANE FLY

Compared to other flies, crane flies are big and clumsy, with a slow, haphazard way of flying. They have a slender body and wings, and are quite fragile. Their long legs break off easily, although losing one or two seems to do them little harm. Adult crane flies do not eat, but their larvae, called leatherjackets, feed on rotting plants and roots. Leatherjackets live under ground or in water and can be serious pests. There are many species of crane flies. *Tipula maxima* is one of the largest, with a wingspan of about 2 in. (5cm).

SCIENTIFIC NAME	*Tipula maxima*
DISTRIBUTION	Europe
SIZE	Up to 1 in. (2.5cm) long, excluding legs

MOSQUITO

There are more than 2,000 species of mosquitoes worldwide, and they live almost everywhere from the tropics to the Arctic. Male mosquitoes eat nectar from flowers, but the females have sharp mouthparts and feed by sucking blood. These small, biting flies often find their way indoors. Their bites are annoying because they itch, but they can also be dangerous because mosquitoes carry diseases. Most common in the tropics, these include yellow fever, dengue fever, and malaria. Female mosquitoes lay their eggs on the surface of stagnant water. The eggs hatch into wriggling larvae that feed on tiny plants and animals. Once the larvae are fully grown, they change into comma-shaped pupae. These mature into adults that eventually fly away.

SCIENTIFIC NAME	*Culex* and other genera
DISTRIBUTION	Worldwide
SIZE	Typical length 0.5 in. (1.2cm)

BITING MIDGE

Many small flies are known as midges. Some are harmless, but others have an irritating bite that seems out of proportion to their tiny size. Many of these biting midges belong to a family of insects that grow up in ditches and boggy ground. As with mosquitoes, the adult males are harmless, but the females need a meal of blood before they can lay their eggs. Biting midges are common in places where the ground is waterlogged. Some attack people, but many suck the blood of caterpillars and other insects.

SCIENTIFIC NAME	*Culicoides* and other genera
DISTRIBUTION	Mainly Northern Hemisphere
SIZE	Typical length 0.1 in. (2.5mm)

Black fly (*Simulium equinum*)

BLACK FLY

Unlike mosquitoes and biting midges, these tiny flies grow up in running water. Their larvae are usually attached to water plants or stones, where they collect food with two tufts of hairs. In early summer, adult black flies float to the surface on bubbles of air. The males fly off to find plants, and the females go in search of blood. Swarms of female black flies can make life uncomfortable for other animals.

SCIENTIFIC NAME	*Simulium* and other genera
DISTRIBUTION	Worldwide
SIZE	Typical length 0.1 in. (2.5mm)

BEE FLY

These furry flies look like bees but do not sting. Adult bee flies feed at flowers. They grip the petals with their front legs, then hover while sucking nectar with their long mouthparts. Female bee flies lay their eggs in or near the nests of solitary bees and wasps. Their larvae eat the food in the nest and also attack the grubs.

SCIENTIFIC NAME	*Bombylius* species
DISTRIBUTION	Worldwide
SIZE	Typical length 1 in. (2.5cm)

Female horse flies are larger than the males

ABOVE
A female horse fly (Tabanus bromius) lays eggs on a rush plant.

Robber fly with outstretched wings

Bristly legs used for grabbing other insects

ROBBER FLY

Fast flying insects with powerful legs, robber flies eat other insects, often catching them in midair. Then the robber fly stabs its prey with its hard mouthparts and sucks it dry. Robber flies have long bristles on their faces—these help protect their eyes when they pounce.

SCIENTIFIC NAME	*Asilus* and other genera
DISTRIBUTION	Worldwide
SIZE	Typical length 2 in. (5cm)

Large eyes spot moving prey

HORSE FLY

Male horse flies feed on nectar and pollen, but the females feed on blood. They are large insects with big eyes, sharp mouthparts, and a painful bite. They attack large mammals, including humans. Some of them make no sound as they fly—a trick that helps them escape notice as they home in to feed. Once a horse fly has landed, it cuts its victim's skin and then sucks up the blood as it oozes out. Horse fly larvae live in mud and wet soil, feeding on small animals.

SCIENTIFIC NAME	*Tabanus* and other genera
DISTRIBUTION	Worldwide
SIZE	Typical length 1 in. (2.5cm)

HOVER FLY

These flies are some of nature's finest mimics. Though harmless, they look very similar to bees or wasps. The resemblance is so strong that many predators are fooled into leaving them alone. They feed at flowers and often hover just above them before landing to eat. During the summer breeding season, males may claim a patch of flowers for themselves. If a rival male tries to visit the flowers, a midair skirmish breaks out.

SCIENTIFIC NAME	*Syrphus* and other genera
DISTRIBUTION	Worldwide
SIZE	Typical length 1 in. (2.5cm)

Hover fly larva

Adult hover fly

LEFT *A robber fly (Asilus crabroniformis) waits on blackberries for prey. Fruit like this often attracts other flies, which the robber fly can grab as they approach.* **ABOVE** *The hover fly Syrphus ribesii is a European species.*

One pair of transparent wings

Feet have claws and pads so the fly can walk upside down on any surface

Body is covered with bristles that sense movement in the air

Metallic blue abdomen

ABOVE *Bluebottles have a keen sense of smell. They quickly gather on the bodies of dead animals, where they lay their eggs.*

CENTER AND ABOVE
House flies have large eyes that take up most of the head. Their mouthparts fold up underneath the head when not in use.

BLUEBOTTLE

This large fly often enters houses in summer, where it buzzes around noisily looking for somewhere to lay its eggs. It gets its name from its bristly abdomen, which has a dark blue sheen. Adult bluebottles feed on rotting meat and open wounds, and they lay hundreds of creamy white eggs where they feed. The eggs produce wriggling larvae, or maggots, that quickly burrow into the food. In hot weather, the bluebottle's entire life cycle takes just over a month. Similar flies, called greenbottles, live in much the same way.

SCIENTIFIC NAME	*Calliphora vomitoria*
DISTRIBUTION	Worldwide
SIZE	0.5 in. (1.2cm) long

HOUSE FLY

This fly is probably one of the most common insects on earth. It has spread with people across the planet and can be seen in places as far apart as New Zealand and the Arctic. Adult house flies feed on anything sweet or rotting, mopping it up with their spongy mouthparts. As they feed, they often leave patches of saliva that turn into "fly spots" when they dry. Their larvae grow up in animal manure and household waste, turning into adult flies in as few as ten days if the weather is warm. House flies do not bite, but they are dangerous because they spread many diseases as they feed.

SCIENTIFIC NAME	*Musca domestica*
DISTRIBUTION	Worldwide
SIZE	Up to 0.25 in. (6mm) long

Bluebottle with wings extended

MEDITERRANEAN FRUIT FLY

Originally from southern Europe, this small, fruit-eating fly is now a serious problem in many warm parts of the world. It lays its eggs on the skin of many kinds of fruit, including oranges, peaches, and cherries. The larvae feed inside the fruit, often causing it to drop to the ground. Like its 1,500 or more close relatives, the "medfly" has a short body, colorful eyes, and mottled wings.

SCIENTIFIC NAME	*Ceratitis capitata*
DISTRIBUTION	Warm places worldwide
SIZE	About 0.2 in. (5mm) long

VINEGAR FLY

This tiny, red-eyed fly is originally from Africa. It breeds in rotting fruit and is strongly attracted by its smell, and also by vinegar and wine. It often flies around drinking glasses and open bottles, sometimes falling in. Vinegar flies are important in science because they are easy to raise in laboratories. They are used to investigate the way in which characteristics are inherited.

SCIENTIFIC NAME	*Drosophila melanogaster*
DISTRIBUTION	Worldwide
SIZE	About 0.1 in. (2.5mm) long

BELOW *These Australian bush flies have settled on a slice of cucumber to drink its moisture.*

Bush flies suck up liquid through a spongy pad

AUSTRALIAN BUSH FLY

A close relative of the house fly, this insect lives in the Australian bush, where it can make outdoor life very uncomfortable during the summer months. At this time of year, bush flies buzz around the eyes and mouths of large animals, including humans. They land to drink their hosts' saliva and tears, which contain water and dissolved substances that bush flies use as food. The females lay their eggs in animal manure. After hatching in the manure, the larvae complete their development in the soil.

SCIENTIFIC NAME *Musca vetustissima*

DISTRIBUTION Australia

SIZE About 0.3 in. (8mm) long

TSETSE FLY

These bloodsucking insects from Africa attack wild mammals, farm livestock, and people. They are dangerous because their bite can spread a disease called sleeping sickness. Adult tsetse flies feed every few days. They track down their victims by sight, then pierce the skin using their sharp mouthparts. Female tsetse flies give birth to fully formed larvae, one at a time.

The larvae burrow into the soil and immediately start to develop into adult flies. Tsetse flies are difficult to control, and in some parts of Africa, sleeping sickness is a major problem.

SCIENTIFIC NAME *Glossina palpalis*

DISTRIBUTION Africa

SIZE About 0.5 in. (1.2cm) long

CARROT FLY

An unwelcome visitor to gardens, this fly lays its eggs on carrots and related plants, such as parsnips and celery. Its larvae eat their way through a carrot's root, leaving it stunted and deformed. Once the larvae are fully grown, they crawl out of the carrot and grow into adults in the soil. Carrot flies can produce two generations in a year, so the same crop can be attacked twice.

SCIENTIFIC NAME *Psila rosae*

DISTRIBUTION Worldwide

SIZE Up to 0.2 in. (5mm) long

SHEEP KED

This insect is a bloodsucking parasite that lives on sheep. It does not have wings, but it can scuttle around quickly on its strong, hooked legs. Sheep keds give birth to fully developed larvae. These immediately turn into pupae, producing adult keds about three weeks later.

SCIENTIFIC NAME *Melophagus ovinus*

DISTRIBUTION Worldwide

SIZE About 0.25 in. (6mm) long

RIGHT *An African tsetse fly drinks a meal of human blood.*

BUTTERFLIES

There are more than 150,000 species of butterflies and moths (page 80–83). Some of them are drab and inconspicuous, but many butterflies have large and brilliantly colored wings. Unlike other insects, butterflies and moths are covered with tiny scales. The scales on their body often look like fur, but the ones on their wings are flat and overlap like tiles on a roof. In many species, these scales reflect light in a particular way, making the wings shimmer. Adult butterflies and moths feed on nectar and other fluids, such as fruit and plant juices. They have long, tubular mouthparts for probing into flowers. Their larvae, called caterpillars, have biting jaws and feed mainly on plants. Butterflies are sun-loving insects and are most common in warm parts of the world.

TIGER SWALLOWTAIL

This insect belongs to a family of spectacular butterflies. It has a long "tail" on each hind wing and is a strong flier. Tiger swallowtails feed from flowers and lay their eggs on trees. Their caterpillars are camouflaged to look like bird droppings when they are young. Later they turn green, with two yellow spots on their backs to scare away predators.

SCIENTIFIC NAME
Papilio glaucus

DISTRIBUTION
North America

SIZE Wingspan
up to 6 in. (15cm)

Forewings are larger than hind wings

Antennae have a club-shaped tip

Mouthparts coiled up during flight

Six jointed legs

Common swallowtail

Common swallowtail
(*Papilo machaon*) caterpillar

LARGE SKIPPER

Skippers are small, fast-flying butterflies that dart from flower to flower. They often rest with their wings half-open, instead of folding them together as most butterflies do. The large skipper is a common species that lays its eggs on grasses. Its caterpillars are blue-green, which helps camouflage them in the grass as they feed. The caterpillars hibernate through the winter and become adults the following spring.

SCIENTIFIC NAME *Ochlodes venatus*

DISTRIBUTION Europe, Asia

SIZE Wingspan up to 1 in. (2.5cm)

PHOEBUS PARNASSIAN

Compared to many butterflies, the Phoebus parnassian copes well with cold weather. It lives on flower-covered mountain slopes and in the tundra, a frozen, treeless area north of the Arctic Circle. It flies slowly and close to the ground. The adults drink nectar from flowers, while the caterpillars eat the leaves of plants, such as stonecrops and saxifrages. The caterpillars hibernate during the winter, which in the tundra can be more than six months long.

SCIENTIFIC NAME *Parnassius phoebus*

DISTRIBUTION Europe, northern Asia, North America

SIZE Wingspan up to 3 in. (8cm)

QUEEN ALEXANDRA'S BIRDWING

Birdwings are the biggest butterflies in the world, and the Queen Alexandra is the largest species of all. The males have metallic blue-green wings and a bright yellow body, but the larger females are black and brown. These giant insects live in dense tropical forest, where they feed on just one species of climbing vine. Because they fly high above the forest floor, they are rarely seen. Butterfly collectors once paid high prices for this species, and as a result it became endangered. Today it is protected by law.

SCIENTIFIC NAME
Ornithoptera alexandrae

DISTRIBUTION Papua New Guinea

SIZE Wingspan up to 11 in. (28cm)

LEFT *This tiger swallowtail is landing on a cluster of lantana flowers. All species of swallowtails have large, boldly marked wings like these.*

Large white in flight

Antennae are used to detect scents in the air

Underside of orangetip's wings are mottled to camouflage it when it rests with its wings folded up

Cabbage white

Cabbage white caterpillar

ABOVE LEFT *The large white's (Pieris brassicae) markings are similar to the cabbage white's.*
LEFT *The cabbage white lays single eggs among cabbage plants. Its well-camouflaged caterpillars feed alone.*

CABBAGE WHITE

This may not be the world's most colorful butterfly, but it is one of the most successful. Its caterpillars feed on cabbage and related plants and have become a garden pest. The cabbage white originally came from Europe, but was accidentally introduced to North America in the 1860s, and to Australia in 1939. Today it is found on all continents except Antarctica. Cabbage whites lay bright yellow eggs, but their caterpillars are pale green, helping them stay hidden as they feed.

SCIENTIFIC NAME	Pieris rapae
DISTRIBUTION	Worldwide
SIZE	Wingspan up to 2 in. (5cm)

ORANGETIP

This is a relative of the cabbage white. The male butterfly has a bright orange tip on its front wings, but the female's wings are white and gray. Orangetips feed on relatives of the cabbage although, fortunately for gardeners, they do not attack cabbages themselves. As caterpillars, orangetips have a dangerous life. When they first hatch, they feed on each other, and the survivors then switch to a diet of plants.

SCIENTIFIC NAME	Anthocharis cardamines
DISTRIBUTION	Europe, Asia
SIZE	Wingspan up to 2 in. (5cm)

ABOVE *The orangetip has many relatives all over the world. Some also have orange wing tips, but others are red or crimson.*

METAMORPHOSIS

Many animals change shape as they mature. This process is called metamorphosis. It can happen gradually as an animal grows, or rapidly at a certain point in its early life. In the insect world, dragonflies, grasshoppers, cockroaches, and true bugs undergo incomplete metamorphosis. This means that they change slightly every time they molt. Their wings do not fully develop until their final molt, but otherwise they resemble their parents when they are young. Young insects that develop in this way are called nymphs.

Butterflies, moths, and many other insects undergo complete metamorphosis. They hatch from eggs as larvae, which include grubs, caterpillars, and maggots. Instead of changing gradually, their bodies are dismantled and rebuilt during a resting stage called a pupa. Larvae also feature in the life cycles of water animals such as crustaceans, echinoderms, and amphibians. By having a larval stage, these animals can use more than one kind of food, which improves their chances of survival.

ABOVE *It takes about four weeks for the monarch butterfly (page 78) to change from an egg into an adult butterfly. The caterpillar feeds and grows quickly before turning into a pupa, protected by a case called a chrysalis. Finally, the adult crawls out, dries off, and flies away.*

ABOVE *The small copper is an energetic little butterfly, and can often be seen darting from flower to flower and chasing other butterflies in meadows and open spaces.*

LARGE BLUE

The large blue has an unusual life story. Like other blues, it produces caterpillars that look like small slugs. These start life feeding on wildflowers, but within a few days, they are "adopted" by ants, which take them into their underground nests. The ants are tricked by the shape and smell of the caterpillars into thinking that they are ant grubs. Once a large blue caterpillar is under ground, it turns into a hungry predator, killing and eating ant grubs. After several months in the nest, it pupates, and the butterfly flies out of the ants' nest to begin its adult life. Despite its name, the large blue is not a large butterfly.

SCIENTIFIC NAME	*Maculinea arion*
DISTRIBUTION	Europe, northern Asia
SIZE	Wingspan up to 1.5 in. (4cm)

Veins in butterflies' wings make them sturdy enough for flight

SMALL COPPER

The small copper is closely related to the large blue. They look different, but both species produce caterpillars that resemble small slugs. The small copper's caterpillars are green with white and red spots. Unlike large blue caterpillars, they are vegetarians, feeding on dock leaves, sorrel, and related plants. Small coppers breed very rapidly. If the summer is warm and dry, they can produce three generations in a single year. In exceptionally warm years, they sometimes manage to squeeze in a fourth.

SCIENTIFIC NAME	*Lycaena phleas*
DISTRIBUTION	Europe, Asia, North America
SIZE	Wingspan about 1 in. (2.5cm)

GRAY HAIRSTREAK

When it is perched on a leaf, this small butterfly looks as if it has a head at each end of its body. Its hind wings have brightly colored spots that resemble eyes, and slender tails that look like antennae. This backward look is shared by many other hairstreaks. It draws attention away from the butterfly's real head and probably helps it to survive attack from birds. The gray hairstreak's caterpillars eat a variety of plants, including cultivated beans.

SCIENTIFIC NAME	*Strymon melinus*
DISTRIBUTION	North, Central, and South America
SIZE	Wingspan up to 1 in. (2.5cm)

EUROPEAN MAP BUTTERFLY

This butterfly gets its name from the intricate, maplike markings on its wings, which are mainly brown and orange. It belongs to a large family of insects called the brush-footed butterflies, or nymphalids, which also includes emperors, admirals, fritillaries, and monarchs. Nymphalids have six legs, but use only four of them for walking. The front pair are much shorter than the others and are held close to the butterfly's head. The European map butterfly's caterpillars are black or brown and are covered with long yellow and black spines to deter predators. They begin life in a group, feeding on nettles and similar plants, but gradually go their separate ways in search of food.

SCIENTIFIC NAME	
	Araschnia levana
DISTRIBUTION	Europe, parts of Asia
SIZE	Wingspan up to 1 in. (2.5cm)

ABOVE *There are several types of map butterfly. The European map butterfly lays its eggs in tiny strings.*

Walking legs

The newly emerged comma holds tightly to the twig

Comma-shaped mark on hind wing gives this butterfly its name

LEFT *This comma butterfly has just left its chrysalis. When butterflies emerge, they rest while the veins in their wings fill with blood, ready for flight.*

The empty pupal case stays fastened to a twig

LEFT *With its wings open, the comma butterfly is much easier for predators to see and attack.*

gardens, particularly in the fall, when they feed on nectar and the juices of rotting fruits.

SCIENTIFIC NAME	*Vanessa atalanta*
DISTRIBUTION	Northern Hemisphere
SIZE	Wingspan up to 2 in. (5cm)

COMMA

The comma's wings have ragged edges, and when they are closed, the butterfly looks like a dead oak leaf. Commas lay their eggs on nettles and hop plants. The caterpillars have a white splash on their backs that makes them look like bird droppings. This disguise allows them to curl up on leaves and avoid being attacked.

SCIENTIFIC NAME	*Polygonia c-album*
DISTRIBUTION	Europe, North Africa, eastward to Japan
SIZE	Wingspan up to 2 in. (5cm)

SILVER-WASHED FRITILLARY

Fritillaries are butterflies with wings that are covered with angular black marks. The silver-washed fritillary is a woodland species. Its caterpillars start life hidden in crevices in the bark of oak trees, later moving to the woodland floor and feeding on violets. Male silver-washed fritillaries have scent glands on their forewings that they use to attract females during courtship.

SCIENTIFIC NAME	*Argynnis paphia*
DISTRIBUTION	Europe, North Africa, Asia
SIZE	Wingspan up to 2.75 in. (7cm)

Red admiral

Purple emperor

Silver-washed fritillary

ABOVE *Like the map and comma butterflies, the red admiral, purple emperor, and silver-washed fritillary belong to the nymphalid family.*

PURPLE EMPEROR

This beautifully colored nymphalid has only two pairs of walking legs. The purple emperor spends its time soaring high above woodlands. The males often battle with each other above the trees. Their caterpillars feed on the leaves of sallow trees and have a pair of horns on the front of their head to ward off attack.

SCIENTIFIC NAME	*Apatura iris*
DISTRIBUTION	Europe and Asia
SIZE	Wingspan up to 3 in. (8cm)

RED ADMIRAL

These black, white, and red butterflies lay their eggs in clusters on the underside of stinging nettles and related plants. Their caterpillars are black with brown and yellow spines. They feed on the nettle leaves and protect themselves by chewing through the leaves and folding them over to make a tent. Adult red admirals are seen in meadows and

Mourning cloak showing yellow-bordered wings

Furlike scales on inner surface of wings

Camouflaged underside to hind wings

ABOVE *The small tortoiseshell hibernates as an adult. It often shelters in buildings, where the heating may wake it up before spring arrives.*

RIGHT *Peacock butterflies have large eyespots on their wings. Attacking birds tend to peck at the eyespots rather than the insect's body, giving it a chance to escape.*

MOURNING CLOAK

This butterfly probably gets its name from its brown-black color, resembling a widow's funeral shawl. Its wings have pale yellow borders that make it easy to identify in flight. The mourning cloak lays its eggs on willows, poplars, and other trees. Its spiny caterpillars live and feed in large groups. When in danger, they jerk their bodies in a threatening-looking way. Where there are many of these caterpillars, they can completely strip young trees of their leaves.

SCIENTIFIC NAME	*Nymphalis antiopa*
DISTRIBUTION	Europe, Asia, North and South America
SIZE	Wingspan up to 3 in. (8cm)

SMALL TORTOISESHELL

This orange and red butterfly is one of the most common species in Europe. It can be seen almost anywhere, from city gardens to seaside cliffs. It lays its eggs on nettles, and once the eggs have hatched, the caterpillars work together to make large silk nests. As the caterpillars grow, they often eat all the leaves around the nest. If their food supplies start to run out, they move to new plants before pupating and becoming adults.

SCIENTIFIC NAME	*Aglais urticae*
DISTRIBUTION	Europe
SIZE	Wingspan up to 2 in. (5cm)

PEACOCK

In the fall, peacock butterflies take shelter in dry places, camouflaged by their mottled hind wings. They wake in the spring. Adult peacocks feed at many kinds of flowers and lay their eggs on nettles.

SCIENTIFIC NAME	*Inachis io*
DISTRIBUTION	Europe, eastward to Japan
SIZE	Wingspan up to 2 in. (5cm)

QUEEN CRACKER

Male cracker butterflies have an unusual way of attracting females—they make a loud clicking sound as they fly. The noise is produced by their forewings, which have a hard ridge that clicks when the wings beat. Cracker butterflies are found only in the American tropics, where there are many different species. The queen cracker, with its brilliant blue and white coloring, is one of the largest examples.

SCIENTIFIC NAME	*Hamadryas arethusa*
DISTRIBUTION	Central and South America
SIZE	Wingspan up to 2.75 in. (7cm)

EIGHTY-EIGHT BUTTERFLY

This small, tropical butterfly gets its name from the markings on the underside of its hind wings, which look like the number 88. The upper side of its wings are a plain brown color. There are nearly 40 species of butterflies related to the eighty-eight, living mostly in the tropical forests of South America.

SCIENTIFIC NAME	*Diaethria clymena*
DISTRIBUTION	South America
SIZE	Wingspan up to 2 in. (5cm)

Fully extended wings, showing the black tips

The underside of the painted lady's wings are as colorful as the upper side

an extra-long tongue to reach nectar deep inside flowers. Toward the end of the summer, the young butterflies head south to escape the winter cold. Many do not survive the journey because they are killed by early frosts.

SCIENTIFIC NAME	*Cynthia cardui*
DISTRIBUTION	Worldwide, except Australia and New Zealand
SIZE	Wingspan up to 2 in. (5cm)

COMMON SNOUT

Snout butterflies are easily recognized by their pair of unusually long mouthparts that look like a slender snout. They use these mouthparts, called palps, to find suitable food plants for their eggs. There are about ten species of these butterflies worldwide. They include the common snout from North America, the nettle-tree butterfly from Europe, and the beak butterfly from Southeast Asia and Australia.

SCIENTIFIC NAME	*Libytheana bachmanii*
DISTRIBUTION	North America
SIZE	Wingspan up to 2 in. (5cm)

INDIAN LEAF

This Asian species is one of the best examples of camouflage in the butterfly world. When it is resting on a twig, it looks exactly like a dry, brown leaf. Its forewings have a sharp point like the tip of a leaf, and its hind wings end in a long tail like a leaf's stalk. The disguise works only when the butterfly's wings are closed. As soon as it opens them to fly, it reveals the bright orange and purple colors on the upper surface of its wings. Leaf butterflies live in tropical forests, and their caterpillars are protected by spines and hairs.

SCIENTIFIC NAME	*Kallima inachus*
DISTRIBUTION	Southern Asia, Far East
SIZE	Wingspan up to 5 in. (12cm)

PAINTED LADY

The painted lady is one of the world's most widespread butterflies. It is also one of the greatest insect travelers. Every summer, billions of these fast-flying insects head north across America and Europe in search of food for their young. They travel through mountain passes and across open water, often reaching areas north of the Arctic Circle. Painted ladies lay their eggs on thistles, nettles, and hollyhocks. Their black and yellow, spiny caterpillars feed on plants inside tents made from folded leaves. The adults have

MONARCH

This large, black and orange insect is one of the best-known butterflies in the world. In North America, it travels more than 2,000 miles (3,200km) between its winter quarters in Mexico and its breeding grounds farther north. In late summer, monarchs return south to escape the winter cold. They spend the winter clustered on trees, jostling for room and a chance to bask in the sun. Monarchs absorb poisons from their diet of milkweeds. The poison is stored in their bodies, making them a dangerous meal for birds that are not deterred by their bright warning colors.

Monarch with open wings

SCIENTIFIC NAME *Danaus plexippus*

DISTRIBUTION Originally from the Americas, now also found in parts of Europe, Southeast Asia, and Australia

SIZE Wingspan up to 4 in. (10cm)

TOP Male monarchs have scent pockets on their hind wings and tufts of scented hairs on the tip of their abdomen. These release a perfume that attracts female monarchs during courtship.
***ABOVE** Morphos skim through forests, flapping their giant wings much more slowly than most other butterflies.*

BLUE MORPHO

Male morphos have beautiful blue wings that flash in the sunlight as they fly through their rain forest home. There are over 50 species of morphos, all from the American tropics. They were once caught in huge numbers so that their wings could be used to make jewelry, but today many species are protected. The male's brilliant color is produced by microscopic ridges on the surface of its scales. These reflect the light in a certain way, making the wings glisten with a metallic blue sheen. Female morphos usually have less blue on their wings, although in some species they are orange or brown.

SCIENTIFIC NAME *Morpho* species

DISTRIBUTION South America

SIZE Wingspan up to 5.5 in. (14cm)

VICEROY

It is not easy to tell this butterfly from the monarch, because the two species are almost identical in shape and color. The similarity is not accidental. Viceroys have come to resemble monarchs because it helps protect them from predators. Viceroys are not poisonous, but because they look like monarchs, birds and other animals avoid them. This kind of defense, called mimicry, is common in the insect world.

SCIENTIFIC NAME *Limenitis archippus*

DISTRIBUTION North and Central America

SIZE Wingspan up to 3 in. (8cm)

GLASSWING

Glasswings have transparent wings. In some species, the wings are covered in see-through scales, but in others the scales fall off soon after the butterfly emerges from its chrysalis. Glasswings are found in tropical climates. Most of them live near the ground in forests, where their clear wings make them difficult to spot.

SCIENTIFIC NAME *Acraea* and other genera

DISTRIBUTION Worldwide

SIZE Typical wingspan 2 in. (5cm)

OWL

This giant butterfly has brown and gray wings and two large eyespots that show when its wings are closed. These look like an owl's eyes and may help scare off hungry birds. Owl butterflies feed mainly on rotting fruit. They lay their eggs on banana plants and flowers called lobster claws. The caterpillars may grow up to 4 in. (10cm) long. They have large appetites, and can cause major problems in banana plantations.

SCIENTIFIC NAME *Caligo idomeneus*

DISTRIBUTION South America

SIZE Wingspan up to 6 in. (15cm)

EVENING BROWN

This tropical butterfly feeds at dusk and hides among fallen leaves during the day. In some parts of the world, evening browns look the same all year round, but in places that have wet and dry seasons, butterflies that emerge at different times have different patterns. In West Africa, the wet-season browns have several eyespots, but the dry-season butterflies have none.

SCIENTIFIC NAME *Melanitis leda*

DISTRIBUTION Africa, southern Asia, Australia

SIZE Wingspan up to 3 in. (8cm)

MEADOW BROWN

This large, plain butterfly is a relative of the evening brown. It lays its eggs on grasses, sometimes dropping them as it flutters overhead. Its caterpillars are bright green—a color that camouflages them as they feed. Meadow browns have eyespots on their forewings, but they are too small to scare off most predators. Instead, they probably work as decoys. Birds peck at the spots instead of the butterfly's body, giving it a better chance to fly away.

SCIENTIFIC NAME *Maniola jurtina*
DISTRIBUTION Europe, North Africa, Middle East
SIZE Wingspan up to 2 in. (5cm)

POSTMAN

The postman belongs to a group of butterflies called the heliconians, which are found only in warm parts of the Americas. Heliconians have long, narrow wings and their colors—red or yellow stripes on a black background—warn birds that they taste unpleasant and are not worth attacking. Like all heliconians, the postman lays its eggs on climbing plants called passionflowers. Heliconians usually ignore plants that already have eggs on them, and some passionflowers grow special decoy eggs to keep these butterflies from laying eggs on their leaves.

SCIENTIFIC NAME
Heliconius melpomene
DISTRIBUTION Central America, tropical South America
SIZE Wingspan up to 3.5 in. (9cm)

Meadow brown with open wings

Meadow brown caterpillar

Long antennae help detect food plants

Hind wings are much shorter than forewings

Coiled tongue

Three pairs of slender legs

Bright colors warn predators that the butterfly tastes unpleasant

ABOVE *The meadow brown is one of the most common butterflies in Europe. Its caterpillars feed at night to avoid being eaten, and the adult butterfly keeps close to the ground, relying on its eyespots for protection.*

LEFT *The postman butterfly lives in hot, damp forests. It flies near the ground on its elegant, rounded wings.*

MOTHS

Butterflies and moths are so closely related that it is sometimes difficult to tell them apart. Like butterflies, moths have a coiled "tongue" and are covered by scales, but their antennae are often feathery, instead of club-shaped. They also fly mostly at night. Moths usually rest with their wings opened flat, while butterflies rest with their wings folded up. Most moths are dull in color, but day-flying species can be as colorful as butterflies. There are more species of moths than of butterflies, and they are more varied.

ABOVE *The peppered moth's speckled wings provide camouflage against tree trunks. Unlike most moths, it rests with its wings partly spread.*

BELOW *The atlas moth's body is dwarfed by its four gigantic wings. This moth spends the first part of its life as a bright green caterpillar covered with long spines.*

PEPPERED MOTH

This insect is a member of a huge family of moths called the geometrids, which includes more than 15,000 species. Like other geometrids, its caterpillars move by forming their bodies into a loop, instead of by walking. The peppered moth demonstrates evolution in action. It is normally speckled black and white, but during the 1800s, a black form evolved near British cities where tree trunks were covered in soot. This black moth was better camouflaged, so it became more widespread.

SCIENTIFIC NAME *Biston betularia*

DISTRIBUTION Europe, Asia

SIZE Wingspan up to 2 in. (5cm)

WINTER MOTH

Unlike most moths, this species is active throughout the winter months. The males have rounded, gray-brown wings, and they often flutter around lighted windows, particularly on mild, damp nights. The females have tiny wings and cannot fly. Winter moth caterpillars feed on trees of all kinds, and they can be a serious pest where apples are grown.

SCIENTIFIC NAME *Operophtera brumata*

DISTRIBUTION Europe, northern Asia, Canada

SIZE Wingspan up to 1 in. (2.5cm)

MADAGASCAN SUNSET MOTH

This day-flying moth is so colorful that it is easily mistaken for a butterfly. It has brilliant, metallic markings, like a spectacular sunset, and long "tails" on its hind wings that make it look like a swallowtail butterfly (page 72). Sunset moths eat poisonous plants, and they are brightly colored to warn birds that they are inedible. The Madagascan sunset moth is a favorite with collectors. It is now raised in captivity to protect the species in the wild.

SCIENTIFIC NAME *Chrysiridia riphearia*

DISTRIBUTION Madagascar

SIZE Wingspan up to 4 in. (10cm)

ATLAS MOTH

With wings wide enough to cover a dinner plate, this is one of the largest moths in the world. Its wings are colored with many shades of brown, and they have triangular "windows" that are almost transparent. Atlas moths live in tropical forests and lay their eggs on a variety of trees.

SCIENTIFIC NAME *Attacus atlas*

DISTRIBUTION India, Southeast Asia, Far East

SIZE Wingspan up to 12 in. (30cm)

There are no scales on the see-through "windows"

Triangular hind wings have rounded tips

Forewings have a streamlined, backswept tip

LEFT *The luna moth often hangs from twigs and plant stems in woodland areas to rest. It was once widespread in North America, but has been endangered by pesticide use and collectors.*

Forewings have a red-purple band along the front edge

Each hind wing has a long, twisted tail

ABOVE *Hummingbird hawkmoths have a short, stubby body and a fan-shaped tail. They spend all day on the move—just like real hummingbirds.*

ABOVE *These silkmoths have just emerged from their cocoons, and two of them are already mating. Soon, the female will lay her eggs.*

DEATH'S-HEAD HAWKMOTH

Hawkmoths are fast and powerful, with heavy bodies and streamlined wings. There are about 1,000 species worldwide, and the death's-head is one of the fastest. It can cruise at about 25 mph (40km/h), or even faster in short bursts. It lays its eggs on potatoes and related plants, and often migrates long distances to breed. The death's-head gets its name from the skull-like markings on its back. If the adult moth is picked up, it can make a loud, squeaking sound. Some people believe that it is bad luck if a death's-head hawkmoth enters their house.

SCIENTIFIC NAME *Acherontia atropos*

DISTRIBUTION Northern Africa, Europe

SIZE Wingspan up to 5.5 in. (14cm)

LUNA MOTH

Moon moths like the luna moth have a plump, furry body and pale wings with long, curling "tails." The luna moth is a ghostly green color and has four bright eyespots—one on each wing. Like many moths, the males have large, feathery antennae. They use these to detect the scent of females, sometimes over distances of more than 2 mi. (3km). This moth lays its eggs on a variety of trees, including hickories and walnuts, and usually produces two generations a year. However, in Canada, where summers are short, luna moths breed just once between May and July. In Mexico, where it is warmer, they may fit up to three generations in a single year.

SCIENTIFIC NAME *Actias luna*

DISTRIBUTION North America, from southern Canada to Mexico

SIZE Wingspan up to 4 in. (10cm)

HUMMINGBIRD HAWKMOTH

When it is feeding, this day-flying hawkmoth flutters its wings so fast that they are little more than a blur. Like its namesake, the hummingbird (page 205), it hovers in front of flowers, takes a quick drink of nectar with its long tongue, and then dashes off to find its next meal. Despite its small size, the hummingbird hawkmoth is an adventurous traveler, migrating north through Europe in early summer to breed. It sometimes crosses the sea to Ireland and Great Britain and ventures as far north as the Arctic Circle.

SCIENTIFIC NAME *Macroglossum stellatarum*

DISTRIBUTION Europe, Asia

SIZE Wingspan up to 2 in. (5cm)

MULBERRY SILKMOTH

This brown or white, flightless moth has been farmed as a source of silk for over 4,000 years. Its caterpillars spin a strand of silk up to 1 mile (1.5km) long when making their cocoons. People harvest the silk by floating the cocoons on water and winding the strands on reels. Silkworms eat the leaves of mulberry trees in silk-producing countries such as China. They are extinct in the wild—only captive silkmoths survive.

SCIENTIFIC NAME *Bombyx mori*

DISTRIBUTION Worldwide

SIZE Wingspan up to 2 in. (5cm)

PINE PROCESSIONARY MOTH

This moth lays its eggs on pine trees, and its caterpillars are serious pests. During the day, the caterpillars crowd together inside ball-shaped tents made of tough silk, setting off to feed at nightfall. The caterpillars move in single file, with as many as 200 traveling head-to-tail. After splitting up to feed on pine needles, the procession reforms, and the caterpillars return to their silky tents. Processionary moth caterpillars follow each other by instinct—if a few are put on the rim of a cup, they crawl around in circles.

SCIENTIFIC NAME	*Thaumetopia pityocampa*
DISTRIBUTION	Southern Europe, northern Africa
SIZE	Wingspan up to 2 in. (5cm)

GYPSY MOTH

The gypsy moth looks harmless enough, but its caterpillars cause tremendous damage in North American forests. They feed on leaves, stripping them so quickly that affected trees can die. Unlike most moths and butterflies, the gypsy moth is not picky about where it lays its eggs. Its caterpillars thrive on a wide range of broad-leaved and evergreen trees. Gypsy moths originally came from Europe. They were introduced to North America in 1869 as a source of silk, but the project failed and the moths escaped into the wild, where they are now common.

SCIENTIFIC NAME	*Lymantria dispar*
DISTRIBUTION	Europe, Asia, North America
SIZE	Wingspan up to 2 in. (5cm)

HORNET MOTH

With its transparent wings and brown and yellow body, this harmless moth looks exactly like a stinging hornet (page 88). To make the disguise even more convincing, it also moves in a hornetlike way. A closer look shows that it has a much smaller head than a hornet, and more important, it does not have a sting. Hornet moths lay their eggs on poplar and willow trees, and the adults feed at flowers. They belong to a family of moths called clearwings, all of which protect themselves by mimicking stinging insects.

SCIENTIFIC NAME	*Sesia apiformis*
DISTRIBUTION	Europe, Asia, North America
SIZE	Wingspan up to 2 in. (5cm)

SIX-SPOTTED BURNET MOTH

Burnet moths fly by day, protected by red and black markings that warn predators that they are poisonous. They fly slowly, never getting far above the ground. Burnets lay their eggs in

Two pairs of slender wings

The burnet moth's antennae have thickened tips

ABOVE AND RIGHT *The brightly colored six-spot burnet moth is easily confused with a butterfly. After climbing out of its cocoon, it rests before taking off.*

Contrasting colors on the wings warn birds that this moth would make an unpleasant meal

grassy places, and their caterpillars eat meadow plants. The caterpillars mature inside papery cocoons. They often find a partner waiting to mate as soon as they emerge.

SCIENTIFIC NAME	*Zygaena filipendulae*
DISTRIBUTION	Europe
SIZE	Wingspan up to 1.5 in. (4cm)

CLOTHES MOTH

This small, dusty-gold moth spends its whole life indoors. It can fly, but it normally prefers to scuttle away if it is disturbed. Clothes moths lay their eggs on anything containing wool or fur, including carpets, blankets, and clothes. Their caterpillars live inside tents made of silk, making holes as they feed. If they are shaken out, they trek across floors or even up windows to find something else to eat. The adult moths live for two or three weeks—just long enough to find a mate and lay the next generation of eggs.

SCIENTIFIC NAME	*Tineola bisselliella*
DISTRIBUTION	Worldwide
SIZE	Wingspan up to 0.6 in. (1.5cm)

Remains of pupal case

FAR LEFT *The garden tiger's bright colors show that it tastes bad and is not worth attacking.*
LEFT *Garden tiger moth caterpillars hibernate inside loose-fitting cocoons and emerge as moths in late spring.*

WHITE PLUME MOTH

Plume moths have spiky legs and narrow wings that branch out to look like a collection of tiny feathers, or plumes. Their forewings are often divided into two plumes and their hind wings into three. The white plume moth rests in a T-shape, with its wings at right angles and partly folded. Most plume moths are brown, but this species is pure white.

SCIENTIFIC NAME *Pterophorus pentadactyla*

DISTRIBUTION Europe

SIZE Wingspan up to 0.6 in. (1.5cm)

GREAT TIGER MOTH

Tiger moths are easy to mistake for small butterflies because they are brightly colored and often fly by day. There are at least 10,000 species found throughout the world. The garden tiger moth has brown and white forewings, spotted orange hind wings, and a large, furry body. Birds avoid it because it feeds on plants that give it an unpleasant taste. The caterpillars also taste bad and are protected by long, black hairs.

SCIENTIFIC NAME *Arctia caja*

DISTRIBUTION Europe, Asia, North America

SIZE Wingspan up to 3 in. (8cm)

WITCHETTY MOTH

This Australian moth is famous for its fat, finger-sized caterpillars called witchetty grubs, which Aborigines traditionally use as food. The caterpillars live in underground tunnels lined with silk and feed on sap from the roots of the witchetty bush. They can be nearly 3 in. (8cm) long and, when dug up and cooked, make a nutritious meal. Although adult moths have plump bodies, they do not feed. They have mottled gray wings and are good fliers.

SCIENTIFIC NAME *Xyleutes leucomochla*

DISTRIBUTION Australia

SIZE Wingspan up to 6 in. (15cm)

ANTS, BEES, AND WASPS

These three types of insects belong to the same group of animals. They have a slender "waist" between the thorax and the abdomen and often have a stinger. Bees and wasps have four narrow, transparent wings. Ants are usually wingless, but many develop winged forms when they reproduce. Most bees get their food from flowers, using their long tongues to suck up nectar. Adult wasps eat similar food, but they feed their young on insects. Ants have the most varied diet. Some are hunters, others are vegetarians, but many are scavengers, collecting whatever food they can find. Most of these insects are social species, living in colonies or family groups. One female, the queen, lays all the colony's eggs, and the other members have different roles. There are more than 100,000 species of ants, bees, and wasps, living all over the world.

BULLDOG ANT

These ants are fierce, with big jaws and powerful stings. If threatened, they sprint toward the enemy, sometimes leaping one foot (30cm) into the air. Bulldog ants live in small colonies, usually of fewer than 1,000 insects. As with most ants, the colonies consist of workers, which collect food and build, and soldiers, which defend the nest. Bulldog ants eat nectar and other insects.

SCIENTIFIC NAME	*Myrmecia* species
DISTRIBUTION	Australia
SIZE	Up to 1 in. (2.5cm) long

WOOD ANT

In the evergreen forests of Europe, large mounds of twigs and pine needles show where wood ants have set up home. Their nests can be 5 ft. (1.5m) high, and they often house several queens. Wood ants feed mainly on small insects. They do not have a stinger, but they have a powerful bite and can squirt formic acid at attackers.

SCIENTIFIC NAME	*Formica rufa*
DISTRIBUTION	Europe
SIZE	About 0.4 in. (1cm) long

HONEYPOT ANT

Insects that live in dry places have to find ways to survive periods of drought. Honeypot ants rely on specialized workers that store water and food. These workers, called repletes, live permanently under ground, hanging upside down. In the wet season, they are fed with nectar and honeydew, a sugary liquid produced by sap-sucking insects. The repletes store this mixture, swelling up like balloons. During a drought, they release the food to their nestmates. Native Americans once used these ants as food.

SCIENTIFIC NAME	*Myrmecocystus melliger*
DISTRIBUTION	North and Central America
SIZE	Workers about 0.4 in. (1cm) long

RIGHT *Wood ants tend a group of aphids high up in a tree. The ants guard the aphids and collect the drops of honeydew that the aphids produce as they feed.*

ABOVE *Weaver ants work together to pull sections of a leaf together to make a treetop nest.*
LEFT *Green tree ants (Oecophylla smaragdina), a species of weaver ant, swarm out of their nest to defend it from a predator.*

ABOVE *Ants, such as this wood ant, use their antennae to taste food and to communicate. The antennae have "elbows" where they bend.*
BELOW *Army ants have tiny eyes and find their prey by touch. Each army of ants can contain over 500,000 insects.*

PHARAOH'S ANT

Despite its size, this tiny, pale brown or reddish ant causes major problems in many parts of the world. It nests near heating pipes and in other warm places in all kinds of buildings, from hotels to hospitals. The pharaoh's ant looks for leftovers to eat, such as breadcrumbs and spilled fruit juice—but it will even tackle shoe polish and soap. As it searches for food, it chews through wood, plaster, and plastic bags. Though its nests are often not much larger than a thimble, there may be several hundred in a single building, which makes them difficult to control.

SCIENTIFIC NAME	*Monomorium pharaonis*
DISTRIBUTION	Worldwide
SIZE	Workers about 0.08 in. (2mm) long

ARMY ANT

Instead of making a permanent nest, army ants keep moving. They pour across the forest floor, using their formidable jaws to overpower animals many times larger than themselves. Army ants spend their nights in temporary camps called bivouacs, which often hang from fallen logs. The ants themselves form the walls of the bivouacs by clinging to each other with their feet. Driver ants, which are found in Africa, live in a similar way.

SCIENTIFIC NAME	*Eciton* species
DISTRIBUTION	Central and South America
SIZE	Up to 0.6 in. (1.5cm) long

WEAVER ANT

Tropical weaver ants have an unusual way of making their nests. They pull leaves together to make a shelter, and once the leaves are close enough, they fasten them using sticky silk. The silk is produced by weaver ant grubs. Each worker holds a grub in its jaws, then moves back and forth across the gap between two leaves, leaving a bonding zigzag of silk. Weaver ants feed mainly on small insects that they find on trees. They can be aggressive if disturbed.

SCIENTIFIC NAME	*Oecophylla* species
DISTRIBUTION	Tropical Africa, southern Asia, Australia
SIZE	About 0.4 in. (1cm) long

LEAF-CUTTER ANT

There are several species of leaf-cutter ants, but they are found only in the Americas. Leaf-cutter ants live in rain forests, where they excavate large, underground nests. They spend the night in their nests, but at dawn, the workers pour out and climb to the treetops, where they cut out pieces of leaves. They carry these pieces back to their nests, following well-worn trails over the forest floor. Instead of eating the leaf-pieces, leaf-cutters use them to build spongy compost heaps under ground. A fungus grows on the heaps, and the ants harvest it as food.

SCIENTIFIC NAME	*Atta* species
DISTRIBUTION	Central and South America
SIZE	Largest workers about 0.5 in. (1.2cm) long

HONEYBEE

Originally from southern Asia, this useful insect has been spread around the world by people, partly because it makes honey and partly because it pollinates flowers, helping to produce fruits and seeds. Worker honeybees have a compact body and strong wings. Each of their back legs has a hair-lined basket that they use for collecting pollen. The queen bee is slightly larger and spends all her time in the nest, laying several hundred eggs a day. In the wild, honeybees nest in hollow trees, raising their young in honeycombs, sheets of wax made up of six-sided cells. Some of the cells contain eggs or larvae, but others store honey, which the bees use for winter food. Beekeepers design beehives to be like a tree hollow, but with a wooden frame so that they can harvest the honey.

SCIENTIFIC NAME	*Apis mellifera*
DISTRIBUTION	Worldwide
SIZE	Workers up to 0.6 in. (1.5cm) long

BUMBLEBEE

Throughout much of the Northern Hemisphere, the year's first bumblebees are a sure sign that spring has arrived. These bees have a large, hairy body and can fly when many other insects are still grounded by the cold. Many bumblebees build small nests under ground. When the eggs hatch, they produce workers that collect food and look after the developing young. Unlike honeybees, bumblebees do not store food for the winter. The queens mate and then hibernate, but when the weather turns cold, the worker bees die.

SCIENTIFIC NAME	*Bombus* and other genera
DISTRIBUTION	Mainly Northern Hemisphere
SIZE	Up to 1.5 in. (4cm)

Six-sided cells make the honeycomb light, but strong

RIGHT *A worker honeybee (in the center of the picture) does a special dance to tell the other workers where there is food. The dance shows which direction the food is and how far away.*

LEFT *A garden bumblebee (Bombus hortorum) uses its long tongue to get nectar from a teasel flower.*

MINING BEE

Unlike honeybees and bumblebees, mining bees are solitary species, not social ones. This means that the bees go their separate ways when they are grown. In the spring, the female mining bee digs a small tunnel in loose ground. After laying her eggs and stocking the tunnel with food, she closes it up and flies away. The larvae develop on their own and eventually emerge from the tunnel as adults. There are hundreds of species of mining bees. They nest in dry ground and in lawns.

SCIENTIFIC NAME	*Andrena* species
DISTRIBUTION	Worldwide
SIZE	Up to 1 in. (2.5cm) long

ABOVE *Mining bees, like this tawny mining bee (Andrena fulva), resemble honeybees, but they are usually hairier and do not have pollen-collecting baskets.*

CARPENTER BEE

Carpenter bees are large insects with a dark, shiny body, hairy legs, and tinted wings. These solitary bees build nest burrows in old timber and dead trees, chewing their way into the wood with their powerful jaws. A typical carpenter tunnels up to 12 in. (30cm) deep and lays its eggs at intervals along its burrow. It gives each egg a stock of pollen, then separates it from the next egg with a partition made of chewed wood. The young bees emerge in sequence, with the ones deepest in the burrow leaving last.

SCIENTIFIC NAME	*Xylocopa* species
DISTRIBUTION	Worldwide
SIZE	Typical length 1 in. (2.5cm)

LEAF-CUTTER BEE

This bee looks like a honeybee, but its abdomen is fringed with golden hairs. It gets its name from the way it slices semicircular pieces out of leaves, which it then takes to its nest. The nest is usually in a hollow stem, although leaf-cutters also nest in crevices and even flowerpots. Inside the nest, the bee rolls up each piece of leaf to make a parcel, then stocks it with pollen and one egg.

SCIENTIFIC NAME	*Megachile centuncularis*
DISTRIBUTION	Europe
SIZE	Up to 0.8 in. (2cm) long

Leaf-cutter bee in flight

ABOVE *A female leaf-cutter bee cuts out a piece of leaf using its sharp jaws like a pair of scissors.*

CUCKOO BEE

Cuckoo bees look like bumblebees, but they raise their eggs in a very different way. Instead of making their own nests, they search out the nests of bumblebees and force their way inside. Once a cuckoo bee has entered a nest, it starts to lay its eggs. The workers look after the cuckoo bee's eggs, while the intruder often attacks and kills the queen bumblebee. Cuckoo bees often resemble their hosts very closely, but unlike bumblebees, they do not have pollen baskets on their legs because they do not collect food.

SCIENTIFIC NAME	*Psithyrus* and other genera
DISTRIBUTION	Mainly Northern Hemisphere
SIZE	Typical length 0.8 in. (2cm)

STINGERS

Animals use stingers to defend themselves and also to attack their prey. A stinger injects poison into another animal's body. The effects range from mild discomfort that soon wears off to severe injury or death.

A scorpion's stinger is easy to see because it is openly displayed on the end of its tail. The stingers of ants, bees, and wasps are also at the end of their bodies, but they are normally hidden away by folding scales. If the insect decides to attack, the scales open up and the stinger slides out. The stinger has two barbed spikes that slide against each other along a central shaft. As the insect pushes the stinger into its victim, the spikes move up and down to work the stinger into its body. Poison flows along a hollow in the center of the stinger and into the animal.

Stinger

Poison sac

A wasp's stinger

What happens next depends on the type of stinging insect. Ants and wasps can easily pull out their stingers because their barbs are small. Bumblebees take a little longer, but honeybees often cannot pull their stingers out at all, because their stingers have large barbs that stick tight in skin. When a honeybee tries to fly away, the stinger is torn from its body, and the bee eventually dies.

LEFT *Potter wasps, like other solitary wasps, feed alone instead of living in family groups or colonies. Their eggs are laid separately, so their young are solitary from the moment they hatch.*

POTTER WASP

Unlike common wasps, potter wasps are solitary insects. They raise their young in nests made of clay. The nests are about the size of a blueberry, and they look like tiny vases stuck to the branches of shrubs. When the female wasp has made a nest, it lays a single egg inside. Then it fills the nest with living caterpillars it has paralyzed with its sting, seals up the pot, and moves on to make another. When the potter wasp larvae hatch, they eat the living caterpillars.

SCIENTIFIC NAME	*Eumenes* species
DISTRIBUTION	Worldwide
SIZE	Typical length 0.5 in. (1.2cm)

TARANTULA HAWK WASP

These solitary wasps hunt large spiders, which they use as food for their young. They rush over the ground in search of their prey, using their long legs to overtake spiders and pin them down. Once a tarantula hawk wasp has trapped a spider, it paralyzes it with its sting and then buries it in sandy ground, laying a single egg on its body. When the wasp grub hatches, it feeds on the buried spider. Other spider-hunting wasps are found all over the world, mainly in the tropics.

SCIENTIFIC NAME	*Hemipepsis ustulata*
DISTRIBUTION	North America
SIZE	Up to 0.8 in. (2cm) long

OAK APPLE WASP

Instead of making nests, oak apple wasps lay their eggs on oak twigs. When the eggs hatch, they cause the tree to form small growths called galls. The oak apple wasp larvae live in the galls and feed on the plant juices inside. Hundreds of types of small wasps live this way on a wide variety of plants. Gall wasps have complicated life cycles, often involving several generations a year. Some gall wasps make two different types of galls, one in the spring and the other in summer. The shape of the gall depends on the species of wasp that lays the egg.

SCIENTIFIC NAME	*Biorrhiza pallida*
DISTRIBUTION	Europe
SIZE	About 0.1 in. (2.5mm) long

TOP *A common wasp feeds on a drop of sugary apple juice.*
ABOVE *Bold yellow and black colors warn that wasps will sting.*

Adult oak apple wasp

Worker hornet showing brown and yellow markings

COMMON WASP

These black and yellow wasps build ball-shaped paper nests in attics or under ground. They are quick to use their stingers, often causing people to panic when they appear in search of sugary food. Common wasps make the paper for their nests by chewing fibers of dead wood to form a paste. A single queen starts the nest, but she soon hands over to a growing band of workers. A nest can house over 5,000 workers and can be over 1.5 ft. (50cm) across. The workers die in the winter, but new queens survive to nest the following spring. Yellow jackets, American relatives of this wasp, live in a similar way.

SCIENTIFIC NAME	*Vespula vulgaris*
DISTRIBUTION	Europe, Asia
SIZE	Workers up to 0.6 in. (1.5cm)

HORNET

These woodland insects nest in hollow trees. They are larger than common wasps, with yellow and brown markings and smoky wings. The adults eat nectar, but they also hunt insects for themselves and their young. Hornets cut the head and legs off their prey before taking the remains to their nest. They have dangerous stings, but they usually avoid people.

SCIENTIFIC NAME	*Vespa crabro*
DISTRIBUTION	Europe, Asia, North America
SIZE	Up to 1 in. (2.5cm)

BELOW *The ruby-tailed wasp is a parasite. It lives off other wasps and bees, laying eggs in their nests so that its grubs can feed on the nest owner's grubs.*

Reinforced body shell is resistant to stings from other wasps and bees

Giant ichneumon wasp with its long ovipositor

GIANT ICHNEUMON WASP

There are over 10,000 species of ichneumons. Giant ichneumon wasps are particularly impressive: the females have long ovipositors that drill through wood to lay their eggs. Like all ichneumons, they lay their eggs inside caterpillars and other insect grubs. When the eggs hatch, the ichneumon larvae eat their hosts alive, leaving only an empty corpse by the time they become adults. This may sound gruesome, but ichneumons are useful in controlling a wide variety of insect pests.

SCIENTIFIC NAME	*Rhyssa persuasoria*
DISTRIBUTION	Europe, Asia
SIZE	Up to 3 in. (8cm) long, including ovipositor

Ovipositor drills deep into wood

RUBY-TAILED WASP

With its brilliant green body and shiny red abdomen, this small but colorful wasp scuttles around busily in the bright sunshine, tapping the surface underfoot with its antennae. Like the cuckoo bee (page 87), it uses the nests of other bees and wasps as foster homes for its young. Its armored body protects it from the occupants' sting when it breaks into a nest.

SCIENTIFIC NAME	*Chrysis ignita*
DISTRIBUTION	Europe, Asia
SIZE	About 0.4 in. (1cm) long

HORNTAIL

Also known as wood wasps, horntails belong to a group of insects called sawflies, which are common in woodland areas. Sawflies are named for the sawlike teeth on their ovipositors, which allow them to bore through wood or tough plants to deposit their eggs. Sawflies differ from true wasps in two important ways: they do not have a stinger or a narrow "waist." Horntail larvae feed on plant matter, spending their early life tunneling through trees and other plants. They are often attacked by ichneumon wasps.

SCIENTIFIC NAME	*Urocerus* and other genera
DISTRIBUTION	Worldwide
SIZE	Typical length 1.5 in. (4cm)

LEFT *This female horntail is about to use her ovipositor to lay an egg inside a fallen branch.*

ECHINODERMS

STARFISH, SEA URCHINS, AND SEA CUCUMBERS ARE TYPES
OF ECHINODERMS. THEY ARE THE ONLY ANIMALS WITH
BODIES BASED ON THE NUMBER FIVE. MANY HAVE FIVE ARMS,
FIVE SETS OF MOUTHPARTS, AND FIVE SETS OF TUBE FEET.

As well as an uncommon shape, echinoderms have unique skeletons made of chalky plates, covered by a thin layer of skin. In some species, the plates are joined to long spines—echinoderm means "spiny skin." Echinoderms live in the ocean, ranging from shallow water to the greatest depths. They feed on plants, small animals such as bivalves, and dead remains. About 6,500 species have been identified.

EDIBLE SEA URCHIN

Sea urchins have round, spine-covered bodies. Their mouths, on their undersides of their bodies, have five pointed teeth for scraping algae from rocks. Their spines protect them from predators. The edible sea urchin has sharp spines that snap off and stick in skin. Others have blunt spines that they use to jam themselves safely into rocky crevices. When sea urchins die, the spines fall off, leaving skeletons called tests.

SCIENTIFIC NAME	*Echinus esculentus*
DISTRIBUTION Northeastern Atlantic Ocean	
SIZE Skeleton up to 8 in. (17cm) wide	

RIGHT *The violet heart urchin (Spatangus purpureus) has short, furlike spines.*

ABOVE *The edible sea urchin has dense pink, red, or purple spines. It gets its name from its edible eggs, or roes.*

HEART URCHIN OR SEA POTATO

Instead of creeping over rocks, heart urchins burrow into seabed sand. They plow slowly beneath the surface, pointed end first, using their tube feet to collect particles of food. On their upper sides, heart urchins have long tube feet that they use to dig tunnels up to the surface of the sand. They use these tunnels as water vents, which enables them to breathe.

SCIENTIFIC NAME	*Spatangus* and other genera
DISTRIBUTION Worldwide	
SIZE Typical length 4 in. (10cm)	

SAND DOLLAR

These sea urchins have flat, circular bodies and short spines. They have a star-shaped pattern of tiny holes on their upper sides, which connect to five rows of tube feet. Sand dollars live on the seabed, where they crowd together near the shore. They produce a sticky mucus that traps particles of food floating in the water.

SCIENTIFIC NAME	*Dendraster* and other genera
DISTRIBUTION Worldwide	
SIZE Typical width 3 in. (8cm)	

SEA CUCUMBER

These sausage-shaped animals creep across the seabed, using a set of frilly tentacles to collect food. Unlike other echinoderms, their mouths are at one end of their bodies. Sea cucumbers are protected by tough skin and a skeleton of chalky spikes. If an enemy comes too close, a threatened sea cucumber has another defense—it turns its anus toward its attacker and ejects a tangle of sticky threads.

SCIENTIFIC NAME	*Stichopus* and other genera
DISTRIBUTION Worldwide	
SIZE Typical length 16 in. (40cm)	

Upper surface
is studded with
thorn-shaped
swellings

LEFT *The northern sea star can be pale
yellow through red to violet in color.
It has five long arms.*

NORTHERN SEA STAR

There are about 1,500 species of sea stars, also called starfish, living in oceans all over the world. Most of them have five arms, but some have as many as 50. Some sea stars have such short arms that they look like five-sided cushions, and most can replace any arms that are broken or bitten off. The northern sea star lives in shallow water, eating mussels and other bivalve mollusks. It creeps over its victims and pries open their shells with its tube feet. Once a small gap has opened up, the sea star slips its stomach inside its prey's shell and digests the soft body.

SCIENTIFIC NAME	*Asterias rubens*
DISTRIBUTION	Atlantic Ocean, Mediterranean Sea
SIZE	Up to 8 in. (20cm) across

LEFT *The
Californian sea
cucumber* (Stichopus
californicus) *lives
in water up to
300 feet deep.*

CROWN-OF-THORNS STARFISH

This tropical starfish has up to 23 arms covered with poisonous spines. It feeds on reef-building corals, eating their soft bodies and leaving the skeletons behind. In recent decades, plagues of these starfish have attacked the Great Barrier Reef off the northeastern coast of Australia, raising fears for the reef's survival. Biologists now think that these plagues are natural events that have occurred many times before. After each onslaught, the starfish die off, and the reefs slowly recover.

SCIENTIFIC NAME	*Acanthaster planci*
DISTRIBUTION	Indian Ocean, Pacific Ocean
SIZE	Up to 16 in. (40cm) across

**Common
brittle star**

COMMON BRITTLE STAR

Brittle stars look like starfish, but they are much more slender and faster on the move. Their arms, joined to a disk-shaped body, are flexible but break off easily if touched. The common brittle star lives near the shore, but other species spend their lives in deep water. They eat dead remains or small particles of food that drift down from the water above.

SCIENTIFIC NAME	*Ophiothrix fragilis*
DISTRIBUTION	Atlantic Ocean
SIZE	Up to 8 in. (20cm) across

RIGHT
*The common brittle
star's five arms are
flanked by rows of
small spines. The
spines help the
brittle star collect
food and fend off
other animals.*

CHORDATES

Leathery trunk is sensitive to touch

ALL CHORDATES SHARE ONE KEY FEATURE: A STRENGTHENING ROD, OR NOTOCHORD, THAT RUNS THE LENGTH OF THEIR BODIES. THIS GROUP OF ANIMALS INCLUDES SIMPLE CREATURES THAT BARELY MOVE, AS WELL AS THE LARGEST, FASTEST, MOST INTELLIGENT ANIMALS ON EARTH.

In simple chordates, such as lancelets and sea squirts, the notochord is the only hard part of the body. But in advanced chordates, such as fish, birds, and mammals, it is surrounded by a column of interlocking bones. These bones, called vertebrae, form part of a complete internal skeleton. After millions of years of evolution, animals with vertebrae now outnumber simple chordates many times over, and they dominate life on our planet.

SIMPLE CHORDATES
There are about 1,300 species of simple chordates found in oceans worldwide. They are all small and easy to overlook. Some of them burrow through sand, but others spend their lives fastened to rocks or drifting in open water. Because simple chordates do not have backbones, they are classified as invertebrates. However, they are invertebrates with a difference, because they have a notochord for all or part of their lives. This feature means that they are related to vertebrates, including humans.

LANCELET
A lancelet looks like a small, transparent fish, with an extremely narrow body. It lurks on the seabed, half-buried in sand, using tentacles to pump water into its mouth. Once the water is inside, sievelike slits filter out small particles of food, and the waste water is pumped away. Lancelets do not have eyes or jaws, and they have only the beginnings of a brain. However, many of the features they do have, such as muscles arranged in blocks, also appear in fish and other vertebrates.

SCIENTIFIC NAME *Branchiostoma* species
DISTRIBUTION Warm seas worldwide
SIZE About 2 in. (5cm) long

SEA SQUIRT
Adult sea squirts live fastened to solid objects and feed by pumping water through their baglike body. Young sea squirts, however, look completely different. They have a tadpole-shaped body, reinforced by a notochord, and swim in open water. They settle on rocks to turn into adults, and their notochord disappears.

SCIENTIFIC NAME *Ciona* and other genera
DISTRIBUTION Worldwide
SIZE Typical height 6 in. (15cm)

Sea squirts often live in colonies of many individuals

VERTEBRATES
Vertebrates are animals that have backbones and a complete internal skeleton. Unlike a shell or exoskeleton, this kind of skeleton can grow to a large size without becoming too heavy or too clumsy to move. Compared to other animals, vertebrates have large brains and elaborate nervous systems, and they often behave in complex ways. There are seven groups, or classes, of vertebrates: three groups of fish, amphibians, reptiles, birds, and mammals. Fish are divided into three classes because they are built in three distinct ways.

ABOVE *The pike (Esox lucius) is a bony fish.*

LEFT *Like most amphibians, the painted frog (Discoglossus pictus) must stay moist to survive.*

LEFT *The common wall lizard (Podarcis muralis) basks in the sun to raise its body temperature.*

LEFT *The common sea squirt* (Ciona intestinalis) *lives on rocks in shallow water. If touched, it instantly contracts.*

Small opening expels water

Large opening sucks in water

JAWLESS FISH

Fish without jaws were the first vertebrates on earth. They lived on the seabed and sucked up their food. Most jawless fish died out more than 300 million years ago, but a few species, called lampreys and hagfish, still exist. They have snakelike bodies, round mouths, and tiny eyes. Their gill openings are shaped like portholes, and they have scaleless and often slimy skin.

ATLANTIC HAGFISH

These deep-sea scavengers feed on dead or dying fish. They find their food using their keen sense of smell, and they often slither right inside thier prey. A hagfish does not have jaws, but it has small teeth that it uses to eat its prey from the inside. As a defense, it secretes an obnoxious, slimy substance. To remove it, the hagfish ties a knot in its body, which it slips down to its tail. Hagfish lay elongated eggs, and their young look like small adults when they hatch.

SCIENTIFIC NAME	*Myxine glutinosa*
DISTRIBUTION	Atlantic Ocean
SIZE	Up to 27.5 in. (70cm) long

SEA LAMPREY

Adult sea lampreys are parasites that feed on the blood of other fish. They have sharp teeth for clamping onto their prey. Lampreys can cling on for weeks, taking so much blood that the victim often dies. Like all lampreys, the sea lamprey breeds in fresh water. Its young, called ammocoete larvae, are blind and toothless. They spend up to six years filtering food from the water before they develop into adults and travel downriver to the sea.

SCIENTIFIC NAME	*Petromyzon marinus*
DISTRIBUTION	Northern Atlantic Ocean, Mediterranean Sea, adjoining rivers and lakes
SIZE	Up to 3 ft. (1m) long

BROOK LAMPREY

Unlike sea lampreys, brook lampreys spend all their lives in fresh water. They are not a threat to other fish because the adults do not feed. The female lays her eggs in gravel or sand. These eggs produce filter-feeding larvae that take about five years to grow into adults. After spawning, the adults die.

SCIENTIFIC NAME	*Lampetra planeri*
DISTRIBUTION	Europe
SIZE	Up to 10 in. (25cm) long

RIGHT *A young brook lamprey slithers over the bed of a stream.*

ABOVE *The Eurasian jay* (Garrulus glandarius) *is a typical bird.*

ABOVE *The European rabbit* (Oryctolagus cuniculus) *is a typical mammal, with dense fur.*

ABOVE *Sea lampreys have seven round gill openings and small fins near the ends of their bodies.*

RIGHT *The sea lamprey's mouth has no jaws, but it is studded with small teeth.*

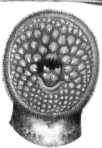

CARTILAGINOUS FISH

SHARKS, SKATES, AND RAYS ARE KNOWN AS CARTILAGINOUS FISH BECAUSE THEIR SKELETONS ARE MADE OF CARTILAGE. THIS SAME RUBBERY SUBSTANCE LINES OUR JOINTS AND GIVES SHAPE TO OUR EARS AND NOSES. CARTILAGE IS WEAKER THAN BONE, BUT IT IS STRONG ENOUGH TO SUPPORT SOME OF THE LARGEST ANIMALS IN THE OCEAN.

Cartilaginous fish have streamlined bodies covered with rough, sandpapery skin and stiff fins that cannot be folded away. Their jaws are powerful and armed with an endless supply of biting or crushing teeth. Most of these fish are predators, but the largest species are filter feeders, scooping up huge numbers of planktonic animals in their gaping mouths as they swim. There are about 600 species of cartilaginous fish living mainly in the sea, with only a few venturing into fresh water. Some lay eggs, but many species give birth to live young.

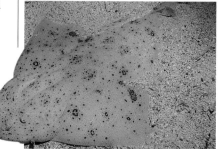

SHARKS

Sharks are the best-known cartilaginous fish and the most feared. There are more than 340 species, and although only about 20 species are known to attack humans, they kill several hundred people every year. Most sharks are shaped for non-stop swimming. They have large, oily livers that work like floats and a keen sense of smell that alerts them to food far away. Most sharks live in the open water, but some are bottom dwellers with effective camouflage colors to protect them from predators.

ANGEL SHARK

This bottom-dwelling shark lives in water as deep as 300 ft. (100m). With its flat body and broad pectoral fins, it resembles a ray (page 100). Angel sharks eat small seabed fish. Like other sharks, they can sense the faint electrical field that surrounds a fish's body, so they can find prey buried in the sand. Angel shark eggs hatch inside the mother's body, producing live young.

SCIENTIFIC NAME	*Squatina squatina*
DISTRIBUTION	Eastern Atlantic Ocean, Mediterranean Sea
SIZE	Up to 6 ft. (2m) long

ABOVE *An angel shark lies on the seabed. Angel sharks have breathing holes on top of their heads so they can lie flat on the sand and still be able to breathe.*

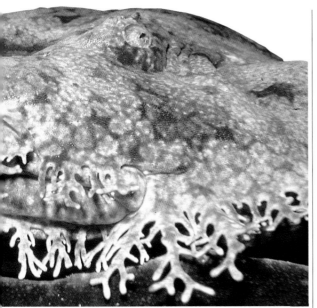

COOKIECUTTER SHARK

Instead of killing and swallowing its prey, the cookiecutter bites off small chunks of flesh. It attacks animals much larger than itself, including dolphins and whales, and has even been known to bite off the rubber fittings of submarines. Cookiecutters live mainly in deep water, traveling to the surface after dark to feed on other fish.

SCIENTIFIC NAME *Isistius brasiliensis*

DISTRIBUTION Indian Ocean, Pacific Ocean, southern Atlantic Ocean

SIZE Up to 20 in. (50cm) long

PORT JACKSON SHARK

With its blunt head, spiny fins, and downward-pointing mouth, this fish looks very different from most other sharks. It feeds after dark on mollusks and crabs, crushing them with its flattened back teeth. Port Jackson sharks breed in shallow water and lay large eggs with tough, spiral-shaped cases. The females sometimes push their eggs into crevices, where they have the best chance of surviving until they hatch.

SCIENTIFIC NAME *Heterodontus portusjacksoni*

DISTRIBUTION Southern Pacific Ocean

SIZE Up to 5 ft. (1.5m) long

Hard spine on dorsal fin

Port Jackson shark

ABOVE *The extraordinary tassels around this spotted wobbegong's body help it hide as it lies on the seabed. From above, its camouflage makes it almost invisible.*

BELOW *The dwarf shark was first discovered in the sea off Japan. It lives in deep water and rises to the surface at night to feed.*

SPOTTED WOBBEGONG

Wobbegongs do not actively search for their prey. Instead, they lie in wait, camouflaged on the seabed. Their shape is broken up by a pattern of light brown markings and by fleshy tassels along the edge of their jaws. Wobbegongs can lie still for hours, but if anything edible comes within range, they strike instantly. Wobbegongs do not normally attack humans, but they can be very dangerous if they are stepped on accidentally.

SCIENTIFIC NAME *Orectolobus maculatus*

DISTRIBUTION Western Pacific Ocean

SIZE Up to 10 ft. (3m) long

DWARF SHARK

This is the world's smallest known shark, with a body that is often shorter than a human hand. Dwarf sharks rise up to shallow water at night and have a luminous underside that they can "turn on" when they feed near the surface of the water. The pale light may help disguise their silhouette from below, making it hard for predators to spot them.

SCIENTIFIC NAME *Squaliolus laticaudus*

DISTRIBUTION Worldwide

SIZE Up to 10 in. (25cm) long

GREENLAND SHARK

This large, cold-water shark feeds on fish, seals, and garbage thrown overboard from fishing boats. It is a sluggish animal that spends much of its time near the seabed. Its flesh is poisonous to humans, but the sharks sometimes eat each other. Adult Greenland sharks usually have finger-sized parasitic crustaceans attached to their eyes. Scientists think that the crustaceans may help lure prey toward the sharks.

SCIENTIFIC NAME *Somniosus microcephalus*

DISTRIBUTION Northern Atlantic Ocean, Arctic Sea

SIZE Up to 20 ft. (6m) long

RIGHT AND BELOW
The whale shark has the huge mouth and tiny eyes typical of a harmless plankton-eater.

WHALE SHARK

The largest fish in the world, this immense shark can weigh more than 20 tons. Its tail can be more than 8 ft. (2.4m) from tip to tip, and its mouth is wide enough to swallow a human swimmer sideways. Fortunately, this giant animal is not interested in people, feeding entirely on plankton and tiny fish. As it cruises near the surface, it takes large gulps of water and filters food from it. Whale sharks sometimes collide with ships, but are otherwise rarely seen. They lay the world's largest eggs, measuring up to 12 in. (30cm) in length. Little is known about how they grow because sightings of young whale sharks are extremely rare.

SCIENTIFIC NAME	*Rhincodon typus*
DISTRIBUTION	Tropical seas worldwide
SIZE	Maximum length unknown, but possibly about 60 ft. (18m)

BASKING SHARK

This is the second largest species of shark, weighing up to four tons. It is a filter feeder, though its shape is more typical of a hunting shark, with a streamlined body and pointed snout. When the basking shark feeds, it opens its mouth until it is almost circular and strains large amounts of water through its huge gills. It swims slowly, as if it is basking in the sunshine, which is how it got its name. Basking sharks give birth to live young after a gestation period of more than a year.

SCIENTIFIC NAME	*Cetorhinus maximus*
DISTRIBUTION	Cool seas worldwide
SIZE	Up to 35 ft. (10m) long

NURSE SHARK

Nurse sharks spend most of their time on the seabed and are found as far north as New York. They have much smaller mouths than most sharks of their size and feed with a vacuum-cleaner action, sucking up mollusks and crustaceans. Nurse sharks look dangerous, but they are generally harmless to people. If they are provoked, however, they can attack. Once a nurse shark has bitten, its jaws often lock shut and have to be forced apart. Nurse sharks give birth to live young.

SCIENTIFIC NAME	*Ginglymostoma cirratum*
DISTRIBUTION	Eastern Pacific Ocean, Atlantic Ocean
SIZE	Up to 13 ft. (4m) long

MEGAMOUTH SHARK

The megamouth shark was discovered in 1976, when the first known specimen was brought ashore in Hawaii. Like the whale shark and basking shark, it is a filter-feeder, but it lives in deep water instead of near the surface. It has a black-brown, tapering body and, true to its name, a huge mouth. Its teeth are tiny, but it has luminous organs inside its mouth that probably help it attract food. The megamouth is seldom seen, and so little is known about its breeding habits or how widespread it is.

SCIENTIFIC NAME	*Megachasma pelagicus*
DISTRIBUTION	Unknown
SIZE	About 13 ft. (4m) long

THRESHER SHARK

Thresher shark showing its long, arched tail

A thresher shark's tail is almost as long as the rest of its body. The lower tail lobe is small, but the upper lobe is large and arched, ending in a pointed tip. Threshers feed alone or in groups on schools of fish. They thrash their tails from side to side to round up or wound their prey. They can even use their tails to knock low-flying seabirds out of the air. Threshers give birth to up to four live young at a time. They produce more, but some of the young eat the others while inside their mother's body.

SCIENTIFIC NAME	*Alopias vulpinus*
DISTRIBUTION	Worldwide
SIZE	Up to 20 ft. (6m) long

BELOW *The basking shark's mouth swells up like a balloon as it filters plankton from the water.*

GREAT WHITE SHARK

The great white is the world's largest and most dangerous predatory shark. It attacks seals, dolphins, and other fish, and eats all kinds of leftovers and remains, including dead whales and garbage thrown from boats. It has a reputation as a man-eater and has been known to attack small boats, biting or punching them with its snout until they sink. The great white's reputation makes it highly prized by sea anglers and by souvenir hunters who collect shark teeth and jaws. As a result, fully grown great white sharks are far less common than they once were.

SCIENTIFIC NAME *Carcharodon carcharias*

DISTRIBUTION Warm waters worldwide

SIZE Up to 25 ft. (8m) long

BELOW *The great white shark's teeth can be more than 2 in. long. They are constantly replaced throughout the shark's life.*

MAKO

With a top speed of nearly 55 mph (90km/h), the mako is the fastest-swimming shark. It needs this speed because it feeds on tuna and mackerel—fish that are also among the swiftest in the seas. Makos have been known to attack people, and they are sought after by sea anglers because they fight back ferociously if hooked. Female makos keep their eggs inside their bodies until they have hatched, then give birth to live young.

SCIENTIFIC NAME *Isurus oxyrhynchus*

DISTRIBUTION Worldwide, mainly in warm waters

SIZE Up to 13 ft. (4m) long

Large dorsal fin

ABOVE *The mako shark uses its large tail to produce spectacular bursts of speed when swimming.*

PORBEAGLE

A close relative of the mako (page 97), the porbeagle is also a swift, surface-dwelling hunter. It feeds on mackerel and herring, and also chases squid. Although sharks are normally cold-blooded, porbeagles and makos can keep their body temperature slightly higher than the water around them. This enables their muscles to contract more quickly, so they can produce a burst of speed. Porbeagles give birth to live young. They feed on their mother's unfertilized eggs before they are born.

SCIENTIFIC NAME	*Lamna nasus*
DISTRIBUTION	Worldwide, particularly common in cold water
SIZE	Up to 10 ft. (3m) long

SMALL-SPOTTED CATSHARK

This slender-bodied fish is Europe's most common shark. Its upper surface is sandy brown with dark spots, and its upright dorsal fin is far down its body, closer to its tail than to its head. Catsharks feed on mollusks, crustaceans, and slow-moving fish, which they hunt on the seabed in shallow water. Like other bottom-dwelling sharks, they have a well-developed electrical sense, so they can find their prey even when it

Sleek shape enables swift movement

is completely buried. Catsharks lay flat, square eggs with spiral tendrils at the corners. These tendrils wind around seaweed, anchoring the eggs until they hatch. The empty cases, called mermaids' purses, often wash up on the shore.

SCIENTIFIC NAME	*Scyliorhinus canicula*
DISTRIBUTION	Eastern Atlantic Ocean, Mediterranean Sea
SIZE	Up to 3 ft. (1m) long

LEOPARD SHARK

Leopard sharks are named for their dark brown spots, which look like the pattern on a leopard's fur. They have large pectoral fins and a series of hard ridges that run the length of their bodies. These common, harmless sharks swim on the seabed, where they feed on clams and other burrowing mollusks. They thrive in captivity and are often kept in marine aquariums.

SCIENTIFIC NAME	*Triakis semifasciata*
DISTRIBUTION	Pacific coast of North America
SIZE	Up to 6 ft. (2m) long

BULL SHARK

This is one of the few sharks that swim up estuaries into fresh water. It can be seen far inland, in the Amazon River in South America, the Zambezi River in Africa, and the Ganges River in India. Bull sharks feed on all kinds of animals, including other sharks. They can be dangerous because they hunt where people swim.

SCIENTIFIC NAME	*Carcharhinus leucas*
DISTRIBUTION	Tropical rivers and coasts
SIZE	Up to 11 ft. (3.4m) long

BLACKTIP SHARK

Many sharks get excited when they sense food, but blacktips get more frantic than most. During "feeding frenzies," they swirl around in chaotic packs, competing for food. They swim near land, but rarely attack people.

SCIENTIFIC NAME	*Carcharhinus limbatus*
DISTRIBUTION	Tropical coasts and seas
SIZE	Up to 7 ft. (2.1m) long

BELOW *The blue shark is a slender and graceful fish, with long pectoral fins. It feeds near the surface and is more tolerant of cold than most sharks. It often ventures into regions where the water temperature is lower than 50°F.*

BELOW *A tiger shark bursts through the water's surface. Compared to other open-water sharks, the tiger shark has an unusually short snout.*

Slit-shaped gill openings

Deep blue back distinguishes this species from most other sharks

Upright dorsal fin

Pectoral fins, used like the wingflaps on an airplane, help the shark change direction

RIGHT *The smooth hammerhead's bizarre head looks more like a handicap than a help, but this fish is an effective and dangerous predator.*

BLUE SHARK

This steel-blue, streamlined fish is one of the most widespread sharks in the world. It has long, curved pectoral fins, which it uses to twist and turn through the water after prey. Blue sharks have a reputation as man-eaters, and they also cause problems for fishermen by raiding nets to feed on trapped fish. They feed both inshore and in the open ocean, often hunting in packs. They can attack and overpower whales and other animals larger than themselves.

SCIENTIFIC NAME *Prionace glauca*

DISTRIBUTION Tropical and temperate waters worldwide

SIZE Up to 13 ft. (4m) long

TIGER SHARK

Some shark specialists believe that this fish is responsible for more attacks on humans than any other species—including the infamous great white (page 97). A huge and formidable hunter, the tiger shark attacks and eats almost anything, from turtles and other sharks to lobster traps and old oil drums. In 1935, one specimen caught off Australia regurgitated a human arm—it was identified by a tattoo, but the rest of the body was never found. Tiger sharks have a striped pattern when they are young, but this fades as they grow. They live both inshore and in the open sea, and give birth to live young.

SCIENTIFIC NAME *Galeocerdo cuvieri*

DISTRIBUTION Warm seas worldwide

SIZE Up to 23 ft. (7m) long

SMOOTH HAMMERHEAD

The ten species of hammerheads are the world's most strangely shaped sharks. They have a typical shark shape except for their heads, which have long flaps that stick out on each side. Scientists do not know for sure what these flaps are for. One possibility is that they help the hammerhead pinpoint its prey; another is that they provide lift as the shark swims. Smooth hammerheads have been known to attack people occasionally. They often swim close to the surface, and can be found near the shore as well as out at sea.

SCIENTIFIC NAME *Sphyrna zygaena*

DISTRIBUTION Warm waters worldwide

SIZE Up to 13 ft. (4m) long

SKATES, RAYS, AND RATFISH

Skates and rays are cartilaginous fish with flattened bodies and winglike fins. Many live on the seabed, where they are often superbly camouflaged, but a few spend most of their lives near the surface, flapping through the sea like underwater birds. Unlike sharks, these fish crush their food with blunt teeth. Their mouths and gill openings are on the undersides of their bodies, and they have breathing holes on their upper surfaces, just behind their eyes. In total, there are more than 300 species of skates and rays, most of which live in the sea. Ratfish belong to a different group of cartilaginous fish. There are about 25 species of ratfish, all marine.

RIGHT *Unlike the skate's upper surface, the underside (shown here) is pale and does not have camouflaged markings.*

Mouth

Row of gill slits

Wide pectoral fins

COMMON SKATE

Skates have diamond-shaped bodies with pointed snouts, wide pectoral fins, and long, spiny tails. Young skates live in shallow water near the shore, but the adults live in water up to 2,000 ft. (600m) deep and feed on fish, crabs, and other crustaceans. They reproduce by laying eggs. The eggs are covered by a tough, yellow case and are rectangular, with a horn at each corner. Common skates are an important source of food for humans, who catch them in trawler nets, which are dragged across the seabed.

SCIENTIFIC NAME *Raja batis*

DISTRIBUTION Eastern North Atlantic Ocean, Mediterranean Sea

SIZE Up to 8 ft. (2.4m) long

ABOVE *The thornback ray (Raja clavata) has prickles on its upper surface and spines along its back and tail.*

MANTA RAY

With a "wingspan" of nearly 23 ft. (7m), the manta ray is the largest ray in the world. Like many of the largest sea animals, it feeds on plankton, which it scoops up as it swims. It has a fleshy paddle on each side of its head to help funnel food into its mouth. In the past, manta rays inspired many legends about sea monsters, but as far as humans are concerned, these enormous fish are totally harmless.

SCIENTIFIC NAME *Manta birostris*

DISTRIBUTION Warm seas worldwide

SIZE Up to 16 ft. (5m) long

STINGRAY

These fish are closely related to skates, but they have a blunter snout. They have one or two spines near the base of their tails that can inject a strong poison if they are attacked. Stingray wounds are rarely deadly to humans, but they can be painful, sometimes paralyzing part of the body until the poison has worn off. Stingrays eat mollusks and crustaceans and produce live young.

SCIENTIFIC NAME *Dasyatis* and other genera

DISTRIBUTION Worldwide

SIZE Typical length 5 ft. (1.5m)

EAGLE RAY

These active swimmers feed on the seabed but often come to the surface, sometimes jumping clear of the water. They have poisonous spines in their tails, which they use for self-defense. Eagle rays eat small seabed animals, flapping their fins to expose them in the sand or mud.

SCIENTIFIC NAME *Myliobatis* and other genera

DISTRIBUTION Worldwide

SIZE Typical length 5 ft. (1.5m)

Atlantic torpedo ray attacking and engulfing a fish

RIGHT *A manta ray glides through the sea, funneling plankton into its mouth. This one is carrying some remoras (page 125).*

LEFT
The Atlantic torpedo ray's pectoral fins give it an almost perfectly circular outline. This electric ray can deliver a severe shock, but it rarely harms people.

Rounded pectoral fins

ATLANTIC TORPEDO RAY

The Atlantic torpedo is the largest electric ray, weighing as much as 200 lb. (90kg). Electric rays are found all over the world. To feed, they trap prey in their fins and give it a powerful electric shock. Two sets of muscles just behind the head can generate a brief jolt of up to 220 volts, which is enough to stun or kill a medium-sized fish.

SCIENTIFIC NAME *Torpedo nobiliana*

DISTRIBUTION Atlantic Ocean, Mediterranean Sea

SIZE Up to 6 ft. (2m) long

Sawfish using its long snout to scatter a school of fish

SAWFISH

The sawfish looks like a cross between a shark and a skate, but its most conspicuous feature is its remarkable, sawlike snout. Shaped like a flattened blade, it can be over 3 ft. (1m) long and is edged with more than 50 sharp teeth. The sawfish uses its snout to attack other fish and to rake the seabed in search of buried animals. Female sawfish produce live young, whose saws are soft. Large adults can weigh more than two tons. Although sawfish look highly dangerous, there are no reliable records of them attacking people.

SCIENTIFIC NAME *Pristis* species

DISTRIBUTION Worldwide

SIZE Up to 23 ft. (7m) long

RATFISH

Roughly translated, this strange looking fish's scientific name means "multi-animal monster." This is an apt description of the ratfish, with its large, bulbous head, rabbitlike mouth, and long, ratlike tail. Ratfish are bottom-feeders, eating mollusks and other seabed animals. Unlike sharks, skates, and rays, the ratfish's gills are hidden by a flap of skin, a feature found more often in bony fish (page 102). Ratfish reproduce by laying eggs. Each egg is enclosed in a long, slender case.

SCIENTIFIC NAME *Chimaera monstrosa*

DISTRIBUTION Eastern North Atlantic Ocean, Mediterranean Sea

SIZE Up to 5 ft. (1.5m) long

BONY FISH

MORE THAN 24,000 SPECIES OF BONY FISH ARE KNOWN TO SCIENCE. SOME WEIGH MORE THAN TWO TONS, WHILE OTHERS WEIGH A FRACTION OF AN OUNCE. BONY FISH LIVE IN EVERY IMAGINABLE WATERY HABITAT, FROM SUNLIT OCEAN SURFACES TO THE PERPETUAL DARKNESS OF UNDERGROUND LAKES.

RIGHT The common sturgeon, like all sturgeons, has a skeleton made of cartilage as well as bone. Sturgeons are primitive bony fish.

These fish have bony skeletons and, in most species, their bodies are covered with scales. Their gills are covered by a movable flap, and they have an internal "float," or swim bladder, which makes them buoyant. Their shapes depend on how they live. Most are streamlined, some are flat, but others have such strange shapes that they hardly look like fish at all. Bony fish usually lay eggs that are fertilized in the water, and they typically leave their young to fend for themselves.

LUNGFISH, BICHIRS, AND BONYTONGUES

This diverse collection of bony fish includes some species that have hardly changed for millions of years, such as coelacanths, the only fish with fleshy fins. Bichirs and their relatives have features in common with sharks. Bonytongues are typical bony fish, although they have some primitive features. There are about 230 species of these fish, living in either fresh water or the ocean.

ABOVE RIGHT, CENTER
The elephant-trunk fish's "trunk" looks like a nose, but it is a long lower jaw with a flexible chin. This fish has an unusually large brain and will play with toys when in an aquarium.

ABOVE RIGHT, BOTTOM
All ten species of bichirs, including this Polypterus ornatus, have eellike bodies and widely separated pectoral and pelvic fins.

SOUTH AMERICAN LUNGFISH

These fish live in places where there is a long dry season each year. As the water evaporates, each lungfish digs a burrow in the mud and breathes air until the wet weather returns. The fish then breaks out of its burrow and resumes its normal life. There are six species of lungfish. South American and African lungfish have two pairs of lungs, but the Australian lungfish has just one and does not dig burrows.

SCIENTIFIC NAME	*Lepidosiren paradoxa*
DISTRIBUTION	Tropical South America
SIZE	Up to 4 ft. (1.2m) long

BICHIR

Bichirs live in large rivers in Africa. They breathe by gulping air. They have long bodies, stubby fins, and a row of finlets along their backs that they can raise or lower like sails. Bichers can also crawl along the riverbed, using their front fins to haul themselves forward. They use this crawling motion to hunt, creeping up on fish and other small water animals.

SCIENTIFIC NAME	*Polypterus* species
DISTRIBUTION	Tropical Africa
SIZE	Up to 3 ft. (1m) long

COELACANTH

Scientists originally thought that this fleshy-finned fish had died out 65 million years ago. Then, in 1938, a museum curator spotted one that had been caught off the coast of South Africa, and had it identified by an expert fish biologist. The discovery caused great excitement because coelacanths are the closest living relatives of vertebrates with legs instead of fins. Coelacanths live close to the coast in water up to 2,500 ft. (750m) deep. They feed on fish and are thought to give birth to live young.

SCIENTIFIC NAME	*Latimeria chalmunae*
DISTRIBUTION	Indian Ocean, off the Comoros islands and Madagascar
SIZE	Up to 6 ft. (2m) long

COMMON STURGEON

Sturgeon are among the largest and most endangered river fish. The common sturgeon can weigh up to 600 lb. (275kg), while the heaviest sturgeon on record—a Russian sturgeon, or beluga—weighed nearly one and a half tons. Sturgeon have sharklike bodies with long, flat snouts and five rows of large, bony plates instead of scales. They feed on the bottom of the sea and in rivers, searching for food with the fleshy barbels, or whiskers, beneath their mouths. Female sturgeons lay millions of sticky, black eggs. People collect these eggs and sell them as caviar, one of the world's most expensive foods.

SCIENTIFIC NAME	*Acipenser sturio*
DISTRIBUTION	European coasts and rivers
SIZE	Up to 10 ft. (3m) long

ELEPHANT-TRUNK FISH

This nocturnal, freshwater fish has a long lower jaw that looks like an elephant's trunk, which it uses to stir up sand and mud, looking for small animals buried beneath the surface. Elephant-trunk fish often live in murky water, but find their way by creating a weak electrical field around themselves. Underwater objects distort the field, and the fish sense this and steer away.

SCIENTIFIC NAME	*Gnathonemus petersi*
DISTRIBUTION	Tropical Africa
SIZE	Up to 9 in. (23cm) long

PIRARUCU OR ARAPAIMA

The pirarucu looks like a gigantic pike (page 107) and is one of the largest fish to spend all of its life in fresh water. This bonytongue fish lives in South American rivers and swamps. The pirarucu feeds mainly on smaller fish, but it also eats snakes, turtles, frogs, and insects. The slow-flowing water in the pirarucu tropical habitat can get very warm and often contains only a little oxygen. The pirarucu survives in these conditions by gulping air. The air enters the swimbladder, which works like a lung.

SCIENTIFIC NAME	*Arapaima gigas*
DISTRIBUTION	South America
SIZE	Up to 8 ft. (2.4m) long

RIGHT *The ornate bichir is a primitive fish. It has diamond-shaped scales and a swim bladder that is connected to the stomach.*

HERRING AND THEIR RELATIVES

This group of fish contains nearly 400 species, including many that provide food for humans and wild animals. They live mainly in the oceans and often form large schools. Schooling protects them by making it harder for predators to single a victim out, but it also means that they are easy to catch in nets. Most of these fish have streamlined, silvery bodies and scales that rub off easily. They feed on planktonic animals, which they filter from the water with their gills. Marine species live near the shore and in shallow seas, and are most varied where the water is warm.

HERRING

Adult herrings live in the open ocean, rising to the surface at night to feed on swarms of plankton. Their teeth are tiny, but their gills work like strainers to trap tiny animals, which they swallow as they swim. Herrings breed by laying eggs, and the female can produce up to 40,000 eggs each year. The eggs sink to the seabed, where many are eaten by haddocks and other predators before they have a chance to hatch. Those that are not eaten produce tiny young fish that swim up toward the surface, attracted by the light. People have fished for herrings since prehistoric times, but in recent years so many have been caught that their numbers have dwindled.

SCIENTIFIC NAME	*Clupea harengus*
DISTRIBUTION	Northern Atlantic Ocean
SIZE	Up to 16 in. (40cm) long

SPRAT

This small fish looks like a miniature herring because it has the same torpedo-shaped, silvery body. Though it is one of the smallest members of the herring family, it is an important source of food for many marine animals. Sprats spawn close to the shore in late winter and spring. Their eggs float on the water.

SCIENTIFIC NAME	*Clupea sprattus*
DISTRIBUTION	Atlantic coast of Europe, Mediterranean Sea
SIZE	Up to 6 in. (15cm) long

NORTHERN ANCHOVY

There are more than 100 species of anchovies, and despite being small and slender, they play an important part in ocean life. These silvery fish live in large schools and are eaten by all kinds of animals, from seabirds to seals. Anchovies themselves eat tiny planktonic animals, but instead of snapping them up one by one, they swim with their mouths open and scoop them up as they go. Northern anchovies live in the Pacific Ocean. A similar species lives near the coasts of Europe.

SCIENTIFIC NAME	*Engraulis mordax*
DISTRIBUTION	Pacific coast of North America
SIZE	Up to 9 in. (23cm) long

SARDINE

Sardines live close to the shore in spring and summer, but move into deeper water during the rest of the year. When they are inshore, they are often attacked by seabirds. They are also caught by people for food. Sardines are attracted to light at night, and in southern Europe, they are lured by fleets of small boats with lamps. When the sardines are close enough to a boat, a net is tightened around them, and the fish are hauled aboard. Because they swim in large schools, sardines are easy to catch.

SCIENTIFIC NAME	*Sardina pilchardus*
DISTRIBUTION	European coasts
SIZE	Up to 10 in. (25cm) long

BELOW Herrings can live to be 20 years old, although their life span depends on where they live. There are several different local varieties of this fish. The smallest kind, which lives in the Baltic Sea, reaches maturity faster than those that live in the Atlantic.

Streamlined body for swimming easily through the water

Large eye

Two-lobed tail, or caudal fin

Scales overlap to cover the whole body

European anchovy
(Engraulis encrasicolus)

TOP *A school of northern
anchovies swims off the
coast of California. A single
school can contain over one
hundred thousand fish,
swimming in a tightly
packed group. These schools
make easy targets for
hungry seabirds.*

ALEWIFE

This North American fish lives along
coasts and in lakes, but it always lays its eggs
in fresh water. Like its close relatives, it has a
silvery body with a row of sharply pointed scales
along its underside. Many alewives travel back
into the sea after they spawn, but those that live
in landlocked lakes or in rivers with dams spend
their whole lives inland. Freshwater alewives are
not as large as their sea-going relatives, and their
numbers vary considerably from year to year.

SCIENTIFIC NAME *Alosa pseudoharengus*

DISTRIBUTION Atlantic coast of North America,
Great Lakes

SIZE Marine fish up to 15 in. (38 cm) long;
freshwater fish up to 10 in. (25cm) long

ALLIS SHAD

Like the alewife, the shad has sharp scales
along its underside, forming a ridge like a small-
toothed saw. It spends most of its life in deep
water offshore, but in the spring, it swims up
rivers to breed. The adults return to the sea after
they have spawned, but the young fish spend
up to two years in rivers before venturing
out to sea.

SCIENTIFIC NAME *Alosa alosa*

DISTRIBUTION European coasts, including
Mediterranean Sea

SIZE Up to 23.5 in. (60cm) long

ATLANTIC MENHADEN

Like herring, Atlantic menhadens live in large
schools. They are always on the move, looking
for plankton-rich waters in which to feed. The
sides of their stocky, silvery bodies are marked
with distinctive black spots. They lay their eggs
in the sea, and their young hatch near the
surface. Menhadens are an important food for
many other fish, seabirds, and humpback whales.

SCIENTIFIC NAME *Brevoorta tyrannus*

DISTRIBUTION Atlantic coast of North America

SIZE Up to 20 in. (50cm) long

SALMON AND THEIR RELATIVES

There are more than 300 species in this group, which includes some of the world's best-known migratory fish. Most of them are predators, either chasing their prey through the water or lurking among water weeds for fish and other animals to come close by. Salmon and their relatives reproduce by laying eggs. In some species, the males change color and shape just before the breeding season begins. This group of fish includes species that are found in both fresh and salt water. They are most common in the Northern Hemisphere.

ABOVE Two Atlantic salmon leap up a waterfall on their way to their spawning grounds. During their journey upstream, the adult salmon do not feed, although they will often snap at flies and fishing lures. They use so much energy that they can lose more than half their body weight during the journey.

ATLANTIC SALMON

This large and powerful fish begins its life in a river, where it eats insect larvae and worms. When it has grown to about 6 in. (15cm) long, it swims downriver to the sea. Adult salmon roam far out into the Atlantic, but after two to four years, they return to fresh water to breed. Using its sense of smell to navigate, each fish finds its way to the river where it developed, fighting its way upstream against the current. Female salmon lay their eggs in riverbed gravel. Once breeding is over, the thin and exhausted adults set off back to the sea, leaving their young to mature on their own. Atlantic salmon are valuable food for humans. Some are caught wild, but many are bred in fish farms.

SCIENTIFIC NAME *Salmo salar*

DISTRIBUTION Northern Atlantic Ocean, Arctic Ocean, adjoining lakes and rivers

SIZE Up to 5 ft. (1.5m) long

SOCKEYE SALMON

Like the Atlantic salmon, this fish spends most of its adult life in the ocean, returning to rivers to breed. At sea, the males are sleek and silvery, but during the breeding season, they turn bright red and develop a humped back and hooked jaws. Sockeye salmon can travel over 1,000 mi. (2,000km) up rivers, leaping up waterfalls and dodging predators. After they have laid their eggs, the adults die.

SCIENTIFIC NAME *Oncorhynchus nerka*

DISTRIBUTION Northern Pacific Ocean

SIZE Up to 3 ft. (1m) long

EUROPEAN SMELT

Smelts are slender-bodied fish with large mouths and long teeth. Like many of their relatives, such as the pike, they have teeth in the roofs of their mouths as well as in their jaws, which makes escape difficult for the fish and crustaceans they eat. Smelts swim up rivers to lay their eggs. The sticky eggs cling to stones and underwater plants.

SCIENTIFIC NAME *Osmerus eperlanus*

DISTRIBUTION Coasts and rivers of northern Europe

SIZE Up to 12 in. (30cm) long

RAINBOW TROUT

Originally from North America, this fast-swimming fish is a favorite with anglers and has been introduced into lakes and rivers in many parts of the world. Wild rainbow trout feed on insects and other small animals, sometimes leaping right out of the water to catch those fluttering above. They lay their eggs in gravelly streams. The adults usually return to the ocean after spawning, but fish in large lakes often spend their whole lives in fresh water.

SCIENTIFIC NAME *Salmo gairdneri*

DISTRIBUTION Northeastern Pacific Ocean, North America; introduced worldwide

SIZE Migratory fish up to 3 ft. (1m) long; nonmigratory fish less than 23.5 in. (60cm) long

NORTHERN PIKE

Pike are fierce freshwater predators that live in quiet lakes and rivers. They hunt by lying in wait for their victims—mainly fish— which they grab with a sudden burst of speed. Their jaws are shaped like a long beak and are strong enough to deal with animals up to a third of the pike's own size. In the spring, a pike's diet may also include ducklings and young coots, which it ambushes from below. Pike have cylindrical bodies and large fins positioned close to their tail.

SCIENTIFIC NAME *Esox lucius*

DISTRIBUTION Throughout the Northern Hemisphere

SIZE Up to 4.5 ft. (1.4m) long

TOP *Rainbow trout originated in North America, but have been introduced into cool, fast-flowing rivers and streams worldwide.*
ABOVE *The brown trout* (Salmo trutta) *is a European fish. Like the rainbow trout, it can spend its whole life in fresh water or migrate between fresh water and the sea.*

GRAYLING

The grayling is easy to recognize by the unusually large fin in the middle of its back. During the breeding season, the male's fin turns red, and he arches it over the female as she lays her eggs on gravel. Graylings live in rivers and lakes. They feed on insect larvae, other small animals, and on other fish's eggs. A similar species, called the Arctic grayling, is found in Canada and in Alaska.

SCIENTIFIC NAME *Thymallus thymallus*

DISTRIBUTION Northern Europe, northern Asia

SIZE Up to 18 in. (46cm) long

ARCTIC CHAR

This member of the salmon family is one of the world's most northerly freshwater fish. It lives in rivers and lakes inland, as well as in the Arctic Ocean, and survives in places where the water's surface is iced over for many months of the year. Arctic chars look similar to trout, but their color varies, depending on where they live. Males usually develop orange-red undersides during the breeding season, and in some lakes they remain this color all year round.

SCIENTIFIC NAME *Salvelinus alpinus*

DISTRIBUTION Seas, lakes, and rivers throughout the far north

SIZE Up to 3 ft. (1m) long

Arctic char with red underside

ABOVE *Although it is young, this northern pike is already a fierce predator. Its large eyes are good for spotting movement.*
LEFT *The grayling is very sensitive to pollution. Graylings quickly disappear from rivers contaminated with chemical fertilizers.*

BRISTLEMOUTHS AND HATCHETFISH

This group of about 250 species includes some of the world's most common saltwater fish. Most of them live in the oceans' depths and are rarely seen. They vary in size and shape, but all of them have hinged teeth and rows of light-producing organs on their bodies. Bristlemouths and hatchetfish feed on other fish or on small animals that drift in plankton. They live in oceans worldwide.

BIOLUMINESCENCE

Sunlight is absorbed by sea water, so the deeper you dive, the darker it gets. Below depths of 3,000 ft. (1,000m), the water is inky black. In these conditions, many fish make their own light. They use it to communicate or to lure prey within striking distance.

Light production by living things is called bioluminescence. Other light-producing animals include jellyfish, sea gooseberries, mollusks, and insects. Some animals glow all over, but most have light-producing organs that they can flash. The light is usually produced by a protein called luciferin, which glows when broken down by oxygen. The flashlight fish from the Indian Ocean uses bacteria to make light. The bacteria are kept in a pouch with a shutter that can cover the pouch to hide the light.

Flashlight fish (Photoblepharon palpebratus)

ABOVE *The viperfish is covered with a layer of slimy jelly, which is thought to make it harder for other fish to catch.*

VIPERFISH

The viperfish got its name from the long fangs that stick out from its jaws, even when its mouth is closed. It has a slender, jet-black body, and one of its fins has a long spine with a luminous tip. The fish probably uses this to lure other animals toward its mouth. Its stomach has an extra-dark lining that works like a curtain, preventing light from its swallowed prey being spotted by other hunters.

SCIENTIFIC NAME	*Chauliodus sloani*
DISTRIBUTION	Worldwide
SIZE	Up to 12 in. (30cm) long

Overlapping teeth

DEEP-SEA HATCHETFISH

About 50 years ago, when sound waves were first used to survey the seabed, scientists were puzzled by echoes that seemed to move up during the night and sink down during the day. These "deep scattering layers" turned out to be schools of deep-sea hatchetfish feeding by night on planktonic animals. Hatchetfish have very narrow, silvery bodies, and their undersides have a sharp edge, like the blade of an ax. The fish communicate with one another using rows of lights, which give off a yellowish glow when seen from below. In turn, hatchetfish have tubular eyes that point up so they can see others swimming above them.

SCIENTIFIC NAME	*Argyropelecus aculeatus*
DISTRIBUTION	Warm seas worldwide
SIZE	Up to 3 in. (8cm) long

DEEP-SEA BRISTLEMOUTH

Although little is known about them, deep-sea bristlemouths are thought to be the most abundant saltwater fish on earth. They feed on small planktonic animals and have bristle-lined jaws to help them scoop up their prey. They have light-producing organs on their undersides that are visible from below.

SCIENTIFIC NAME	*Cyclothone* species
DISTRIBUTION	Worldwide
SIZE	About 2 in. (5cm) long

EELS

With their long, snakelike bodies, eels look very different from most other fish. Most eels do not have scales, but many do have a ribbon-shaped fin that runs along their backs, around their tails, and underneath their bodies. True eels live in fresh and salt water, but they all start life as transparent, leaf-shaped larvae that drift in the surface waters of the oceans. Some species migrate back to rivers to breed, an epic journey that can take several years. There are 700 species of eels found all over the world.

ABOVE *The gulper eel has an enormous mouth. Scientists do not know if the eel actively hunts or lies in wait for fish.*

EUROPEAN EEL

These eels spend most of their adult lives in fresh water, where they feed on small animals. For many years, their life cycle was a mystery, but in 1920, a research expedition showed that the adults travel across the Atlantic Ocean to breed in the Sargasso Sea. The adults then die, leaving the tiny larvae to make their way back to Europe—a journey that takes three years. A similar eel lives in North America. Its journey from the Sargasso Sea takes only one year.

RIGHT *During its lifetime, the European eel travels nearly 6,000 miles.*

BELOW *The conger's snakelike shape allows it to slide through rocky crevices in search of its prey.*

SCIENTIFIC NAME
Anguilla anguilla

DISTRIBUTION Europe, northern Atlantic Ocean

SIZE Up to 3 ft. (1m) long

CONGER EEL

This eel's gray body is thicker than a man's arm. It lives in shallow water close to the shore, but during the day it hides in rocky crevices and old wrecked ships, with only its head exposed. At night, it swims out of its lair to feed on fish, crabs, octopuses, and sometimes lobsters caught in fishermen's lobster traps. In summer, fully mature congers migrate to the open sea to breed.

SCIENTIFIC NAME *Conger conger*

DISTRIBUTION Northern Atlantic Ocean

SIZE Up to 9 ft. (2.7m) long

MORAY EEL

Brightly colored and highly aggressive, moray eels spend most of their adult lives half-hidden in rocky lairs. They feed by grabbing fish that come within reach, using a swift, snakelike action, and sometimes bite divers' hands and feet. Moray bites can be dangerous because they easily become infected. There are more than 200 species of these eels, and they are most common in the tropics, particularly on coral reefs.

SCIENTIFIC NAME *Muraena* and other genera

DISTRIBUTION Worldwide

SIZE Up to 10 ft. (3m) long

Lower jaw much shorter than the upper jaw

GULPER EEL

The gulper eel has a slender body and a huge mouth—fully open, it could swallow a football. Gulper eels live in the deep sea, and it is not known how they feed. They either trap fish by swimming with their mouths open or use light to lure them into their jaws.

SCIENTIFIC NAME *Eurypharynx pelecanoides*

DISTRIBUTION Warm seas worldwide

SIZE Up to 23.5 in. (60cm) long

SPINY EEL

Unlike true eels, spiny eels have scales and underslung mouths. They also have a row of spines along their backs, which is how they got their name. These fish live on seabed mud in deep water and feed on slow-moving animals.

SCIENTIFIC NAME *Macroganthus* and other genera

DISTRIBUTION Worldwide

SIZE Typical length 3 ft. (1m)

Small pectoral fin

ABOVE
Spiny eels are found in tropical and temperate waters. They live on soft seabed sediment, often at great depths.

CARP AND THEIR RELATIVES

Carp and their relatives are among the world's most numerous freshwater fish. They are found all over the world except in South America, Australia, and New Zealand, and range in size from two-inch (5-cm) minnows to fish more than 6 ft. (2m) long. Carp eat a wide variety of food, including other fish, water snails, and water plants. They do not have teeth in their jaws, but they do have them at the back of their mouths. These teeth push against a hard pad, grinding up any food that they swallow. There are about 2,000 species of these fish, all of which reproduce by laying eggs.

COMMON CARP

This deep-bodied fish lives in lakes and slow-flowing rivers, where it feeds by sucking up animals and small plants from the mud. It has four fleshy feelers, or barbels, at the corners of its mouth that help it find food in murky water. Carp have been bred by people for food since ancient times, and over the centuries, several different varieties have evolved. One type, the mirror carp, has lines of extra-large scales along its back and sides. Another, the golden carp, is bright orange. Carp can live for up to 40 years—a long time for a freshwater fish.

SCIENTIFIC NAME	*Cyprinus carpio*
DISTRIBUTION	Originally from central Asia; introduced into many parts of the world
SIZE	Up to 3 ft. (1m) long

Common goldfish

Comet

ABOVE *Goldfish have been specially bred in captivity longer than any other kind of fish.*

GRASS CARP

In the Far East, the slender, silvery grass carp is one of the most important "farmed" freshwater fish. It is easy to raise because it feeds on water plants and can survive in small ponds. Grass carp have large appetites, and in the wild, they help keep rivers and lakes from becoming clogged up with vegetation. They have been introduced into Europe and North America for this reason.

SCIENTIFIC NAME	*Ctenopharyngodon idella*
DISTRIBUTION	Originally from China; introduced into other parts of Asia, Europe, North America
SIZE	Up to 4 ft. (1.2m)

BELOW *The rudd usually feeds near the surface because its sloping mouth prevents it from picking up food from the bottom.*

RUDD

With its bright red fins and olive-yellow body, this common freshwater fish looks as though it should be easy to spot, but it is actually well camouflaged in murky water. Rudd live in lakes and slow-flowing rivers, eating plants and small animals, such as worms and insect larvae. In late spring, the females lay as many as 200,000 eggs. The eggs stick to underwater plants, and the young fish hatch about a week later.

SCIENTIFIC NAME	*Scardinius erythrophthalmus*
DISTRIBUTION	Originally from Europe, parts of Asia; introduced into North America
SIZE	Up to 12 in. (30cm) long

GOLDFISH

Goldfish are the world's most popular ornamental fish. Over the past thousand years, hundreds of varieties have been bred. Some have bright colors and patterns, while others have bulging eyes and misshapen bodies and fins. Wild goldfish live in pools and lakes. They are gray when young, but turn orange as they grow.

SCIENTIFIC NAME	*Carassius auratus*
DISTRIBUTION	Originally from Europe, Asia; now kept in ornamental ponds worldwide
SIZE	Up to 12 in. (30cm) long

FAR LEFT *Golden carp are often kept in lakes and ornamental ponds. They are descended from the common carp and are specially bred for their color.*
LEFT *The finger-sized European minnow is common in clean rivers and streams. It is caught by kingfishers, which dive into the water to catch fish near the surface.*

EUROPEAN MINNOW

This small, dark-colored fish lives in cool, fast-flowing streams, where it feeds on water plants, insect larvae, and shrimp. Because it lives in clear water, it relies on speed for protection, darting away at the first sign of danger. European minnows gather in schools to spawn, and they lay their eggs among gravel and stones.

SCIENTIFIC NAME *Phoxinus phoxinus*
DISTRIBUTION Europe, northern Asia
SIZE Up to 4 in. (10cm) long

BITTERLING

Bitterlings are small, silvery fish that have a remarkable way of reproducing. Instead of laying eggs in open water, the female uses a long egg tube, or ovipositor, to lay them inside the shell of a live freshwater mussel. The male then sheds his sperm into the mussel and guards the mussel while the eggs develop inside. When the eggs hatch, the young leave their nursery and swim away. Bitterlings lay far fewer eggs than other fish in the carp family, but their unusual behavior gives their eggs a much better chance of survival.

SCIENTIFIC NAME *Rhodeus sericeus*
DISTRIBUTION Europe, northeast Asia; introduced into North America
SIZE Up to 3.5 in. (9cm) long

COMMON SHINER

This is a widespread river fish of eastern North America. It is covered with silvery scales and has an olive-colored back, although the male turns pink just before the breeding season begins. There are more than 100 species of shiners in North America, and it can be difficult to tell them apart. To make matters more complicated, several species, including the common shiner, interbreed with other species.

SCIENTIFIC NAME *Luxilus cornutus*
DISTRIBUTION North America
SIZE Up to 7 in. (18cm) long

TOP *A female bitterling lays her eggs inside a freshwater mussel while a male waits nearby.*
ABOVE *The common shiner lives in rocky pools in rivers, and sometimes in lakes.*

ZEBRA DANIO

Danios are tiny, highly active freshwater fish found in streams and lakes in India and other warm parts of Asia. They have slender bodies, often with a silvery sheen. This particular species got its name from the horizontal stripes that run from its head to the tip of its tail and across its fins. It is a popular aquarium fish, and several ornamental varieties have been bred.

SCIENTIFIC NAME	*Brachydanio rerio*
DISTRIBUTION	India
SIZE	Up to 2 in. (5cm) long

TENCH

This green-brown, heavy-bodied fish feeds on the bottom of slow-moving lakes or rivers, where it finds its prey by touch and smell. The tench has leathery skin covered with a layer of slippery mucus. Female tench can lay nearly a million eggs a year, but many are eaten, and only a tiny fraction survive to become adult fish.

SCIENTIFIC NAME	*Tinca tinca*
DISTRIBUTION	Originally from Europe, parts of northern Asia; widely introduced elsewhere
SIZE	Up to 2.25 ft. (70cm) long

COLORADO SQUAWFISH

Squawfish are the largest North American carp. They have streamlined bodies, long heads, and large mouths, and they feed mainly on other fish. The Colorado squawfish is the largest of all, weighing more than 75 lb. (35kg). The building of dams has caused the population to dwindle, and it is now an endangered species.

SCIENTIFIC NAME	*Ptychocheilus lucius*
DISTRIBUTION	Southwestern United States
SIZE	Up to 6 ft. (2m) long

BARBEL

This slender freshwater fish has a round body with a flat underside to suit its bottom-dwelling lifestyle. It is named after the four fleshy feelers, or barbels, that hang from its jaws. The feelers have taste-sensitive tips, and are used to probe riverbeds for insect larvae and other small animals. Barbels lay their eggs in gravel or on stones.

SCIENTIFIC NAME	
Barbus barbus	
DISTRIBUTION	Europe
SIZE	Up to 3 ft. (1m) long

ABOVE *The barbel is a typical bottom-feeder, with a downward-facing mouth.* **BELOW** *The red-tailed black shark will often fight if it is kept with others in an aquarium.*

RED-TAILED BLACK SHARK

Despite its name, this small freshwater fish is not a shark, but it does have an aggressive streak. It lives in streams and feeds on algae, which it rasps off plants and stones. The most striking thing about this fish is its color. Its body is jet-black, its tail is bright red, and its fins are sometimes orange. The red-tailed black shark has many close relatives living in rivers in Africa and Asia.

SCIENTIFIC NAME	*Labeo bicolor*
DISTRIBUTION	Southeast Asia
SIZE	Up to 6 in. (15cm) long

LONGNOSE SUCKER

Suckers are freshwater fish with a downward-pointing mouth and large, suckerlike lips. They live on the bottoms of rivers and lakes, sucking up their prey like vacuum cleaners. There are about 100 species of suckers, almost all of them in North America. The longnose sucker is one of the few that is also found in Asia. It lives in rivers in the far north and survives in waters right up to the edge of the Arctic Ocean.

SCIENTIFIC NAME *Catastomus catastomus*

DISTRIBUTION North America, northern Asia

SIZE Up to 23.5 in. (60cm) long

JAPANESE WEATHERFISH

Although they live in water, fish are sometimes affected by conditions outside. The Japanese weatherfish is one of these species. It is most active when the atmospheric pressure is low and when the weather is changing. In the past, it was sometimes kept as a living weather forecaster because it warned of approaching rain—the atmospheric pressure often drops before it begins to rain, and the weatherfish signals the change ahead. Weatherfish live in mud on the bottoms of lakes and streams, where they sometimes burrow beneath the surface.

SCIENTIFIC NAME *Misgurnus anguillicaudatus*

DISTRIBUTION Originally from Far East; introduced into North America

SIZE Up to 4 in. (10cm) long

CLOWN LOACH

Loaches are bottom-dwelling fish that live in streams. Some have a snakelike shape, but the clown loach is thickset with clear orange and black markings. There are about 200 species of loaches worldwide, and some of them, including the clown loach, are popular aquarium fish. Because loaches feed on the bottom, they stay out of the way of other fish and help keep the aquarium gravel clean.

SCIENTIFIC NAME *Botia macracantha*

DISTRIBUTION Indonesia, Papua New Guinea

SIZE Up to 12 in. (30cm) long

BELOW *Clown loaches normally feed at night. Like many other loaches, they defend themselves with two spines, one underneath each eye.*

Dark, vertical bands of color

Small scales give the skin a smooth texture

Defensive spine is usually folded flat, but flips up if the fish is threatened

Downward-facing mouth

CHARACINS AND THEIR RELATIVES

Characins are freshwater fish that live in warm parts of the Americas and in tropical Africa. Some are small and highly active with jewellike colors, but this group also includes fish that are large, slow-moving, and well camouflaged. Characins often have sharp teeth, and they eat a wide range of different foods. Many are vegetarians, but predatory characins include highly aggressive piranhas, which hunt in packs and can strip large fish and other animals down to their bones. Characins usually scatter their eggs among water plants, and they leave their young to develop on their own. There are about 1,400 species of characins, mostly in South America.

RED PIRANHA

There are more than 50 species of piranhas, all of them living in the rivers of South America. Many eat fruit, but the red piranha is a highly efficient predator. It has a blunt face with an underslung lower jaw—an ideal shape for biting pieces of flesh out of animals much larger than itself. Red piranhas hunt in large schools, normally feeding on fish. However, if a large land animal becomes stranded in the water, a piranha school will attack in a deadly feeding frenzy. Although piranhas usually ignore humans, their unpredictable nature makes them dangerous. In the early 1980s, more than 300 people died in a piranha attack after a boat overturned in a Brazilian river.

SCIENTIFIC NAME	*Serrasalmus nattereri*
DISTRIBUTION	South America
SIZE	Up to 12 in. (30cm) long

RIGHT *A red piranha peers out from some waterside vegetation. Its upper and lower teeth fit together exactly when it closes its jaws, so it can chop out pieces of flesh.*

STRIPED HEADSTANDER

Headstanders are small, South American fish that spend most of their lives head-down on riverbeds. This position is convenient for getting to the riverbed plants they eat, but headstanders often stay like this even when they are resting. The striped headstander has dark bands running the length of its body and a narrow mouth for probing into riverbed mud for food.

SCIENTIFIC NAME *Anostomus anostomus*
DISTRIBUTION South America
SIZE Up to 7 in. (18cm) long

GIANT TIGERFISH

This African fish is one of the largest characins, often weighing more than 65 lb. (30kg). It is built for speed, with a streamlined body and a deeply forked tail. The giant tigerfish lives in slow-flowing rivers and lakes, where it feeds on other fish. Tigerfish are naturally aggressive and put up a furious fight if they are hooked by an angler.

SCIENTIFIC NAME *Hydrocynus goliath*
DISTRIBUTION Central Africa
SIZE Up to 6 ft. (2m) long

MARBLED HATCHETFISH

Not to be confused with the deep-sea hatchetfish (page 108), this small, deep-bodied characin is one of the few fish in the world that is capable of powered flight. If it is chased by a predator, it leaps clear of the water and beats its pectoral fins to skim just above the surface. Marbled hatchetfish cannot fly far, but their brief airborne journey is often enough to help them escape being eaten by a larger fish.

SCIENTIFIC NAME *Carnegiella strigata*
DISTRIBUTION Tropical South America
SIZE Up to 2 in. (5cm) long

NEON TETRA

With its electric-blue sides and bright red tail, the tiny neon tetra is easily recognized. In the wild, neon tetras live in the upper reaches of the Amazon River in Brazil. They feed in schools, and like other characins, they scatter their eggs among plants. Their placid nature means that they are easy to keep in aquariums.

SCIENTIFIC NAME *Pracheirodon innesi*
DISTRIBUTION Tropical South America
SIZE Up to 1.5 in. (4cm) long

X-RAY FISH

Instead of being brightly colored, the x-ray fish is almost transparent. It has see-through muscles and skin, and its backbone is clearly visible, as in an x-ray picture. Its other organs are surrounded by a silvery covering that glints as it catches the light. X-ray fish live in rivers and feed on plants and water animals.

SCIENTIFIC NAME *Pristella maxillaris*
DISTRIBUTION South America
SIZE Up to 1 in. (2.5cm) long

BLIND CAVE CHARACIN

The blind cave characin lives in water under ground. It has a pale pink body with colorless fins, but its most remarkable feature is that it has no eyes. It finds its food by smell and navigates using its lateral line, a row of sensors down each side of its body that warn it of anything nearby. Most fish have a lateral line, but in the cave characin, it is highly developed.

SCIENTIFIC NAME *Astyanax fasciatus*
DISTRIBUTION Mexico
SIZE Up to 3.5 in. (9cm) long

TOP *The neon tetra is a popular aquarium fish.*
ABOVE *The x-ray fish was named for its see-through body.*

ABOVE *As blind cave characins swim, they sense faint waves of pressure that bounce back from nearby objects.*

Deeply forked tail

Deep body stabilizes fish during takeoff

Metallic scales

LEFT
The marbled hatchetfish has a low-slung body and two pectoral fins high up near its back. It uses these fins as wings to flutter over the surface of the water.

CATFISH AND ELECTRIC EELS

Catfish spend their lives on the bottoms of rivers and lakes. Most are nocturnal. They probe for food with the threadlike barbels that hang from their lips and jaws like whiskers. Catfish do not have scales, but their pectoral fins are armed with sharp spines that make it uncomfortable for other animals to swallow them. In some species, these spines are poisonous, giving the catfish extra protection. There are at least 2,500 species of catfish, and they are found in most parts of the world, except where it is extremely cold. Although they look very different, electric eels are related to catfish, not to other eels.

RIGHT *The glass catfish is active during the day. Being transparent helps it avoid being seen by predators, such as herons and other fishing birds.*

BELOW *The upside-down catfish, seen here the right way up, has three pairs of long barbels that it uses to find its food.*

GLASS CATFISH

Many fish have see-through bodies, but the glass catfish is remarkable for being almost transparent. Its muscles contain oil that makes them nearly as clear as glass, so it is easy to see its bones, intestines, reproductive organs, and eyes. The glass catfish lives in streams and rivers, where it feeds on plants and small animals such as water fleas. It usually lives in schools.

SCIENTIFIC NAME	*Kryptopterus bicirrhis*
DISTRIBUTION	Southeast Asia
SIZE	Up to 4 in. (10cm) long

UPSIDE-DOWN CATFISH

Instead of finding its food in riverbed mud, as most catfish do, this African species often feeds at the surface of the water. It swims upside down, which makes it easier for it to eat flies and other insects that have landed on the water. It even rests this way under water plants and overhanging branches. This catfish has a mottled pattern that helps camouflage it from predators as it feeds.

SCIENTIFIC NAME	*Synodontis multipunctatus*
DISTRIBUTION	Lake Tanganyika in tropical Africa
SIZE	Up to 4 in. (10 cm) long

Long barbels attached to upper lip

Short central barbels attached to lower lip

RIGHT *The electric eel's "batteries" extend all the way down its body. Unlike a true eel (page 109), it has a long fin on its underside only.*
BELOW *The wels has a slimy body without scales and two long barbels under its chin. This giant freshwater fish feeds mainly at night.*

TOADFISH AND ANGLERFISH

These two groups of fish contain some of the strangest-looking animals in the oceans. Most of them hunt on the seabed or in open water, using a combination of stealth and camouflage to catch unwary prey. Some look like pieces of living seaweed, while others resemble stones or sediment, but all of them have large mouths that can open in a split-second to suck in their victims. There are about 70 species of toadfish, mostly living in shallow water near the coast. Anglerfish are more varied, with at least 300 species. They live in a range of habitats from shallow water to the deep ocean floor.

WELS

The wels is one of the largest freshwater fish in the world. The heaviest one ever caught, in Russia in the 1800s, weighed over 725 lb. (330kg), although it is unlikely that such examples still exist today. Wels live in large, slow-flowing rivers and feed entirely on animals. Fish are the most important items on their menu, but they also eat crayfish and ducks, and have been reputed to tackle dogs. They breed in mid-summer, when the male excavates a "nest" in the mud. The female can lay more than 100,000 eggs, and the male guards them until they hatch.

SCIENTIFIC NAME	*Silurus glanis*
DISTRIBUTION	Europe, parts of central Asia
SIZE	Up to 15 ft. (4.6m) long

ELECTRIC EEL

This South American river fish can produce strong electric currents. When it is hunting, it can stun other fish with a shock of up to 550 volts. Once the fish has been stunned, the eel turns off the current and swallows its prey. Like the elephant-trunk fish (pages 102–103), the electric eel uses special muscles as batteries. Large eels have the largest batteries—a shock from one can knock a person off their feet.

SCIENTIFIC NAME	*Electrophorus electricus*
DISTRIBUTION	South America
SIZE	Up to 8 ft. (2.4m) long

Long barbels have sensitive tips for finding food

ATLANTIC MIDSHIPMAN

A member of the toadfish family, the Atlantic midshipman lurks on the bottom in shallow water, feeding on crustaceans and other fish. Unusually for an inshore fish, it produces light to lure its victims. Like many toadfish, it can make grunting and squeaking sounds with its swim bladder, and it is particularly noisy when it breeds. The females fasten their eggs to rocks, and the males guard them until they hatch.

SCIENTIFIC NAME	*Porichthys porosissimus*
DISTRIBUTION	Western Atlantic Ocean
SIZE	Up to 9 in. (23cm) long

EUROPEAN ANGLERFISH

With its huge, flat head and stumpy tail, this grotesque fish looks as if it has been squashed flat. Its body is superbly camouflaged, and it has a row of leafy flaps around the edge, helping it blend in with the seabed. When the anglerfish hunts, the only part of its body that moves is a special spine on its head. The fleshy tip of the spine jiggles and entices fish. The anglerfish's mouth opens and shuts so quickly that its victims appear to vanish into thin air.

SCIENTIFIC NAME	*Lophius piscatorius*
DISTRIBUTION	Northeastern Atlantic Ocean
SIZE	Up to 6 ft. (2m) long

SARGASSUMFISH

The Sargassumfish is an anglerfish that lives close to the surface of the sea. It hides among rafts of floating weeds and is camouflaged so well that it is seldom spotted. Its body is the same color and pattern as seaweed, and for extra effect, it is covered with leafy flaps. Like other anglerfish, the Sargassumfish catches its prey with the help of a lure on its head.

SCIENTIFIC NAME	*Histrio histrio*
DISTRIBUTION	Warm seas worldwide
SIZE	Up to 8 in. (20cm) long

ABOVE *The European anglerfish lurks on the seabed, often in shallow water. Many smaller anglerfish hunt in the dark depths of the open sea, attracting prey with luminous lures.*

CODFISH AND THEIR RELATIVES

There are about 500 species of codfish. They are found mainly in the cool seas of the Northern Hemisphere, mostly near the seabed or in open water, although a few live in lakes and rivers inland. These fish are all carnivorous, and they eat a wide range of water animals. Codfish have small scales, but their eyes are often large—an essential feature for animals that hunt partly by sight. Compared to other fish, codfish lay vast numbers of eggs, but they abandon them once they have been laid. The young fish usually drift in the plankton, and only a tiny fraction survive. As adults, they face another threat—many of them are caught to feed people.

ATLANTIC COD

This thick-bodied creature is one of the world's most important commercial fish, and nearly two million tons are caught each year. In some places, so many fish have been caught that stocks have been badly damaged and may take many years to recover. The cod often feeds near the seabed, in water up to 2,000 ft. (600m) deep. During the breeding season, large schools gather in shallow waters, where the females lay as many as nine million eggs each. The eggs float up and the young start life feeding close to the surface. The largest cod on record weighed more than 200 lb. (90kg), but today's fish are much smaller.

SCIENTIFIC NAME *Gadus morhua*

DISTRIBUTION North Atlantic Ocean

SIZE Up to 4 ft. (1.2m) long

WHITING

Unlike many of its relatives, the whiting usually stays close to the shore. This sleek, silvery-sided fish eats other fish and shrimp, catching its food both in open water and on the seabed. It is often caught by anglers and by fishing-boats out at sea. Newly hatched whiting feed on plankton. When they are big and strong enough to swim against the current, they often live among the tentacles of jellyfish. As they are immune to jellyfish stings, this protects them from predators.

SCIENTIFIC NAME *Merlangius merlangus*

DISTRIBUTION European coasts

SIZE Up to 2 ft. (60cm) long

HADDOCK

Haddock live near the seabed in water up to 11,000 ft. (300m) deep. They feed on worms, mollusks, and other small animals. They have a dark patch on each side of their bodies and pointed dorsal fins. Haddock eggs float on the water for about two weeks until they hatch.

SCIENTIFIC NAME *Melanogrammus aeglefinus*

DISTRIBUTION North Atlantic Ocean

SIZE Up to 29.5 in. (75cm) long

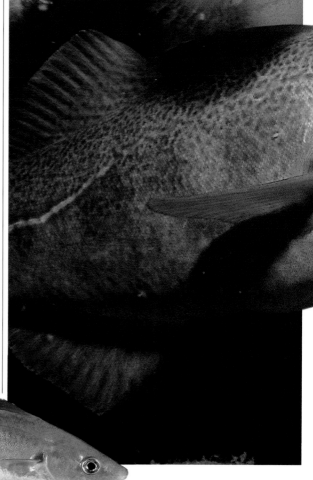

RIGHT
*The whiting
is one of the most
common sea fish in the
northeastern Atlantic Ocean.*

HAKE
Unlike some of their relatives, which have three fins on their backs, hake have only two, but their rear fins reach as far as their tails. They have sharp teeth and a black lining on the inside of their mouths. Hake are fierce predators, preying on smaller fish, including their own young. They usually live in deep water, but they come close to the shore to spawn.

SCIENTIFIC NAME
Merluccius merluccius

DISTRIBUTION European coasts

SIZE Up to 29.5 in. (75cm) long

COMMON LING
The ling has a completely different shape from its relative the cod. It is slender and eellike, with two extra-long fins along the top and underside of its body. Adult ling live in water up to 1,300 ft. (400m) deep. They hide among rocks and sunken ships, where they attack fish and other animals. They spawn in deep water, but their eggs drift to the surface.

Single barbel under the chin

SCIENTIFIC NAME *Molva molva*

DISTRIBUTION North Atlantic Ocean

SIZE Up to 6 ft. (2m) long

Large gill covers

Burbot showing its long dorsal fin

BURBOT
This long-bodied fish is one of the few codfish relatives that live in fresh water. A bottom-dweller, it is found in rivers and lakes, as well as in salty water near the ocean. Burbots feed on other fish, attacking after dark. They do most of their feeding in winter months and spend the summer resting in deep pools. Female burbots can lay as many as five million eggs. Their eggs would float if they were laid in the ocean, but in fresh water they sink to the bottom.

ABOVE
The Atlantic cod eats worms, crustaceans, and also other fish.

SCIENTIFIC NAME *Lota lota*

DISTRIBUTION North America, Europe, northern Asia

SIZE Up to 3 ft. (1m) long

ROUGH-HEADED GRENADIER
The grenadier belongs to a group of fish called rattails, which live in water up to 20,000 ft. (6,000m) deep. They all have large heads with large eyes and downward-pointing mouths. They got their name because their bodies quickly taper away to thin and spindly tails. Rattails are just as common as many of their edible relatives, but because they are harder to catch, less is known about how they live. The rough-headed grenadier feeds on the seabed. It has powerful jaws, which it uses to crush mollusks and deep-water starfish. Like other species of rattails, it can use its swim bladder to make noises.

SCIENTIFIC NAME *Macrourus berglax*

DISTRIBUTION Northern Atlantic Ocean

SIZE Up to 3 ft. (1m) long

LIONFISH, DORIES, AND OARFISH

These three groups of fish are only distantly related and very different in size. There are more than 1,200 species of lionfish and their relatives, about 40 kinds of dories, and only about 20 species of oarfish. Lionfish and their relatives live in both fresh and salt water and are particularly common in coral reefs. Some of these reef species are brilliantly colored, and many have highly poisonous spines. Dories live in shallow water close to coasts, while oarfish and their relatives usually live out in the open ocean. As well as having a very narrow body, oarfish are immensely long and brightly colored, making them some of the world's most spectacular fish.

LIONFISH

Lionfish have fan-shaped fins and eye-catching brown, red, and white vertical stripes. They live on coral reefs, eating small fish and shrimp. Their fins are tipped with sharp spines that can inject poison into an attacker's skin. If they are threatened, lionfish stay in the open with their fins spread out wide. By facing up to an enemy, they show that they will fight back if attacked.

SCIENTIFIC NAME	*Pterois* species
DISTRIBUTION	Indian Ocean, Pacific Ocean
SIZE	Typical length 12 in. (30cm)

STONEFISH

This is one of the deadliest animals in the sea. Unlike its relative the lionfish, it is well camouflaged among coral and rocks. The fins on its back have sharp spines, and if the stonefish is accidentally stepped on, the spines can inject a poison strong enough to kill a person. The stonefish feeds on fish that come within reach of its large, upturned mouth.

Stonefish hidden on a coral reef

SCIENTIFIC NAME	*Synanceia verrucosa*
DISTRIBUTION	Indian Ocean, Pacific Ocean
SIZE	Up to 12 in. (30cm) long

RED GURNARD

Gurnards are bottom-dwelling members of the lionfish group. They are usually red or gray, and have a large, bony head, a slender body, and spiky fins. They have three rays on their pectoral fins that can move like fingers, which they use to "walk" on the seabed, feeling for food. Red gurnards make a grunting noise, which probably helps them communicate with each other.

SCIENTIFIC NAME	*Trigla lucerna*
DISTRIBUTION	European coasts
SIZE	Up to 29.5 in. (75cm) long

LUMPFISH

The lumpfish lives in shallow water close to the coast, where it feeds on worms and other small animals. It has a plump body and a small mouth and is covered with knobbly lumps. Its most interesting feature is its pelvic fins. Located underneath the deepest part of its body, they form a powerful sucker used to fasten the fish to rocks. In spring, female lumpfish lay about 200,000 eggs among rocks near the shore. The male guards the eggs with great devotion and fans water over them until they hatch.

SCIENTIFIC NAME	*Cyclopterus lumpus*
DISTRIBUTION	Northern Atlantic Ocean
SIZE	Up to 23.5 in. (60cm) long

JOHN DORY

The John Dory is shaped like a plate standing on its edge. Its body is deep but extremely narrow, with a central black spot, and is edged at the top and bottom by large, spiny fins. Its face is flat and bony with a large, drooping mouth. John Dories eat other fish, but they are not built for speed. Instead, they hunt by stealth, shooting out their mouths and swallowing their food in a fraction of a second.

SCIENTIFIC NAME	*Zeus faber*
DISTRIBUTION	Eastern North Atlantic Ocean
SIZE	Up to 25.5 in. (65cm) long

ABOVE *The red gurnard is one of the few fish to use its fins to feel for food.*
LEFT *John Dories are solitary hunters, feeding at depths of up to 650 ft. When they are young, they often lurk in seaweed.*

ABOVE *These two species of lionfish, the common lionfish (Pterois volitans) on the left and the clearfin lionfish (Pterois radiata) on the right, are protected from most predators by their poisonous spines.*

OARFISH

The oarfish looks like a gigantic, silvery ribbon edged with a single, brilliant red fin. Despite its immense length, this fish is rarely seen as it normally keeps out of sight well beneath the surface. The oarfish swims by rippling its body. It is harmless to people; it has no teeth and feeds on small crustaceans and fish, which it catches in its funnellike mouth. This ocean-going fish grows to such an enormous size that it is easily mistaken for a sea monster.

SCIENTIFIC NAME	*Regalecus glesne*
DISTRIBUTION	Worldwide
SIZE	Up to 55 ft. (17m) long

OPAH

Like the oarfish, the opah spends most of its time in the middle depths of the ocean and is hardly ever seen near the surface. It has a bright blue body with bright red fins, lips, and eyes. Although it looks narrow when seen head-on, it is a heavy fish with a deep body. Large examples can weigh as much as 155 lb. (70kg). Opahs are fast-moving creatures that chase squid and other fish, catching them with their beaklike mouths.

SCIENTIFIC NAME	*Lampris guttatus*
DISTRIBUTION	Warm waters worldwide
SIZE	Up to 4 ft. (1.2m) long

FLYINGFISH, GRUNIONS, AND SEAHORSES

These three groups contain some freshwater fish, but most of the species live in the ocean. Flyingfish are famous for gliding over the water on outstretched fins, while grunions wriggle onto sandy beaches to lay their eggs. Seahorses never leave the water, but they are poor swimmers and live mainly among water weeds. Altogether, these fish total about 900 species, most commonly found in warm parts of the world.

ABOVE *An Atlantic flyingfish bursts into the air. This fish can "fly" at a height of more than 16 ft.— high enough to land accidentally on small boats.*

BELOW *The leafy seadragon lives in seaweed off the coast of Australia. It has tiny fins and is an extremely slow swimmer.*

ATLANTIC FLYINGFISH

Many fish jump out of the water to escape danger, but flyingfish go even farther—they soar through the air on their outstretched fins for up to 650 ft. (200m). After takeoff, flyingfish often trail the bottom lobe of their tails in the water. It works like a ship's propeller, pushing them along. Flyingfish all have large pectoral (or shoulder) fins, and many species fly using these alone. The Atlantic flyingfish also has large pelvic fins to give it extra lift as it skims along.

SCIENTIFIC NAME	*Cypselurus melanurus*
DISTRIBUTION	Warm seas worldwide
SIZE	Up to 16 in. (40cm) long

HOUNDFISH

The houndfish is a relative of flyingfish, but its shape could hardly be more different. It has a slender, spearlike body with small fins and a needle-sharp, tooth-filled "beak." Houndfish are predators, using their long jaws to grab other fish side-on. They have a habit of leaping at bright lights after dark and have been known to impale people aboard boats, occasionally even killing them.

SCIENTIFIC NAME	*Tylosurus crocodilus*
DISTRIBUTION	Warm seas worldwide
SIZE	Up to 5 ft. (1.5m) long

SEAHORSE

Seahorses are like no other fish. They are covered in bony armor and they swim upright, pushed along by tiny fins. They have angular, horselike heads at right angles to their bodies and grasping, or prehensile, tails that can wrap around rocks and weeds. Seahorses feed on minute animals that they suck up through their tiny mouths. When they breed, the males and females pair up during a long and complicated courtship dance. The female then passes her eggs to the male, who incubates them in a special pouch on his front. After hatching, the young swim out through a hole at the top of the pouch.

SCIENTIFIC NAME	*Hippocampus* and other genera
DISTRIBUTION	Worldwide, except in cold regions
SIZE	Typical length 6 in. (15cm)

LEAFY SEADRAGON

Seadragons are closely related to seahorses. They have the same overall shape as seahorses, but they are disguised by some of the most elaborate camouflage in the animal world. Their bodies have a collection of leafy flaps that make them almost impossible to see in the beds of underwater weeds where they live.

Camouflage pattern extends across the eyes

Tubular mouth sucks up microscopic animals

Leafy flaps mimic seaweed

Seadragons do not have prehensile tails. They are sometimes washed ashore in storms.

SCIENTIFIC NAME	*Phycodurus eques*
DISTRIBUTION	Australia
SIZE	Up to 12 in. (30cm) long

Tubular mouth

Slender, wormlike body

Eggs fastened to the underside of the body

RIGHT *A male worm pipefish* (Nerophis lumbriciformis) *with a batch of eggs. This pipefish lives in shallow water along northeastern Atlantic coasts. It can sometimes be found under stones at low tide.*

PIPEFISH

A pipefish is like a seahorse that has been stretched out until its body is perfectly straight. It has the same kind of bony armor, a tubular mouth, and tiny fins. Some pipefish swim vertically, but most swim horizontally, gliding slowly through eelgrass and other underwater plants. Pipefish share another feature with seahorses—when they breed, the male carries the eggs until they hatch. Pipefish live close to the shore, relying mainly on their camouflage to avoid being attacked.

SCIENTIFIC NAME *Nerophis and other genera*

DISTRIBUTION Worldwide

SIZE Typical length 10 in. (25cm)

THREESPINE STICKLEBACK

This freshwater fish got its name from the three spines on its back. During the breeding season, the green-brown males develop bright red undersides. Each male builds a nest from underwater plants. He lures females into the nest to lay their eggs and then guards the young fish. Despite their small size, male sticklebacks are pugnacious fish, and fights often break out between rivals.

SCIENTIFIC NAME *Gasterosteus aculeatus*

DISTRIBUTION Europe, North America

SIZE Up to 3 in. (8cm) long

CALIFORNIA GRUNION

This small, silvery fish lives in schools and is famous for the unusual way in which it breeds. On spring and summer nights, during extra-high tides, thousands of adult grunions wriggle ashore on sandy beaches. The females lay eggs in the wet sand. After 15 days, the next series of high tides wets the eggs and they hatch. The young grunions then make their way out to sea.

SCIENTIFIC NAME *Leuresthes tenuis*

DISTRIBUTION Pacific coast of southern California and Mexico

SIZE Up to 7.5 in. (19cm) long

ABOVE *Male threespine sticklebacks develop bright colors in the spring.*

PARENTAL CARE

Seahorses, pipefish, and sticklebacks take care of their eggs, and sometimes of their young when they hatch. Although they lay only a few eggs each time they breed, careful parenting gives each one a good chance of survival. The jewel cichlid (page 126) is also a good parent, but most other fish are not. Fish usually lay thousands, or even millions, of eggs, but because they leave them to develop on their own, only a small percentage of their young survive.

Parental care varies throughout the animal world. Most invertebrates have little to do with their eggs or young, but there are exceptions, such as scorpions, spiders, and some insects. Amphibians and reptiles often abandon their eggs once they have been laid, but some of these animals stand guard over them until they hatch, and a few even carry their young to the water. With birds and mammals, parental care is an important part of life. Compared to other animals, birds and mammals have small families, but they put much more effort into helping their young survive.

Male common seahorse "giving birth" to young

PERCH AND THEIR RELATIVES

There are about 9,500 species of these fish—more than a third of the world's total—making them the largest single group of fish. They live in a wide range of habitats, from mountain streams to the open ocean. The largest species can grow to more than 15 ft. (4.6m) long, while the smallest species, measuring just 0.4 in. (1cm) long, is the shortest vertebrate. Perch and their relatives have a bewildering variety of shapes, but they all have a spiny dorsal fin—the front, and sometimes only, fin on their backs. They reproduce by laying eggs. Some species scatter their eggs in the water, so most do not survive, but other species are much more careful parents, looking after their young both before and after they hatch.

NILE PERCH

The Nile perch is the largest freshwater fish in Africa, weighing as much as 285 lb. (130kg). It lives in rivers and lakes and is often caught for food. Nile perch have olive-gray bodies, large mouths, and spiny front dorsal fins. They feed mainly on other fish and have decimated species where they have been introduced.

ABOVE The European perch lives in lowland rivers, lakes, and ponds, usually in small schools close to tree roots or weed beds.

SCIENTIFIC NAME   *Lates niloticus*

DISTRIBUTION   Nile River; widely introduced into other parts of Africa

SIZE   Up to 6 ft. (2m) long

EUROPEAN PERCH

Compared to some of its exotic relatives, the European perch is an inconspicuous fish. It has a deep body, and its color camouflages it well among water plants. It has two fins on its back. The rear one is soft, but the front one has strong spines. Perch hunt other fish by lurking among underwater plants. Their usual technique is to rush out from cover to grab a passing fish by the tail. Once the fish has been disabled, the perch turns it around so that it can swallow it headfirst. Perch lay thousands of eggs in long strings, wrapping them around plants and stones.

SCIENTIFIC NAME   *Perca fluviatilis*

DISTRIBUTION   Europe, northern Asia; introduced into other parts of the world

SIZE   Up to 1.5 ft. (50cm) long

GIANT GROUPER

Groupers are warm-water fish that often live on coral reefs. Heavy and slow-moving, they have stocky bodies and wide, fleshy mouths with lots of teeth. Many of them are striped or spotted, and their markings often change as they grow. Of the more than 400 species of these impressive carnivorous fish, the giant grouper is the largest, weighing up to 650 lb. (300kg). It feeds on lobsters and fish, including small sharks. Groupers are reported to have

Large eyes for efficient hunting of other fish

Marbled coloration

RIGHT *The Nile perch has been introduced into many of Africa's lakes. In Lake Victoria, it had a disastrous effect on local fish, driving many species to the brink of extinction.*

attacked divers, but they are probably not as dangerous as they look. Because they move slowly, they are easy targets for spear-fishers, and many species are now endangered.

SCIENTIFIC NAME
Epinephalus lanceolatus

DISTRIBUTION Red Sea, Indian Ocean, Pacific Ocean

SIZE Up to 9 ft. (2.7m) long

Sucker seen from above

Spotted pattern

ABOVE *The giant grouper is the largest bony fish that lives in coral reefs. It often lurks in caves and shipwrecks.*

ABOVE
The remora's sucker has two rows of ridges. When the remora presses the sucker against another fish, the ridges flatten and the sucker sticks tightly.

Ridges are flattened because the sucker is fastened to a tank

PILOTFISH
Pilotfish spend their adult lives swimming close to large sea animals, such as sharks, rays, turtles, and whales. Their hosts seem to ignore them completely, although they are brightly striped and often swim right in front of their mouths. At one time, people thought that pilotfish acted as guides to lost animals. A more likely explanation is that pilotfish gain protection from the larger animals. They do not share their host's food, but they do dart after any small fish that swim away as a host animal approaches.

SCIENTIFIC NAME *Naucrates ductor*

DISTRIBUTION Warm seas worldwide

SIZE Up to 2.25 ft. (70cm) long

DOLPHIN-FISH
This relative of the remora has a confusing name. It is not a true dolphin, but probably got this name because it feeds on flyingfish, often bursting out of the water like a dolphin as it chases its prey. Dolphin-fish have very narrow bodies that are brilliant yellow-green, with a metallic sheen. They have large, pointed tails that give them an impressive swimming speed of up to 40 mph (65km/h).

SCIENTIFIC NAME *Coryphaena hippurus*

DISTRIBUTION Warm seas worldwide

SIZE Up to 6 ft. (2m) long

REMORA OR SHARKSUCKER
The remora gets a free ride through the seas by fastening itself with an oval sucker to animals such as sharks, whales, and porpoises. The sucker is a specially modified fin just behind the top of its head. It locks tightly when the remora presses against its host, but it loosens if the remora swims ahead to feed. The sucker is amazingly strong—if a remora is put in a bucket of water, the whole bucket can be lifted up by holding on to the remora's tail.

SCIENTIFIC NAME *Echeneis naucrates*

DISTRIBUTION Warm seas worldwide

SIZE Up to 3.5 ft. (1.1m) long

SPANGLED EMPEROR
Emperors are coastal fish with long, sloping foreheads and large, staring eyes. They feed mostly at night, catching other fish or crunching up crabs and mollusks with their powerful jaws. There are about 40 species of emperor fish, but they can be difficult to identify because they are able to change color extremely quickly. The spangled emperor is one of the largest species. It lives on coral reefs and among beds of seagrass, and often feeds in schools.

SCIENTIFIC NAME *Lethrinus nebulosus*

DISTRIBUTION Indian Ocean, Pacific Ocean

SIZE Up to 33.5 in. (85cm) long

Imperial angelfish
in adult colors

Red mullet, a
bottom-feeder
with a down-
turned mouth

Forceps fish
uses beak
to probe
into
crannies

Jewel cichlid showing
speckled coloration

RED MULLET
Mullet, also known as goatfish, are mainly
tropical fish that live on the seabed in shallow
water. They have two long feelers, or barbels,
which they use to stir up the sand in search
of food. They eat worms and other bottom-
dwelling creatures, and after they feed, they fold
away their barbels into grooves underneath their
jaws. The red mullet is one of the few species
found along the shores of Europe.

SCIENTIFIC NAME *Mullus surmuletus*

DISTRIBUTION Eastern North Atlantic Ocean,
Mediterranean Sea

SIZE Up to 16 in. (40cm) long

COMMON ARCHERFISH
The archerfish is an unusual hunter. It lives
along muddy coasts, estuaries, and in mangrove
swamps, feeding on insects and other small
animals. It sometimes jumps out of the water
to catch its prey, but it can also knock insects
off overhanging branches by spitting at them.
To do this the archerfish closes its gill covers
suddenly. This forces a mouthful of water past
its tongue and jaws, and out in a well-aimed
jet. The fish can hit animals 3 ft. (1m)
above the surface.

SCIENTIFIC NAME *Toxotes chatareus*

DISTRIBUTION Indian Ocean

SIZE Up to 16 in. (40cm) long

IMPERIAL ANGELFISH
Angelfish live in coral reefs and are famous
for their striking patterns and colors. Young
imperial angelfish are dark blue with white rings,
but the adults are yellow with pale blue stripes—
so different that they look like a separate species.
Like all angelfish, they feed on coral and
sponges. They have small, beaklike mouths
and narrow bodies, which helps them
squeeze between coral branches.

SCIENTIFIC NAME *Pomacanthus imperator*

DISTRIBUTION Indian Ocean, Pacific Ocean

SIZE Up to 12 in. (30cm) long

FORCEPS FISH
The forceps fish lives on the seaward edge of
coral reefs, where breakers roll in from the open
ocean. Its mouth looks like a pair of forceps or
tweezers. With this precision instrument, the
forceps fish can pick up small animals
from seemingly inaccessible places,
such as among sea urchin spines. This
fish has a dark spot near its tail. The
spot looks like an eye and probably helps
divert predators away from its head.

SCIENTIFIC NAME *Forcipiger longirostris*

DISTRIBUTION Indian Ocean, Pacific Ocean

SIZE Up to 7 in. (18cm) long

CLOWN ANEMONE FISH
A brilliant orange body marked with three
broad white bands makes this small fish one
of the brightest in the seas. It shelters and
feeds among the stinging tentacles of large
sea anemones. Here it is safe from most of its
enemies, and its skin produces chemicals that
keep the anemones from attacking it. While the
fish clearly benefits from the partnership, it is
not known if anemones get anything in return.

SCIENTIFIC NAME *Amphiprion percula*

DISTRIBUTION Great Barrier Reef, coasts
of New Guinea

SIZE Up to 4 in. (10cm) long

JEWEL CICHLID
Cichlids are freshwater fish of tropical Africa,
India, and Central and South America. The
jewel cichlid lives in streams and eats a variety
of food, including plants and small animals such
as water fleas. As with all cichlids, it is a careful
parent. Once the young have hatched, both
adults protect them by sheltering them in their
mouths. There may be more than 2,000 species
of cichlids, but counting them is difficult because
many are found in only one river or lake.

SCIENTIFIC NAME *Hemichromis bimaculatus*

DISTRIBUTION Western Africa

SIZE Up to 4 in. (10cm) long

Clown anemone fish
among the stinging
tentacles of an anemone

MUDSKIPPER

These small fish live in mangrove swamps and on muddy coasts. When the tide rises, they hide in burrows, but at low tide, they skip across the mud on their fins and even climb up tree roots. They survive out of water because they breathe partly through their gills and partly through their skin. Their eyes are on top of their heads, helping them spot food and watch for danger.

SCIENTIFIC NAME	*Periophthalmus* and other genera
DISTRIBUTION	Warm coasts worldwide
SIZE	Typical length 6 in. (15cm)

Protruding eyes give all-around vision, and the mudskipper keeps them moist by rolling them back into the sockets

BELOW *A mudskipper peers out of the water. This fish can stay out of the water for hours at a time, as long as it keeps its skin moist. Mudskippers carry water in their gill chambers, which enables them to live in air.*

Skin absorbs oxygen from the air

Pectoral fins act like legs

PARROTFISH

These beautifully colored fish got their name from their teeth, which are joined together to form a shape like a parrot's beak. They use their teeth to bite off plants and pieces of the coral reefs in which they live. They have a second set of teeth inside their throat for grinding up their food, and their loud crunching sounds can be heard several yards away. Parrotfish come out to feed during the day. At night, they wrap themselves in a "sleeping bag" of mucus, which helps keep their enemies at bay.

SCIENTIFIC NAME	*Scarus* and other genera
DISTRIBUTION	Tropical seas worldwide
SIZE	Typical length 12 in. (30cm)

ABOVE *Spectacled parrotfish (Scarus perspicillatus) live around the Hawaiian Islands.* **LEFT** *A juvenile twin-spot wrasse is brightly colored.*

TWIN-SPOT WRASSE

Wrasse are slender fish with several strange features. They often change color as they grow, and like parrotfish, they sometimes change sex as well. The twin-spot wrasse starts life with a pale yellow body with black and red spots on its back. Adult females are also yellow, although they do not have spots, but adult males are green-black. Twin-spot wrasse live in coral reefs and feed on mollusks, crabs, and sea urchins. At night, they hide away in sand.

SCIENTIFIC NAME	*Coris aygula*
DISTRIBUTION	Indian Ocean, Pacific Ocean
SIZE	Up to 4 ft. (1.2m) long

NORTHERN STARGAZER

The stargazer has an almost vertical mouth and eyes on the top of its head. It keeps its thick body partly buried in sand, lying in wait for animals to swim nearby. Stargazers can produce mild electric shocks using "batteries" behind their eyes. They probably use the electric shocks to help them catch their prey.

SCIENTIFIC NAME	*Astroscopus guttatus*
DISTRIBUTION	Atlantic Ocean
SIZE	Up to 22 in. (55cm) long

LEFT *The surgeonfish (Acanthurus leucosternon) has blades that can cut through skin.*

SURGEONFISH

The surgeonfish looks harmless as it feeds among coral reefs. But if threatened, it can fight back with hidden weapons—two foldaway blades at the base of its tail. The surgeonfish slashes its blades from side to side and can inflict a painful wound. Surgeonfish have deep, narrow bodies and are often beautifully colored. They eat plants, usually feeding in small schools. Like many coral reef fish, they scatter their eggs in the water, then leave their young to develop on their own.

SCIENTIFIC NAME	*Acanthurus* and other genera
DISTRIBUTION	Tropical seas worldwide
SIZE	Typical length 10 in. (25cm)

SIAMESE FIGHTING FISH

This small freshwater fish is famous for its territorial behavior. The placid females are inconspicuous, but the males are brightly colored with large fins. They are also much more aggressive than the females. If one male swims into another's territory, a fight almost always breaks out. The territory's resident holds out his fins like fans, and if the intruder does not give way, he launches an attack. Males on home ground usually win. Fighting fish are often kept in aquariums. Many breeds have been developed, and in some, the males' fins are much longer than their bodies.

SCIENTIFIC NAME	*Betta splendens*
DISTRIBUTION	Southeast Asia
SIZE	Up to 2 in. (5cm) long

ABOVE *Female Siamese fighting fish have small fins and are not aggressive. They lay their eggs in rafts of bubbles made by the males.*

Narrow snout

LEFT *With its fins spread out, this male Siamese fighting fish is ready to fend off any rivals. When two males fight, they lunge at each other, trying to bite off their opponent's scales or pieces of their fins.*

Trailing pectoral fins

SYMBIOSIS

In coral reefs, many fish improve their chances of survival by forming partnerships with other animals. For example, clown anemone fish (page 126) shelter in the tentacles of sea anemones, while small fish called cleaner wrasse remove parasites and damaged scales from larger fish. This kind of teaming-up is known as symbiosis. In some symbiotic partnerships, only one partner benefits, but in most partnerships, both of the partners gain. This is the situation with cleaner wrasse—the cleaner benefits by getting a meal, and in return, it helps its "clients" stay healthy. Symbiotic partnerships occur not just with fish, but throughout the living world. Many animals use symbiotic microbes to help them digest food, and many plants use animals to spread their pollen. In some partnerships, the partners can live without each other if they have to, but other partners depend on each other for survival.

Cleaner wrasse (*Labroides* species) with a "client"

CLIMBING PERCH

Climbing perch are close relatives of Siamese fighting fish, and like them, they live in slow-flowing rivers and coastal lagoons. The water in these habitats often contains little oxygen, and both types of fish survive by breathing air as well as using their gills. Climbing perch are particularly good at this and can survive out of the water for long periods, provided they stay wet. Like some catfish (page 116), climbing perch can crawl overland, using their front fins like legs. They tend to come out on land when it is raining, but they will crawl over land to a new home if their surroundings start to dry up.

SCIENTIFIC NAME *Anabas testudineus*

DISTRIBUTION Southeast Asia

SIZE Up to 10 in. (25cm) long

GREAT BARRACUDA

With its lean, torpedo-shaped body, jutting lower jaw, and sharp, daggerlike teeth, the great barracuda is a highly dangerous predator. Although stories about these fish are often exaggerated, they are known to attack divers and swimmers, particularly those carrying shiny objects that look like fish. Barracuda hunt in packs, and they live in a wide range of habitats, from inshore water to the open ocean. They are sometimes caught and eaten—a dangerous practice, because their flesh can be poisonous.

SCIENTIFIC NAME	*Sphyraena barracuda*
DISTRIBUTION	Warm seas worldwide
SIZE	Up to 6 ft. (2m) long

ATLANTIC MACKEREL

Mackerel look like small-scale versions of the barracuda, with the same sleek and slender shape. They are camouflaged by iridescent blue and green stripes. Their fins can be flattened against their body—an adaptation that helps them swim at speed. Atlantic mackerel live in large schools that migrate into shallow water to breed. They are well-known for snapping at almost anything that moves, from fish to pieces of brightly colored plastic.

SCIENTIFIC NAME	*Scomber scombrus*
DISTRIBUTION	Atlantic Ocean
SIZE	Up to 23.5 in. (60cm) long

ABOVE *The Atlantic mackerel begins life in open water, where it feeds on tiny animals in the plankton. Females lay up to half a million eggs each time they spawn.*

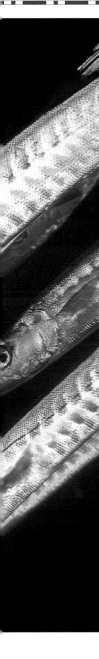

RIGHT AND BELOW *Three of the fastest fish in the world are the sailfish, the blue marlin, and the swordfish. All these fish have two different types of muscle. One type is used for steady cruising, the other for bursts of speed. Like tuna, these fish can keep their bodies warmer than the water around them.*

Swordfish

Blue marlin

Sailfish

SAILFISH

Over short distances, the metallic blue sailfish is probably the fastest fish in the sea. It can reach an amazing 68 mph (109km/h). A sailfish can manage these bursts of speed because its body is superbly streamlined and packed with muscle. Its stiff, crescent-shaped tail is ideal for hitting high speeds, and its high dorsal fin, or "sail," slices through the water like a knife. A sailfish's snout tapers to a sharp, spearlike point.

SCIENTIFIC NAME	*Istiophorus platypterus*
DISTRIBUTION	Warm seas worldwide
SIZE	Up to 12 ft. (3.6m) long

BLUE MARLIN

A close relative of the sailfish, the blue marlin is one of the largest predatory fish in the world. Using its sharply pointed snout, it slashes its way through schools of smaller fish, swallowing them once they are stunned. Blue marlins are not as fast as sailfish—the top speed on record is 50 mph (80km/h)—but they can beat most other fish for speed in open water.

SCIENTIFIC NAME	*Makaira nigricans*
DISTRIBUTION	Warm seas worldwide
SIZE	Up to 15 ft. (4.6m) long

SWORDFISH

From a distance, the swordfish looks like a blue marlin because of its purple-blue color and streamlined shape, but its snout is flattened like a sword and can be up to 4.5 ft. (1.4m) long. The swordfish probably uses its snout to kill or stun its prey. It has a reputation for being dangerous, which may come from accidental collisions with old sailing ships. In the early 1800s, one swordfish stabbed through a ship's hull, penetrating a layer of copper plating and a foot (30cm) of solid oak.

SCIENTIFIC NAME	*Xiphias gladius*
DISTRIBUTION	Warm seas worldwide
SIZE	Up to 16 ft. (4.9m) long

SKIPJACK TUNA

Tuna live in schools and are known for their speed and their long migrations. In the 1950s, a tagged tuna was caught after swimming from Mexico to Japan, a distance of at least 5,600 mi. (9,000km). Tuna can manage feats like this because they keep their bodies warmer than the water around them. The warmth makes their muscles work more effectively, but they have to keep moving to get the oxygen that their muscles need. There are more than six species of these fish. Some of them are becoming rare because they are heavily fished for food.

SCIENTIFIC NAME	*Euthynnus pelamis*
DISTRIBUTION	Warm seas worldwide
SIZE	Up to 3 ft. (1m) long

ANTARCTIC COD

This fish is one of only about 120 species that manage to survive in the icy waters close to Antarctica. It lives on the seabed, where it feeds on mollusks and crustaceans that thrive in a cold but clean environment. Around Antarctica, the temperature on the seabed is often slightly below freezing point, and the sea would freeze solid if it did not contain dissolved salt. To cope with these conditions, the Antarctic cod has a natural antifreeze in its blood.

SCIENTIFIC NAME	*Notothenia coriiceps*
DISTRIBUTION	Southern Ocean
SIZE	Up to 23.5 in. (60cm) long

ICE FISH

Antarctica's ice fish are the only vertebrates that do not have hemoglobin, the red pigment that normally carries oxygen in blood. Their blood is almost colorless, and it collects oxygen in the same way that water does—by simply dissolving it. Ice fish have to survive with about a tenth as much oxygen as normal fish, which they do by swimming slowly and by remaining motionless for long periods. They live on the seabed, feeding on small animals such as crustaceans.

SCIENTIFIC NAME	*Chaenocephalus aceratus*
DISTRIBUTION	Southern Ocean
SIZE	Up to 3.5 in. (60cm) long

Spines stand on end when the fish swells up

Tough jaws can crush shelled animals

ABOVE *This porcupine fish is relaxed, with its spines folded flat.*

TRIGGERFISH

Triggerfish and their relatives have a remarkable variety of shapes—some look like boxes, while others are more like balls or dinner plates. They share a number of features that are sometimes difficult to see, such as a small mouth, unusual teeth, and relatively few vertebrae in their backbone. There are about 350 species of these fish, and they are found around the world. Most of them live in shallow water near coasts, but the largest, the ocean sunfish, roams far out to sea.

PICASSO TRIGGERFISH

Triggerfish got their name from two spines on their back. One spine can hinge upright, and the other works like a trigger, locking the first spine in place. Many of these fish have extraordinary colors and markings, as if they had been painted by an artist. The Picasso triggerfish lives on coral reefs and sandy seabeds. It feeds on sea urchins, which it turns upside down by blowing water at them. It can then reach the spineless undersides.

TOP *The Picasso triggerfish has a large head with a tiny mouth.*
ABOVE *Like all its relatives, the blue boxfish (Ostracion lentiginosum) is a slow swimmer. It has few enemies because of its effective "armor."*

SCIENTIFIC NAME	Rhinecanthus aculeatus
DISTRIBUTION	Indian Ocean, Pacific Ocean
SIZE	Up to 12 in. (30cm) long

BOXFISH

Also known as trunkfish, these fish are covered with hard, bony plates that protect them from attack. This is not their only form of defense—a powerful poison oozes over the surface of their skin. There are many species of boxfish, almost all of them living on coral reefs.

SCIENTIFIC NAME	Ostracion and other genera
DISTRIBUTION	Warm seas worldwide
SIZE	Typical length 8 in. (20cm)

PORCUPINEFISH

Porcupinefish have blunt heads and large eyes, and a remarkable way of fending off their enemies. If one of these fish is threatened, it swallows a large amount of water, swelling up like a balloon. The fish's skin is covered with large spines that stand on end, making it almost impossible for predators to eat it. The only disadvantage of this survival technique is that the puffed-up fish is far too cumbersome to swim. Porcupinefish live among rocks and seaweed close to the shore.

SCIENTIFIC NAME	Diodon hystrix
DISTRIBUTION	Warm seas worldwide
SIZE	Up to 3 ft. (1m) long, often much smaller

OCEAN SUNFISH

The sunfish is one of the world's largest and most strangely shaped fish. Its body is round and flat, like an immense saucer. It has a long, pointed fin on top and underneath, but its tail is almost nonexistent, making the fish look as if it has been cut off at the back. The ocean sunfish feeds mainly on jellyfish, which it scoops up with its tiny mouth. It often basks on the surface of the water and, despite its clumsy shape, sometimes jumps right out of the water.

SCIENTIFIC NAME	Mola mola
DISTRIBUTION	Warm seas worldwide
SIZE	Up to 13 ft. (4m) long

FLATFISH

Flatfish begin life in the open sea, but most of them spend their adult lives on the seabed, lying on one side. As a flatfish grows, its body changes. It starts to lean over, and its downward-pointing eye moves around its head until it is next to the eye that points up. The side that will be on top develops camouflage colors, while the other side turns pale. There are about 500 species of flatfish. Most live in shallow sea water, from the tropics to much colder regions in the far north and south.

PLAICE

An adult plaice lies on its left-hand side, which means that both of its eyes are on its right. It has smooth scales and distinctive bright orange spots on its upper side. The plaice swims in characteristic flatfish fashion, by rippling along close to the seabed. It feeds on bottom-living invertebrates and finds food mainly by touch, using the sensitive skin on the left-hand side of its head.

SCIENTIFIC NAME	Pleuronectes platessa
DISTRIBUTION	Eastern Atlantic Ocean
SIZE	Up to 3 ft. (1m) long

DAB

Like the plaice, this small fish feeds in shallow water and ranges north beyond the Arctic Circle. Its breeding technique is typical of flatfish. It releases its eggs into the water, and they float up to the surface. The young fish drift among the plankton and are already lopsided by the time they are 0.8 in. (2cm) long. Once they have changed shape, they leave the surface and lie on the seabed.

SCIENTIFIC NAME	Limanda limanda
DISTRIBUTION	Eastern Atlantic Ocean
SIZE	Up to 16 in. (40cm) long

PEACOCK FLOUNDER

This colorful flatfish belongs to a family called the left-eye flounders, which have their eyes on their left-hand sides. This side of their bodies has a pattern of bright blue rings that stretch from the mouth to the tail. Peacock flounders live along shallow coasts and on coral reefs.

SCIENTIFIC NAME	Bothus lunatus
DISTRIBUTION	Western Atlantic Ocean, Caribbean Sea
SIZE	Up to 17.5 in. (45cm) long

Dab

Plaice

ATLANTIC HALIBUT

This is the world's largest flatfish, weighing up to 650 lb. (300kg). Unlike most other flatfish, it is an active predator that feeds in open water, instead of living on the seabed. It has a large mouth with sharp teeth, and its eyesight is unusually good. Atlantic halibut have been fished for centuries, partly because they grow so big. Today, specimens over 385 lb. (175kg) are rare, and the species is endangered because of overfishing.

SCIENTIFIC NAME	Hippoglossus hippoglossus
DISTRIBUTION	Northern Atlantic Ocean
SIZE	Up to 8 ft. (2.4m) long

Mouth twisted around to one side

Left eye moved around to the right side, now the upper side, of the fish

BELOW *The plaice lives on sand and gravel on the seabed, up to 650 ft. deep.*

ABOVE *The peacock flounder is difficult to see when it lies on the seabed.*

AMPHIBIANS

AMPHIBIANS INCLUDE FROGS, TOADS,
NEWTS, AND SALAMANDERS, AS WELL AS SOME
LESSER-KNOWN ANIMALS CALLED CAECILIANS.
MOST OF THEM START LIFE AS LEGLESS
TADPOLES THAT LIVE IN WATER AND
BREATHE THROUGH GILLS.

COMMON FROG

This green-brown frog spends almost all of its adult life on land, but in early spring, it returns to ponds and ditches to breed. Each female lays up to 4,000 jelly-coated eggs, which float in masses called frogspawn. When the tadpoles hatch, they fasten themselves to underwater plants. Like other amphibians, the common frog's development depends partly on the water temperature. If it is warm, the tadpoles can turn into froglets within six weeks, but in cold weather this process takes much longer.

SCIENTIFIC NAME *Rana temporaria*

DISTRIBUTION Europe, parts of Asia

SIZE Up to 4 in. (10cm) long, excluding legs

Large, circular eardrum just behind the eye

During their early lives, amphibians slowly change shape to prepare for life on land. Tadpoles often eat tiny water plants, but the adults gulp down small animals such as insects and slugs. Adult amphibians rarely stray from damp places because they have to keep their skin moist, and they usually return to water to breed. There are about 4,350 species of amphibians. They are most common in warm places. They are cold-blooded, which means that their bodies stay at the same temperature as their surroundings.

ABOVE
Like most amphibians, the common frog changes shape completely as it develops from tadpole to adult.
1 *The female lays eggs in early spring.* **2** *The eggs hatch into legless tadpoles with tails.* **3** *A few weeks later, the tadpoles develop hind legs.* **4** *The tadpoles develop front legs.* **5** *The tail and gills are absorbed, and the tadpoles become small adults with lungs, ready for life on land.*

FROGS AND TOADS

Frogs and toads make up about nine tenths of all the world's amphibians. They are easy to recognize by their short, tailless bodies and powerful back legs. Their back feet have webs between the toes, which they use for swimming as well as jumping. Frogs usually move by hopping and live either on the ground or in trees. Toads normally move by crawling and nearly always live on the ground. Many of these animals have loud calls, which they use during the breeding season to attract a mate.

Front feet have four toes

ABOVE *Like many amphibians, the common frog breathes partly through its lungs and partly through its skin. It cannot suck air into its lungs; instead, it takes it in by gulping with its mouth. Common frogs hunt mainly by sight, lunging at any small animals that move, including insects and spiders.*

RIGHT *The whistling frog is so small that it could fit inside a matchbox. The male has a whistlelike courtship call.*

BELOW *A horned frog lies in wait for its prey. This predator is large enough to swallow small mammals.*

Webbed back feet

on insects and other small animals. Leopard frogs have green skin, but they got their name from the black spots that are scattered over their legs and backs.

SCIENTIFIC NAME	*Rana pipiens*
DISTRIBUTION	North America
SIZE	Up to 3.5 in. (9cm) long, excluding legs

GOLIATH FROG

This is the world's largest frog, with a body almost the size of a dinner plate. The heaviest one ever found weighed more than 7.75 lb. (3.5kg) and had a legspan of 3 ft. (1m). Goliath frogs live in the rivers of tropical western Africa and were once quite common. Today, they are threatened with extinction, because man-made dams have reduced their habitat, and because they are hunted and sold as unusual pets.

SCIENTIFIC NAME	*Conraua goliath*
DISTRIBUTION	Cameroon and neighboring countries
SIZE	Up to 12 in. (30cm) long, excluding legs

WHISTLING FROG

This tiny frog is unusual because it lays its eggs on land and its young hatch out as miniature adults, but with tiny tails. The female lays about 25 eggs at a time, usually among damp, fallen leaves. This way of reproducing allows it to live in forests and other habitats where standing water is hard to find. The whistling frog has about 400 relatives that also breed on land. All these frogs come from Central or South America or from islands in the Caribbean.

SCIENTIFIC NAME	*Eleutherodactylus johnstonei*
DISTRIBUTION	Caribbean islands, northern South America
SIZE	Up to 1.5 in. (4cm) long, excluding legs

AMERICAN BULLFROG

Adult bullfrogs are the largest frogs in North America. They lurk in the weed-choked shallows of lakes and streams, where they eat anything they can swallow. Their diet includes fish, turtles, rats, and even bats and young waterbirds, which they hunt mainly by night. This is also when they call. The males have a pouch under their chin that blows up like a balloon to amplify the sound.

SCIENTIFIC NAME	*Rana catesbiana*
DISTRIBUTION	Eastern and central North America; introduced into parts of Europe
SIZE	Up to 8 in. (20cm) long, excluding legs

NORTHERN LEOPARD FROG

Unlike the bullfrog, this streamlined North American frog often wanders away from water, although it goes back to breed. It lives in a wide range of habitats, from mountain meadows to coastal swamps, and feeds

HORNED FROG

This large, fat-bodied frog has a huge mouth and two protruding eyes topped by stubby "horns." It has electric blue and brilliant green markings, though these are usually hidden because the frog buries itself in mud, with only its eyes visible. It stays completely still and lies in wait for an insect or other animal to wander within range. Then it bursts out of the mud and swallows its victim. Unlike most frogs, the tadpoles of the horned frog are also predatory.

SCIENTIFIC NAME	*Ceratophrys cornuta*
DISTRIBUTION	South America
SIZE	Up to 8 in. (20cm) long, excluding legs

ABOVE *A red-eyed treefrog clings to a twig high up in the canopy of a Central American rain forest.*

RED-EYED TREEFROG

Treefrogs spend most of their lives high above the ground in trees. They have long, spindly legs, and their fingers and toes end in flat pads that work like suction cups. A treefrog can stick to a vertical leaf and can even climb up a pane of glass. The red-eyed treefrog lives in rain forests, where the females lay their eggs on large leaves overhanging pools. The tadpoles drop into the water when they hatch and climb up into the trees as froglets.

SCIENTIFIC NAME	*Agalychnis callidryas*
DISTRIBUTION	Central America
SIZE	Up to 2.75 in. (7cm) long, excluding legs

EUROPEAN GREEN TREEFROG

Most treefrogs live in the tropics, where there are insects to eat all year round. This species lives as far north as Holland and Denmark and hibernates for several months each year. During the spring, the females lay eggs in ponds and water tanks. The males attract them to good laying sites at night by making a loud, ducklike quacking noise.

SCIENTIFIC NAME	*Hyla arborea*
DISTRIBUTION	Central and southern Europe
SIZE	Up to 2 in. (5cm) long, excluding legs

SPRING PEEPER

The high-pitched call of this North American treefrog signals that spring is on the way. Spring peepers live among plants close to the water, though unlike most treefrogs, they rarely climb far from the ground. They form a loud chorus when it rains, but because they are small and brown, they are very difficult to find. Female peepers lay their eggs one by one on water plants. After the tadpoles hatch, they take about three months to turn into froglets and move onto land.

SCIENTIFIC NAME	*Pseudacris crucifer*
DISTRIBUTION	Eastern North America
SIZE	Up to 1 in. (2.5cm) long, excluding legs

ABOVE *Using an inflatable sac under its throat, a gray treefrog (Hyla versicolor) calls to attract a mate.*
BELOW *The European green treefrog often climbs up rushes and reeds. This one is preparing to jump from its perch.*

Smooth skin

Slender toes with pads at tips

Treefrog's toe pads give it a firm grip on a slippery sheet of glass

Moist skin sticks to smooth surfaces

ROCKET FROG

This small, Australian frog belongs to the treefrog family, but it spends much of its life on the ground. It has a sharply pointed nose, well-developed back legs, and dark stripes running down its body. The rocket frog is exceptionally agile—it jumps for cover at the first sign of trouble, disappearing into the undergrowth or into water. Rocket frogs breed in streams or in grassland flooded by storms in the wet season.

SCIENTIFIC NAME	*Litoria nasuta*
DISTRIBUTION	Northern and eastern Australia
SIZE	Up to 2 in. (5cm) long, excluding legs

WHITE'S TREEFROG

Also known as the green treefrog, this amphibian is a relative of the rocket frog, but it is not so streamlined. It is one of Australia's most widespread frogs and is often seen in gardens. Compared to most other treefrogs, it survives well in dry conditions, thanks to its thick skin.

SCIENTIFIC NAME	*Litoria caerulea*
DISTRIBUTION	Australia
SIZE	Up to 4 in. (10cm) long

WATER-HOLDING FROG

The water-holding frog lives in deserts, a remarkable habitat for any amphibian. It spends most of its life under ground, coming to the surface only after heavy rain. Like many desert species, it breeds in temporary pools created after rare storms. Between the storms, the frog digs into the ground, burying itself up to 3 ft. (1m) deep. It has a water supply in its bladder and seals itself inside a watertight cocoon.

SCIENTIFIC NAME	*Cyclorana platycephalus*
DISTRIBUTION	Australia
SIZE	Up to 2.75 in. (7cm) long, excluding legs

MARSUPIAL FROG

This plump, South American treefrog raises its young in an unusual way. The male helps the female gather her eggs into a pouch on her back, which is covered by a flap of skin. The female frog carries the eggs for three or four months. When the tadpoles are ready to live on their own, the female reverses into a pool and uses her back feet to push them into the water.

SCIENTIFIC NAME	*Gastrotheca marsupiata*
DISTRIBUTION	South America
SIZE	Up to 1.5 in. (4cm) long, excluding legs

BELOW *The bright green color of White's treefrog camouflages it well among leaves. With its slender legs and toes, it moves agilely through trees.*

COMMUNICATION

Most animals have to communicate with their own kind. Often the message is a simple one—it may show that an animal is ready to breed or is about to launch an attack. But whatever the message, it is vital that it gets across.

Animals communicate in many different ways. Visual signals are very common, particularly with animals that have good eyesight. Many animals also signal by scent, which has the added advantage that it can work at close quarters or at a distance, and the message remains when the animal that left it has moved on. Sound is also a good way of sending signals, particularly in dense areas such as forests, where trees get in the way of other methods. Frogs and toads are experts at communicating by sound. They amplify their calls by inflating throat pouches or vocal sacs, which swell up like miniature balloons. Although their calls can sound alike to us, each species has its own "song," a set of signals understood only by others of the same species.

Male peacock *(Pavo cristatus)* displaying its tail feathers to attract females

Black ants *(Lasius niger)* communicating by touching antennae

Edible frog *(Rana esculenta)* calling with inflatable air sacs

FLYING FROG

Flying frogs cannot really fly, but they are experts at gliding from tree to tree in their rain forest home. They manage this remarkable trick by using their hands and feet as parachutes. For their size, flying frogs have huge fingers and toes, linked together by webs of skin. They also have flaps of skin that stick out from their legs. Together, these webs and flaps slow their fall, enabling them to glide through the air. Flying frogs lay their eggs high above the ground in nests of foam, which they whip up by mixing mucus with rainwater.

SCIENTIFIC NAME *Rhacophorus nigripalmatus*
DISTRIBUTION Southeast Asia
SIZE Up to 1.5 in. (4cm) long, excluding legs

GLASS FROG

There are about 60 species of glass frogs living along rain forest streams, often in cloud-draped mountains. Most of them have semitransparent skin, and as a result, some of their internal organs can be clearly seen. Like many rain forest frogs, they lay their eggs on leaves overhanging shallow pools, and their tadpoles drop into the water when they hatch. *Centrolenella fleischmanni* has bright red tadpoles that bury themselves in submerged mud and decaying leaves.

SCIENTIFIC NAME *Centrolenella* species
DISTRIBUTION Central and South America
SIZE Typical length 2 in. (5cm), excluding legs

ARROW POISON FROG

Arrow poison frogs live on the rain forest floor, where predators are all around. But these tiny frogs do not hide—instead, they feed in broad daylight, showing off their brilliant colors. They can be bold because their skin contains poisons so deadly that they are used by forest people to poison the tips of arrows for hunting. The bright colors warn predators to keep away. There are more than 100 species of these frogs. The most dangerous, *Phyllobates terribilis*, was discovered in Colombia in 1973. Arrow poison frogs have an unusual life cycle. The female lays her eggs on damp ground. When the tadpoles hatch, the male carries them on his back. Once they are large enough to fend for themselves, the male carefully releases them into water.

SCIENTIFIC NAME *Dendrobates* and other genera
DISTRIBUTION Central and South America
SIZE Up to 1.5 in. (4cm) long, excluding legs

ABOVE *With its feet spread out, a flying frog glides through the air far above the forest floor.*

RIGHT *These two Surinam toads are preparing to mate. Once the female has laid her eggs, the male will press them into the soft skin on her back.*

BELOW *Arrow poison frogs exhibit a variety of showy colors. Males use their colors to defend their territories, as well as to warn predators that they are poisonous.*

Mottled skin provides camouflage in muddy streams

ABOVE *A male mouth-brooding frog sits with a froglet that has just emerged from its vocal sac.*

MOUTH-BROODING FROG OR DARWIN'S FROG

For all amphibians, the early part of life is the most dangerous. The male mouth-brooding frog helps its tadpoles survive by swallowing them as they start to hatch. The tadpoles shelter in the frog's vocal sac, feeding on the yolk from their eggs. Three weeks later, when the tadpoles have become small adults, the male spits them out into water. This frog lives in streams in the forests of the southern Andes Mountains. It is small and well camouflaged, but its sharply pointed nose makes it easy to identify.

SCIENTIFIC NAME *Rhinoderma darwinii*
DISTRIBUTION Chile, Argentina
SIZE Up to 1 in. (2.5cm) long, excluding legs

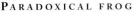

Star-shaped fingertips help the toad find food

RIGHT *A young Surinam toad emerges from a pouch on its mother's back. It is far smaller than its mother, but otherwise it looks like an adult.*

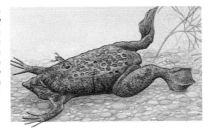

touch, using its slender fingers. This toad also has another remarkable feature—the female acts as a living nursery for her eggs. When the female lays her eggs, the male uses his body to press them into the spongy skin on her back. The skin then grows over the eggs, protecting them from predators. Three or four months later, the eggs hatch, producing up to 100 tiny but fully formed toads.

SCIENTIFIC NAME	*Pipa pipa*
DISTRIBUTION	Northern South America
SIZE	Up to 8 in. (20cm) long, excluding legs

AFRICAN CLAWED TOAD

This flat-bodied toad lives in ponds and lakes in southern Africa. Like its close relative the Surinam toad, it spends its entire life in water. Its eyes and nostrils face upward above the surface, allowing it to see and breathe. Females lay their eggs one by one on water plants or pieces of wood, and their tadpoles feed on microscopic plants, insect larvae, and other animals.

SCIENTIFIC NAME	*Xenopus laevis*
DISTRIBUTION	Southern Africa
SIZE	Up to 5 in. (12cm) long, excluding legs

PARADOXICAL FROG

A paradox is something that seems absurd but is true. With this frog, the paradox is that the tadpoles are three times as long as their parents. Adult paradoxical frogs are small enough to sit in a coffee cup, but the largest tadpole on record was 10 in. (25cm) long. Adult paradoxical frogs spend most of their lives in water. No one knows why they have such large young.

SCIENTIFIC NAME	*Pseudis paradoxus*
DISTRIBUTION	South America
SIZE	Adult up to 2 in. (5cm) long, excluding legs

SURINAM TOAD

With its flattened body, triangular head, and warty skin, the Surinam toad is one of South America's most unusual amphibians. It lives in rivers and streams and finds food partly by

BELOW *The African clawed toad has a wedge-shaped body with a narrow head and large back legs. Like the Surinam toad, it does not have a tongue.*

Front legs feel for food

Egg-laying
and fertilization
happen in water

Female's body
is swollen
with eggs

LEFT *Gripping his
partner with his front
legs, a male common toad
stays with his mate until
she has laid her eggs. The
male will fertilize the eggs
as they are laid so that
they can start to develop.*

COMMON TOAD

Unlike frogs, most toads have
warty skin and short back
legs and spend most
of their adult lives on
land. They usually
feed at night,
when the air is
damp, and hide
away during the day. The common toad, one
of the largest toads in Europe, has a dark brown
body and golden eyes. In cold places, these toads
hibernate during the winter. The adults gather at
ponds to breed in the early spring. Each female
lays a double string of up to 4,000 eggs, which
she wraps around underwater plants.

*Male grasps the female
under her front legs with
rough pads to help him
maintain his grip*

BELOW *As in
most toads, the
giant toad
has poison-
producing
parotid glands
behind each eye.
Large giant
toads can squirt
poison at an
attacker.*

SCIENTIFIC NAME *Bufo bufo*

DISTRIBUTION Europe, northern Asia

SIZE Up to 6 in. (15cm) long, excluding legs

AMERICAN TOAD

The American toad lives in a wide variety
of habitats and is a frequent visitor to gardens
and backyards. It is a useful guest because,
during its nocturnal wanderings, it eats many
small garden pests, such as insects and slugs. The
females produce up to 8,000 eggs in early spring,
laying them in all kinds of places, from swamps
to temporary pools. Many toads have croaky
voices, but this species is much more musical—
in spring, it makes a long, trilling sound.

SCIENTIFIC NAME *Bufo americanus*

DISTRIBUTION Eastern North America

SIZE Up to 4 in. (10cm) long, excluding legs

GIANT TOAD OR CANE TOAD

This is the world's largest toad.
In the wild, females often weigh
more than 2 lb. (1kg), and in captivity,
they can grow to more than twice this
weight. They feed at dusk with little fear
of predators because their skin contains
glands that produce a powerful
poison. Giant toads originally
come from the American tropics,
but because they eat so many
insects, they have been introduced
into other parts of the world—
often with disastrous results.
They were released in Australia
in 1935 to control beetles that
were destroying sugar cane crops,
but they ate lizards, frogs, and
small rodents as well. Because they had
no natural predators, they multiplied
rapidly and have seriously harmed
many native Australian animals.

SCIENTIFIC NAME *Bufo marinus*

DISTRIBUTION Central and South
America; introduced into the West Indies,
Hawaii, the Philippines, Australia

SIZE Up to 10 in. (25cm) long, excluding legs

**American toad
with red parotid glands**

The green toad is well camouflaged

The natterjack toad is brown, gray, or green in color

BELOW AND BOTTOM
Male midwife toads carry their partner's eggs. Midwife toads have good eyesight, and emerge only after dark.

GREEN TOAD

This toad has patches of bright green on a pale brown background, like military camouflage. In warm places, it often lives near houses, and adults sometimes gather around street lamps to feed on insects that have fallen to the ground. Green toads sound like crickets when they call. They lay their eggs in ponds and shallow lakes.

SCIENTIFIC NAME *Bufo viridis*

DISTRIBUTION Eastern and southern Europe, northern Africa, parts of Asia

SIZE Up to 4 in. (10cm) long, excluding legs

NATTERJACK TOAD

The European natterjack is easy to recognize because it has a bright yellow stripe running down its back. Its exceptionally loud call sounds like a piece of machinery. Each burst of sound lasts for only a few seconds, but on still evenings, it can be heard up to 1.25 mi. (2km) away. This toad often lives in sandy places near the sea.

SCIENTIFIC NAME *Bufo calamita*

DISTRIBUTION Europe

SIZE Up to 4 in. (10cm) long, excluding legs

Male carries up to 60 eggs wrapped around his back legs

FIRE-BELLIED TOAD

From above, this small toad is an unremarkable gray-green color, but underneath it has a startling scarlet and black pattern. If it is threatened by a predator, it arches its head and raises its legs to show these bright markings, which warn that it is poisonous and dangerous to attack. Fire-bellied toads live in ditches and ponds and often float on the water.

SCIENTIFIC NAME *Bombina bombina*

DISTRIBUTION Eastern Europe, parts of Asia

SIZE Up to 2 in. (5cm) long, excluding legs

MIDWIFE TOAD

Midwife toads mate and lay their eggs on land. The female produces a string of eggs, and after they have been fertilized, the male wraps them around his back legs. For a month or more he carries the eggs, protecting them from predators and dipping them in water to keep them wet. Just before they are ready to hatch, he lowers them into shallow water. Midwife toads live in woodlands and rocky places and spend the day hiding in holes and crevices.

SCIENTIFIC NAME *Alytes obstetricans*

DISTRIBUTION Western Europe

SIZE Up to 2 in. (5cm) long, excluding legs

SPADEFOOT TOAD

Spadefoot toads are expert burrowers. They have a ridge of hard skin on each back foot, which they use like a spade to dig into loose, sandy ground. Spadefoot toads live in dry places, often spending months hidden under ground. If it rains, they scramble to the surface, where they mate and lay their eggs. Spadefoot tadpoles can turn into toadlets in just two weeks, helping them survive in places where water soon dries out. There are ten species of spadefoot toads.

SCIENTIFIC NAME *Scaphiophus* and *Pelobates* species

DISTRIBUTION North America, Europe, northern Africa, Middle East

SIZE Typical length 2 in. (5cm), excluding legs

LEFT *Couch's spadefoot toads* (Scaphiophus couchii) *can spend up to nine months under ground.*

SALAMANDERS AND CAECILIANS

Unlike frogs and toads, salamanders and caecilians keep their tails when they are adults. These two groups of animals also look very different and behave in different ways. Salamanders have long bodies and four, or occasionally two, legs. As adults, some live in damp woods, but many spend their lives in ponds and streams. There are nearly 400 species of salamanders, and they are found all over the world. Caecilians are rarer, with about 150 species. They look like giant earthworms because they have no legs and their bodies are divided into rings. Caecilians live mainly in the tropics. Some live in water, but most of them burrow through soil.

CHINESE GIANT SALAMANDER

This is the largest amphibian in the world. It has a large, broad head, small eyes, and dark, wrinkled skin. It lives in cool mountain streams, where it eats insects, frogs, and fish. Chinese giant salamanders are very rare. They are threatened by pollution, and they are also collected for food and for use in traditional medicine.

SCIENTIFIC NAME *Andrias davidianus*

DISTRIBUTION China

SIZE Up to 6 ft. (2m) long, including tail

AXOLOTL

This pale pink salamander has a remarkable life cycle—it can breed without fully growing up. Instead of losing its gills and developing into an adult shape, it often remains a giant, four-legged tadpole all its life. Axolotls are sometimes kept in aquariums. Their only natural habitat is in lakes near Mexico City, where they are now rare.

SCIENTIFIC NAME *Ambystoma mexicanum*

DISTRIBUTION Mexico

SIZE Up to 12 in. (30cm) long, including tail

Soft, rubbery skin

ABOVE *In water, axolotls breathe through their deep red, feathery gills.*

RIGHT *The warty newt returns to water to breed in the spring. Like most newts, the male carries out a complicated courtship dance.*

Bright colors on underside only

Five toes on hind feet

The male has a silver stripe down its webbed tail

Each male has a unique pattern of spots

HELLBENDER

North America is home to a large proportion of the world's salamanders, and the hellbender is the largest and possibly the ugliest of them all. A close relative of the Chinese giant salamander, it has a similar shape, with short legs, an oversized head, and wrinkled, slimy skin. Hellbenders live in fast-flowing rivers and streams, hiding under rocks by day. In summer, female hellbenders lay strings of eggs on the riverbed, and the male guards them until they hatch.

SCIENTIFIC NAME *Cryptobranchus alleganiensis*

DISTRIBUTION Eastern North America

SIZE Up to 27.5 in. (70cm) long, including tail

WARTY NEWT OR GREAT CRESTED NEWT

Newts are small or medium-sized salamanders that often have webbed tails as adults. During the breeding season, the male warty newt also develops a jagged crest that runs all the way down his back. His underside is orange or yellow, with contrasting black spots. Warty newts carry out their courtship under water, and the female lays about 300 eggs. She fastens them individually to the leaves of water plants, using a sticky fluid to fold the leaf around the egg.

SCIENTIFIC NAME *Triturus cristatus*

DISTRIBUTION Europe

SIZE Up to 6 in. (15cm) long, including tail

FIRE SALAMANDER

The brilliantly colored fire salamander spends its adult life on land, living in forests and other damp habitats. Fire salamanders emerge at night, often after rain, to hunt prey such as earthworms. Their yellow and black markings warn that their skin is poisonous, which keeps enemies at bay as they search for food. They mate on land, but female fire salamanders give birth to live young in pools and streams.

SCIENTIFIC NAME
Salamandra salamandra

DISTRIBUTION Europe, except British Isles and Scandinavia

SIZE Up to 11 in. (28cm) long, including tail

RED SALAMANDER

The red salamander is equally at home in and out of water and is found in springs, woodlands, and wet meadows. When it has newly reached maturity, it is brilliant red, though its color fades with age. The red salamander is one of about 200 species that do not have lungs as adults. Lungless salamanders breathe through their skin or through the lining of their mouths. Almost all of the world's lungless salamanders live in the Americas.

SCIENTIFIC NAME *Pseudotriton ruber*

DISTRIBUTION Eastern North America

SIZE Up to 7 in. (18cm) long, including tail

CAECILIAN

Compared to other amphibians, little is known about caecilians because their burrowing behavior keeps them out of sight. Most live in the leaf litter and soft soil on the floor of tropical rain forests. They have blunt heads and small eyes, and they push head-first through the soil, finding their food mainly by touch. Caecilians are carnivorous, but their prey depends on their size. The smallest ones eat insects, centipedes, and worms, but the largest species can tackle frogs and snakes. Some caecilians give birth to live young, but most species have swimming tadpoles—a feature that demonstrates their links with salamanders, frogs, and toads.

SCIENTIFIC NAME *Siphonops* and other genera

DISTRIBUTION Central America, South America, tropical Africa, India, Southeast Asia

SIZE Up to 5 ft. (1.5m) long

Only the male has a crest

Four toes on front feet

TOP AND ABOVE *Fire salamanders are marked with yellow lines or spots. The poison in their skin burns the mouth and eyes of any animal that tries to eat them.*

LEFT *A female South American caecilian (Siphonops annulatus) curls around her newly laid eggs.*

REPTILES

REPTILES WERE THE FIRST ANIMALS WITH
BACKBONES TO BECOME FULLY EQUIPPED
FOR LIFE ON DRY LAND. DURING THE AGE
OF THE DINOSAURS, REPTILES RULED THE
EARTH AND INCLUDED THE LARGEST
ANIMALS THE WORLD HAS EVER SEEN.

U nlike amphibians, reptiles have a tough skin
covered by scales, and their eggs have waterproof
shells. These two features allow them to live away
from water in some of the driest habitats on earth.
Although reptiles are cold-blooded, they can warm
themselves by basking in sunshine—once they are warm,
they can move around quickly. In total, there are nearly
6,000 species of reptiles. They are found in most parts
of the world, except places where it gets very cold.

CROCODILES AND ALLIGATORS

This group of about 23 species includes the largest reptiles alive
today. Crocodiles and alligators have armored scales and long jaws
with sharp teeth. They live in or near water. When they swim, they
are almost invisible because only their eyes and nostrils break the
surface—an adaptation that helps them ambush animals coming
down to drink. Crocodiles and alligators lay leathery-shelled eggs,
often carrying their young to water when they have hatched. These
animals are hunted for their skins, and many are endangered.

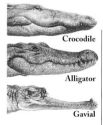

Crocodile

Alligator

Gavial

ABOVE *Crocodiles and
alligators have broad
snouts, but the gavial's
snout is very narrow
for catching fish.*

ESTUARINE CROCODILE
Known in Australia as the "saltie," this is the
world's largest and most dangerous crocodile.
Unlike other crocodiles, it lives in sea water as
well as in lakes and rivers. The female lays up
to 90 eggs in a mound of sand and leaves. She
guards the nest fiercely, but when her young
hatch, she gently carries them to water. Fully
grown estuarine crocodiles can kill animals as
large as water buffaloes and may be responsible
for as many as 1,000 human deaths each year.

SCIENTIFIC NAME *Crocodylus porosus*

DISTRIBUTION Bay of Bengal, Southeast Asia,
northern Australia

SIZE Up to 20 ft. (6m) long

ABOVE *The estuarine crocodile
is famous for its aggressive nature.*

NILE CROCODILE
This freshwater crocodile lives in
lakes and rivers. It preys on animals
that come to drink, dragging them
under water and drowning them. It
twists around in the water to rip its food
apart. The Nile crocodile has a spectacular
courtship display. The male defends a stretch of
bank, roaring at any intruders. When a female is
attracted by the noise, the male thrashes his body
and shoots water into the air from his nostrils.

SCIENTIFIC NAME *Crocodylus niloticus*

DISTRIBUTION Africa, Madagascar

SIZE Up to 17 ft. (5m) long

DWARF CROCODILE
This is the smallest and least known of the
world's crocodiles. It lives in rain forest rivers
and swamps, climbing up tree trunks to bask in
the sun. The female lays up to 17 eggs and guards
them for three months. Unusually, it has armored
scales on its underside as well as its back.

SCIENTIFIC NAME *Osteolaemus tetraspis*

DISTRIBUTION Western and
central Africa

SIZE Up to 6 ft.
(2m) long

GAVIAL

This large, freshwater crocodile has an extremely slender snout equipped with many small but needle-sharp teeth. Although its snout looks fragile, it is ideal for catching fish, the gavial's main food. Once it has made a catch, the gavial lifts its snout into the air, then flicks the fish around so it can swallow it head first. Compared to other crocodiles, gavials spend a lot of time in the water. Their back feet are fully webbed.

SCIENTIFIC NAME *Gavialis gangeticus*
DISTRIBUTION Pakistan, India, Bangladesh, Nepal
SIZE Up to 23 ft. (7m) long

ABOVE *Like most of their relatives, Nile crocodiles spend many hours each day basking in the sunshine.*

BELOW *American alligators hunt when the temperature is above 70°F. When it is colder, they become sluggish.*

AMERICAN ALLIGATOR

The American alligator is the largest reptile in the Western Hemisphere. In the 1960s, after decades of being hunted, it was declared an endangered species. It has since made a spectacular recovery. Alligators live in rivers and swamps, eating anything they can overpower, from turtles to birds. During the summer, they often wallow in water-filled hollows called "gator holes," but in winter, they hibernate in shallow dens. Alligators are very similar to crocodiles. The easiest way to tell them apart is that a crocodile's lower front teeth protrude when its mouth is closed, while an alligator's fit into sockets in its upper jaw.

SCIENTIFIC NAME *Alligator mississippiensis*
DISTRIBUTION Southeastern United States
SIZE Up to 18 ft. (5.5m) long

SPECTACLED CAIMAN

A caiman is a small crocodile from Central and South America. There are five different species, of which the spectacled caiman is the most common. It lives in rivers, lakes, and swamps, and it can survive droughts by burrowing into the mud. The spectacled caiman got its name from the ridges around its eyes, which look like a pair of glasses.

SCIENTIFIC NAME *Caiman crocodilus*
DISTRIBUTION Central America, South America
SIZE Up to 6 ft. (2m) long

Spectacle-shaped ridges around the eyes

Blunt snout

Small teeth

Pale underside

LEFT *The spectacled caiman often lounges at the water's edge. There are several varieties of this widespread reptile.*

LIZARDS AND TUATARAS

Lizards make up just over half of the world's reptiles. There are about 3,500 species, and most of them live in places with warm climates. Lizards usually have long legs and tails. In emergencies, many can escape attack by shedding their tail—later, they grow a new one in its place. Most lizards live on the ground and feed on insects, although these reptiles also include many nimble climbers, such as geckos and chameleons. Lizards normally reproduce by laying small, leathery-shelled eggs, but some species give birth to live young. Tuataras look like lizards, but they belong to a different group of reptiles that first appeared more than 200 million years ago. There are only two species, both in New Zealand.

BELOW *Tuataras grow slowly and take about 20 years to reach breeding age—a record for reptiles. It is thought that they can live for as long as 100 years.*

TUATARA

These powerfully built animals have large heads, stocky feet, and a spiky crest running down their backs. They resemble lizards on the outside, but they have unusually shaped skulls and backbones, and their teeth are permanently fixed to their jaws, instead of being set in sockets. Tuataras are nocturnal. They hide in burrows during the day, emerging at night to eat birds' eggs and small animals such as insects. Compared to lizards, they are long-lived and cope well with the cold. Tuataras were once common in New Zealand, but are now among the rarest animals in the world. They live only on a few islands, where they are carefully protected against rats and other introduced mammals.

SCIENTIFIC NAME *Sphenodon punctatus* and *Sphenodon guntheri*

DISTRIBUTION New Zealand

SIZE Up to 25.5 in. (65cm) long

Iguanas have good eyesight

Ear opening

COMMON IGUANA

This impressive animal is one of the world's largest plant-eating lizards. It spends most of its time basking high up in waterside trees. It has powerful feet with sharp claws and a long, muscular tail. Despite its size, it can be difficult to see, because its green color keeps it well camouflaged. Adult iguanas are large enough to defend themselves against most attackers, but if taken by surprise, they have an unusual way of escaping—they leap out of the trees and crash into the water, quickly swimming away.

SCIENTIFIC NAME *Iguana iguana*

DISTRIBUTION Central America, South America

SIZE Up to 6 ft. (2m) long

RIGHT AND ABOVE *Although it has a fearsome appearance, the common iguana is a harmless vegetarian.*

CHUCKWALLA

Chuckwallas are plant-eating lizards that live in deserts and rocky places. They have broad, red and gray bodies with fat tails and loose skin covered with rough, sandpapery scales. Chuckwallas feed during the day. If they are threatened, they often run into rocky crevices and then gulp air—this makes them swell up, wedging them in place. Female chuckwallas lay clutches of about ten eggs, and like most lizards, they leave their young to fend for themselves.

SCIENTIFIC NAME	*Sauromalus obesus*
DISTRIBUTION	Southern United States, Mexico
SIZE	Up to 16 in. (40cm) long

MARINE IGUANA

This remarkable reptile is the world's only seagoing lizard. It feeds on seaweed that grows around the rocky shores of the Galapagos Islands. The water around the Galapagos is cold, but the iguana survives the low temperatures by slowing its heart rate when it dives, so that its blood does not lose too much heat through its skin. Marine iguanas are shaped for their unusual way of life—they have blunt heads, wide jaws, and a flattened tail that works like a cross between a propeller and a rudder. They can stay under water for up to 20 minutes.

SCIENTIFIC NAME	*Amblyrhynchus cristatus*
DISTRIBUTION	Galapagos Islands
SIZE	Up to 5 ft. (1.5m) long

HORNED LIZARD

Most lizards run away if threatened, but horned lizards stand their ground. Their squat bodies are protected by an array of horns and spines, and they can squirt blood from their eyes at an attacker. Also known as horned toads, horned lizards live in deserts in North America. There are 14 species, most of which feed on ants.

SCIENTIFIC NAME	*Phrynosoma* species
DISTRIBUTION	North America, from southern Canada to Mexico
SIZE	Up to 7 in. (18cm) long

BASILISK OR CRESTED WATER DRAGON

The bright green basilisk has an eye-catching bony flap on its head, as well as a crest on its back and tail. But the most unusual thing about it is that it can run on its two back legs. It only does this in emergencies, but it can splash its way across several yards of water, as well as running on dry land. Basilisks are able to do this because they have large back feet with a fringe of scales

on each of their toes. These lizards live in forests, and they find their food on the ground as well as in trees.

SCIENTIFIC NAME	*Basilicus plumifrons*
DISTRIBUTION	South America
SIZE	Up to 31.5 in. (80cm) long

ANOLE

Anoles are small, bright green lizards with slender bodies and long tails. They feed on insects they find in trees. They can race along branches with amazing speed because their fingers and toes have rounded pads and sharp claws, giving them a good grip. Most male anoles have a brightly colored flap that can fold underneath their chin, which they use to attract females during the breeding season. There are more than 250 species of anoles, found only in the Americas.

SCIENTIFIC NAME	*Anolis* species
DISTRIBUTION	Southeastern United States, Central America, South America
SIZE	Up to 8 in. (20cm) long

LEFT *Chuckwallas jam themselves tightly into crevices to keep predators from removing them.*
BELOW *With its tail up and its throat-flap extended, a male anole tries to attract a mate.*

ABOVE *Marine iguanas bask on the shores of the Galapagos Islands.*

BELOW *The Texas horned lizard (Phrynosoma cornutum) usually stays out in the open, but it can bury itself in loose soil.*

LEFT *The basilisk uses its tail for balance as it runs on two legs.*

GALAPAGOS LAND IGUANA

Unlike the marine iguana (page 147), this large lizard stays on dry land. It feeds almost entirely on the leaves and fruit of the prickly pear cactus, breaking off the cactus's spines with its jaws before swallowing the rest. Female land iguanas bury their eggs in the ground. They leave the dry lowlands and trek up mountains to find the moist ground they need for a nesting site.

SCIENTIFIC NAME	*Conolophus subcristatus*
DISTRIBUTION	Galapagos Islands
SIZE	Up to 4 ft. (1.2m) long

FRILLED LIZARD

This is one of Australia's most spectacular lizards. Its color varies from dull red to brown, but if the lizard is cornered, it responds with a striking threat display. It unfurls a brilliant red and yellow frill around its neck and opens its bright red mouth. At the same time, it sways and hisses, making it look as if it is about to attack. This is often enough to make the lizard's enemies back away, but if not, it folds up its frill and runs up the nearest tree.

SCIENTIFIC NAME	*Chlamydosaurus kingii*
DISTRIBUTION	Australia
SIZE	Up to 20 in. (50cm) long

FLYING DRAGON

This lizard lives in forests, where it glides from tree to tree. Its "wings" are specially enlarged ribs that open out like the struts of a fan, stretching a flap of loose skin. After flight, the ribs hinge back along its body to fold the wings away. Flying dragons feed on small insects and lay their eggs on the ground.

SCIENTIFIC NAME	*Draco volans*
DISTRIBUTION	Southeast Asia
SIZE	Up to 9 in. (23cm) long

THORNY DEVIL

The thorny devil lives in the deserts of western Australia, where it feeds mainly on ants. Its body is covered with prickles and spines that extend from its head to its tail and along its legs. It needs these because ants take time to eat, and while it is feeding it is vulnerable to attack.

SCIENTIFIC NAME	*Moloch horridus*
DISTRIBUTION	Australia
SIZE	Up to 6 in. (15cm) long

BELOW *With its frill opened out like an umbrella, a frilled lizard tries to bluff its way out of trouble with a spectacular defensive display.*

FLAP-NECKED CHAMELEON

This African lizard is one of about 90 species of chameleons, all adapted for life in trees. Like other chameleons, its body is humped and narrow, and its eyes can swivel independently. It can also change color, either to match its background or to show its mood. If it spots an insect, it shoots out its sticky-tipped tongue, which is as long as the rest of its body. Some chameleons give birth to live young, but this particular species lays eggs.

SCIENTIFIC NAME	*Chamaeleon dilepis*
DISTRIBUTION	Southern Africa
SIZE	Up to 14 in. (35cm) long

RIGHT *Jackson's chameleon (*Chamaeleon jacksoni*) catches a moth. It is fast and accurate with its long, sticky tongue.*

Turret-shaped, swiveling eyes

Long tongue retracts into the chameleon's throat when not in use

Color changes as pigment moves in or out of the outer layers of skin

ABOVE *The protective spikes on a thorny devil serve another purpose too. In the desert, dew condenses on them, and the water drips into the lizard's mouth.*

Fingers and toes are specially designed for grasping twigs and branches

SIX-LINED RACERUNNER

Racerunners are among the world's fastest lizards. Over short distances, they can reach speeds of 20 mph (30km/h)—almost as fast as the best human sprinters. They live in grassland, sand dunes, and other open places, relying on speed to keep out of trouble. They have slender bodies with very long tails. Racerunners belong to a family of lizards called whiptails, which total more than 200 species, and are found only in the Americas. Some are of particular interest to scientists because they are all female and can breed without having to mate.

SCIENTIFIC NAME *Cnemidophorus sexlineatus*

DISTRIBUTION Central and eastern United States

SIZE Up to 8 in. (20cm) long

Large eyes spot prey in the dark

Toes have sharp claws and narrow pads

LEFT *The flap-necked chameleon uses stealth to catch food. Perfectly camouflaged on a branch, it waits patiently for food to come within reach of its long tongue.*

TOKAY GECKO

Across much of Southeast Asia, the tokay gecko is a common visitor to houses. At night, it scuttles up walls in search of insects and other lizards and can even run across ceilings upside down. It can grip so well because it has flattened toe pads covered with up to a million microscopic, clinging hairs. This acrobatic animal is one of more than 800 species in the gecko family, most commonly found in the tropics. They often gather around lights after dark to catch their prey. Most lay two eggs at a time. These are soft and sticky at first, but soon harden.

SCIENTIFIC NAME *Gekko gekko*

DISTRIBUTION Southern and Southeast Asia

SIZE Up to 11 in. (28cm) long

LEAF-TAILED GECKO

When pressed flat against a tree, the leaf-tailed gecko is almost impossible to see because of its superb camouflage. Its body has a mottled pattern that looks like patches of lichen growing on bark. It also has a leaf-shaped tail that helps break up its outline. Like most geckos, this forest lizard cannot blink—instead, it uses its tongue to clean its eyes.

SCIENTIFIC NAME *Phyllurus cornutus*

DISTRIBUTION Australia

SIZE Up to 7 in. (18cm) long

Prehensile tail can wrap around branches for extra grip

TOP *This tokay gecko is in a defensive posture.*
ABOVE *A leaf-tailed gecko uses its long tongue to clean its eyes. Geckos have larger eyes than most lizards, which helps them see their prey after dark.*

Long, snakelike body

ABOVE *The sand skink, like its relatives, has smooth, flat scales that allow it to burrow without getting dirty.*

BELOW AND BOTTOM *The green lizard is one of the largest in Europe. It can shed its tail and grow a new one if it is attacked. The close-up shows how the green lizard's scales vary in size across its body.*

Tail breaks off at this point

COMMON BLUE-TONGUED SKINK

Skinks make up one of the largest families of lizards, with at least 1,000 species. Most of them have smooth, shiny scales and small legs, and almost all of them live on the ground. The common blue-tongued skink, a large species from eastern Australia, often comes into backyards. It has a large head and a short tail, but its most conspicuous feature is its blue tongue. If threatened, it sticks its tongue out and makes a hissing noise. This performance frightens off many predators—and some humans as well. There are several kinds of blue-tongued skinks, and they all give birth to live young.

SCIENTIFIC NAME *Tiliqua scincoides*

DISTRIBUTION Eastern Australia

SIZE Up to 20 in. (50cm) long

SAND SKINK

The sand skink is one of North America's strangest lizards. It has a long, streamlined body and a sharply pointed nose, and its legs are so small that they are often difficult to see. Its back feet each have two toes, but its front feet have just one. Sand skinks spend much of their lives under ground. Instead of digging with their legs, they wriggle their bodies and "swim" through the sand. They are very sensitive to movement. This helps them find termites and insect grubs to eat.

SCIENTIFIC NAME *Neoseps reynoldsi*

DISTRIBUTION Florida

SIZE Up to 5 in. (12cm) long

GREEN LIZARD

This handsome, bright green lizard has a tail almost twice as long as its body. It lives on the ground and in trees, feeding on insects, spiders, and occasionally young birds. Green lizards breed by laying eggs. During the winter months, they hibernate in tree hollows and rocky crevices. The viviparous lizard *(Lacerta vivipara)*, a small brown relative of this species, is the only lizard that breeds north of the Arctic Circle. The word "viviparous" means that it gives birth to live young, unlike its relative the green lizard.

SCIENTIFIC NAME *Lacerta viridis*

DISTRIBUTION Central and southern Europe

SIZE Up to 17.5 in. (45cm) long

Ear opening

Large scales cover the head

SLOWWORM

The slowworm looks like a small snake, but it is actually a lizard with no legs. Slowworms differ from snakes in many ways. They can close their eyes, and they shed their tails if attacked. They also have bony plates beneath their scales, which make their bodies hard and stiff. Slowworms come out at dawn and dusk, often after rain. They feed on insects, spiders, and slugs. Females produce up to 12 eggs that hatch as they are being laid.

Slowworm curled like a snake

SCIENTIFIC NAME	*Anguis fragilis*
DISTRIBUTION	Europe, Asia, northern Africa
SIZE	Up to 20 in. (50cm) long

Tongue is deeply forked

GILA MONSTER

The fat and lumbering Gila monster is one of only two poisonous lizards in the world—the other is the Mexican beaded lizard *(Heloderma horridum)*. Its bright orange and black colors warn other animals to leave it alone. Gila monsters live in deserts and other dry places. Their tails work like a camel's hump, storing fat for times when food is scarce. They hunt small mammals and other lizards after dark, gripping them in their jaws and injecting venom as they chew. Although their bite is extremely painful, it is rarely fatal to humans.

SCIENTIFIC NAME	*Heloderma suspectum*
DISTRIBUTION	Southwestern United States, northern Mexico
SIZE	Up to 23.5 in. (60cm) long

KOMODO DRAGON

The Komodo dragon is the world's largest lizard. A meat-eater, it feeds by hunting and scavenging and is strong enough to bring down a horse. Komodo dragons belong to a group of giant lizards called monitors, which have powerful legs and long, forked tongues. They use their tongues to taste the air for living prey or dead remains. Komodo dragons once roamed over a large part of Indonesia, but they now live on only a handful of islands. There are about 5,000 left, and they are protected by law.

SCIENTIFIC NAME	*Varanus komodoensis*
DISTRIBUTION	Komodo and neighboring Indonesian islands
SIZE	Up to 10 ft. (3m) long

Loose skin hangs from the lower jaw

GOULD'S MONITOR OR GOULD'S GOANNA

Australia has more monitor lizards, or goannas, than anywhere else in the world, and Gould's monitor is the most widespread species. It is brown or golden in color, with a small head, but it has large, powerful feet and claws for ripping apart its prey. Its long, thick tail acts as a prop when the lizard stands on its back legs to look for food. Gould's monitor eats mammals, snakes, and other lizards, and was itself once an important source of food for Australian Aborigines.

SCIENTIFIC NAME	*Varanus gouldii*
DISTRIBUTION	Australia
SIZE	Up to 5 ft. (1.5m) long

WORM LIZARD OR AMPHISBAENID

Worm lizards are burrowing reptiles with blunt heads, tiny eyes, and scales arranged in rings. Most of them have no legs, but three species—all from Mexico—have small front legs with five strong toes. These bizarre animals are not true lizards, and they live very differently. They build a system of underground tunnels by using their heads to bulldoze through the soil, and they feed on insects and worms. There are about 130 species of these reptiles. Some lay eggs, but others give birth to live young.

SCIENTIFIC NAME	*Amphisbaena* and other genera
DISTRIBUTION	Worldwide, mainly in warm regions
SIZE	Typical species about 12 in. (30cm) long

ABOVE *Gould's monitor can detect dead animals more than half a mile away by tasting the air with its forked tongue.*

BELOW *The Gila monster has a slow, lumbering walk, but it can suddenly lunge forward to inflict a poisonous bite.*

ABOVE *The Komodo dragon is bulkier than other monitors, and also more dangerous. It can weigh more than 200 lb., and its tail takes up about half its length.*

has made an attack, the boa hangs in the air while clinging on with its tail. After it has constricted and swallowed its prey, it pulls itself back up. The green tree python *(Chondropython viridis)* from Australia is also bright green and hunts in a similar way.

SCIENTIFIC NAME	*Corallus caninus*
DISTRIBUTION	South America
SIZE	Up to 4 ft. (1.2m) long

SNAKES

Snakes are legless reptiles that hunt other animals and swallow their prey whole. They can eat animals wider than they are because they have flexible jaws that inch forward around the victim's body. Unlike lizards, snakes cannot move their eyelids, their ears are not visible, and their vision is poor. They have an excellent sense of smell, flicking out their forked tongues to pick up scents in the air. Some snakes kill their prey by constriction—squeezing them to death—but most use their teeth. Some inject poison, or venom, through special teeth called fangs to stun or kill their victims. Most snakes lay eggs, which often hatch as soon as they are laid. There are about 2,300 species of snakes. They are most common in warm climates.

Emerald tree boa coiled on a branch

Body curled around a branch for support

TOP *This emerald tree boa has almost finished swallowing a rat whole. While it is swallowing, its windpipe is pushed out of the way. If this did not happen, the snake would not be able to breathe.*
ABOVE *A boa constrictor swallows its prey. Although snakes cannot chew their food, they can digest almost everything they eat, except fur, feathers, and claws.*

BOA CONSTRICTOR

Like all the snakes on these two pages, the boa is not venomous. It kills by constriction, tightening its coils around its victims until they cannot breathe. Contrary to what people often imagine, boas do not crush their prey, and few bones are broken. Boas are among the six largest snakes in the world. They live in a variety of habitats, from deserts to dense forests. Their markings vary, but they are always well camouflaged. Boas prey mainly on birds, mammals, and sometimes farm livestock. They produce up to 50 eggs a year, which hatch as they are laid.

SCIENTIFIC NAME	*Boa boa*
DISTRIBUTION	Central and South America
SIZE	Up to 18 ft. (5.5m) long

EMERALD TREE BOA

This beautifully colored rain forest snake spends most of its life in trees. With its bright green body clamped around a branch, it waits for birds and other animals to come within range. Once it

ANACONDA OR WATER BOA

The olive-green anaconda is one of the world's longest and heaviest snakes. One captive anaconda measured more than 28 ft. (8.6m) from head to tail, but it is not known what size this snake can reach in the wild. Though the anaconda is a good climber, it spends much of its time in or near water, catching animals that come to drink. Capybaras (page

BELOW *A fully grown anaconda can weigh almost 450 lb. Its dark colors camouflage it both on the ground and in water.*

257) are among its favorite prey, but it also eats turtles and caimans. When young anacondas are born, they can be 3 ft. (1m) long.

SCIENTIFIC NAME	*Eunectes murinus*
DISTRIBUTION	Tropical South America
SIZE	Up to 28 ft. (8.5m) long, possibly more

BURMESE PYTHON

This is one of the most common pythons in Southeast Asia. The true Burmese python is dark in color, but a subspecies called the Indian python is paler and smaller. Burmese pythons hunt both day and night for rodents, young deer, and other animals. They have been known to bite humans, but like other pythons, they are not venomous.

SCIENTIFIC NAME	*Python molurus*
DISTRIBUTION	Southeast Asia
SIZE	Up to 20 ft. (6m) long

RETICULATED PYTHON

This is the longest snake in the world, and it is the only snake that is known to have reached a length of 33 ft. (10m). Reticulated pythons live in tropical forests, where they prey on birds and small mammals. Like other pythons, they have a pair of heat-sensitive pits on their snouts to help them track down their prey. They lay up to 100 eggs, which the female guards until they hatch.

SCIENTIFIC NAME	*Python reticulatus*
DISTRIBUTION	Southeast Asia
SIZE	Up to 33 ft. (10m) long

ANIMAL EGGS

Most of the world's animals reproduce by laying eggs. Water animals usually lay jellylike eggs. On land, eggs like these would dry out, so most land animals lay eggs with waterproof shells. The smallest shelled eggs, laid by insects, can be seen only with a microscope, but the largest, laid by ostriches, can be 8 in. (20cm) long, with shells as thick as a plate. Once an egg has been laid, the animal inside often needs warmth to develop. Birds incubate or sit on their eggs, but because reptiles are cold-blooded, they rely on warmth from their surroundings. In cold places, snakes seek out "hot spots" such as compost heaps in which to lay their eggs. Pythons are the only snakes that are known to incubate their eggs. They wrap their bodies around them and twitch their muscles to produce heat.

A common kingsnake (*Lampropeltis getulus*) hatching from its egg

WART SNAKE

There are three species of wart snakes, found from India to northern Australia. Wart snakes are thick and heavily built, and their baggy skin looks as if it is several sizes too large. They spend their lives in shallow water in rivers and estuaries or the ocean, and have great difficulty moving around on land. They feed on fish, killing them with a powerful bite. *Acrochordus javanicus*, sometimes known as the Javan wart snake, is the largest species. It gives birth to live young.

SCIENTIFIC NAME	*Acrochordus* species
DISTRIBUTION	Southeast Asia, northern Australia
SIZE	Up to 8 ft. (2.4m) long

BELOW *The Burmese python's coloring camouflages it well in the dappled light on the forest floor.*
BOTTOM *Like other large snakes, the reticulated python can go for months between meals. Because it is cold-blooded, it uses relatively little energy for its size.*

Interlocking scales produce a smooth surface

Heat sensitive pit

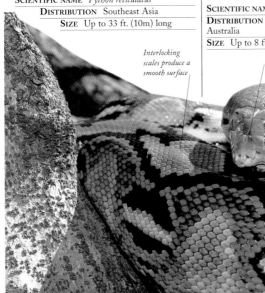

COMMON KINGSNAKE

This widespread North American snake is one of the most varied in color. In California, it is often black or brown with white bands, but farther south it is much paler. Kingsnakes kill their prey by constriction. Like all the snakes on these two pages, they belong to a family called the colubrids, which includes more than three fourths of the world's snake species. Colubrids have solid teeth rather than true fangs, and most of them are harmless.

SCIENTIFIC NAME *Lampropeltis getulus*

DISTRIBUTION North and Central America

SIZE Up to 6 ft. (2m) long

ABOVE *The common kingsnake's head is barely wider than the rest of its body, a common feature of the colubrid family of snakes.*
BELOW *This rat snake is swallowing a vole. It stretches its jaws slowly around its prey.*

ABOVE *With its mouth gaping open, this grass snake is trying to avoid attack by playing dead. Grass snakes also have another defense—they can expel a fluid with a very unpleasant smell.*

GRASS SNAKE

The grass snake is a daytime hunter and spends much of its time near water. It is a good swimmer and feeds mainly on frogs and toads, although it also eats small mammals and young birds. Its olive-green body is well camouflaged, and its slender shape is ideal for slipping through waterside vegetation. If a grass snake is threatened out in the open, it defends itself in an unusual way—it stays completely still and pretends to be dead. Many predators avoid dead animals, so this ruse sometimes saves the snake's life. Grass snakes reproduce by laying clutches of up to 40 eggs, which can take two months to hatch.

SCIENTIFIC NAME *Natrix natrix*

DISTRIBUTION Europe, northern Africa, northern Asia

SIZE Up to 6 ft. (2m) long

RAT SNAKE

The rat snake can be plain or striped, and black, yellow, gray, or brown, but it has one characteristic feature—its underside is completely flat, turning up at sharp corners along its flanks. Rat snakes climb well. They eat mice and rats, which makes them useful visitors on farms. Rat snakes kill their prey by constriction. If a rat snake is in danger, it rears up, hissing.

SCIENTIFIC NAME *Elaphe obsoleta*

DISTRIBUTION North America

SIZE Up to 8 ft. (2.5m) long

COMMON GARTER SNAKE

This North American snake is named for its stripes, which look like the patterns on old-fashioned garters. It is very widespread and is found farther north than any other North American reptile, within a few hundred miles of the Arctic Circle. There, large numbers of snakes gather in writhing heaps during the fall mating season. After mating, they hibernate together, which helps them survive in places with freezing winters. Garter snakes give birth to live young.

SCIENTIFIC NAME *Thamnopsis sirtalis*

DISTRIBUTION North America

SIZE Up to 4.25 ft. (1.3m) long

Unusually
small teeth

Spines inside the
throat break the
egg's shell

Jaws dislocate when
the egg is swallowed

Skin between the scales stretches
so that the mouth can expand

The tongue
can sense food,
danger, and
potential mates

WESTERN WHIP SNAKE

This green-yellow snake is a daytime
hunter with well-developed eyes. It
lives on rocky hillsides and in scrub
and specializes in catching lizards.
Compared to many snakes, it is
fast and agile—characteristics
needed for hunting fast-moving
prey. Whip snakes lay about
12 eggs each time they breed,
hiding them in crevices
among the rocks.

Snakes
constantly
flick their
tongues in
and out to
taste the air

SCIENTIFIC NAME *Coluber viridiflavus*

DISTRIBUTION Southern and western Europe

SIZE Up to 5 ft. (1.5m) long

ABOVE *Snakes use their
tongues to smell. They
collect a tiny amount of
scent with their tongues
and carry it to a sensitive
pit in the roofs of their
mouths. Here, a common
garter snake (above center)
and a western whip snake
(above) sample the air.*

MEXICAN VINE SNAKE

Vine snakes live in trees and mainly eat lizards.
They are long but very slender, with pointed
snouts. Their shape allows them to creep up
on their prey. Vine snakes inject venom through
grooved teeth at the back of their jaws. "Back-
fanged" snakes are rarely dangerous to humans,
as most of them can bite only small animals.

SCIENTIFIC NAME *Oxybelis aeneus*

DISTRIBUTION Southern Arizona, Central
and South America

SIZE Up to 6 ft. (2m) long

EGG-EATING SNAKE

This snake is a rare exception to the rule that
snakes hunt things that move. It feeds on birds'
eggs, and it has become so well adapted for this
unusual diet that it rarely eats anything else. Like
other snakes, it cannot chew, so it swallows the
eggs whole. As an egg moves down its neck, the
snake arches its body, and downward-pointing
spines on its backbone break the shell open.
The contents of the egg travel into the snake's
stomach, but the snake regurgitates the pieces
of broken shell. There are six species of egg-
eating snakes, all of them found in Africa.

SCIENTIFIC NAME *Dasypeltis scaber*

DISTRIBUTION Africa

SIZE Up to 29.5 in. (75cm) long

BOOMSLANG

The African boomslang is one of the few
members of the colubrid snake family that
has a bite poisonous enough to kill people.
Like the vine snake, it lives in trees, but its
venom is far stronger, and its fangs are set
further forward, making it easier for it to strike
and bite. Boomslangs are camouflaged brown or
green. They lie in wait in the trees for their prey,
often with the front of their bodies sticking out
in the air. Birds sometimes mistake them for
branches and land on them, only to become
an easy meal for the snake.

SCIENTIFIC NAME *Dispholidus typhus*

DISTRIBUTION Central and southern Africa

SIZE Up to 6 ft. (2m) long

KING COBRA OR HAMADRYAD

This giant cobra is the largest venomous snake in the world. The largest on record, which was kept at London Zoo in England, reached a length of almost 18 ft. (5.5m). King cobras produce large quantities of highly toxic venom and prey entirely on other snakes. They are generally secretive, but they can be aggressive, sometimes attacking people without provocation. King cobras are unusual in the snake world because they make nests out of sticks and leaves. After laying up to 40 eggs, the female remains on top of the nest until her young slither out.

SCIENTIFIC NAME	*Ophiophagus hannah*
DISTRIBUTION	India, Southeast Asia
SIZE	Up to 18.75 ft. (5.7m) long

RINGHALS OR SPITTING COBRA

The ringhals is one of three cobras that defend themselves by spitting venom. The ringhals's fangs have venom ducts that open forward, so the venom squirts out of its open mouth. It can spray its venom up to a distance of 8 ft. (2.4m), leaning its head back to aim the venom at its enemy's eyes. The effect is extremely painful and can sometimes cause permanent blindness. This snake eats rodents and frogs. It is one of the few members of the cobra family that give birth to live young.

SCIENTIFIC NAME	*Haemachatus haemachatus*
DISTRIBUTION	Southern Africa
SIZE	Up to 3 ft. (1m) long

BELOW *The king cobra can lunge more than 6 ft. when it strikes, making it dangerous to approach. Its spread hood warns that it is preparing to attack.*

BELOW AND RIGHT *Also known as the Asian cobra, the Indian cobra has more than ten different color forms.*

ABOVE *A death adder bites a lizard. Before antidotes became available, people often died after being bitten by this snake.*

INDIAN COBRA

For centuries, this poisonous snake has been popular with Indian snake charmers. When disturbed, it rears up and spreads out its ribs to form a hood, preparing to strike. It cannot hear, so it responds to snake charmers' movements rather than their music. Cobras have hollow fangs at the front of their mouths. They make a quick stab and hold their prey until the poison has taken effect. Indian cobras lay 20 or 30 eggs, which the female guards until they hatch.

SCIENTIFIC NAME	*Naja naja*
DISTRIBUTION	India, Southeast Asia
SIZE	Up to 7.25 ft. (2.2m) long

largest poisonous snake and is unpredictable when threatened. The taipan has a dark brown body and a slim, cream-colored head. It lives in the sparsely populated north of Australia, and although it sometimes hunts in sugar cane fields, it rarely attacks people.

SCIENTIFIC NAME	*Oxyuranus scutellatus*
DISTRIBUTION	Australia
SIZE	Up to 10 ft. (3m) long

EASTERN CORAL SNAKE
Coral snakes are nocturnal, and they spend much of their time under leaves or logs. They have cylindrical bodies and small heads, and their black, yellow, red, or white hoops are often so bright that they look freshly painted. No one knows why burrowing, nocturnal snakes should be so vividly colored—it is most likely that the colors warn predators that the snakes are dangerous. There are about 40 species of true coral snakes, all from warm parts of the Americas.

SCIENTIFIC NAME	*Micrurus fulvius*
DISTRIBUTION	Southeastern United States, Mexico
SIZE	Up to 4 ft. (1.2m) long

BLACK MAMBA
The black mamba is the largest poisonous snake in Africa. It is actually gray rather than black, and it hunts in trees and bushes as well as on open ground. Black mambas are probably the fastest-moving land animals without legs. In short bursts, they can move at up to 12 mph (20km/h)—fast enough to overtake someone running away.

SCIENTIFIC NAME	*Dendroaspis polylepis*
DISTRIBUTION	Africa, south of the Sahara Desert
SIZE	Up to 14 ft. (4.3m) long

YELLOW-BELLIED SEA SNAKE
About 40 species in the cobra family live in the sea. They have flat tails that work like paddles, nostrils that shut when they dive, and highly toxic venom. Huge groups of yellow-bellied sea snakes are sometimes seen hundreds of miles out to sea, though no one knows why so many gather together. Some sea snakes lay their eggs on land, but the yellow-bellied sea snake gives birth to live young and never comes ashore.

SCIENTIFIC NAME	*Pelamis platurus*
DISTRIBUTION	Tropical seas worldwide
SIZE	Up to 3 ft. (1m) long

ABOVE
The eastern coral snake has powerful venom, but its mouth and teeth are small, making it difficult for it to bite people.

DEATH ADDER
This highly venomous snake is not a true adder, but an unusually short and fat member of the cobra family. It feeds on rodents, lizards, and birds and spends the day coiled up beneath leaves or in loose soil. Like a real adder, it often lies in wait for prey instead of searching it out. Its body tapers very sharply into a narrow tail, which it waves to attract animals within range. Death adders are dangerous because they strike instantly if they are disturbed.

SCIENTIFIC NAME	*Acanthopis antarcticus*
DISTRIBUTION	Australia
SIZE	Up to 20 in. (50cm) long

TAIPAN
Nine tenths of Australia's snakes belong to the venomous cobra family but the taipan is probably the most dangerous of all. It is the world's third-

ABOVE *Raising its head above the grass, a black mamba investigates its surroundings. Black mambas are extremely venomous—fortunately, they live in places that are thinly populated.*

COMMON VIPER

Vipers do not pursue their prey, but wait for food to come their way, then strike with deadly efficiency. The common viper is a typical member of this small group of poisonous snakes. It has a large head, narrow neck, and thick body with a zigzag pattern for camouflage. Its fangs are normally folded away, but they swing forward as the snake attacks. Once a viper has struck, it waits for its venom to work, feeding only when its prey is dead. The common viper eats lizards, frogs, and small mammals. The female produces up to 20 young in late summer.

SCIENTIFIC NAME	*Vipera berus*
DISTRIBUTION	Europe, northern Asia
SIZE	Up to 20 in. (50cm) long

ABOVE *The body of a fully grown puff adder is thicker than a man's arm.*
RIGHT *Compared to its larger relatives, the common viper is rarely a threat to humans, but it attacks small animals with deadly efficiency.*

Zigzag pattern along back

ABOVE *A Gaboon viper waits for passing animals to come within reach of its giant fangs.*

GABOON VIPER

This rain forest snake is one of the fattest vipers and one of the best camouflaged. Its back is covered with intricate, brown and black, wedge-shaped markings, making it very difficult to see among fallen leaves. Its eyes face upward, an adaptation that helps it spot other animals as it lies on the forest floor. The Gaboon viper's fangs can be up to 2 in. (5cm) long, and they are sharp enough to stab through clothes and shoes. Like the common viper, it produces eggs that hatch as, or just after, they are laid.

SCIENTIFIC NAME	*Bitis gabonica*
DISTRIBUTION	Western, central, and southern Africa
SIZE	Up to 6 ft. (2m) long

PUFF ADDER

The puff adder is one of Africa's most dangerous snakes because it often lies in wait on roads and tracks after dark, staying still but fully alert. It is then all too easy to step on it. It lives in a wide range of habitats, from woodlands to semidesert, and feeds on ground-living animals, such as reptiles and rodents. This snake got its name from its habit of puffing itself up if it is threatened.

SCIENTIFIC NAME	*Bitis arietans*
DISTRIBUTION	Africa, Middle East
SIZE	Up to 6 ft. (2m) long

FER-DE-LANCE

This large, dangerous snake belongs to a family of reptiles called the pit vipers. Pit vipers track down warm-blooded animals using heat-sensitive pits between their eyes and nostrils. This works so well that many of them can strike accurately in total darkness. The fer-de-lance, one of the largest pit vipers, is responsible for more human deaths than any other snake in the American tropics. It lives in low-lying areas and often hunts in fields and sugar plantations.

SCIENTIFIC NAME	*Bothrops atrox*
DISTRIBUTION	Central and South America
SIZE	Up to 8 ft. (2.4m) long

EYELASH VIPER

This small pit viper is one of a handful of species that live and feed in trees. Many eyelash vipers are green or brown, but some are gold with speckles of red. Eyelash vipers eat lizards and frogs, but they also lurk near flowers to catch hummingbirds as they hover and feed.

SCIENTIFIC NAME	*Bothrops schlegelii*
DISTRIBUTION	Central America, northern South America
SIZE	Up to 3 ft. (1m) long

RIGHT
The western diamondback rattlesnake has a reputation for being dangerous. The pair of snakes (right) are rival males fighting during the breeding season. The single diamondback (far right) is getting ready to strike. Its jaws can open to almost a 180-degree angle.

Rival males wrestle, but do not bite each other

Rattle gets longer each year

Wide scales on the underside grip the ground

WESTERN DIAMONDBACK

The western diamondback is one of the largest and most dangerous of the 35 species of rattlesnakes. These snakes are pit vipers with built-in rattles at the tips of their tails. Rattles consist of up to 12 loose, bony rings that make a buzzing or rattling sound when the tail vibrates. They are used to warn enemies to keep away, but they may also help distract small animals while the snake gets ready to strike. The western diamondback lives in dry places and woodlands and eats mammals, birds, and lizards. Like all rattlesnakes, it gives birth to live young.

SCIENTIFIC NAME *Crotalus atrox*

DISTRIBUTION Southern United States, Mexico

SIZE Up to 6 ft. (2m) long

SIDEWINDER

This desert rattlesnake lives in sandy places, where the loose surface makes it difficult to slither. Instead, it throws its body sideways across the sand, leaving a series of parallel, J-shaped tracks. This way of moving, called sidewinding, uses less energy than creeping, and helps the snake keep cool. Sidewinders also have another adaptation to desert life— a pair of horns over their eyes that work like visors.

SCIENTIFIC NAME *Crotalus cerastes*

DISTRIBUTION Southwestern United States, northwestern Mexico

SIZE Up to 31.5 in. (80cm) long

FANGS AND VENOM

Vipers and pit vipers have fangs that fold away when not in use. Most of these snakes can eat small animals without using their fangs, but they bring them into action to deal with larger prey. Unlike other snakes, their fangs are at the front of their mouths— ideal for making a quick, deadly stab. Snake venom contains many substances, and the way it works varies from one group of snakes to another. Viper venom breaks down the prey's blood cells, but cobra venom acts on the victim's nervous system. The Gaboon viper produces more venom than any other snake—about .02 oz. (0.5g) with each bite, enough to kill ten people.

Venom sac

Hole in tip of fang

TURTLES AND TORTOISES

Turtles and tortoises are the only living reptiles with hard shells. Their shells are made of solid bone covered by large, thin scales, and they protect the whole of the animal's body apart from the head, legs, and tail. Most turtles and tortoises can pull their heads inside their shells if they are threatened; many can also pull in their legs and tails. Land-dwelling tortoises have stubby legs with blunt claws, while sea-going turtles have flat legs that work like flippers. Freshwater and coastal species have legs that can be used for swimming, walking, and sometimes climbing. There are about 230 species of turtles and tortoises, all of which reproduce by laying eggs. Many species have become endangered in recent years.

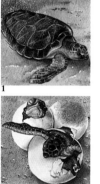

1

2

3

4

LEFT *Although they live in the sea, green turtles lay their eggs on land.* **1** *The female uses her front flippers to haul herself onto a sandy beach.* **2** *After digging a nest, she lays a clutch of soft-shelled eggs.* **3** *The young turtles usually hatch beneath the sand, tearing open their eggs with their snouts.* **4** *Once they have reached the surface of the sand, they instinctively head toward the sea.*

BELOW *Leatherbacks feed on jellyfish and can dive more than 5,000 ft. to catch their food.*

GREEN TURTLE

This is one of seven turtles that spend almost all of their lives at sea. Like other marine species, its shell is smooth and streamlined, and its front legs beat like wings to pull it through the water. It can stay under water for over half an hour without surfacing to breathe. It feeds on seagrass and seaweed, nipping off mouthfuls with its sharp-edged jaws. Green turtles nest on sandy beaches, hauling themselves ashore under the cover of darkness. Each female lays about 100 eggs. Three months later, the baby turtles dig to the surface and scuttle toward the waves. This is the most perilous moment of a turtle's life; seabirds often attack young turtles before they can swim away. Green turtle nesting sites are often in remote places, and adult turtles may travel over 1,000 mi. (1,600km) to breed. Scientists think that they navigate the same way fish do—by recognizing the taste of the water where they hatched.

SCIENTIFIC NAME   *Chelonia mydas*

DISTRIBUTION   Warm seas worldwide

SIZE   Up to 4 ft. (1.2m) long

LEATHERBACK TURTLE

The leatherback is the world's largest turtle, sometimes weighing more than half a ton. Its enormous, winglike front flippers can measure 8 ft. (2.4m) from tip to tip. Unlike other marine turtles, its scaleless shell has a rubbery feel, with deep grooves running from front to back. Leatherbacks are great travelers and may wander far out into the ocean. One leatherback tagged off South America turned up on the opposite side of the Atlantic Ocean—nearly 4,300 mi. (7,000km) away. The leatherback is now critically endangered because it has been hunted extensively by people.

SCIENTIFIC NAME   *Dermochelys coriacea*

DISTRIBUTION   Worldwide, in temperate or warm water

SIZE   Up to 6 ft. (2m) long

WOOD TURTLE

This North American turtle is equally at home on land and in water. It hibernates in ponds and lakes, but in the summer, it often wanders across farms and through woods, looking for fruit and animals such as insects and worms. It is a good swimmer, but it also climbs well and sometimes clambers up tree trunks. Wood turtles have rough shells, and their scales look as if they have been cut into steps. The skin on their neck and forelegs is often orange.

SCIENTIFIC NAME   *Clemmys insculpta*

DISTRIBUTION   Northeastern United States; adjoining areas of Canada

SIZE   Up to 9 in. (23cm) long

DIAMONDBACK TERRAPIN

Terrapins are small turtles that live in or near water. Most of them are freshwater animals, but the diamondback lives in estuaries and saltmarshes, where it feeds mainly on worms and snails. Its colors can vary greatly, but like most terrapins, its underside is usually much more eye-catching than the top of its shell, often with orange or yellow streaks and patches of black. Diamondback terrapins nest above the high-tide mark. The females dig several nests, laying up to a dozen eggs in each one. The young terrapins are only about 1 in. (2.5cm) long when they hatch, and they mature slowly. They often do not breed until they are 10 years old.

SCIENTIFIC NAME *Malachlemys terrapin*

DISTRIBUTION Atlantic and Gulf coasts of the United States

SIZE Up to 9 in. (23cm) long

ALLIGATOR SNAPPING TURTLE

This giant turtle is the largest freshwater species and the most dangerous. It has a knobbly shell, a spiked neck, and a long tail. It lurks on the bottom of rivers and lakes with its mouth open wide, wiggling a pink, wormlike thread of skin at the end of its tongue. If a fish approaches to investigate, the turtle's massive jaws snap shut. Because the turtle stays so still, it uses very little oxygen, and it can stay under water for hours without surfacing to breathe. No one knows exactly how large these turtles can grow. One example, seen in 1948, probably weighed more than 500 lb. (225kg) and was said to be as large as a kitchen table.

SCIENTIFIC NAME *Macrochlemys temmincki*

DISTRIBUTION Mississippi River Basin

SIZE Up to 4 ft. (1.2m), including tail

SPUR-THIGHED TORTOISE

There are about 40 kinds of land tortoises; this medium-sized species is one of the few that lives in Europe. It got its name from the small spur on each of its front legs. Spur-thighed tortoises live in scrub and rocky places. They spend the morning and evening looking for plants to eat and rest during the hottest part of the day. The females lay two or three eggs each year, which take about three months to hatch. In the past, these tortoises were collected and sold as pets, but they are now protected by law.

SCIENTIFIC NAME *Testudo graeca*

DISTRIBUTION Southern Europe

SIZE Up to 12 in. (30cm) long

GALAPAGOS GIANT TORTOISE

Weighing up to 800 lb. (350kg), the Galapagos giant tortoise looks almost too heavy to move. It is one of only two species of giant tortoises in the world—the other lives on the remote Aldabra islands, north of Madagascar. Galapagos giant tortoises feed on cactus and other plants. The tortoises vary from one island to another, and some have extra-long necks that help them reach their food. These huge animals can live for more than 100 years, but they face an increasing struggle to survive. In the past, they were often used as food by sailors, and now only a few thousand are left.

SCIENTIFIC NAME *Geochelone elephantopus*

DISTRIBUTION Galapagos Islands

SIZE Up to 4 ft. (1.2m) long

Jaws have razor-sharp edges for slicing prey

ABOVE *Wiggling its tongue, an alligator snapping turtle lures a fish into its mouth. It swallows small fish whole; larger ones are often cut in two.*

BELOW *Tearing open their eggs, two baby spur-thighed tortoises begin life in the outside world. Like other tortoises and turtles, they look like miniature versions of their parents when they hatch, complete with tiny shells.*

Tortoise's shell hardens soon after hatching

BIRDS

APART FROM BATS, BIRDS ARE THE ONLY
ANIMALS WITH BACKBONES THAT CAN FLY.
THEY ARE THE UNRIVALED EXPERTS OF
FLIGHT, TRAVELING FARTHER AND FASTER
THAN ANY OTHER LIVING CREATURE.

Birds have several features that help them get off the ground. Hollow bones, slender legs, and a beak instead of heavy jaws and teeth all save weight, enabling flight. But their most important features are feathers and wings. Feathers are useful in a number of ways—they provide lift and make the birds' bodies streamlined so they can slip through the air, but they also help keep in body heat. There are about 9,000 species of birds. They all reproduce by laying hard-shelled eggs, and most of them look after their young.

FLIGHTLESS BIRDS

Over millions of years, some birds have gradually lost the ability to fly. These flightless birds include giant species, such as the ostrich and the emu, as well as kiwis and penguins. On land, flightless birds move by walking or running on their powerful legs. Penguins have short legs, so they cannot run fast, but they use their wings like flippers to speed through seawater.

LEFT *Male ostriches have black and white plumage, but the females are brown-gray.*

OSTRICH

The ostrich is the world's largest bird and the only one with two-toed feet. It lives on open plains, where its height gives it a good view of approaching predators. Ostriches can run at up to 45 mph (70 km/h), but if they are cornered, they kick out with their feet, using their claws as weapons. Ostrich eggs are the largest of any bird, measuring as much as 8 in. (20cm) long. Each female lays up to 12 eggs, with several females often laying in the same nest. When the eggs hatch, the male takes charge of the young and may gather several families of young together. Because they are easily tamed, ostriches are often kept in captivity. In the wild, they feed mainly on seeds and fruit, but captive birds will swallow almost anything.

SCIENTIFIC NAME	*Struthio camelus*
DISTRIBUTION	Africa
SIZE	Up to 9 ft. (2.7m) high

GREATER RHEA

Rheas are like small ostriches and live in the open plains of South America. There are two species, the greater and the lesser rhea (*Pterocnemia pennata*). Both have brown plumage and both live in flocks. Like ostriches, rheas use shared nests, with up to six females laying their eggs in the same hollow in the ground. Unusually for birds, the females take no part in incubating the eggs or looking after the young. The males do it all instead.

SCIENTIFIC NAME	*Rhea americana*
DISTRIBUTION	Southern South America
SIZE	Up to 5 ft. (1.5m) high

EMU

The emu is Australia's tallest bird. It has brown-gray plumage with a distinctive, pale blue throat. Emus feed on seeds and insects and can be serious pests on farmland. In the 1930s, a team of army machine-gunners tried to keep emu flocks out of the wheat-growing region of western Australia, but emus still managed to thrive. Emus lay dark green eggs. The male incubates them on his own, and the striped chicks hatch after about eight weeks.

SCIENTIFIC NAME	*Dromaius novaehollandiae*
DISTRIBUTION	Australia
SIZE	Up to 6 ft. (2m) high

COMMON CASSOWARY

Cassowaries are solitary birds that live in rain forests. They have black plumage, blue and red necks, and a large, bony shield called a casque on top of their heads. Cassowaries are more unpredictable and dangerous than other flightless birds. Instead of running away from people, they may attack with

LEFT *The cassowary's casque and coarse plumage protect it as it runs through dense undergrowth.*

their claws, sometimes fatally. Cassowaries lay their eggs on a bed of leaves on the forest floor. The male takes care of incubation, but both parents look after the chicks.

SCIENTIFIC NAME
Casuarius casuarius

DISTRIBUTION
New Guinea, northern Australia

SIZE Up to 6 ft. (2m) high

RIGHT *Magellanic penguins (Spheniscus magellanicus) lay their eggs in burrows and sleep under ground.*

BELOW *Emperor penguin chicks grow extremely quickly to enable them to survive in the Antarctic climate.*

ABOVE *At 12 in. high, the little penguin (Eudyptula minor) is the smallest penguin. It breeds on the coasts of Australia and New Zealand.*

BROWN KIWI

Kiwis live in New Zealand's forests, where they come out to feed after dark. They eat earthworms and other small animals, and unusually for birds, they sniff out their food using nostrils at the ends of their beaks. Their wings are tiny, but their hairlike plumage provides protection from the rain. Female kiwis often lay just one egg, which can be a fourth of the female's total weight.

A kiwi finds food mainly by smell

SCIENTIFIC NAME *Apteryx australis*

DISTRIBUTION New Zealand

SIZE Up to 20 in. (50cm) long

EMPEROR PENGUIN

The world's largest penguin, this is also one of the few that breeds on the Antarctic ice. The female lays one egg in late fall, then swims out to sea. The male protects the egg through the winter, warming it under a flap of skin on his feet. When the female returns in early spring, the chick has hatched, and the male urgently needs food. Emperor penguins can dive to a depth of 850 ft. (250m) to find fish and krill to eat.

SCIENTIFIC NAME
Aptenodytes forsteri

DISTRIBUTION Antarctica, Southern Ocean

SIZE Up to 4 ft. (1.2m) high

LOONS, GREBES, AND PETRELS

These birds spend most of their lives on or over water. Loons and grebes live mainly on lakes and rivers, where they catch fish below the surface. Their legs are set far back on their bodies, and their webbed feet work like propellers, helping them dive and swim. Petrels and their relatives live at sea. They also have webbed feet, but they snatch up food as they flutter or glide over the waves. Some of these birds stay close to shore. Others, such as albatrosses, wander across the oceans, returning to land only to breed. There are four species of loons and about 20 species of grebes. Petrels and their relatives make up a larger group of birds, containing more than 100 species.

RIGHT *The common loon's calls sound like ghostly howling or eerie laughter.*
BELOW *Like its relatives, the southern giant petrel has tubular nostrils and a well-developed sense of smell.*

Nostrils open near the end of the beak

COMMON LOON

The loon's loud cry is one of the most haunting sounds in the lonely northern lakes where it feeds and breeds. It has a long, sharp beak and handsome black and white breeding plumage. Loons are expert swimmers and fast fliers, but their legs are set so far back that they have difficulty moving on land. They spend the spring and summer on rivers and lakes, but after raising a pair of chicks, they usually head for the coast for the winter months.

SCIENTIFIC NAME *Gavia immer*

DISTRIBUTION Northern North America, Iceland, northwestern Europe

SIZE Up to 3 ft. (1m) long

GREAT CRESTED GREBE

During the breeding season, this grebe's feathery crest makes it one of the most elegant birds on the water. It shows off the crest during its courtship displays, then molts it once the breeding season is over. Grebes are not deep divers, but they are very agile. Their toes have individual webbing, and if danger threatens, they can sink like submarines until only the tops of their heads are visible above the water. Great crested grebes usually raise three or four chicks a year. The chicks often ride on their parents' backs, held underneath their wings, and they stay on board even during a dive.

SCIENTIFIC NAME *Podiceps cristatus*

DISTRIBUTION Europe, Asia, Africa, Australia, New Zealand

SIZE Up to 19 in. (48cm) long

PIED-BILLED GREBE

This small, pale brown grebe is named for the black ring around its beak, which appears just before the breeding season begins. Compared to the great crested grebe, it has a stocky body and a short neck. It feeds on freshwater insects and snails as well as fish. It builds its nest in typical grebe fashion, by heaping water plants into a soggy, floating pile.

SCIENTIFIC NAME *Podylimbus podiceps*

DISTRIBUTION North, Central, and South America, from Canada to Argentina

SIZE Up to 14 in. (35cm) long

SOUTHERN GIANT PETREL

The southern giant petrel is a scavenger, feeding on the shore as well as out at sea. It looks like a heavy brown seagull, with a powerful, hooked beak, which it uses to tear open dead animals and to carry off seabird chicks. Its nostrils form two tubes along the top of its beak, a feature all petrels and their relatives share. Giant petrels nest on the ground. If anything comes too close, they can defend themselves by spitting a foul-smelling oil.

SCIENTIFIC NAME *Macronectes giganteus*

DISTRIBUTION Southern oceans and coasts, as far south as Antarctica

SIZE Up to 3 ft. (1m) long

NORTHERN FULMAR
Holding out its wings stiffly from its sides, the fulmar rides the wind over rocks and waves, soaring and swooping with amazing agility. This gray and white bird nests on cliffs, where it lays its eggs on rocky ledges. The adults feed their chicks on regurgitated, half-digested food. They often follow fishing-boats to eat waste thrown overboard, and the species has become common because modern boats produce a lot of waste.

SCIENTIFIC NAME *Fulmarus glacialis*

DISTRIBUTION Northern Pacific Ocean, northern Atlantic Ocean

SIZE Up to 19 in. (48cm) long

SHORT-TAILED SHEARWATER
Shearwaters roam the open oceans, skimming over the waves as they search for food. They are common all over the world, but they often go unnoticed—partly because they come ashore only at night. They nest in burrows on rocky islands, laying just one egg each time they breed. Shearwaters are great travelers, and the short-tailed shearwater flies farther than any other bird on its annual migration. It breeds on islands near Tasmania, and each year the adults fly a figure-eight loop around the whole Pacific Ocean— a distance of about 20,000 mi. (32,000km).

SCIENTIFIC NAME *Puffinus tenuirostris*

DISTRIBUTION Pacific Ocean

SIZE Up to 17 in. (43cm) long

WANDERING ALBATROSS
This giant seabird has the largest wingspan of any flying animal—up to 12 ft. (3.6m). Its wings are long and narrow, and it uses them to glide on storm-force winds in the southern oceans, snatching jellyfish and other animals from the waves. Its flight is so efficient that it rarely has to beat its wings. Wandering albatrosses nest on remote islands, laying a single egg each time they breed. Their eggs are the

largest of any seabird and take more than 80 days to hatch. This is the longest incubation period of any bird. Wandering albatrosses take a long time to mature and are almost a year old before they are ready to fly.

SCIENTIFIC NAME *Diomedea exulans*

DISTRIBUTION Southern Ocean

SIZE Up to 4.5 ft. (1.4m) long

Northern fulmar in flight

ABOVE *The northern fulmar is often mistaken for a seagull, but its tubular nostrils show that it belongs to the petrel family.*
BELOW *The wandering albatross glides on air that rises from the waves.*

COURTSHIP
Before animals mate, they have to make sure they have found the right partner. Many birds do this by carrying out courtship displays, which are like dances with precise movements. The great crested grebe's displays are among the most complicated in the bird world. During one of the dances, the two partners paddle toward each other until they are almost touching, then shake their heads from side to side. In another dance, called the weed ceremony, they suddenly dive down to the lake bed and surface with weeds in their beaks. Paddling furiously, they tread water, with their bodies and necks bolt upright. Displays like these enable both partners to show that they are healthy and that they belong to the same species. They also help them get used to each other—an important step if they are to raise a family together.

ABOVE *These great crested grebes are in the middle of a courtship dance, while a rival male looks on from the right.*

PELICANS AND THEIR RELATIVES

Pelicans are famous for their enormous beaks, but they also have another unusual feature—unlike most waterbirds, they have webs of skin connecting all four of their toes. This is also true of cormorants, gannets, and frigatebirds, which are among the pelican's closest relatives. All these birds feed on fish, and most of them live at sea. They are all strong fliers, but many find it difficult to move around on land. There are about 60 species in this group of birds. Some are found all over the world, but tropicbirds and frigatebirds are found only where it is warm.

RIGHT *Friendly with each other, Northern gannet pairs are aggressive toward their neighbors.*

Pouch for catching fish hangs beneath huge beak

LEFT *While one white pelican feeds, the other rests with its closed beak propped on its chest.*

ABOVE *Brown pelicans always fish close to the coast. They often follow fishing boats into port in the hope of catching scraps.*

ABOVE *A blue-footed booby watches over its eggs. These birds lay their eggs on bare rock and keep them warm with their feet.*

GREAT WHITE PELICAN

This pelican has a wingspan of up to 10 ft. (3m), making it one of the world's largest freshwater birds. It is a powerful and skillful flier, but it is even more impressive when it sets out to catch a meal. Great white pelicans live and feed in flocks. They form circles around schools of fish and drive them together to make them easier to catch. Each pelican lunges after its food, filling its pouch with up to 4 gallons (15 liters) of water. Once the water has drained from its beak, the pelican swallows its prey.

SCIENTIFIC NAME	*Pelecanus onocrotalus*
DISTRIBUTION	Southern Europe, Africa, Asia
SIZE	Up to 6 ft. (2m) long

BROWN PELICAN

Instead of scooping the water for food, brown pelicans act more like low-level dive-bombers. They cruise along in long lines close to the shore, watching for fish below. If they spot a school, the lead bird swoops up and then dives, and all the others follow suit. Within seconds, the pelicans are bobbing back up to the surface of the sea, usually with fish in their pouches. Brown pelicans nest on rocky ground or in low trees, and they lay two or three eggs.

SCIENTIFIC NAME	*Pelecanus occidentalis*
DISTRIBUTION	Pacific and Atlantic coasts of North, Central, and South America
SIZE	Up to 4.25 ft. (1.3m) long

NORTHERN GANNET

Gannets and boobies are the bird world's record high-divers. They dive at fish from a height of 100 ft. (30m) or more, folding back their narrow wings just before they slice through the surface of the sea. A streamlined shape, strong skull, and air pockets under the skin, allows them to hit the water at great speed. Northern gannets nest on rocky islands in the northern Atlantic Ocean. Young birds are speckled brown, but after four or five years, they develop their adult plumage, with white bodies and black wing tips.

SCIENTIFIC NAME	*Sula bassana*
DISTRIBUTION	Northern Atlantic Ocean
SIZE	Up to 3 ft. (1m) long

BLUE-FOOTED BOOBY

This close relative of the northern gannet has a gray beak, brown wings, and bright blue, webbed feet. Like the gannet, it catches fish by plunge-diving, though the booby often dives at a more gentle angle. Its close-set eyes enable it to look directly ahead as it drops toward the water. Blue-footed boobies are experts at catching flyingfish (page 122) disturbed by boats.

SCIENTIFIC NAME	*Sula nebouxii*
DISTRIBUTION	Pacific coast of Central and South America, Galapagos Islands
SIZE	Up to 33 in. (84cm) long

RED-BILLED TROPICBIRD

Tropicbirds often wander far out to sea, soaring and flapping their way across hundreds of miles of open water. They usually hover for a few seconds before diving into the water for fish and squid to eat. There are three species of these birds, all of which are mainly white, with two long tail feathers that look like streamers.

The red-billed tropicbird is the largest of the three. It nests on rocky coasts and remote islands and raises a single chick each year.

SCIENTIFIC NAME *Phaethon aethereus*

DISTRIBUTION Tropical eastern Pacific and Atlantic Oceans, Arabian Sea, Persian Gulf

SIZE Up to 3.5 ft. (1.1m) long, including tail

AMERICAN DARTER, ANHINGA, OR SNAKE-BIRD

Darters are sleek relatives of cormorants that live in lakes and swamps. They often swim with most of their bodies submerged, leaving just their heads and necks above the surface. Their beaks are straight and sharp—unlike the cormorant's, which is hooked—and they use them to impale fish under water. Once a darter has made a catch, it surfaces, flicks its prey into the air, and swallows it headfirst. Darters nest in trees, and their young can swim before they can fly.

SCIENTIFIC NAME *Anhinga anhinga*

DISTRIBUTION Southeastern United States, Central America, tropical South America

SIZE Up to 3 ft. (1m) long

GREAT CORMORANT

Cormorants are fish-eating birds that chase their prey under water. They propel themselves mainly with their feet and can dive for more than a minute, reaching a depth of about 33 ft. (10m). Unlike most waterbirds, cormorants' feathers are not completely waterproof, so they hold their wings out to dry when they return to land. There are about 30 species of cormorants, and the great cormorant is by far the most widespread. It lives in lakes and estuaries as well as on coasts, building its nest on cliffs or in trees. Apart from its white throat, it is almost entirely black.

SCIENTIFIC NAME
Phalacrocorax carbo

DISTRIBUTION Freshwater and seacoasts worldwide, except South America

SIZE Up to 3 ft. (1m) long

RIGHT *The great cormorant spends much of its time perched at the water's edge.*

MAGNIFICENT FRIGATEBIRD

Frigatebirds' wingspans can exceed 6 ft. (2m), but their skeletons can weigh as little as 4 oz. (115g)—less than the weight of their feathers. This amazing combination of size and lightness enables them to soar effortlessly over the ocean, where they keep a watchful eye on other birds. If a frigatebird sees another bird catching a fish, it immediately sets off in pursuit. It snaps at the bird until it drops its catch, then deftly catches the food before it hits the water. Frigatebirds nest in trees and shrubs. The males attract females by inflating throat pouches that look like red balloons. They rarely land on water.

SCIENTIFIC NAME
Fregata magnificens

DISTRIBUTION Tropical eastern Pacific and Atlantic Oceans

SIZE Up to 3.5 ft. (1.1m) long

BELOW *Perched in a bush, a male magnificent frigatebird inflates his throat to attract a mate. Frigatebirds nest in groups, using twigs to make platform-shaped nests.*

Great cormorant holding out its wings to dry

HERONS AND THEIR RELATIVES

These birds all share two eye-catching features—long legs and equally long necks. Most of them feed by wading into shallow water, where they either watch for fish or use their beaks to feel for small animals such as mollusks and crabs. Flamingos strain their food from the water, using bent beaks that work like strainers. Storks look as if they should wade too, but they rarely feed in water. Instead, most of them stride across open ground, catching small animals, including insects and frogs. There are about 120 species of herons and their relatives all over the world. Where wetlands have been drained, many of these birds have become rare.

GRAY HERON

This is the largest heron in Europe, with a wingspan of up to 5.5 ft. (1.7m). It catches fish by stealth, wading into the shallows and then waiting for its prey to swim within reach. When a fish comes close enough, the heron flicks out its neck and impales the fish on the end of its long, pointed beak. Like other herons, this bird folds its neck into an S shape when it flies and rests. It nests in groups, usually high in trees. Males and females greet each other by making loud, clattering sounds with their bills.

SCIENTIFIC NAME *Ardea cinerea*

DISTRIBUTION Europe, Africa, Asia

SIZE Up to 4.25 ft. (1.3m) long

BLACK-CROWNED NIGHT-HERON

When most birds are settling down for the night, this small heron comes out to feed. Compared to some of its relatives, it looks short and squat, but it is just as effective at finding food. Night-herons patrol the water's edge, watching for fish and other small animals. They nest in trees and bushes, making flimsy platforms out of sticks.

SCIENTIFIC NAME *Nycticorax nycticorax*

DISTRIBUTION Worldwide, but absent from cool regions of Northern Hemisphere and Australia

SIZE Up to 25 in. (63cm) long

EURASIAN BITTERN

Bitterns live in reedbeds, where their brown plumage blends in against the dead reed stalks. When threatened, they stretch out their necks and sway like reeds blowing in the wind. In the breeding season, male Eurasian bitterns make booming calls that sound like someone blowing across an empty bottle. They can be heard up to 3 mi. (5km) away.

SCIENTIFIC NAME *Botaurus stellaris*

DISTRIBUTION Europe, parts of central Asia and Africa

SIZE Up to 31.5 in. (80cm) long

RIGHT The blue heron stands motionless in shallow water, waiting for prey to approach.

BELOW AND RIGHT
The Eurasian bittern is a secretive bird that feeds mainly on frogs and fish. Although it flies well, it spends most of its time creeping through its marshy reedbed home. During the last 100 years, many reedbeds have been drained and turned into farmland, so this bird is less common than it once was.

S-shaped curve of neck

ABOVE
Balancing on one leg, a gray heron stretches its wings.
RIGHT *The black-crowned night-heron has strong toes and is a good climber. It often perches on overhanging branches to watch for fish or frogs.*

Gray wings with black flight feathers

Brown plumage matches the stems of dead reeds

RIGHT
With its legs sticking out behind it, a greater flamingo sits on its nest.
BELOW *The white stork has bright red legs and a red, dagger-shaped beak.*

ABOVE *Young scarlet ibises are gray with white undersides. Their scarlet plumage develops when they are old enough to breed.*

WHITE STORK

This large, migratory bird is sometimes thought of as a symbol of good luck. In northern Europe, it often nests on rooftops. It feeds in fields and open places, where the ground is damp and full of animal life. Changing farming methods have made this kind of ground harder to find, so white storks are not as common as they once were. In the fall, European white storks fly south to Africa. They return in spring, often to the same nest they left six months earlier.

SCIENTIFIC NAME *Ciconia ciconia*

DISTRIBUTION Breeds in Europe, northern Asia; migrates to Africa, southern Asia in the winter

SIZE Up to 3 ft. (1m) long

MARABOU STORK

This huge, bald-headed bird is a stork that behaves like a vulture. It has larger wings than almost any other land bird, and it soars over the African plains looking for dead remains and edible waste. It is majestic in the air, but on the ground, its hunched body, pink head, and fleshy pouch give it an ugly look. The pouch hangs from its neck and is probably used in courtship.

SCIENTIFIC NAME *Leptoptilos crumeniferus*

DISTRIBUTION Africa

SIZE Up to 5 ft. (1.5m) long

SCARLET IBIS

This bird has one of nature's most breathtaking color schemes—an intense, all-over scarlet. It lives along muddy coasts and in mangrove swamps, and feeds and nests in groups. Scarlet ibises eat small mollusks and crustaceans, feeling for them in the mud with their curved beaks.

SCIENTIFIC NAME *Eudocimus ruber*

DISTRIBUTION Northeastern coast of South America

SIZE Up to 24 in. (61cm) long

WHITE SPOONBILL

It is easy to see how this bird got its name. Its beak has a rounded tip, making it look like a spoon. As it wades through lakes or lagoons, the spoonbill dips its beak beneath the surface of the water and sweeps its head from side to side. Its sensitive beak snaps shut instantly if it touches anything that might be food.

SCIENTIFIC NAME *Platalea leucorodia*

DISTRIBUTION Southern Europe, Asia, northern and western Africa

SIZE Up to 3 ft. (1m) long

GREATER FLAMINGO

Flamingos are the only birds that filter-feed, a method of eating also used by many whales (page 26). Flamingos dip their beaks in the water and collect tiny plants and animals by pumping water through slits on their beaks and tongues. There are five species of flamingos, and this is the most common. It feeds in shallow lakes, sometimes in flocks of more than a million.

SCIENTIFIC NAME *Phoenicopterus ruber*

DISTRIBUTION Southern Europe, Africa, southern Asia, Central America, Caribbean islands

SIZE Up to 5 ft. (1.5m) long

SWANS, GEESE, AND DUCKS

Swans, geese, and ducks are also known as waterfowl because they spend their lives on or near water. They have flat, shovel-shaped beaks, and most of them get their food either from the water itself or from underwater mud. Geese are exceptions to this rule—they feed on land, pulling up grass and other plants with their beaks.

Waterfowl have webbed feet and waterproof feathers. Most nest on the ground, and their chicks can swim only a few hours after hatching. There are more than 150 species of these birds. Ducks are found all over the world, but most geese live in the Northern Hemisphere and breed in the Arctic.

BLACK SWAN

This Australian bird is the world's only all-black swan, although it does have white wing tips. It lives on large, shallow lakes and mudflats and is highly sociable, often gathering in flocks thousands strong. Black swans nest near the water's edge or on small islands. The parent birds are careful to nest just beyond pecking distance of their neighbors. Black swans were introduced into New Zealand in the 1860s, where they are now widespread.

SCIENTIFIC NAME *Cygnus atratus*

DISTRIBUTION Australia; introduced into New Zealand

SIZE Up to 4.5 ft. (1.4m) long

Red beak with pale tip

Long, muscular neck

Flight feathers have curled edges

White wing tips

MUTE SWAN

This elegant, all-white bird originally comes from the lakes of central Asia, but it is now common on parkland lakes all over the world. It uses its long neck to reach water plants, mollusks, and other bottom-living animals, often tipping up on end as it feeds. Its young, called cygnets, are gray-brown when they hatch. It takes them nearly a year to turn white. Mute swans fly well, but they need a long running start to take off. They usually come in to land on water, using their large, black feet as brakes.

SCIENTIFIC NAME *Cygnus olor*

DISTRIBUTION Europe, central Asia; semitame birds also in North America, Australia, New Zealand

SIZE Up to 5.25 ft. (1.6m) long

SNOW GOOSE

These geese breed in the Arctic tundra of North America. They fly up from the south each spring, and their young hatch when the days are getting longer and the food supply is at its best. Even in late spring, the tundra can be very cold, so the geese line their nests with feathers to keep their eggs warm. Snow geese have two different color variations. Many are white all over, apart from their black wing tips, but some are blue-gray.

SCIENTIFIC NAME *Anser caerulescens*

DISTRIBUTION Breeds in North American Arctic; migrates to southeastern and southwestern United States, northern Mexico in the winter

SIZE Up to 33 in. (84cm) long

FAR LEFT *Black swans are nomadic birds. They are constantly on the move, searching for good places to feed.*
LEFT *Mute swans are often seen in pairs, but will gather in flocks in the winter.*
BELOW LEFT *Snow geese may fly 3,000 mi. to breed.*
BELOW RIGHT *In parts of Europe, Canada geese are common parkland birds.*

CANADA GOOSE

This handsome goose has a brown and white body and a black head, with a white "chinstrap" on its throat. It breeds near lakes and in wetlands throughout Canada and the northern United States, and its size varies according to where it lives. The largest geese, from the American Great Plains, can be seven times heavier than those from Alaska—a record difference for the same species of bird. In the early evening, Canada geese usually return to water to roost. They make a loud, honking noise as they fly.

SCIENTIFIC NAME *Branta canadensis*

DISTRIBUTION North America; introduced into northern Europe, New Zealand

SIZE Up to 3.5 ft. (1.1m) long

GREYLAG GOOSE

Greylags breed near water across Europe and central Asia, flying as far south as India and China for the winter. They have gray-brown bodies with pink legs and feet, and heavy beaks that are good for pulling up grass and water weeds. They are the ancestors of most farmyard geese.

SCIENTIFIC NAME *Anser anser*

DISTRIBUTION Breeds from Iceland eastward to China; migrates to Great Britain, southern Europe, southern Asia in the winter

SIZE Up to 3 ft. (1m) long

MIGRATION

Every year, millions of geese travel north to the Arctic to breed. They fly in a V-formation, and they make their long journey for one reason—food. In warm parts of the world, the days are about the same length all year round, and the food supply depends mainly on how much rain there is. Farther north and south, the days are much longer in the summer than they are in the winter. In winter it is dark and cold, but in summer, long days mean that plants can grow rapidly, producing plenty of food for animals to eat. For geese and many other birds, this huge but short-lived surge of food makes it worth traveling a long way. Animal travelers are called migrants. Migratory species include whales, antelope, turtles, butterflies, and fish, but birds migrate farthest— up to 20,000 mi. (32,000km) a year.

ABOVE When they migrate, greylags and other geese often fly in a V-shaped formation. This saves energy because each bird is helped along by air currents produced by the one in front. The geese take turns to lead.

The horny crest helps males attract females

LEFT The magpie goose is one of the world's most primitive waterfowl. It is easy to tell the males from the females because the males have a high, bony crown on the top of their heads.

MAGPIE GOOSE OR PIED GOOSE

The black and white magpie goose is unusual in several ways. It has much longer legs than most geese, and its feet are only slightly webbed. It is also the only waterfowl species that feeds its young—the others simply lead their chicks to food. Magpie geese live in large flocks close to rivers, in swamps, and in grassland. They feed on land and in water, and although they live in open places, they are good at perching in trees.

SCIENTIFIC NAME *Anseranas semipalmata*

DISTRIBUTION Australia, New Guinea

SIZE Up to 33.5 in. (85cm) long

Soft down feathers are hidden beneath outer plumage

Feathers are kept waterproof by a special oil

Male mallard in breeding plumage

ABOVE AND RIGHT *Like all ducks, mallards spend a lot of time making sure that their feathers are clean and waterproof.*

Female mallard with wings spread

MALLARD

The mallard is one of the world's most widespread ducks. It lives on almost any patch of fresh water, from the fringes of the Arctic to suburban lakes and ponds. To feed, it either "dabbles" at the surface or tips up on end to reach food on the bottom. Like most ducks, the males and females look quite different. During the breeding season, the males have bright green heads and curly tails. Females are brown all year round, providing camouflage when they nest.

SCIENTIFIC NAME *Anas platyrhynchos*

DISTRIBUTION Throughout the Northern Hemisphere; introduced into Australia, New Zealand

SIZE Up to 25.5 in. (65cm) long

MANDARIN

During the breeding season, the male mandarin has a bright red beak, orange "whiskers," and two orange wing feathers that stick up like a pair of sails. Mandarins come from forested rivers and lakes in the Far East, and they nest in holes in trees. Within a day of hatching, the ducklings leave the nest to follow their mother to water. They cannot fly, but they are light and covered with soft down, so the jump is not as dangerous as it sounds.

SCIENTIFIC NAME *Aix galericulata*

DISTRIBUTION Russian Far East, China, Japan; introduced into the British Isles

SIZE Up to 20 in. (50cm) long

Male

Female

Male

Female

Male

Female

ABOVE TOP *Northern shovelers often swim in circles to stir up food.*
ABOVE CENTER *In the winter, pintails will feed in fields of harvested corn.*
ABOVE *Tufted ducks have a distinctive backswept crest on their heads.*

NORTHERN SHOVELER

Shovelers are easy to recognize from their oversized, shiny black beaks. They use them to strain tiny plants and animals from the surface of lakes and ponds. Unlike other freshwater ducks, they rarely tip up on end. There are four species of shovelers—in addition to this species, there is one in South America, one in South Africa, and another in Australia. The northern shoveler is the most widespread, and it migrates as much as 3,700 mi. (6,000km) to breed.

SCIENTIFIC NAME *Anas clypeata*

DISTRIBUTION Breeds in northern North America, Europe, Asia; migrates to United States coast, Central America, southern Europe, Africa, southern Asia, Japan in the winter

SIZE Up to 20 in. (50cm) long

PINTAIL

In its breeding plumage, the male pintail is one of the most elegant freshwater ducks, with a chocolate-brown head, gray and white body, and long, pointed tail. Pintails breed near rivers and on marshy ground, where they feed by dabbling on the water's surface and by up-ending. Like most ducks, they are good fliers. They can take off almost vertically when alarmed and speed through the air on powerful, fast-beating wings.

SCIENTIFIC NAME *Anas acuta*

DISTRIBUTION Breeds in northern North America, Europe, Asia; migrates to southern United States, Central America, southern Europe, Africa, southern Asia, Japan in the winter

SIZE Up to 23 in. (58cm) long

TUFTED DUCK

This black and white duck lives on lakes, but instead of feeding from the surface of the water, it dives for food. It disappears completely with a splash, then bobs back to the surface with water plants and small animals, such as mollusks and insects, that it has collected from the bottom. Adult tufted ducks usually feed in water up to 6 ft. (2m) deep. The ducklings can also dive for food within a few hours of leaving the nest.

SCIENTIFIC NAME *Aythya fuligula*

DISTRIBUTION Breeds in northern Europe, northern Asia; migrates to southern and western Europe, Africa, southern Asia in the winter

SIZE Up to 18.5 in. (47cm) long

RED-BREASTED MERGANSER

Mergansers are called saw-billed ducks because their beaks have serrated edges for gripping slippery fish. They live on fresh water and on the coast, and they dive after their prey, bringing it to the surface to eat it. Compared to other ducks, they have long, slender bodies and untidy, backswept crests. Red-breasted mergansers lay up to 12 eggs in a nest hidden among plants. The female covers her eggs with feathers when she leaves the nest to feed.

SCIENTIFIC NAME *Mergus serrator*

DISTRIBUTION Breeds in northern North America, Europe, Asia; migrates to coasts in North America, southern Europe, Far East in the winter

SIZE Up to 23 in. (58cm) long

COMMON EIDER

Eiders live on rocky coasts, where they feed on crabs and other small animals. They have stocky bodies, powerful, sloping beaks, and some of the warmest plumage in the world. Eiders need good insulation because they breed farther north than any other birds. They nest on the ground, and they keep their eggs warm by lining their nests with down. Before synthetic fibers were invented, eider down was used to stuff pillows and bedding. Small amounts are still collected today.

SCIENTIFIC NAME *Somateria mollissima*

DISTRIBUTION Breeds on northern coasts, including edges of Arctic Sea; migrates to coasts in North America, Iceland, northern Europe in the winter

SIZE Up to 28 in. (71cm) long

FALKLAND ISLANDS STEAMER DUCK

There are four species of steamer ducks, all living on the cold coasts around the tip of South America. Like most steamer ducks, the Falkland Islands steamer duck has difficulty flying. To escape danger, it usually paddles away instead. The duck dives in beds of seaweed to find small animals and water plants to eat.

SCIENTIFIC NAME *Tachyeres brachypterus*

DISTRIBUTION Falkland Islands

SIZE Up to 29 in. (73cm) long

Female
Male
Female
Male

TOP *Red-breasted mergansers are very good at catching fish, which makes them unpopular with anglers.*

ABOVE *The common eider duck has a distinctive profile, with a flat forehead that merges with its beak.*

BELOW *The Falkland Islands steamer duck nests in tussock grass on coasts and lagoons near the shore. It is very territorial and chases away any other ducks that come too close.*

Close-fitting feathers are fully waterproof

Wings are small compared to body

BIRDS OF PREY

Birds of prey hunt other animals, particularly those that take speed and strength to overpower. They catch their prey with their feet, which are armed with needle-sharp claws called talons. Once they have made a kill, they use their hooked beaks to tear their food into pieces small enough to swallow. Unlike owls (page 200), which hunt after dark, birds of prey are active during the day. Most swoop down to snatch their victims on the ground, although some can catch animals in midair. There are about 280 species of birds of prey worldwide. They include eagles, hawks, kites, falcons, and vultures, which feed on dead remains.

Powerful neck muscles for tearing up prey

Sharp talons for gripping and piercing

Good forward vision helps with judging distances

Sharply hooked beak tip

ABOVE AND RIGHT
Like all birds of prey, the golden eagle has superb eyesight. Its hooked beak looks dangerous, but comes into play only once it has made a kill. Its real weapons are its talons.

GOLDEN EAGLE

An inhabitant of wild, mountainous country, the golden eagle preys on rabbits, marmots, and other mammals, as well as on other birds. It often makes a fast, low-level attack, catching its prey from behind. Golden eagles nest on crags or in trees, making a large platform out of sticks. They lay two eggs a year and often use the nest for many years in succession, adding more nesting material each time they breed. Though people have always admired the golden eagle's power, its reputation for attacking lambs and gamebirds has led to its persecution. As a result, and because its eggs are sometimes stolen from nests by collectors, this magnificent bird of prey is now quite rare.

SCIENTIFIC NAME *Aquila chrysaetos*

DISTRIBUTION Europe, northern Asia, Middle East, North America

SIZE Up to 3 ft. (1m) long

Head feathers are gold in color, and body plumage is brown

MARTIAL EAGLE

This powerful bird is Africa's largest eagle. It attacks a wide range of animals, including hyraxes and snakes, usually by diving on them from high in the air. Like many birds of prey, male and female martial eagles differ in size, with the females being larger than their mates. Martial eagles nest high up in trees and often use the same nest for many years.

SCIENTIFIC NAME *Polemaetus bellicosus*

DISTRIBUTION Africa, south of the Sahara Desert

SIZE Up to 3 ft. (1m) long

WEDGE-TAILED EAGLE

The wedge-tailed eagle lives in a wide range of habitats, from open plains to dense forest. With a wingspan of over 8 ft. (2.4m), it can catch animals as large as young kangaroos, launching its attack either from the air or from a perch high up in a tree. Before rabbits were introduced to Australia, wedge-tailed eagles there ate mostly marsupials, but they now eat rabbits as well. They also gather around dead sheep and other animal remains.

SCIENTIFIC NAME *Aquila audax*

DISTRIBUTION Australia, Tasmania, New Guinea

SIZE Up to 3 ft. (1m) long

AMERICAN HARPY EAGLE

Harpy eagles live in tropical forests. Their short, broad wings make them slow but highly maneuverable. Harpy eagles fly over the forest canopy, snatching prey from the treetops. They eat monkeys and lizards, but they specialize in attacking sloths. Female harpy eagles, which are larger than the males, can lift animals weighing 12 lb. (5.5kg)—about the same as their own body weight. Deforestation has had a severe effect on these birds, and particularly in Central America, they are now extremely rare.

SCIENTIFIC NAME *Harpia harpyja*

DISTRIBUTION Central America, tropical South America

SIZE Up to 3.5 ft. (1.1m) long

PHILIPPINE EAGLE

The Philippine eagle is one of the world's most endangered birds of prey, with perhaps as few as 150 birds left in the wild. Like the American harpy eagle, it lives in dense forest and has been brought to the edge of extinction by the rapid

RIGHT *Like other large birds of prey, the Philippine eagle needs access to large areas of undisturbed forest to survive. If deforestation continues, its future looks bleak.*

Strong beak can tear large animals apart

BELOW *With its talons at the ready, an American harpy eagle swoops through the trees to catch a monkey. Harpy eagles build their nests at the top of rain forest trees, so their chicks start life up to 225 ft. above the ground.*

ABOVE *The bald eagle takes five years to develop its black and white adult plumage. It does not always hunt live prey; dead or dying animals, especially salmon, make up a large part of its diet.*

clearance of its forest home. The Philippine eagle attacks monkeys, squirrels, pigs, and flying lemurs, or colugos. It searches for food either by flying above the trees or by perching beneath the treetops, where it silently watches, waiting for any animals to come within reach.

SCIENTIFIC NAME *Pithecophaga jefferyi*

DISTRIBUTION The Philippines

SIZE Up to 3 ft. (1m) long

BALD EAGLE

The bald eagle is the national bird of the United States of America. It is also one of the world's largest birds of prey. It lives near rivers, lakes, and coasts and feeds mainly on fish, though it also eats other birds. There were once about 50,000 bald eagles in North America, but by the 1970s, the numbers had dropped to 2,000 due to poisoning from the pesticide DDT. DDT has now been banned, and the eagles are making a gradual recovery.

SCIENTIFIC NAME *Haliaeetus leucocephalus*

DISTRIBUTION North America

SIZE Up to 3.5 ft. (1.1m) long

AFRICAN FISH EAGLE

With its white head and chest and its loud yelping call, this eagle is a distinctive bird of prey. It perches on waterside trees, watching the water for signs of food. If it sees a fish, it glides down and snatches up the prey with one foot before returning to its perch to eat.

SCIENTIFIC NAME *Haliaeetus vocifer*

DISTRIBUTION Africa, south of the Sahara Desert

SIZE Up to 30 in. (76cm) long

Flight feathers splay out like fingers

Powerful, feathered legs

ABOVE *With its wings spread wide, this black kite shows the long outer flight feathers that help it soar.*

BELOW *The red-tailed hawk is closely related to the Eurasian buzzard and has the same powerful build.*

EURASIAN BUZZARD

Over large parts of Europe and Asia, the buzzard can often be seen soaring high in the air. Even when it is far away, its high-pitched, mewing cry is easy to hear. It feeds on a wide range of live animals, from rabbits to earthworms, and will also eat dead remains. At the start of the breeding season, in early spring, buzzards perform spectacular courtship displays. The male and female pass sticks to each other in midair and sometimes lock their feet together and tumble toward the ground. The turkey vulture (page 178) is sometimes called a buzzard, but it is not a close relative of the Eurasian buzzard.

SCIENTIFIC NAME	*Buteo buteo*
DISTRIBUTION	Asia, parts of Africa
SIZE	Up to 21.5 in. (54cm) long

Streamlined head helps the hawk glide smoothly

Only the male has gray wing feathers

ABOVE *Northern harriers have slender bodies and legs. Unlike most birds of prey, harriers glide with their wings held up in a V shape.*

RED-TAILED HAWK

This heavily-built bird of prey is the most common hawk in North America. It is also one of the most variable, with more than 12 local varieties, each different in size and color. Red-tailed hawks live in woods, open plains, and deserts. They feed mainly on rodents. In Canada, red-tailed hawks are summer visitors, but in most of the United States, they stay all year round.

SCIENTIFIC NAME	*Buteo jamaicensis*
DISTRIBUTION	North and Central America, Caribbean islands
SIZE	Up to 25 in. (63cm) long

BLACK KITE

An efficient hunter and scavenger, the black kite is one of the world's most widespread birds of prey. It is also the one that is least afraid of people. In Asia, it often lives in towns and cities, where it swoops down to snatch up scraps of food, even where there is busy traffic. The black kite also follows bush fires, looking for animals flushed out by the smoke and flames. Like other kites, it has a forked tail, which it uses like a rudder to help it dodge any obstacles in its path.

SCIENTIFIC NAME	*Milvus migrans*
DISTRIBUTION	Central and southern Europe, Africa, Asia, Australia
SIZE	Up to 23.5 in. (60cm) long

SNAIL KITE OR EVERGLADE KITE

This remarkable bird feeds entirely on freshwater snails. It has an unusually long and slender beak that is ideal for prying the snails from their shells. It finds its food by flapping along low over marshes and reedbeds. When it locates a snail, it picks it up with one foot, then carries it to a perch to feed.

SCIENTIFIC NAME	*Rostrhamnus sociabilis*
DISTRIBUTION	Florida, Caribbean islands, Central America, tropical South America
SIZE	Up to 17 in. (43cm) long

NORTHERN HARRIER OR MARSH HAWK

Harriers hunt by flying low over the ground, flapping and gliding back and forth across the same stretch of country. If they spot food—a mouse or a young bird, for example—they drop to the ground and snatch it up with their feet. Unusually for birds of prey, harriers nest on the ground, and both parents feed the nestlings until they are ready to fly. Female northern harriers are brown, but the slightly smaller males are light gray.

SCIENTIFIC NAME	*Circus cyaneus*
DISTRIBUTION	North and South America, Europe, northern Asia; migratory in north of range
SIZE	Up to 23 in. (58cm) long

RIGHT *A male common kestrel clutches a mouse in its talons.*

A peregrine falcon diving with its wings folded down at its sides

Small beak with narrow hook

Prey is held tight in strong talons

Narrow wing tips

PEREGRINE FALCON

The peregrine falcon is the world's fastest bird. It dives on other birds in midair, reaching speeds of more than 100 mph (160km/h) as it plummets toward its prey. It can knock a pigeon from the air with a single slash of its talons. Like other falcons, the peregrine has a slender body, a long, narrow tail, and pointed wings. It usually breeds on mountains or cliffs, but some live in cities, nesting on window ledges.

SCIENTIFIC NAME *Falco peregrinus*

DISTRIBUTION Worldwide, except Greenland, Central and South America

SIZE Up to 19 in. (48cm) long

GYRFALCON

There are about 50 species of falcons, and this Arctic species is the largest of them all. Females can weigh more than 4 lb. (2kg)—twice as much as many of the males. Gyrfalcons live in and near the Arctic, where they feed on ptarmigans, ducks, and other birds. They also prey on hares and rodents, speeding close to the ground to make a kill. Some gyrfalcons have gray plumage, but others are largely white—a useful feature in a snow-covered landscape.

SCIENTIFIC NAME *Falco rusticolus*

DISTRIBUTION Breeds north of the Arctic Circle; migrates farther south in the winter

SIZE Up to 25 in. (63cm) long

COMMON KESTREL

Kestrels are small falcons that eat rodents and insects. They have superb eyesight and hover over open ground watching for food, with their tails splayed out and their wings beating rapidly. Kestrels are the largest birds that can hover for long periods. Unlike hummingbirds (pages 204-205), they need a gentle headwind to keep them in the air. Common kestrels may take over other birds' nests. They lay up to five eggs a year in one clutch, and the nestlings can fly a month after hatching.

SCIENTIFIC NAME *Falco tinnunculus*

DISTRIBUTION Most of Europe, Asia, Africa; migratory in north of range

SIZE Up to 14 in. (35cm) long

TURKEY VULTURE

Vultures are birds of prey that feed on dead remains instead of catching live animals. They have extremely good eyesight, and they watch for food from the air, soaring high in the sky. The turkey vulture, often mistakenly called a buzzard, is the most widespread vulture in the Americas. It lives in a variety of habitats and can often be seen over roads, where it watches for animals that have been hit by cars. Like other vultures, it has a bald head, an adaptation that helps it stay clean when it feeds. Adult turkey vultures have bright red heads, which contrast with their dark brown plumage.

SCIENTIFIC NAME *Cathartes aura*

DISTRIBUTION North, Central, and South America, from Canada to Tierra del Fuego

SIZE Up to 31.5 in. (80cm) long

Bald head avoids feathers becoming matted with blood

ANDEAN CONDOR

The Andean condor is the largest vulture in the world. Its wings can measure up to 10.5 ft. (3.2m) from tip to tip, a size equaled by only one other land bird, the marabou stork (page 169). Its head and neck are bald, but it has a white, feathery "collar" and black and white wings. Condors soar over high mountains, nesting and roosting on inaccessible ledges. They lay one to three eggs a year. Their young take up to six months to leave the nest.

SCIENTIFIC NAME *Vultur gryphus*

DISTRIBUTION South America

SIZE Up to 4.25 ft. (1.3m) long

CALIFORNIA CONDOR

Andean condors are still common, but their largest living relative, the California condor, is in danger of extinction. This giant vulture once

lived throughout the mountains of central and southern California, but today only about 30 birds are left, mostly in captivity. A program is underway to breed captive condors and release their young into the wild.

SCIENTIFIC NAME *Gymnogyps californianus*

DISTRIBUTION California

SIZE Up to 4 ft. (1.2m) long

RUPPELL'S GRIFFON

This vulture is one of more than six species that soar over the African plains. It takes off shortly after sunrise, when the air has began to warm, and finds its food partly by watching the ground below, partly by watching other vultures. If one vulture spots a carcass and drops down to feed, others quickly arrive from many miles around. Ruppell's griffons are stronger than most other African vultures, and they push aside the smaller species to feed.

SCIENTIFIC NAME *Gyps ruepellii*

DISTRIBUTION Tropical Africa

SIZE Up to 3 ft. (1m) long

BEARDED VULTURE

This species is unlike other vultures in appearance and in the way it feeds. It has a feathered head and neck and a "beard" of bristles around its beak. It specializes in eating the tough parts of carcasses, such as the skin and bone. It drops the bones from high up in the air. The bones smash when they land, allowing the birds to feed on the marrow inside.

Bearded vulture perched on a rock

SCIENTIFIC NAME *Gypaetus barbatus*

DISTRIBUTION Southern Europe, Africa, central Asia

SIZE Up to 4 ft. (1.2m) long

EGYPTIAN VULTURE

This small, off-white vulture is one of the few animals that use tools to get their food. It normally eats insects and dead remains, but if it finds an ostrich egg, it throws a stone at the egg until it breaks. Egyptian vultures often gather on garbage dumps near cities.

SCIENTIFIC NAME *Neophron percnopterus*

DISTRIBUTION Southern Europe, Africa, Middle East, southern Asia

SIZE Up to 27.5 in. (70cm) long

RIGHT *A crested caracara guards its nest. Caracaras build their nests in trees or on rocky ledges, and they lay either two or three eggs at a time. They often feed alongside vultures, harassing them and forcing them to give up their food.*

CRESTED CARACARA

Caracaras feed mainly on dead animals, but they are not true vultures. Their closest relatives are the falcons (page 177). Like falcons, they usually fly by flapping their wings instead of soaring, but their long legs make them good at walking on the ground. The crested caracara lives on the edge of forests and in open country, where it often feeds on animals killed on roads.

SCIENTIFIC NAME *Polyborus plancus*

DISTRIBUTION North, Central, and South America, from southern United States to Tierra del Fuego

SIZE Up to 21 in. (53cm) long

Relatively short hook at tip of beak

SECRETARY BIRD

The secretary bird is a bird of prey, but it is so unusual that biologists classify it in a family all its own. It has a hooked beak, a red face, and a feathery crest, but its most distinguishing features are two extremely long legs that end in relatively small feet. The secretary bird lives on the ground, but it flies well and nests on the tops of trees. It often stamps its prey to death. It eats frogs, lizards, and small rodents, but snakes are its favorite food. When it attacks a snake, it uses its wings as shields, making it difficult for the snake to strike.

SCIENTIFIC NAME *Sagittarius serpentarius*

DISTRIBUTION Africa, south of the Sahara Desert

SIZE Up to 5 ft. (1.5m) long

Crest of feathers is raised when the bird is excited or trying to attract a mate

ABOVE AND RIGHT *The secretary bird got its name from the long feathers on its head. These look like the old-fashioned quill pens that secretaries used to tuck behind their ears. Unlike other birds of prey, the secretary bird can run fast, but its feet are too small to pick up prey.*

GAMEBIRDS

Gamebirds got their name because many were hunted for food or sport. Some are still hunted today, but several species are raised on farms. Gamebirds have plump bodies and short legs. Most of them feed on the ground. They eat seeds, insects, and grubs, often using their feet to scratch for food. They can fly short distances, but many run when threatened. Most gamebirds are ground-nesters that lay large numbers of eggs. There are more than 230 species, found in various inland habitats from tropical forests to Arctic tundra.

Many gamebirds have brightly colored flesh on their heads, which is used in courtship displays

BELOW *The mallee fowl's shape is typical of most gamebirds. Its plump body is supported by sturdy legs.*

Long, fleshy wattles hang down over the beak

Fleshy neck pouches

MALLEE FOWL

This Australian gamebird and its relatives do not incubate their eggs. Instead of sitting on them to keep them warm, they bury them in gigantic nest-mounds made of sand and fallen leaves. As the leaves begin to rot, the mounds warm up, allowing the eggs to develop. Every day, the male tests his mound's temperature with his beak. By opening the mound or building it up, he keeps the eggs at a steady 91°F (33°C). Mallee fowl chicks take about seven weeks to hatch. The young chicks dig their way to the surface of the mound and are left to look after themselves.

SCIENTIFIC NAME	*Leipoa ocellata*
DISTRIBUTION	Southern and western Australia
SIZE	Up to 24 in. (61cm) long

GREAT CURRASOW

Unlike most other gamebirds, currasows nest in trees, and they also fly up into trees if disturbed. They lay fewer eggs than most gamebirds—usually between two and four—but their young develop quickly and can fly within a few days of hatching. The great currasow is one of the most spectacular species, with long legs and a feathery crest. The males are black, and the females are rusty red with black and white heads.

SCIENTIFIC NAME	*Crax rubra*
DISTRIBUTION	North, Central, and South America, from Mexico to Colombia
SIZE	Up to 3 ft. (1m) long

WILD TURKEY

Wild turkeys are woodland birds that eat acorns, other seeds, and insects. Both the males and females have bare heads and copper-colored plumage, but the males also

LEFT AND CENTER *Male wild turkeys display to females by fluffing out their feathers and fanning their wings and tails. Their calls can be heard over a mile away.*

have fleshy flaps called wattles hanging from their heads and necks, and a tuft of feathers dangling from their chests. Wild turkeys were first domesticated in Mexico more than 1,000 years ago, but by the early 1900s, they had disappeared from large parts of the United States. In recent years, turkeys have been reintroduced into places where they once lived, and they have staged a successful comeback.

SCIENTIFIC NAME *Meleagris gallopavo*

DISTRIBUTION United States, Mexico

SIZE Up to 4 ft. (1.2m) long

GREATER PRAIRIE-CHICKEN
Many gamebirds carry out impressive courtship displays, but the display of the prairie-chicken is one of the most remarkable of all. The males have an inflatable yellow sac on each side of their necks, which they pump full of air to attract potential mates. At the same time, they make a loud, booming sound as they dance up and down. These displays take place at courtship grounds called leks, which are often used for many years. Unfortunately for prairie-chickens, much of their habitat has been turned into farmland, so they are becoming increasingly rare.

SCIENTIFIC NAME *Tympanuchus cupido*

DISTRIBUTION Central United States

SIZE Up to 17 in. (43cm) long

GRAY PARTRIDGE
Partridges are small gamebirds that often feed in fields. They usually live in flocks, scuttling away at the first sign of danger or speeding low over the ground on whirring wings. The gray partridge is one of the most widespread European species. Its body is actually brown, but it got its name from its gray legs. Gray partridges can lay more than 20 eggs each time they breed, making them among the most prolific egg-laying birds in the world. However, many of their chicks are eaten by predators.

SCIENTIFIC NAME *Perdix perdix*

DISTRIBUTION Western and central Europe

SIZE Up to 12 in. (30cm) long

HIMALAYAN SNOWCOCK
The snowcock resembles a giant partridge, and it is one of the partridge's closest relatives. Though it can weigh as much as 6.5 lb. (3kg), its white and gray plumage helps hide its bulk against snow and rocks. Snowcocks live in flocks of up to 20 birds. In their bleak mountain

ABOVE AND LEFT Like all gamebirds, gray partridges feed on the ground. They keep a constant lookout for predators.

Female   Male

ABOVE The top pair of willow ptarmigans are in their summer plumage. The other pair are in their winter whites. The red grouse, a British form, stays brown all year round.

Male   Female

habitat, where food is scarce, Himalayan snowcocks are always on the move, searching for food. They nest on the ground under overhangs and in caves.

SCIENTIFIC NAME *Tetraogallus himalayensis*

DISTRIBUTION Himalaya Mountains

SIZE Up to 22 in. (55cm) long

WILLOW PTARMIGAN
Willow ptarmigans are among the world's hardiest birds. They live in the Arctic tundra, where they eat leaves, twigs, and seeds. In winter, they dig into snowbanks to keep out of the freezing wind. To help them survive, their feet are covered with warm feathers, and the birds change color to stay camouflaged all year. In the summer, they are mottled brown, but their winter plumage is white, except for a black-tipped tail.

SCIENTIFIC NAME *Lagopus lagopus*

DISTRIBUTION Worldwide in Arctic, except Greenland

SIZE Up to 15 in. (38cm) long

Main plumage color can vary from gray to brown

Teardrop-shaped crest

Female

Male

A pair of common quail, camouflaged in dead grass

One leg tucked up under plumage

CALIFORNIA QUAIL

With its dainty, forward-pointing crest, the California quail is one of the most elegant small gamebirds in North America. Its plumage is neat and tidy, with speckles and stripes on its face, neck, and underside. The California quail lives mainly on open ground and in woodlands, but it sometimes ventures to the edges of cities. It feeds in small groups during the breeding season, but in the winter, birds gather together, forming flocks up to 300 strong. These winter flocks have a better chance of avoiding attack than lone birds because while some birds are feeding, others are on the lookout for danger.

SCIENTIFIC NAME	*Callipepla californica*
DISTRIBUTION	Western North America, from British Columbia to Baja California
SIZE	Up to 10 in. (25cm) long

COMMON QUAIL

The tiny, stubby-tailed common quail is one of the few gamebirds that migrates to breed. It spends the winter as far south as central Africa, but breeds thousands of miles away in Europe and parts of western Asia. Despite being such an experienced traveler, it usually runs from danger instead of flying away. Common quail feed in grassy places and cornfields. They are so small that they are difficult to find, but their soft, three-note calls sometimes give them away. They nest in hollows in the ground and lay up to 12 camouflaged eggs.

SCIENTIFIC NAME	*Coturnix coturnix*
DISTRIBUTION	Europe, Africa, Middle East, central Asia, India
SIZE	Up to 7 in. (18cm) long

Male

LEFT *The male common pheasant has a more colorful head and a much longer tail than the female.*

Female

RING-NECKED PHEASANT

Pheasants are gamebirds with long, trailing tails. Female ring-necked pheasants are brown all over, but males have coppery bodies, an iridescent green-purple neck, and a patch of bright red skin around their eyes. Ring-necked pheasants originally come from Asia, but they have been introduced into many other parts of the world for sport and for food. Though their natural homes are forests and open grasslands, they adapt well to life in wooded farmland and fields.

SCIENTIFIC NAME	*Phasianus colchicus*
DISTRIBUTION	Originally from central and Southeast Asia; introduced into North America, Europe, Australia, New Zealand
SIZE	Up to 32.5 in. (82cm) long

a peahen, is mainly brown and white with a short tail. The male bird, called a peacock, has a brilliant blue body, and his tail has up to 150 extra-long feathers, each tipped with an iridescent "eye." When a peacock courts a peahen, he opens these feathers to make a fan and shakes them so they rustle. The male also has a distinctive, piercing call. Peacocks are kept in parks and gardens worldwide.

SCIENTIFIC NAME *Pavo cristatus*

DISTRIBUTION Originally from India, Sri Lanka; semicaptive birds introduced into many parts of the world

SIZE Up to 7.25 ft. (2.2m) long

RED JUNGLEFOWL
The red junglefowl is the ancestor of domestic chickens, which are raised all over the world. It lives on the edges of forests, finding seeds and insects by scratching up the ground with its feet. Male junglefowl look similar to farmyard roosters, and they make the same noisy, crowing sound. The hens are slimmer than domesticated chickens, and they are always brown. Domesticated junglefowl now outnumber wild ones many times over.

SCIENTIFIC NAME *Gallus gallus*

DISTRIBUTION Northern India, Southeast Asia

SIZE Up to 22 in. (55cm) long

HELMETED GUINEA FOWL
Guinea fowl live in plains and forests, where they eat seeds, edible roots, and insects. They have dark blue bodies with light blue spots, short tails, and powerful legs. All species of guinea fowl have bare, blue heads, and the helmeted guinea fowl also has a hard shield, or casque, on the top of its head. Originally from Africa, the helmeted guinea fowl is bred for food all over the world. Even in captivity, it reacts to danger with a piercing alarm call that sounds like the screeching of broken machinery.

SCIENTIFIC NAME *Numidia meleagris*

DISTRIBUTION Tropical Africa

SIZE Up to 23 in. (58cm) long

GREAT ARGUS PHEASANT
This rain forest pheasant is one of the most spectacular gamebirds in Southeast Asia. The male and female both have blue heads and gray-brown bodies, but the male also has giant flight feathers along the rear edges of his wings, decorated with eyespots. The male opens them out during his courtship display to form a gigantic fan. As with many other spectacular birds, the male puts all his effort into attracting females. He plays no part in building a nest or raising young.

SCIENTIFIC NAME *Argusianus argus*

DISTRIBUTION Thailand, Malaysia, Indonesia

SIZE Up to 6 ft. (2m) long

PEAFOWL OR PEACOCK
Male gamebirds are usually more impressive than their mates, but with the peafowl, these differences reach amazing extremes. The female bird, called

ABOVE *A peacock fans out his tail feathers in a spectacular display.*

Female

Male Lady Amherst's pheasant

Female

Male golden pheasant

ABOVE *Male Lady Amherst's pheasants (Chrysolophus amherstiae) and golden pheasants (Chrysolophus pictus) are brightly colored.*

CRANES AND THEIR RELATIVES

Cranes and their relatives include some birds that stand as high as an adult human, as well as others that could easily nestle in the palm of a hand. Despite their outward differences, they have similar internal features, such as the shape of their skeletons, that show that they are closely related. Many of these birds live near water or on marshy ground, and most of them have long necks and legs. When they fly, they hold their necks out straight, and their legs usually trail behind them. Most of these birds nest on the ground. There are about 200 species, including some of the most endangered birds in the world.

COMMON CRANE

Cranes are birds of open places. They stride across the ground on their long legs, snapping up seeds and insects with their sharply pointed beaks. They live in flocks, and many of them, including the common crane, migrate long distances to breed. Like other cranes, the common crane pairs up for life and has a spectacular courtship display. The males and females strut, bow, and leap high into the air. Cranes have a very long windpipe, or trachea, and their loud, trumpeting sounds can be heard over a mile (1.5km) away. Common cranes were once widespread, but their numbers have declined because they need an undisturbed habitat to survive.

SCIENTIFIC NAME *Grus grus*

DISTRIBUTION Breeds in Europe, Asia; migrates to southern Europe, Asia, northern Africa in the winter

SIZE Up to 3.5 ft. (1.1m) long

Common crane standing on one leg

GREAT BUSTARD

Bustards are long-legged, ground-dwelling birds that live in open, grassy places. Most of them are found in Africa, but the great bustard comes from the plains of Europe and Asia. It weighs up to 40 lb. (18kg), making it one of the heaviest flying birds in the world. Male and female great bustards look similar, with gray heads and brown and white bodies, and the males put on a spectacular display during the breeding season, puffing out their chests and turning their tails over their backs. Great bustards have been hunted for centuries and are now much rarer than they once were.

SCIENTIFIC NAME *Otis tarda*

DISTRIBUTION Spain, central Europe, central and eastern Asia

SIZE Up to 3 ft. (1m) long

WHOOPING CRANE

This stately, white bird is the rarest crane in North America and also the largest, with a wingspan of about 7 ft. (2.1m). Though it once lived in marshes across the western side of the continent, today only about 200 birds are left. Most of them breed in Wood Buffalo National Park in Canada and spend the winter on the coast of the Gulf of Mexico. The whooping crane gets its name from its loud call, which sounds like a high-pitched trumpeting.

SCIENTIFIC NAME
Grus americana

DISTRIBUTION
Canada, United States

SIZE Up to 4.5 ft. (1.4m) long

RIGHT *The whooping crane will sometimes wade into water, but it finds most of its food on land.*

EURASIAN COOT

Coots are small, solidly built, freshwater birds with short beaks and jet-black plumage. They spend most of their time on the water, picking food from the surface or diving to the bottom. Although their feet are not webbed, their toes are edged with flexible flaps that push against the water as they swim. These noisy, aggressive birds often chase each other across the water during the breeding season and sometimes eat the young of other waterbirds. Coots build their nests close to the water's edge, where they lay up to ten camouflaged eggs at a time. A very similar species lives in North America.

Flexible flaps along sides of toes

SCIENTIFIC NAME *Fulica atra*

DISTRIBUTION Originally from Europe, Asia, Australia; introduced into New Zealand

SIZE Up to 17 in. (43cm) long

TOP *When it is in danger, a moorhen can sink like a submarine, until only its beak is above the surface.* **ABOVE** *If caught out in the open, the water rail will "freeze" to avoid being seen.* **LEFT** *Moorhen chicks leave the nest when they are just two or three days old. At this age, they are already good swimmers.*

Speckled pattern camouflages eggs

Gray- black plumage

ABOVE *Unlike ducks, male and female coots look exactly the same. The females usually raise one family a year, but they often lay eggs in their neighbors' nests as well as in their own.*

COMMON MOORHEN

The moorhen looks similar to the coot, but it is a smaller, more timid bird, and also more secretive. Though it swims well, it finds much of its food on land, in damp mud and grassy fields. At the first sign of danger, it runs for cover, hiding away among waterside plants. During the breeding season, moorhens and coots are easy to tell apart, because moorhens have red beaks.

SCIENTIFIC NAME	*Gallinula chloropus*
DISTRIBUTION	Worldwide, except Australia, New Zealand, the far north
SIZE	Up to 13 in. (33cm) long

TAKAHE

The takahe is a large, flightless relative of the moorhen. It has a dark blue body, red legs, and a powerful, bright red beak. It uses its beak to eat tussock grass, holding the stems down with one foot while it feeds. Takahes are found only in New Zealand. At one time, they were thought to have been driven to extinction by introduced mammals such as cats, but in 1948, a small group was discovered in the Murchison Mountains of South Island. These birds are now protected, and the species looks likely to survive.

SCIENTIFIC NAME	*Porpyrio mantelli*
DISTRIBUTION	South Island of New Zealand
SIZE	Up to 25 in. (63cm) long

WATER RAIL

Rails are narrow-bodied birds that live among waterside plants. Their shape is ideal for slipping through dense vegetation, but they are cautious about coming into the open. Although they are usually hidden away, they reveal themselves with their loud and unearthly calls. The water rail's call sounds like a squealing and grunting pig— an amazingly loud sound for a small bird.

SCIENTIFIC NAME	*Rallus aquaticus*
DISTRIBUTION	Europe, central Asia, Far East, northern Africa
SIZE	Up to 11 in. (28cm) long

Shorebirds

Shorebirds, also known as waders, live on coasts, lakes, marshes, and meadows all over the world. Most of them are small or medium-sized birds with slender legs and long, sensitive beaks.

They often probe wet sand, mud, or grass, finding worms, mollusks, and other small animals to eat mainly by touch. Shorebirds lay their eggs on the ground and are careful parents. There are more than 200 species of these birds worldwide. Many breed in the far north, migrating in flocks tens of thousands strong.

ABOVE Jacanas often make their nests on floating water plants. The male looks after the nest and the young.

Winter

Summer

CENTER Even when they are resting, oystercatchers are always on the lookout for danger.
ABOVE In the summer, the male pied stilt has a black head.

COMB-CRESTED JACANA

Jacanas live on plant-covered lakes and ponds. Although they can swim if they have to, they usually trot and flutter across the surface, using lily pads and leaves as floating steppingstones. Jacanas can do this because their immensely long toes help spread out their weight. The comb-crested jacana has a brown and white body and a fleshy crest on its head. Like other jacanas, it has a sharp spur on the front edge of each wing, which it uses when it fights.

SCIENTIFIC NAME *Irediparra gallinacea*
DISTRIBUTION Philippines, Indonesia, New Guinea, Australia
SIZE Up to 10 in. (25cm) long

EURASIAN OYSTERCATCHER

Oystercatchers are large, noisy birds that live on rocky coasts and beaches, or sometimes near water inland. There are 11 species, most of which are either black or brown and white, with long, orange or red beaks. Eurasian oystercatchers use their beaks in two ways. Some birds use them to hammer open the tough shells of mussels and cockles, but others use them like pincers to pull worms out of the sand. Oystercatchers nest on gravel beaches and lay up to four camouflaged eggs each year.

SCIENTIFIC NAME *Haematopus ostralegus*
DISTRIBUTION Breeds in Europe, central Asia, Far East; migrates to western and southern Europe, parts of Africa, Middle East, India in the winter
SIZE Up to 17 in. (43cm) long

PIED STILT

Compared with the rest of its body, the pied stilt has the longest legs of any bird. They are bright pink, and they trail far beyond its tail when it flies. Stilts live on insect larvae and other small animals, using their long legs to wade into lakes and lagoons, where they feed on the surface of the water. They nest on open mud, and when they sit down to incubate their eggs, their legs stick out behind them like a pair of backward knees.

SCIENTIFIC NAME *Himantopus himantopus*
DISTRIBUTION Breeds in North America, Europe, central Asia; migrates to areas throughout the Southern Hemisphere in the winter
SIZE Up to 15 in. (38cm) long

PIED AVOCET

Avocets are the only shorebirds with sharply upturned beaks. Instead of probing for their food, they stride through shallow water, sweeping the tips of their beaks from side to side just below the surface. If an avocet touches anything edible, it grabs it using its beak like a pair of tweezers and quickly swallows the food. Avocets live on lagoons and brackish lakes, and they nest on muddy islands. The pied avocet is the most widespread of the four avocet species. During the northern winter, tens of thousands gather on some lakes in East Africa.

SCIENTIFIC NAME
Recurvirostra avosetta
DISTRIBUTION
Breeds in Europe, central Asia, parts of Africa; migrates mainly to Africa, Persian Gulf in the winter
SIZE Up to 17.5 in. (45cm) long

LEFT Like many other shorebirds, the pied avocet can find food simply by feeling with its beak. This highly developed sense of touch allows it to feed in muddy water.

Beak has thickened tip

Double band around breast

RIGHT *A killdeer stands over its nest. If a predator comes too close, the parent bird will lure it away by pretending to have a broken wing. This trick is used by many shorebirds.*
BELOW *Eurasian lapwings are not as common as they once were because their habitat is often drained and plowed up.*

KILLDEER
This brightly marked shorebird is named for its piercing call, which sounds like "kill-dee, kill-dee." It has a slender body and conspicuous stripes on its breast, and it lives in a wide variety of habitats, including fields, riverbanks, and shores. Killdeers nest on gravel, and they sometimes lay their eggs on flat roofs.

SCIENTIFIC NAME *Charadrius vociferus*
DISTRIBUTION Breeds throughout North America, except the Arctic; migrates to southern North America, Central America, parts of South America in the winter
SIZE Up to 10 in. (25cm) long

EURASIAN LAPWING
Unlike most shorebirds, lapwings usually live inland. The Eurasian lapwing prefers damp, grassy fields, but other species live closer to water. The Eurasian lapwing has an elegant crest, a green-black back, and a short, sharply pointed beak. During the breeding season, the males perform spectacular aerial displays, tumbling down from the sky toward the ground. Because lapwings build their nests on the ground, they always have to be on the lookout for predators. If a crow or fox appears near the nest, the parent

birds immediately go on the attack to try to drive it away.

SCIENTIFIC NAME *Vanellus vanellus*
DISTRIBUTION Breeds in northern Europe, central Asia; migrates to western and southern Europe, northern Africa, Middle East, southern Asia in the winter
SIZE Up to 12 in. (30cm) long

LESSER GOLDEN-PLOVER
This small shorebird carries out one of the longest migrations of any land-living bird. It spends the winter in central South America, then flies north to the high Arctic to breed. This journey is mostly over land, but on the return trip, the adult birds follow a shorter, more hazardous route. They head out over the Atlantic Ocean off eastern Canada and fly due south until they reach Brazil. This shortcut saves energy, but it means flying nearly 2,500 mi. (4,000km) nonstop. These plovers are a golden color during the breeding season, but gray the rest of the year.

SCIENTIFIC NAME *Pluvialis dominica*
DISTRIBUTION Breeds in Alaska, northern Canada; migrates to South America in the winter
SIZE Up to 10.5 in. (27cm) long

ABOVE *American lesser golden-plovers prepare themselves for their southward migration by fattening up on berries along the Canadian coast. They cannot fly back along the same route because spring comes very late in this part of the world. The ground is frozen, making food very difficult to find.*

R U D D Y   T U R N S T O N E
This small, solidly built shorebird lives on rocky coasts and feeds in an unusual way. Using its short beak, it flicks stones and seaweed aside to reveal animals hidden underneath. There are two species of turnstones: the black turnstone (*Arenaria melanocephala*) lives on the Pacific coast of North America, and the ruddy turnstone can be seen from Alaska to Australia.

SCIENTIFIC NAME   *Arenaria interpres*

DISTRIBUTION   Breeds throughout the Arctic; migrates to western Europe, southern North America, Australia, New Zealand, throughout the tropics in the winter

SIZE   Up to 9 in. (23cm) long

BELOW The ruddy turnstone has quick reactions. When it flicks away a stone or pebble, it can peck up insects and beach fleas before they escape.

G R E E N S H A N K
Every spring, large flocks of greenshanks fly north to the Siberian tundra to breed. These birds have gray wings, white undersides, and olive green legs, from which they got their name. Greenshanks nest in boggy ground or forest clearings, and as with all shorebirds, they have fast-developing young. Their chicks can feed themselves soon after they hatch, and they instinctively crouch down if any predators fly overhead.

SCIENTIFIC NAME   *Tringa nebularia*

DISTRIBUTION   Breeds in northern Europe, Siberia; migrates mainly to Africa, southern Asia, Australia in the winter

SIZE   Up to 13.5 in. (34cm) long

E U R A S I A N   C U R L E W
Curlews, one of the the largest shorebirds, have speckled brown or gray plumage and long, downcurved beaks. They live on coasts and in damp inland places and are experts at finding worms and other animals hidden in wet sand and mud. When a curlew is searching for food, it probes the ground with its beak closed.

If it feels food, it can open just the tip of its beak, gripping the animal and pulling it to the surface of the mud. Eurasian curlews nest in damp grassland and other boggy places. They are known for their beautiful, bubbling call.

SCIENTIFIC NAME   *Numenius arquata*

DISTRIBUTION   Breeds in northern Europe, northern Asia; migrates to western and southern Europe, Africa, southern Asia in the winter

SIZE   Up to 23.5 in. (60cm) long

W R Y B I L L
The wrybill is the only bird in the world to have a beak with a sideways bend. It lives in New Zealand, spending the summer on stony riverbanks in South Island and the winter on the North Island coast. With its bend to the right, the wrybill's beak is an ideal tool for getting at insect larvae and other animals hidden beneath stones. The bird sweeps its beak in a clockwise direction, flipping over stones and quickly snapping up its meal. Wrybills nest on bare river gravel and lay just two eggs a year.

SCIENTIFIC NAME   *Anarhychus frontalis*

DISTRIBUTION   New Zealand

SIZE   Up to 8.25 in. (21cm) long

R E D - N E C K E D   P H A L A R O P E
As a general rule, most male birds are more brightly colored than the female, and the female does most of the work of raising the young. With the red-necked phalarope, things are the other way around. During the breeding season, the female has a bright red neck, and she uses her colorful plumage to attract a mate. Once the eggs have been laid, the male takes sole charge of the incubation of the clutch and the care of the young. Though they are waders, phalaropes are also unusual because they swim to feed— most waders walk instead.

SCIENTIFIC NAME   *Phalaropus lobatus*

DISTRIBUTION   Breeds in northern regions, the Arctic; migrates to tropical seas in the winter

SIZE   Up to 7 in. (18cm) long

RIGHT In the winter, both male and female red-necked phalaropes have pale plumage. In the summer, the female is brighter then her mate.

TOP With a beak up to 7.5 in. long, the Eurasian curlew can reach worms buried deep in wet mud.
ABOVE When a wrybill hatches, its beak is short and straight. It develops a bend to the right as the bird matures.

RUFF

During the winter, ruffs look much like other shorebirds, but in the spring, the males develop extraordinary feathery "ruffs" around their necks, with extra tufts over their heads. These ruffs have many different colors, and the males show them off at their traditional display grounds, or leks, where they compete for the chance to mate. Once a female has mated, she leaves the display ground and raises her young alone. Ruffs live in marshland and grassy places, feeding mainly on insects.

ABOVE *In their summer breeding plumage, male ruffs are unmistakable.*

SCIENTIFIC NAME
Philomachus pugnax

DISTRIBUTION Breeds in northern Europe, Siberia; migrates mainly to Africa in the winter

SIZE Up to 11.5 in. (29cm) long

Male ruff in winter

Female ruff in winter

BELOW *A female common snipe settles down on her nest.*

PURPLE SANDPIPER

The purple sandpiper feeds on rocky shores, where it dodges the surf to pick up mollusks exposed by the tide. This small, dumpy bird nests on some of the most northerly land on earth, within 600 mi. (1,000km) of the North Pole. Unlike other Arctic shorebirds, the purple sandpiper does not migrate very far south. Some individuals stay close to the Arctic Circle even through the winter, when there are only a few hours of daylight each day.

SCIENTIFIC NAME *Calidris maritima*

DISTRIBUTION Breeds in high Arctic; migrates to northeastern North America, Iceland, northwestern Europe in the winter

SIZE Up to 9 in. (23cm) long

COMMON SNIPE

The common snipe is a small, secretive bird with brown plumage and a long, straight beak. It lives in woodlands and other damp places, leaving trails of small holes in damp mud where it has been feeding. Snipe are well camouflaged, but if they are caught unawares, they burst into the air with a sudden screech, disappearing in a zigzag flight. During the breeding season, male snipe make a remarkable humming sound as they plunge through the air. This sound is made by their two outermost tail feathers, which vibrate as the air rushes past them.

SCIENTIFIC NAME *Gallinago gallinago*

DISTRIBUTION Breeds in North America, northern Europe, northern Asia; migrates to North and Central America, western and southern Europe, Africa, southern Asia in the winter

SIZE Up to 10.5 in. (27cm) long

JAEGERS, GULLS, AND TERNS

There are seven species of jaegers, and about 85 species of gulls and terns. Jaegers breed mainly in cold places, but gulls and terns are found on or near coasts around the world, and sometimes far inland. They all have webbed feet and waterproof feathers and are skillful fliers. Terns live by fishing, but most gulls scavenge on the shore or in garbage thrown from boats. Gulls and terns can be bold, but jaegers are even more aggressive. They eat eggs and chicks, and often steal food from other seabirds.

ABOVE *The great skua often steals food from larger birds.*

PARASITIC JAEGER

The parasitic jaeger is a skillful airborne pirate. It will hunt rodents or steal eggs, but it gets most of its food by making other seabirds drop any fish they have caught, grabbing the fish in midair. Parasitic jaegers breed in groups in treeless tundra or open ground near the sea. They spend the winter flying over the ocean.

SCIENTIFIC NAME *Stercorarius parasiticus*

DISTRIBUTION Breeds in the far north; migrates as far south as the Southern Ocean in the winter

SIZE Up to 18 in. (46cm) long

ABOVE *Parasitic jaegers vary in color. Some are dark brown all over, but others have brown backs and pale undersides.*
BELOW *Herring gulls crack open mollusk shells by dropping them from the air.*

GREAT SKUA

This powerfully built, dark brown seabird makes its living largely at the expense of other birds. It eats young seabirds and eggs, and chases adult birds to make them regurgitate their catch. It also eats dead animals, ripping open their remains with its hooked beak. Great skuas nest on the ground and usually produce two eggs each time they breed. The great skua is closely related to the Antarctic skua, which lives in the Southern Ocean and often attacks penguin chicks. These two birds are so similar that they were once thought to be the same.

SCIENTIFIC NAME *Catharacta skua*

DISTRIBUTION Northern Atlantic Ocean

SIZE Up to 26 in. (66cm) long

HERRING GULL

This noisy, quarrelsome bird is one of the most widespread and adaptable gulls in the Northern Hemisphere.

It feeds on fields and around garbage dumps as well as along the shore, and often follows fishing boats and ferries, waiting for any scraps that are thrown overboard. Herring gulls breed in groups and make their nests out of seaweed and other plants. They usually nest on the ground, but in some coastal towns they make their homes on rooftops. If anything comes too close to their eggs or chicks, the parent gulls circle overhead, producing a deafening chorus of loud, yelping cries.

Powerful beak

SCIENTIFIC NAME *Larus argentatus*

DISTRIBUTION Coasts and inland areas throughout the Northern Hemisphere

SIZE Up to 23.5 in. (60cm) long

GREAT BLACK-BACKED GULL

This is one of the world's largest gulls, with a wingspan of up to 5.5 ft. (1.7m). It has a powerful, yellow beak, a white body and head, and a black back and wings. Black-backed gulls scavenge for dead remains, but they are

Great black-backed gull on the ground

also highly effective predators. They can kill animals as large as rabbits and can swallow seabird chicks and ducklings whole. Unlike the herring gull, this bird often hunts on its own or in pairs. It nests on rocky coasts and lays three eggs a year.

SCIENTIFIC NAME *Larus marinus*

DISTRIBUTION Northern Atlantic Ocean

SIZE Up to 31 in. (79cm) long

COMMON BLACK-HEADED GULL

In the winter, this small gull is almost totally gray and white, but when it is wearing its breeding plumage, it looks as if its head has been dipped in dark brown ink. Black-headed gulls sometimes feed on the coast, but they are just as much at home inland. They often follow plows to pick up earthworms and other small animals. They roost on lakes and reservoirs and nest on marshy ground.

SCIENTIFIC NAME *Larus ridibundus*

DISTRIBUTION Breeds in Europe, northern Asia; migrates throughout Europe, northern Africa, Asia, east coast of North America in the winter

SIZE Up to 14 in. (35cm) long

LEFT *Great black-headed gulls* (Larus ichthyaetus) *breed around the inland seas of central Asia. Like most of their relatives, their heads turn gray in the winter.*
BELOW *These common black-headed gulls are scavenging for food around European bison. They catch insects and other small animals that are disturbed by the bison.*

Juvenile

Breeding adult

Winter adult

KITTIWAKE

Kittiwakes got their name from their call, a shrill "kitti-week, kitti-week." They are smaller and daintier than many gulls and get almost all of their food from the sea. Kittiwakes breed in noisy groups on steep cliff ledges. Unlike most of their relatives, they build elaborate, cup-shaped nests, using mud to cement them to the rock. After they have raised their chicks, parent kittiwakes go their separate ways, but they return to the same breeding site the following year and pair up again to raise their next family.

SCIENTIFIC NAME *Rissa tridactyla*

DISTRIBUTION Northern Atlantic Ocean, northern Pacific Ocean

SIZE Up to 16 in. (40cm) long

SILVER GULL OR RED-BILLED GULL

This seabird is the most common gull in Australia. It has a rounded, white body with a silver-gray back and wings and a bright red beak and legs. Silver gulls are versatile creatures, as much at home in cities and on inland lakes as they are far out at sea. They often gather in fields and around garbage dumps to feed, particularly in stormy weather. Silver gulls nest on the ground and lay one to three eggs each year.

SCIENTIFIC NAME *Larus novaehollandiae*

DISTRIBUTION Australia, New Zealand

SIZE Up to 17 in. (43cm) long

ABOVE *Kittiwakes have sharp claws, which help them cling to rocky ledges when they nest.*
BELOW *Measuring just 10 in. long, the little gull* (Larus minutus) *is the world's smallest gull.*

ARCTIC TERN

Terns are more graceful than gulls and have pointed beaks, narrow wings, and forked tails. Instead of scavenging for food along the shore, they flutter over the water, diving down to catch small fish. These lightly built birds are tireless fliers, and the Arctic tern is one of greatest travelers of them all. Arctic terns breed in cool parts of the Northern Hemisphere, laying their eggs in hollows scraped in gravel. Once they have finished breeding, they fly all the way to the Southern Ocean. During the northern spring, they fly north again, completing a round-trip journey over 22,000 mi. (35,000km) long.

SCIENTIFIC NAME	*Sterna paradisea*
DISTRIBUTION	Breeds in northern Europe, northern North America, along shores of the Arctic Sea; migrates to Southern Ocean in the winter
SIZE	Up to 14 in. (35cm) long

INCA TERN

Many terns have white and gray plumage, but the Inca tern has a completely different color scheme. Its beak and feet are bright red, and its body is dark gray, but it has white plumes that sprout from the base of its beak like a pair of long, curling whiskers. Inca terns feed in large flocks. They often catch fish trying to escape from cormorants and sea lions.

SCIENTIFIC NAME	*Larosterna inca*
DISTRIBUTION	Pacific coast of South America
SIZE	Up to 16.5 in. (42cm) long

WHITE TERN

This all-white tern flutters across the vastness of the open ocean. It is unusually tame and often circles boats before continuing on its way. White terns breed on remote islands, laying a single egg each year. Instead of laying on the ground as most terns do, they lay their eggs on the bare branches of low trees. The parent holds the egg in position with its body, and the chick jumps to the ground a few days after hatching.

SCIENTIFIC NAME	*Gygis alba*
DISTRIBUTION	Tropical oceans worldwide, except eastern Pacific Ocean
SIZE	Up to 13 in. (33cm) long

BLACK SKIMMER

Skimmers are the only birds with a lower beak that is much longer than the part on top. They skim the surface of lakes and lagoons with their beaks open, and if the beak touches a fish or other small animal, the top part snaps shut, and the bird swallows its catch. There are three species of these birds. The black skimmer is the largest.

SCIENTIFIC NAME	*Rhyncops niger*
DISTRIBUTION	North, Central, and South America
SIZE	Up to 20 in. (50cm) long

ABOVE *Arctic terns share the work of feeding their chicks. Here, one parent returns with a fish while the other keeps the chick warm.*
BELOW *This Atlantic puffin has a beak full of sand-eels for its chick. Puffins abandon their young when they are about six weeks old, leaving them to flutter down to the sea.*

Narrow wings for fast, agile flight

FAR LEFT *White terns lay just one egg each time they breed, and the parents share the task of incubation. They have to change places with care to keep the egg from falling from the precarious nest site.*
LEFT *An Inca tern spreads its wings and calls. Inca terns breed on desert coasts and lay their eggs in rocky crevices or burrows made by other birds.*

AUKS

There are no penguins in the Northern Hemisphere, but auks look like them and feed in a similar way. Like penguins, they have dumpy bodies, and they speed through the water by beating their wings. There are about 22 species in the auk family, most of which nest on rocky ledges or in burrows, although a few nest in trees. Unlike true penguins, auks can fly, and they soar over the water on whirring wings. The largest auk ever known, called the great auk, was completely flightless. It became extinct in 1844.

Beak is at its brightest during the breeding season

Fish arranged head to tail

ATLANTIC PUFFIN

With their bright red feet and multicolored beaks, puffins are comical-looking seabirds. They nest in burrows on rocky coasts, eating sand-eels and other small fish. During the breeding season, puffins speed back to their burrows with fish for their chicks. They catch up to 12 fish on each trip, holding them in their beaks. Remarkably, a puffin can add to its catch without dropping any of the fish it has already caught.

SCIENTIFIC NAME *Fratercula arctica*

DISTRIBUTION Northern Atlantic Ocean

SIZE Up to 12.5 in. (32cm) long

DOVEKIE

The tiny, black and white dovekie is one of the most common seabirds on the edges of the Arctic. It has a short beak and a plump body with its legs set far back. Dovekies feed on planktonic animals, and they sometimes bob up and down on the water in large flocks. They nest in rocky crevices or burrows and, like most other auks, lay just one egg a year.

SCIENTIFIC NAME *Alle alle*

DISTRIBUTION Northern Atlantic Ocean, Arctic Ocean

SIZE Up to 8.25 in. (21cm) long

RAZORBILL

These large auks have flat, hooked beaks. They nest on ledges and in crevices on rocky coasts, laying single eggs. Razorbill chicks leave their nesting ledges when they are about two weeks old, still with plenty of growing to do. Once they are safely at sea, one of their parents feeds them until they are able to feed themselves.

SCIENTIFIC NAME *Alca torda*

DISTRIBUTION Northern Atlantic Ocean

SIZE Up to 16 in. (40cm) long

Dovekies (left) and razorbills (right) in summer and whiter winter plumage

Summer

Winter

Common murres in summer and winter plumage

COMMON MURRE

Murres are the largest auks, with streamlined bodies and long, pointed beaks. They breed on inaccessible rocky ledges, crowding together just a few yards above the waves. Murres lay single eggs directly on the rock, and the parents take turns to incubate it. The eggs are sharply pointed, so they roll in circles instead of rolling off the edge into the sea.

SCIENTIFIC NAME *Uria aalge*

DISTRIBUTION Northern Atlantic Ocean, northern Pacific Ocean

SIZE Up to 17.5 in. (45cm) long

PIGEONS AND DOVES

Pigeons and doves are
plump-bodied birds
with small heads that flick
back and forth when they walk.
They have short beaks, and most of
them are vegetarians, feeding on seeds,
fruit, or leaves. Apart from the largest species,
all of them are strong fliers, exploding into the air
at the first sign of danger and speeding away on
fast-flapping wings. They nest in trees, on ledges,
or sometimes on the ground, making flimsy
nests out of sticks and twigs. One of their most
unusual features is that they feed their young
on a milky fluid made in their throats.
Flamingos (page 169) are the only other
birds known to behave in this way. Pigeons
and doves are unique in that they can suck up
water when they
drink—all other birds
have to take a mouthful and then tip
their heads back. There are about 300
species in the pigeon and dove family,
and the greatest variety is found in
Southeast Asia and Australia.

ABOVE LEFT *The wood
pigeon (Columba
palumbus) is a farmland
pest in parts of Europe.*
ABOVE RIGHT *Stock doves
(Columba oenas) are
smaller than wood pigeons,
with shorter tails.*

ROCK DOVE

The slate-gray rock dove is the original
ancestor of all the world's street pigeons.
Centuries ago, rock doves were kept for food,
but over the years many of them escaped. The
escaped birds learned how to find food in urban
areas, and they have been increasingly successful
ever since. Wild rock doves nest on cliff ledges,
often near the ocean. Street pigeons have
inherited this head for heights. They treat
buildings like cliffs, nesting on high window
ledges or under bridges. In the wild, rock doves
lay two eggs at a time and often raise two or
three families each year. In cities, where food
is easy to find, street pigeons may breed all
through the year.

SCIENTIFIC NAME *Columba livia*

DISTRIBUTION Rock dove: southern Europe,
northern Africa, southern Asia;
street pigeon: worldwide

SIZE Up to 13 in. (33cm) long

MOURNING DOVE

The mourning dove is well known for its call.
It makes a soft, mournful cooing sound, which
is how it got its name. Mourning doves nearly
always feed in pairs or small flocks, and they are
common in many different habitats, including
fields, farmyards, and gardens. They have brown
wings, pink-brown bodies, and long, sharply

pointed tails. During the breeding season, male mourning doves perform special display flights, climbing high on noisily clapping wings, then gliding down to the ground.

SCIENTIFIC NAME *Zenaida macroura*

DISTRIBUTION North and Central America, Caribbean islands

SIZE Up to 12.5 in. (32cm) long

TURTLEDOVE

Like the mourning dove, this dove is famous for its call—a purring sound that can be heard wherever it nests. As with most pigeons and doves, the males and females look very similar, with pink-gray bodies and brown and black wings. Turtledoves spend the winter in Africa, but they fly north to Europe and central Asia to breed.

SCIENTIFIC NAME *Streptopelia turtur*

DISTRIBUTION Breeds mainly in Europe, Middle East; migrates to Africa in the winter

SIZE Up to 10.5 in. (27cm) long

Broad wings with long flight feathers

DIAMOND DOVE

Diamond doves live in dry parts of Australia. Like many other birds that live in dry places, they are nomadic, moving on whenever food becomes scarce. Diamond doves have blue-gray bodies and are named for the diamond-like flecks of white on their wings. They feed on the ground and fly to waterholes in the late afternoon before roosting for the night.

SCIENTIFIC NAME *Geopelia cuneata*

DISTRIBUTION Northern, western, and central Australia

SIZE Up to 8.25 in. (21cm) long

SPINIFEX PIGEON

This Australian pigeon lives in open country dotted with clumps of spinifex grass, a tough, drought-resistant plant with spear-shaped leaves. Spinifex grass grows only after rain, but it produces large crops of seeds that can keep the

pigeon fed during dry weather. Spinifex pigeons are small, with spiky, upright crests and brown markings that blend in with the ground. If they are disturbed, they often scuttle away around the spinifex instead of flying to safety.

SCIENTIFIC NAME *Petrophassa plumifera*

DISTRIBUTION Central and western Australia

SIZE Up to 9 in. (23cm) long

SUPERB FRUIT-DOVE

Compared to most doves and pigeons, fruit-doves are richly colored. The superb fruit-dove has a lime-green body, orange shoulders, and a bright purple patch on its head. It lives in tropical and subtropical forests and feeds mainly in the treetops, only occasionally coming to the ground. Fruit-doves eat small, oily fruits, which they usually swallow whole. They digest the flesh, but they scatter the seeds in their droppings, helping trees spread.

SCIENTIFIC NAME *Ptilinopus superbus*

DISTRIBUTION Northeastern Australia, New Guinea and adjacent islands

SIZE Up to 9.5 in. (24cm) long

VICTORIA CROWNED PIGEON

This extraordinary and rare bird is one of the largest members of the pigeon family. The size of a chicken, it has lustrous, turquoise plumage and a fan-shaped crest of lacy feathers that stays up all the time. Crowned pigeons live in rain forests, feeding on fallen fruit on the forest floor. Like most pigeons, they are popular as food, and hunting has severely reduced their numbers.

SCIENTIFIC NAME *Goura victoria*

DISTRIBUTION New Guinea

SIZE Up to 33 in. (84cm) long

ABOVE *The collared dove (Streptopelia decaocto) originally lived in Asia.*

BELOW *Turtledoves feed mainly on small seeds in fields and open places.* **BOTTOM** *Australia is home to over 24 kinds of pigeons and doves. The diamond dove, shown here, is one of the smallest.*

PARROTS

The parrot family includes some of the world's most colorful and distinctive birds. They have strong, sharply hooked beaks and strong feet for climbing and for picking up food. Most parrots eat fruit, seeds, or nectar, either in trees or on the ground. Parrots usually nest in holes in trees and lay a small number of white, almost round eggs. There are about 300 species of parrots, mostly found in the Southern Hemisphere. Deforestation and illegal hunting are taking their toll on many species, and some face extinction.

SULFUR-CRESTED COCKATOO

Cockatoos are the only parrots with feathery, fanlike crests. They can raise or lower these crests to show their mood. The sulfur-crested cockatoo has a bright yellow crest, and the rest of its plumage is white—an unusual color for a parrot. It lives in a range of habitats, from forests to farmland, roosting high up in eucalyptus trees. It is a popular pet because it can imitate human speech.

SCIENTIFIC NAME	
Cacatua galerita	
DISTRIBUTION	Originally from northern and eastern Australia, New Guinea; introduced into New Zealand
SIZE	Up to 20 in. (50cm) long

GALAH

This attractive, pink and gray cockatoo is one of Australia's best-known parrots. Flocks of galahs can be seen in parks and on beaches, but they are particularly common in wooded country and farmland, where they sometimes cause damage by eating grain. Even by parrot standards, galahs are noisy and energetic birds, particularly when hundreds of them speed through the air, twisting and turning with split-second coordination. Galahs usually nest in holes in trees, but unlike most parrots, they line the hole with leaves and twigs before laying their eggs.

SCIENTIFIC NAME	*Cacatua roseicapilla*
DISTRIBUTION	Australia, except Tasmania
SIZE	Up to 15 in. (38cm) long

COCKATIEL

This popular cage bird is Australia's smallest cockatoo and the only one with a long, pointed tail. Cockatiels have gray and white bodies and yellow crests. The male's face is more brightly colored than the female's. Wild cockatiels live in flocks, feeding mostly on the ground. They lay up to seven eggs in a tree hole by water, and the parents share the work of incubation.

SCIENTIFIC NAME	*Nymphicus hollandicus*
DISTRIBUTION	Australia, except far north and coastal regions
SIZE	Up to 13 in. (33cm) long

LEFT *Sulfur-crested cockatoos often live in city parks and gardens, screeching noisily as they fly through the trees.* RIGHT *A pair of cockatiels sit on a branch. When they fly, cockatiels fold their crests flat against their heads.*

White plumage tinged with yellow under the tail

BUDGERIGAR

Commonly called a parakeet, this small, Australian parrot is one of the world's most popular cage birds. Pet budgerigars can be a variety of colors, including blue, yellow, and white, but wild budgerigars are always yellow and green. Wild budgerigars live in Australia's interior, where the food supply depends on rainfall. If it is dry, flocks of budgerigars wander hundreds of miles looking for food. Budgerigars nest in dead trees or fallen logs, lining their nest-holes with wood chips. They lay up to eight eggs at a time.

SCIENTIFIC NAME	*Melopsittacus undulatus*
DISTRIBUTION	Central Australia
SIZE	Up to 8 in. (20cm) long

RAINBOW LORIKEET

Instead of feeding on seeds or fruit, lorikeets eat mainly nectar and flower pollen. Their tongues have a brushlike tip that helps them lap up their food. The rainbow lorikeet, one of the most widespread species, is vividly colored with a mixture of blue, yellow, red, and green. Like other lorikeets, it sets off to find food at sunrise, screeching loudly as it clambers around high up in the trees. Rainbow lorikeets are easy to tame, and in some places they visit gardens to feed at the flowers.

SCIENTIFIC NAME	*Trichoglossus haematodus*
DISTRIBUTION	New Guinea and adjacent islands, parts of Indonesia, northern and eastern Australia, Tasmania
SIZE	Up to 10 in. (25cm) long

ECLECTUS PARROT

Male and female parrots can look similar, but in this species they are easy to tell apart. The males are bright green, but unusually for a bird, the females are even more colorful, with bright red heads, blue chests, and deep-red backs. Eclectus parrots live in forests, eating fruit, flowers, and buds. Compared to other parrots, their flight is slow, but they have the typical parrot habit of calling as they fly along. They nest high up in trees and usually lay just two eggs at a time.

SCIENTIFIC NAME	*Eclectus roratus*
DISTRIBUTION	New Guinea and adjacent islands, Cape York Peninsula in northeastern Australia
SIZE	Up to 17 in. (43cm) long

Featherless patch around the eye

Two budgerigars on a perch

GRAY PARROT

This large, African parrot is unusual in having mainly gray plumage, apart from its bright red tail. It lives in forests and mangrove swamps, and although it spends most of its life in the treetops, it sometimes lands in fields to feed on grain. Gray parrots fetch high prices as cage birds because they are experts at copying human speech—some have been taught a vocabulary of more than 750 words. This makes them seem highly intelligent, though, as with all "talking" birds, they repeat words without understanding their meaning. Gray parrots are bred in captivity, but birds are also collected illegally in the wild and smuggled abroad for sale.

SCIENTIFIC NAME	*Psittacus erithacus*
DISTRIBUTION	Tropical western and central Africa
SIZE	Up to 13 in. (33cm) long

TOP *Like all parrots, budgerigars have four toes. Two point forward and two point backward, giving them a good grip.*
ABOVE *Many large parrots, such as this African gray, have a patch of bare skin around their eyes. Compared to other birds, parrots have small eyes, although they are still good at spotting food.*

LEFT *Like all their relatives, blue and yellow macaws (Ara ararauna) are noisy birds, screeching loudly as they skim over the treetops.*
BELOW *A scarlet macaw's beak is a multipurpose tool, used for preening feathers and cracking open food.*

SCARLET MACAW

Macaws are the world's largest parrots. They live in Central and South America, often flying in pairs over forests and open woodland as they look for nuts and seeds on the trees below. They have long, tapering tails and powerful wings. There are about 15 species of these magnificent birds, and although all of them are under threat, the scarlet macaw is probably the most numerous. It feeds high up in trees and is a messy eater, dropping pieces of fruit on the ground. When macaws start to feed, agoutis (page 257) and other animals soon arrive to eat this fallen feast. Scarlet macaws usually raise two chicks a year, and it is about three months before the chicks leave the nest.

SCIENTIFIC NAME *Ara macao*
DISTRIBUTION Central America, northern South America
SIZE Up to 33.5 in. (85cm) long

HYACINTH MACAW

This South American macaw is the largest member of the parrot family. It is deep blue all over, except for a bright yellow patch around each eye and beneath its chin. It lives mainly among palm trees close to the banks of rivers. Even for a macaw, its beak is unusually large, and it uses it to pick palm nuts and crack open their tough shells. Hyacinth macaws are a protected species, but they are still sometimes trapped and sold as pets. Fewer than 3,000 of these birds survive in the wild.

SCIENTIFIC NAME *Anodorhynchus hyacinthinus*
DISTRIBUTION Brazil, Bolivia
SIZE Up to 3 ft. (1m) long

A pair of scarlet macaws on a branch

HAWK-HEADED PARROT OR RED-FAN PARROT

This parrot got its name from its large beak and slender shape, which give it a hawklike look. When it is excited or alarmed, it shows off a more unusual feature—a ruff of red feathers that lifts up around the back of its head like a fan. Despite its name, it is a harmless vegetarian, feeding on fruit, seeds, and nuts. Hawk-headed parrots live in forests and wooded grassland and nest in tree holes made by woodpeckers.

SCIENTIFIC NAME *Deroptyus accipitrinus*
DISTRIBUTION Northern South America, from Colombia to Brazil
SIZE Up to 14 in. (35cm) long

as a roosting site, particularly in the winter when the nights can turn cold.

SCIENTIFIC NAME	*Myiopsitta monachus*
DISTRIBUTION	Originally from central South America, from Bolivia to Argentina; introduced into North America, some Caribbean islands
SIZE	Up to 8.5 in. (22cm) long

BLUE-CROWNED HANGING PARROT

Smaller than a sparrow, this blue-headed bird is one of the world's tiniest parrots. It got its name from the way it hangs upside down to rest. It lives in dense forest, and it flies fast and climbs well. Hanging parrots eat nectar, flowers, and fruit, lapping up their food with their tongues. They nest in tree holes and line their nests with leaves, which they carry in the feathers on their rumps.

SCIENTIFIC NAME	*Loriculus galgulus*
DISTRIBUTION	Malaysia, Indonesia
SIZE	Up to 5 in. (12cm) long

KEA

The kea is a large, heavily built parrot from the mountains of New Zealand. Unlike other parrots, it eats dead animals and insects, as well as fruits and seeds. It has dark green plumage, a large beak, and strong feet for walking on the ground. Keas are inquisitive and will help themselves to picnics and leftover food. They will also tug at shoelaces and car windshield wipers. They used to be shot for apparently attacking sheep, but they are now protected.

SCIENTIFIC NAME	*Nestor notabilis*
DISTRIBUTION	South Island of New Zealand
SIZE	Up to 19 in. (48cm) long

KAKAPO

The kakapo is the heaviest parrot and the only one that cannot fly. It emerges after dark to feed on flowers, seeds, and leaves. In the breeding season, male kakapos go to mating grounds, or leks, every night, where they call the females with a booming sound that can be heard over half a mile away. Kakapos have no defenses against introduced mammals, and are now among the most endangered parrots in the world.

SCIENTIFIC NAME	*Strigops habroptilusi*
DISTRIBUTION	Islands offshore of New Zealand
SIZE	Up to 25.5 in. (65cm) long

ROSE-RINGED PARAKEET

Parakeets are small or medium-sized parrots with slim bodies and long tails. Like many parakeets, the rose-ringed parakeet is mainly green, but the male has a thin, black and red ring around its neck. This parakeet is one of the few species that is found in Africa as well as Asia, and in recent years, it has also made its home in North America and Europe. In North America, escaped rose-ringed parakeets live around the cities of Los Angeles and Miami, and in Europe, they can be found as far north as London, England.

SCIENTIFIC NAME	*Psittacula krameri*
DISTRIBUTION	Originally from central and eastern Africa, India, Sri Lanka; introduced into parts of North America, Europe
SIZE	Up to 16 in. (40cm) long

MONK PARAKEET

This green and gray parakeet has a bad reputation with South American farmers because it lives in large, noisy flocks and often raids fields and orchards for food. While a flock is feeding, some birds act as lookouts, giving the alarm if they spot anything dangerous coming their way. Monk parakeets are the only parrots that make nests in the branches of trees. They usually nest very close together, making a giant structure high off the ground. They use their group nests

LEFT *Hyacinth macaws do not start to breed until they are about seven years old, and in an average year each pair manages to raise just one chick. This explains why this species is so easily endangered when its chicks are collected as pets.*

BELOW *The rose-ringed parakeet has managed to adapt to life in cities. In its native home, it lives in large flocks.*

ABOVE *There are only about 50 kakapos left in the wild. They live on islands off the New Zealand coast, where their progress is carefully monitored.*

OWLS

Owls hunt live animals, and most of them catch their prey at night. They have large, forward-facing eyes, well-developed ears, and powerful feet with sharp claws. Many species have soft fringes on their wing feathers, helping them fly almost silently, so they can hear squeaks or rustling on the ground. They hide during the day. There are about 130 species of owls spread across most of the world.

GREAT HORNED OWL

This is North America's largest owl, large enough to kill a fully grown skunk or goose. It has staring, yellow eyes, feathery feet, and two feathery tufts on its head. These tufts are easily mistaken for ears, but they are not used for hearing—the owl's true ears are hidden beneath short feathers on either side of its head. Great horned owls sometimes lay their eggs in holes in trees or rocky crevices, but they usually take over nests abandoned by birds of prey. They lay two or three eggs, which often hatch several days apart.

Adult great horned owl with prey

SCIENTIFIC NAME *Bubo virginianus*

DISTRIBUTION North, Central, and South America, from the Arctic to Tierra del Fuego

SIZE Up to 22 in. (55cm) long

BARN OWL

The barn owl is one of the world's most widespread birds. It has a pale underside and a flat, heart-shaped face, giving it a distinctive silhouette as it flaps slowly over the ground. Barn owls live in a wide variety of habitats, from pastures to semidesert. They feed almost entirely on small rodents, hovering above the ground before dropping down to make a kill. They lay their eggs in holes in trees or in old buildings, but they do not make nests.

ABOVE
The barn owl's ears are so sensitive it can hunt in complete darkness, pinpointing its prey by sound alone.

SCIENTIFIC NAME *Tyto alba*

DISTRIBUTION Worldwide, except the extreme north, central Asia, Far East

SIZE Up to 16 in. (40cm) long

TAWNY OWL

This adaptable owl normally lives in woodland, but it is equally at home among trees in parks and leafy gardens. The male's call is a deep hoot,

All owls have large eyes and can see well, even in the dark

ABOVE AND LEFT *Tawny owls can be brown or gray. Like other owls, tawny owl chicks hatch in sequence, a few days apart. If food is scarce, only the oldest and largest chicks survive.*

while the female's reply is a high-pitched "kee-wick." Tawny owls feed mainly on small mammals, but they are also fond of earthworms. Their hearing is so good that they can hunt their prey in complete darkness.

SCIENTIFIC NAME *Strix aluco*

DISTRIBUTION Europe, northern Africa, central Asia, Far East

SIZE Up to 15 in. (38cm) long

SNOWY OWL
The snowy owl lives in the Arctic tundra, where daylight lasts around the clock in the summer. The owl's white plumage makes it almost invisible against the melting snow. Snowy owls nest on the ground, laying up to eight eggs each time they breed. They feed on lemmings and hares, as well as on other birds. If lemmings are scarce, snowy owls may leave the Arctic altogether during the winter months.

SCIENTIFIC NAME *Nyctea scandiaca*

DISTRIBUTION High Arctic worldwide

SIZE Up to 26 in. (66cm) long

ELF OWL
The elf owl is the smallest owl in the world. It lives in deserts and on wooded hillsides, where it eats grasshoppers, moths, and other insects, often swooping down on them from its perch. With its short tail and tiny feet, the elf owl is small enough to nest and roost in holes made by woodpeckers. In woodlands, these holes are in trees, but in the desert, they are in saguaro cacti.

SCIENTIFIC NAME *Micrathene whitneyi*

DISTRIBUTION Southwestern United States, Mexico

SIZE Up to 6 in. (15cm) long

BURROWING OWL
Burrowing owls live in open places, where there is no cover for rearing a family. They dig burrows for shelter or take over those made by other animals. They have long, slender legs and use their feet and beaks to scratch at the ground. Burrowing owls hunt at night, but they spend much of the day standing by the entrances to their homes. If disturbed, they make a call that sounds like a rattlesnake shaking its tail.

SCIENTIFIC NAME *Athene cunicularia*

DISTRIBUTION North, Central, and South America

SIZE Up to 10 in. (25cm) long

LEFT Female snowy owls, like this one, have white plumage with black marks, but the males are often completely white.

BELOW An elf owl sits in front of its nest hole with a moth in its beak.

BOOBOOK OWL
This dark brown, fully nocturnal owl got its name from its high-pitched, two-note call. It perches on branches and fences, flying out to catch its prey. Boobooks eat insects and other small animals and sometimes catch their food around streetlights in towns.

SCIENTIFIC NAME *Ninox novaehollandiae*

DISTRIBUTION Australia, New Zealand, New Guinea and adjacent islands

SIZE Up to 14 in. (35cm) long

BROWN FISH OWL
Several of the world's owls, including the brown fish owl, prey on frogs and fish. Most of these owls have bare legs and feet, with sharp scales on their toes to keep hold of their prey. The brown fish owl hunts at dusk, swooping over the water's surface or wading into the shallows to find food.

SCIENTIFIC NAME *Bubo zeylonensis*

DISTRIBUTION India, Southeast Asia

SIZE Up to 22 in. (55cm) long

ABOVE The burrowing owl is easy to recognize because it stands like a sentry by its burrow. These birds nest in all kinds of open places, including golf courses and airports.

NIGHTJARS AND FROGMOUTHS

Nightjars, also known as nighthawks, are nocturnal birds that catch insects on the wing. They have small beaks, but their mouths open up like funnels to scoop up their prey in midair. During the day they often rest on the ground, but their excellent camouflage keeps them safely out of sight. Frogmouths are similar to nightjars, but they catch their food on the ground and usually roost in trees. There are about 70 species of nightjars and 12 species of frogmouths. Nightjars are found in warm areas all over the world, while frogmouths live only in Southeast Asia and Australia. The oilbird, a remarkable relative of these strange birds, is found only in South America.

EUROPEAN NIGHTJAR

After dark, the male European nightjar makes a soft, churring noise, clapping his wings to attract a mate. European nightjars feed over scrubland and roost on the ground during the day. With their wings and eyes closed, their gray and brown plumage makes them look like pieces of fallen wood.

Male

Female

SCIENTIFIC NAME	*Caprimulgus europaeus*
DISTRIBUTION	Breeds in Europe, central Asia; migrates to Africa in the winter
SIZE	Up to 11 in. (28cm) long

ABOVE *Male and female European nightjars have slightly different patterns.*
BELOW *A tawny frogmouth sits on its nest with two recently hatched chicks. The nest is a flimsy platform of sticks.*

COMMON NIGHTHAWK

This widespread, American bird starts hunting before sunset, which makes it easy to spot. It has slim, gray-brown wings, with a splash of white near the tips that can be seen when it flies. During the breeding season, the male carries out courtship flights as the light fades, swooping down to the ground and making a booming sound with his wings. Nighthawks normally nest on the ground or on tree stumps, but in some areas, they nest on flat roofs as well. They lay two camouflaged eggs at a time.

SCIENTIFIC NAME	*Chordeiles minor*
DISTRIBUTION	Breeds in North and Central America; migrates to South America in the winter
SIZE	Up to 9.5 in. (24cm) long

TAWNY FROGMOUTH

If this gray or red bird is approached on its daytime perch, it camouflages itself as a piece of wood. It flattens its feathers, points its beak skyward, and stays absolutely still. It closes its eyes until they are almost shut, leaving a gap so it can see what is happening. The tawny frogmouth lives in forests and open woodland, where it feeds mainly on insects, though it also eats lizards and mice. It hunts after dark and often catches its food along roads.

SCIENTIFIC NAME	*Podargus strigoides*
DISTRIBUTION	Australia, Tasmania
SIZE	Up to 18.5 in. (47cm) long

OILBIRD

Oilbirds feed on oily fruit from rain forest trees. They breed and roost on ledges deep inside caves, making their nests out of their own droppings. When they return from their nightly feeding trips, oilbirds fly as much as 2,600 ft. (800m) under ground. They find their way as bats do (pages 240-241), using bursts of sound to judge distances. Despite the darkness, oilbirds can find their own chicks among the hundreds or thousands in the cave.

SCIENTIFIC NAME	*Steatornis caripensis*
DISTRIBUTION	Panama, northern South America, Trinidad
SIZE	Up to 19 in. (48cm) long

CUCKOOS AND THEIR RELATIVES

Cuckoos are best known for their habit of laying their eggs in other birds' nests. This way, they avoid the hard work that goes into feeding and looking after their young. In reality, only about 50 species actually use other birds as foster parents—the rest raise their own young. There are about 130 species of cuckoos, most of which live in trees. Turacos are relatives of cuckoos that live in forests in Africa. There are about 20 species, and unlike cuckoos, almost all of them are beautifully colored.

Adult European cuckoo

Juvenile European cuckoo

COMMON CUCKOO

Throughout Europe and northern Asia, this bird's call—a loud "cu-koo"—is a sign that spring is well underway. It lays its eggs in the nests of warblers and other small birds, fluttering down when the parents are away. The cuckoo lays just one egg in each nest it visits, and its chick is often the first to hatch. The chick pushes the other eggs out of the nest so that it can get all the food. Amazingly, the foster parents do not realize that they have been tricked, even though the cuckoo chick grows to be several times their own size.

SCIENTIFIC NAME   *Cuculus canorus*

DISTRIBUTION   Breeds in Europe, northern Asia; migrates to Africa, southern Asia in the winter

SIZE   Up to 13 in. (33cm) long

GREATER ROADRUNNER

The roadrunner is one of a small group of cuckoos that spend most of their time on the ground. It lives in semidesert and scrub, speeding after lizards and snakes on its long legs. It has a long tail and short, broad wings, which it uses to swerve around rocks and bushes faster than most people can run. Roadrunners build nests in cacti or thorn bushes, laying up to six eggs at a time.

SCIENTIFIC NAME   *Geococcyx californianus*

DISTRIBUTION   Southern United States, northern Mexico

SIZE   Up to 23 in. (58cm) long

GREAT BLUE TURACO

This is the largest turaco, with a body as large as a pheasant's. Like other turacos, it has silky plumage and nests high up in trees. It feeds mainly on fruit, and although it is not a good flier, it is an expert at hopping or running along branches to get to its food. Turaco chicks have tiny claws on their wings, which they use to clamber among the branches near their nests.

SCIENTIFIC NAME   *Corythaeola cristata*

DISTRIBUTION   Central and western Africa

SIZE   Up to 29.5 in. (75cm) long

HOATZIN

The South American hoatzin is one of the world's most eccentric birds. It has a long neck and a spiky crest and lives in dense forest near rivers and lakes. It feeds entirely on leaves—a bulky diet that gives it a strong smell and makes it difficult for it to fly. Like young turacos, hoatzin chicks have claws on their wings. If they are threatened, the chicks drop into the water below their nests, clambering back up again when the coast is clear.

SCIENTIFIC NAME   *Opisthocomus hoatzin*

DISTRIBUTION   Northern South America

SIZE   Up to 25.5 in. (65cm) long

ABOVE AND ABOVE INSET *Young cuckoos soon grow larger than their foster parents—in this case, a reed warbler (page 216).*

ABOVE *The roadrunner can sprint at nearly 15 mph—faster than the snakes it pursues. It beats them on the ground before eating them.*

SWIFTS AND HUMMINGBIRDS

Swifts spend more time in the air than any other flying animals—they catch insects, drink, and even sleep on the wing. Their wings are long and slender, and their feet are so small that they cannot perch, but cling to rough surfaces instead. Hummingbirds, close relatives of swifts, also have tiny feet. These minute, jewel-colored birds feed on nectar, hovering in front of flowers as they feed. There are nearly 100 species of swifts. They are found all over the world, often as summer visitors. There are about 340 species of hummingbirds, but they are found only in the Americas.

BELOW *This young Eurasian swift has only recently left its nest, but it is already a good flier.*

EURASIAN SWIFT

During its lifetime, this sleek, black bird spends more time in the air than any other species that lives over land. After leaving its nest, it spends three or four years in the air, until the time comes for it to breed. Swifts migrate north in the spring to breed and produce two or three young each year. In the summer, small flocks often hurtle over rooftops and along city streets, screaming as they speed through the air.

SCIENTIFIC NAME *Apus apus*

DISTRIBUTION Breeds in Europe, Asia; migrates mainly to Africa in the winter

SIZE Up to 7 in. (18cm) long

ABOVE *The alpine swift* (Apus melba) *is a common summer visitor to southern Europe.*

CHIMNEY SWIFT

This small, brown swift originally roosted and nested in hollow trees, but it now uses barns and chimneys. In late summer, some chimneys get crowded when flocks of migrating birds use them as rest stops on their way south. Like most swifts, these birds make their nests from feathers and dust snatched up in midair, which they glue together with their sticky saliva. Chimneys make ideal nesting sites, so chimney swifts are more common than they once were.

SCIENTIFIC NAME *Chaetura pelagica*

DISTRIBUTION Breeds in eastern Canada, eastern United States; migrates to Central America, northern South America in the winter

SIZE Up to 5 in. (13cm) long

Each wing can beat independently at a different speed

Grooves in front of the eyes allow the bird to see ahead

RUBY-THROATED HUMMINGBIRD

During the summer, this mostly green hummingbird flies as far north as Canada, feeding on nectar from flowers and on small insects. Like all hummingbird species, it has a tube-shaped beak and laps up its food with its tongue. It makes its nest out of leaves and lichen tied together with spiders' silk. It lays two white eggs at a time, each smaller than a pea. Despite being so tiny, hummingbirds are fearless and will chase away rivals in noisy, midair fights.

SCIENTIFIC NAME *Archilochus colubris*

DISTRIBUTION Breeds in eastern North America; migrates to Florida, Central America in the winter

SIZE Up to 3.5 in. (9cm) long

Small, densely packed feathers

Tiny feet cannot be used for perching

Tail feathers fan out to slow the bird down

RIGHT *At top speed, the ruby-throated hummingbird's wings beat more than 70 times a second—so fast that they seem to disappear into a blur.*

RIGHT *The sword-billed hummingbird can feed at flowers that are too large for other hummingbirds to reach into. Although its beak looks unwieldy, the hummingbird is also good at catching insects in midair.*

SWORD-BILLED HUMMINGBIRD

This hummingbird's beak is almost as long as its body—a record for any bird. The bird uses it to collect nectar from downward-hanging flowers, hovering beneath them as it feeds. When it perches, the sword-billed hummingbird holds its beak almost vertically, which makes it easier to support. This hummingbird lives high up in trees and rarely comes down to the ground.

SCIENTIFIC NAME *Ensifera ensifera*

DISTRIBUTION Andes Mountains in northern South America

SIZE Up to 10 in. (25cm) long

BEE HUMMINGBIRD

This rarely seen hummingbird is the tiniest bird in the world. Without its feathers, it would be smaller and lighter than many bumblebees, though it chases away butterflies several times its own size. Its eggs can be as small as 0.25 in. (6mm) long, and it lays them in a nest smaller than an egg-cup. Bee hummingbirds feed from a wide range of flowers and catch insects to feed to their young.

SCIENTIFIC NAME *Calypte helenae*

DISTRIBUTION Cuba

SIZE About 2 in. (5cm) long

GIANT HUMMINGBIRD

Though only the size of a starling, this plain, brown bird is by far the largest hummingbird. It cannot hover as well as its relatives and often perches next to flowers to feed. The giant hummingbird lives in mountains, where its size helps it cope with the nighttime cold.

SCIENTIFIC NAME *Patagona gigas*

DISTRIBUTION Andes Mountains in South America

SIZE About 8.5 in. (22cm) long

TROGONS AND MOUSEBIRDS

Trogons are forest birds found in the tropics. There are about 35 species scattered across the Americas, Africa, and Asia, including some of the most beautiful birds in the world. Despite their flamboyant colors, trogons are difficult to see because they spend much of their time perched motionless high in the treetops. Mousebirds are not related to trogons, and they look rather dowdy in comparison. There are six species, all from Africa. They got their name from their habit of scurrying around in trees.

RESPLENDENT QUETZAL

This Central American bird is the most showy member of the trogon family. The males have red underparts and green heads and backs, but their most spectacular feature is a three-foot-long train of lacy, green plumes that hangs down over their tails. Quetzals live in mountain forests, where they feed on oil-rich fruit. They nest in holes in trees, and both parents share the work of incubating the eggs. The female can fit inside the nest, but the male has to turn around after he has climbed in, so his tail plumes hang out of the entrance.

SCIENTIFIC NAME *Pharomachrus mocinno*

DISTRIBUTION Central America, northern South America

SIZE Up to 4.5 ft. (1.4m) long, including tail plumes

BLUE-NAPED MOUSEBIRD

Mousebirds have long, slender tails and unusual feet with outer toes that can swivel forward or backward. They feed on leaves, seeds, and insects, scuttling along branches or hanging upside down to get to their food. The blue-naped mousebird is one of the most widespread species. It lives in small flocks that flutter noisily from tree to tree, and its young begin to creep among the branches soon after they hatch.

SCIENTIFIC NAME *Colias macrourus*

DISTRIBUTION Tropical Africa

SIZE Up to 14 in. (35cm) long

ABOVE *High in the treetops, a male quetzal rests on a lichen-covered perch. Although they are brilliantly colored, quetzals are unobtrusive birds. Unlike some fruit-eating birds, such as parrots (pages 196-199), they feed quietly and on their own.*

BELOW *With a fish firmly grasped in its beak, this European kingfisher is on its way back to its perch to feed. Like other waterbirds, kingfishers swallow fish headfirst.*

Wings beat rapidly during flight

Blue-green back provides camouflage in the shade

Small, bright orange legs and feet

Common kingfisher watching for food

BELTED KINGFISHER

This is the only kingfisher in most of North America. The males are blue-gray and white, but the females have a rust-colored "belt" across their undersides. This kingfisher watches for food from branches above the water. If it spots a fish, it dives to catch it, then carries it back to its perch and stuns it against a branch before swallowing it.

Belted kingfisher on a perch

SCIENTIFIC NAME *Megaceryle alcyon*

DISTRIBUTION Breeds throughout North America; migrates to southern United States, Central America, Colombia in the winter

SIZE Up to 13 in. (33cm) long

EUROPEAN KINGFISHER

With its turquoise and orange plumage, this bird looks like it belongs in the tropics, but it is found as far north as Scandinavia. Its hunting technique is similar to the belted kingfisher's, though the smaller European kingfisher catches much smaller fish. It uses its beak and claws to dig a nest burrow in the riverbank, and it is careful to make the burrow slope upward, so rain or river water cannot get in. Kingfishers do not use nesting material, but their burrows soon become cluttered with fish bones.

SCIENTIFIC NAME *Alcedo atthis*

DISTRIBUTION Europe, northern Africa, central and southern Asia

SIZE Up to 6 in. (15cm) long

KINGFISHERS AND THEIR RELATIVES

This varied group of birds includes kingfishers, rollers, hoopoes, bee-eaters, and hornbills. All of these birds have partially joined front toes, and many of them are brightly colored. Kingfishers are found on every continent, but only about half of the 92 species actually feed on fish. The rest live away from water, snatching lizards and other animals from the ground. Their relatives also live mainly by catching animals, although hornbills often eat fruit. Rollers, hoopoes, bee-eaters, and hornbills are mainly tropical birds, though none of them live in the Americas.

Laughing kookaburra overpowering a snake

LAUGHING KOOKABURRA

This giant Australian kingfisher is famous for its call, which sounds like crazy laughter. It often lives in family groups, and if one bird starts to call, the others soon follow suit. Laughing kookaburras live in dry forests. They catch their prey on the ground. They eat insects, lizards, and small birds, and are also adept at catching snakes. Like waterside kingfishers, they usually stun their prey before swallowing it, either by dropping it on the ground or by battering it against a branch.

Kookaburras usually nest in hollow tree trunks. Young birds often help their parents for several breeding seasons by bringing food to the nest.

SCIENTIFIC NAME *Dacelo novaeguineae*

DISTRIBUTION Eastern and southwestern Australia

SIZE Up to 18.5 in. (47cm) long

EUROPEAN ROLLER

Rollers resemble jays (page 229), but they are more closely related to kingfishers. Many of them, including the European roller, are brown and bright blue. Most feed on insects, catching them on the ground or sometimes in the air. Rollers get their name from the male's aerobatic courtship display. He flies high into the air and then dives down, twisting as he falls. European rollers nest in unlined tree holes and lay up to five white eggs at a time.

SCIENTIFIC NAME *Coracias garrulus*

DISTRIBUTION Breeds in Europe, Siberia; migrates to Africa in the winter

SIZE Up to 12.5 in. (32cm) long

HOOPOE

The hoopoe is a ground-feeding bird with a pink body and black and white wings. It has a crest that it can flick over its head and a long, curved beak. It uses its beak to probe grass and animal dung for worms and grubs. Hoopoes nest in holes in trees and walls and are famously unhygienic. While the female incubates the eggs, she and her nest give off a strong smell that may help keep predators away.

SCIENTIFIC NAME *Upupa epops*

DISTRIBUTION Europe, southern Asia, Africa

SIZE Up to 11.5 in. (29cm) long

CARMINE BEE-EATER

Vividly colored bee-eaters live in Europe, Africa, Asia, and Australia, and they specialize in eating bees. They snatch them in midair in their long, curved beaks and carry them back to a perch. Then they wipe the bees against the perch to squeeze the poison from the bees' stingers, making them safe to eat.

SCIENTIFIC NAME *Merops nubicus*

DISTRIBUTION Central Africa

SIZE Up to 13 in. (33cm) long

GREAT INDIAN HORNBILL

Hornbills live in Africa and southern Asia and feed on small animals and fruit. They got their name from their massive, curved beaks, which are often topped with a hard shield, or casque. The great Indian hornbill is one of the largest species, with a wingspan of about 6 ft. (2m). Hornbills nest in tree holes, and the female incubates the eggs. Once she is in the nest, the male seals the entrance with mud, leaving a small hole through which he can pass food. The female stays imprisoned for up to three months, until her nestlings are ready to venture out. This remarkable behavior helps protect the chicks from snakes and other predators.

SCIENTIFIC NAME *Buceros bicornis*

DISTRIBUTION India, Southeast Asia

SIZE Up to 4 ft. (1.2m) long

Rusty brown back

Raised crest

Hoopoe

European roller

Great Indian hornbill

BELOW LEFT *The European roller watches for food from high lookout posts, such as telephone poles and dead trees.*

BELOW CENTER *A hoopoe uses its eyecatching crest to show its mood. This bird's raised crest shows it is alert.*

BELOW RIGHT *Great Indian hornbills eat anything they can collect or overpower. This bird has caught a lizard, which it will swallow whole.*

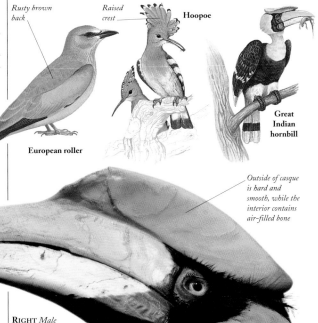

Outside of casque is hard and smooth, while the interior contains air-filled bone

RIGHT *Male hornbills, such as this great Indian hornbill, have larger casques than females. The casques show the birds' age and sex. In some species, they help amplify the birds' calls.*

WOODPECKERS AND TOUCANS

Woodpeckers and toucans both live in trees, but they feed in very
different ways. Most woodpeckers hack at wood with their beaks so
they can reach insect grubs hidden inside. They are good climbers, clinging
to the bark with their sharp claws while they brace themselves with their
stubby tails. Toucans feed mainly on fruit, and they perch on top of branches
instead of climbing up them. Their vividly colored beaks are enormous, but also
surprisingly light. Toucans use them like pincers, craning forward to reach their
food. There are about 200 species of woodpeckers, and they live all over the world,
except in Madagascar and Australia. The toucan
family contains only about 35 species, all
in Central or South America.

GREEN WOODPECKER

Instead of feeding in trees, this green and
yellow woodpecker finds most of its food on the
ground. Ants are its favorite prey, and it collects
them by pushing its tongue deep into their nests.
All woodpeckers have long tongues, often with
spiny tips. The green woodpecker's tongue is
spiny and sticky, which helps it collect its prey.
Most woodpeckers signal to each other by
drumming their beaks against trees, but this
one uses its loud, laughing call instead.

SCIENTIFIC NAME	*Picus viridis*
DISTRIBUTION	Europe
SIZE	Up to 12.5 in. (32cm) long

BLACK WOODPECKER

This is one of the world's largest
woodpeckers, and it has an exceptionally
powerful peck. When searching for food,
it can chisel its way through 6 in. (15cm) of
solid wood, scattering wood chips the size of
clothespins. As with other woodpeckers, its
brain is specially cushioned inside its skull.
Without this protection, its brain would
soon be damaged by the impact of the beak
smashing into trees. Black woodpeckers feed
mainly on insect grubs, but they also break open
nests in tree holes to eat the young birds inside.

SCIENTIFIC NAME	*Dryocopus martius*
DISTRIBUTION	Europe, Asia
SIZE	Up to 17.5 in. (45cm) long

ACORN WOODPECKER

Acorn woodpeckers live in family groups of
up to 15 birds. They eat insects in the summer,
but in the winter, they eat acorns. To ensure
they have enough acorns to stay well fed, they
store them in holes pecked in dead trees, called
"granary trees." Each hole is large enough for
only one acorn, and thousands of holes are
drilled all the way up the trunk. The

ABOVE
*Watched by her
mate, a female black
woodpecker peers out
of her nest hole.*
LEFT *Strong feet and a
stiff tail give this green
woodpecker a steady grip.*

RIGHT *An adult
acorn woodpecker
returns with food for
its young. Its nest is
surrounded by acorns
that have been wedged
into holes in the bark.*

woodpeckers hammer the acorns very tightly into the wood, then keep a close watch on their food stores, chasing other birds away before they can steal anything.

SCIENTIFIC NAME *Melanerpes formicivorus*

DISTRIBUTION Western North America, Central America

SIZE Up to 9 in. (23cm) long

NORTHERN FLICKER

Flickers are ground-feeding woodpeckers that live throughout the Americas. Like the green woodpecker, they are fond of ants and have sticky tongues. The northern flicker breeds in North America, chiseling nest holes in trees, telephone poles, and sometimes in the walls of wooden houses. During the spring, it makes a loud, drumming sound by hammering on dead branches and roofs.

SCIENTIFIC NAME *Colaptes auratus*

DISTRIBUTION North and Central America, Caribbean islands

SIZE Up to 12.5 in. (32cm) long

TOCO TOUCAN

This extraordinary bird is the largest toucan, with a bright yellow beak and a blue ring around its eyes. Its beak is about as long as a banana, but it contains many air-filled spaces that make it less heavy and cumbersome than it looks. Toco toucans hop along branches on their pale blue, scaly feet, feeding on fruit and small animals such as insects. Scientists are not sure why toucans' beaks are so huge. They are useful for reaching food, but they may also help the birds recognize members of their own species, because each species has its own beak colors.

SCIENTIFIC NAME *Rhamphastos toco*

DISTRIBUTION Tropical South America

SIZE Up to 23.5 in. (60cm) long

KEEL-BILLED TOUCAN

The keel-billed toucan is slightly smaller than the toco toucan, but it has an even showier beak, colored brown, orange, green, and blue. It lives in forests and in wooded areas near farms. Like other toucans, it flies by alternately flapping its wings and then closing them by its sides, dipping up and down in the air. Toucan chicks take a long time to develop. The keel-billed toucan's young take a month to start growing their

Patch of bare skin around eyes

White throat patch

Both halves of the beak have serrated edges

feathers and do not leave the nest hole until they are nearly two months old.

SCIENTIFIC NAME *Rhamphastos sulfuratus*

DISTRIBUTION North, Central, and South America, from Mexico to Venezuela

SIZE Up to 22 in. (55cm) long

GREEN ARACARI

Aracaris are medium-sized toucans with relatively small, slender beaks. There are about 11 species, and the green aracari is one of the brightest, with a green back and a bright yellow chest. Like its larger relatives, it nests in tree holes, laying between two and four eggs a year. Aracaris are the only toucans that use tree holes as overnight roosts as well as places to breed. Several birds often use the same roost. In order to fit, they make themselves more compact by turning their beaks over their backs.

SCIENTIFIC NAME *Pteroglossus viridis*

DISTRIBUTION Tropical South America

SIZE Up to 12 in. (30cm) long

BLUE-THROATED BARBET

Barbets, small birds with strong beaks and thickset bodies, are related to woodpeckers and toucans. There are about 80 species throughout the tropics, many of which have long, repetitive calls. They got their name from the bristles, or barbs, around the bases of their beaks. The blue-throated barbet lives in forests and gardens, where it feeds on fruit and insects.

SCIENTIFIC NAME *Megalaima asiatica*

DISTRIBUTION India, Southeast Asia

SIZE Up to 9 in. (23cm) long

Two toes point forward and two backward

TOP *Like all large toucans, this keel-billed toucan has a black body, a bright throat patch, and a giant beak.*
ABOVE *Different species of toucans sometimes feed together. Here, two keel-billed toucans look on as a toco toucan carefully leans forward to pick a berry.*

PERCHING BIRDS

More than 5,000 species of birds—over half the world's total—belong to a group called the passerine, or perching, birds. Most of them are small, and all of them have slender, unwebbed toes that can fold around branches, twigs, or wires. When these birds rest on a perch, their toes lock into position so they cannot fall off, even when they are asleep. There are more than 60 families of perching birds, and almost all of them nest in trees. Their nestlings, blind and helpless when they hatch, are fed by their parents until they are fully fledged and able to find food for themselves. Perching birds are found worldwide, but few live on water. Primitive perching birds, which are featured on these two pages, are often poor singers, but songbirds (pages 212–229) include the best singers in the world.

RUFOUS OVENBIRD OR RUFOUS HORNERO

This small, brown bird is unremarkable to look at, but it is famous for its extraordinary nests. It uses wet mud and straw to build a structure shaped like an old-fashioned clay oven, which becomes rock-hard as it slowly dries. The nest's entrance leads into a spiral passageway that crosses over a low threshold before opening into the nesting chamber itself. The nest is usually positioned on a branch or on top of a fencepost, often where it is easy to see. Ovenbirds use their nests for just one breeding season and make new ones each year.

SCIENTIFIC NAME	*Furnarius rufus*
DISTRIBUTION	Central South America
SIZE	Up to 7 in. (18cm) long

LOVELY COTINGA

This small, pretty bird lives in the forests of Central America, where it feeds on fruit and insects. The females are dark brown, but the males are richly colored, with sky-blue feathers all over, except for a lilac patch on their throats and chests. There are about 90 species of cotingas, and almost all of them live in trees. They are common throughout warm parts of the Americas, but are not found anywhere else.

SCIENTIFIC NAME	*Cotinga amabilis*
DISTRIBUTION	Central America
SIZE	Up to 8 in. (20cm) long

THREE-WATTLED BELLBIRD

Bellbirds live in dense forest and are often difficult to see. However, there is no mistaking their call—a sudden explosion of sound that can be heard up to 2,600 ft. (800m) away. The male

TOP *This Rufous ovenbird is standing in a half-built nest. It will finish the nest with a roof to protect the chicks.*
ABOVE *A three-wattled bellbird prepares to call from his display perch in a forest in Costa Rica.*

three-wattled bellbird has another striking feature—three black, wormlike wattles that hang from the top and sides of its beak. Bellbirds belong to the cotinga family. There are four species, each with its own colors and calls.

SCIENTIFIC NAME	*Procnias tricarunculata*
DISTRIBUTION	Central America
SIZE	Up to 12 in. (30cm) long

UMBRELLABIRD

This all-black cotinga is the largest species in its family, with a body the size of a crow's. It got its name from its flattened crest, which looks like an umbrella or hat. The feathery pouch that hangs from its throat is inflatable, and in males it can be more than 12 in. (30cm) long when fully extended. The male lets his pouch hang over a branch when he broadcasts his courtship call.

SCIENTIFIC NAME	*Cephalopterus ornatus*
DISTRIBUTION	Northern South America
SIZE	Up to 20 in. (50cm) long

GUIANAN COCK-OF-THE-ROCK

Many cotingas are brightly colored, and the cock-of-the-rock is one of the most beautiful species of all. Though the female is black, the male is an intense orange—a rare color even in tropical birds. The male birds are made even more striking by their semicircular, orange crests, which fold out to reach the tips of their beaks. During the breeding season, the males gather at traditional courtship grounds, or leks, to carry out noisy displays. The females watch the performance and select the most impressive males as their mates.

SCIENTIFIC NAME	*Rupicola rupicola*
DISTRIBUTION	Northern South America
SIZE	Up to 12.5 in. (32cm) long

Slender display feathers on wings

RIGHT *Standing on a log, a male Guianan cock-of-the-rock shows off his spectacular plumage. Once a male has mated, he takes no part in building a nest or raising the young.*

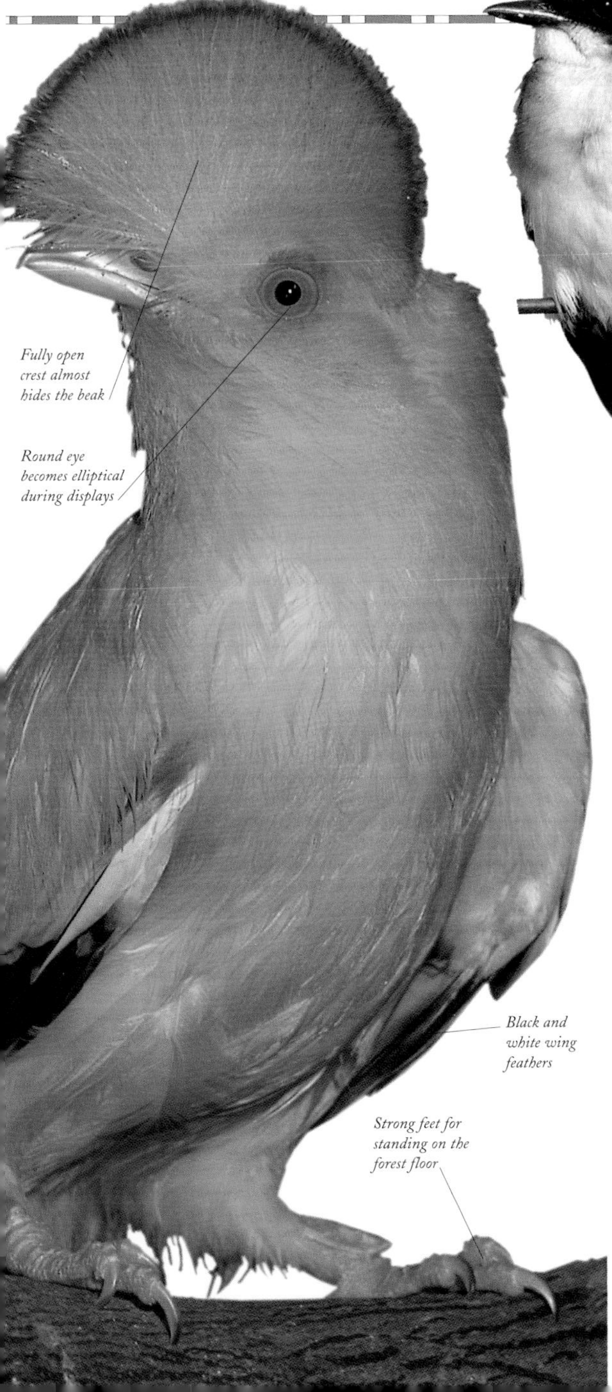

Fully open crest almost hides the beak
Round eye becomes elliptical during displays
Black and white wing feathers
Strong feet for standing on the forest floor

LEFT *An Eastern kingbird watches for flying insects from its perch on an overhead wire.*

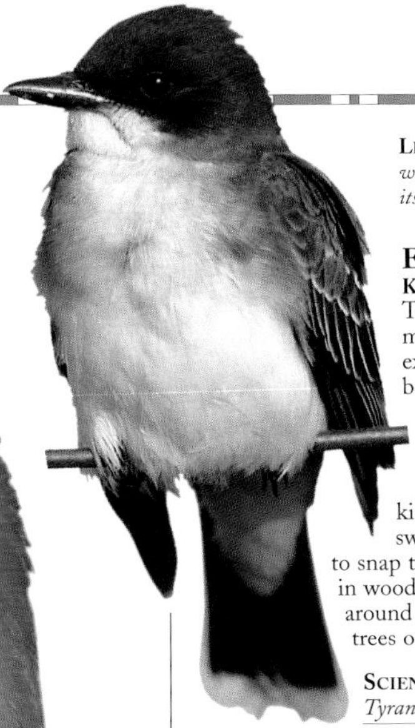

EASTERN KINGBIRD

This bird breeds across most of North America, except the far west. It belongs to a family called the tyrant flycatchers, named for the fearless way these birds defend their nests. The Eastern kingbird feeds on insects, swooping out from a perch to snap them up in midair. It lives in woodland clearings and around farms, and nests in trees or on fenceposts.

SCIENTIFIC NAME *Tyrannus tyrannus*

DISTRIBUTION Breeds in North America; migrates to Central America, South America in the winter

SIZE Up to 8.5 in. (22cm) long

EASTERN PHOEBE

Phoebes get their name from their song, a sharp-sounding "fee-bee, fee-bee, fee-bee." Like other tyrant flycatchers, they fly out from a perch to catch insects. Eastern phoebes are brown and white, with small whiskers around their beaks. They often live near water and originally nested on cliffs or banks. Today, many nest in buildings or under bridges.

SCIENTIFIC NAME *Sayornis phoebe*

DISTRIBUTION Breeds in eastern North America; migrates to southeastern United States, Mexico in the winter

SIZE Up to 7 in. (18cm) long

SUPERB LYREBIRD

This Australian bird has large legs and a plump body covered in gray and brown feathers. The female's tail is long and thin, but the male's has four curved feathers and lacy plumes that spread open and tip forward during the bird's courtship display. Lyrebirds live in forests, feeding on insects and other small animals they find on the ground. They are skillful mimics and can copy many sounds, from birdsong to machinery.

SCIENTIFIC NAME *Menura novaehollandiae*

DISTRIBUTION Southeastern Australia, Tasmania

SIZE Up to 3 ft. (1m) long, including tail

SKYLARK

Larks are small, brown and gray birds that feed and nest on the ground. Many of them are good singers, but the skylark outshines all the others. It sings while it climbs into the sky and keeps singing from high up in the air. Skylarks tuck their cup-shaped nests out of sight in grassy fields, where they raise two or three families a year. They eat insects and seeds.

SCIENTIFIC NAME *Alauda arvensis*

DISTRIBUTION Europe, Asia, northern Africa

SIZE Up to 7 in. (18cm) long

ABOVE *Skylarks have been badly affected by changes in farming practices because they need undisturbed pasture for nesting. This kind of habitat can be hard to find on modern farms.*

BELOW AND BOTTOM
A barn swallow's tail feathers show how old it is. This one has short feathers, showing that it is less than a year old.

HOUSE MARTIN

This airborne insect-eater is a close relative of the barn swallow and is sometimes mistaken for it. However, unlike the barn swallow, it has a short tail and a large, white patch on its deep blue back. Its underside is completely white. House martins make their nests out of mud, with tiny entrance holes. They usually nest under overhanging eaves, where they are protected from the rain, but they also build nests under bridges and on rock faces and cliffs.

SCIENTIFIC NAME *Delichon urbica*

DISTRIBUTION Breeds in Europe, Asia; migrates to Africa, India, Southeast Asia in the winter

SIZE Up to 5 in. (12cm) long

BARN SWALLOW

The barn swallow is one of the world's best-known migrants. It feeds on insects, which it catches in midair. Its streamlined, blue and white body is shaped for fast, long-distance flight, and its narrow wings and forked tail make it highly maneuverable, so that it can twist and turn after its prey.

SCIENTIFIC NAME
Hirundo rustica

DISTRIBUTION Breeds in the Northern Hemisphere; migrates to the Southern Hemisphere in the winter

SIZE Up to 7.5 in. (19cm) long

Food in beak shows that this house martin is raising a family

RIGHT AND FAR RIGHT
House martins often feed in the same areas as barn swallows, but they usually fly higher up. This keeps the two species from competing for the same food.

Legs tucked up during flight

Short tail feathers

PURPLE MARTIN

Every spring, millions of purple martins fly north to the United States and Canada to return to the places where they bred or hatched the previous year. Unlike most other martins and swallows, these birds vary in color according to their sex. The males are shiny purple all over, but the females are gray underneath. Purple martins normally nest in tree holes and on rocky ledges, but they are also attracted to purpose-built birdhouses, particularly in the east.

SCIENTIFIC NAME *Progne subis*

DISTRIBUTION Breeds in North America; migrates to northern South America in the winter

SIZE Up to 7.5 in. (19cm) long

PIED WAGTAIL

Whether they are walking or standing still, wagtails constantly bob their tails up and down. This tail-wagging probably helps them balance as they move around, watching the ground for insects to eat. There are eight species of wagtails, all with slender bodies, narrow beaks, and long legs and toes. Pied wagtails are black, gray, and white. They live on open ground, around farms, and in gardens, and often nest on ivy-covered walls.

SCIENTIFIC NAME *Motacilla alba*

DISTRIBUTION Europe, northern Africa, Asia

SIZE Up to 7 in. (18cm) long

ROCK PIPIT

Pipits are small, brown birds that spend most of their lives on the ground. Most are found inland, but the rock pipit lives along the shore, where it feeds on small snails, beach fleas, and tiny flies that breed in rotting seaweed. The rock pipit nests in crevices in cliffs, making its cup-shaped nest out of

Long, narrow wings provide speed and maneuverability

grass. Like many songbirds, it often collects hair or wool caught on fences to give its nest a warm lining.

SCIENTIFIC NAME *Anthus petrosus*

DISTRIBUTION Western Europe

SIZE Up to 6.75 in. (17cm) long

RED-EYED BULBUL

In Africa and southern Asia, bulbuls feed in open woodlands, parks, gardens, and other places where there are insects and ripe fruit. There are more than 100 species of bulbuls. The red-eyed bulbul is a typical example, with a whistling call and busy, self-assured manner. It has a gray-brown body, a black head, and bright red rings around its eyes, from which it got its name. Like most other bulbuls, it nests in low trees and bushes. The parents take turns incubating the eggs, and both parents feed their young.

SCIENTIFIC NAME *Pycnonotus jocosus*

DISTRIBUTION Southern Africa

SIZE Up to 8.25 in. (21cm) long

RED-BACKED SHRIKE

Although they are songbirds, shrikes behave more like miniature birds of prey. They attack insects, lizards, birds, and small rodents, killing them with their hooked beaks. If they kill more animals than they need, they store the surplus food by impaling it on thorns or sometimes on the spikes of barbed-wire fences. The red-backed shrike is one of several species that migrate north to Europe every year. It has a gray head, a rusty-red back, and a black stripe running across its eyes, like a mask. It nests in thorny bushes and lays up to six eggs at a time.

SCIENTIFIC NAME *Lanius collurio*

DISTRIBUTION Breeds in Europe, western Asia; migrates mainly to Africa in the winter

SIZE Up to 7 in. (18cm) long

TOP *The pied wagtail feeds on the ground, but it is an expert at catching insects that try to fly away. This one is collecting food for its nestlings.*
ABOVE *A red-eyed bulbul pants in the midday heat. Birds cannot lose heat by sweating because they do not have sweat glands. Instead, many of them pant when they get too hot.*

MOCKINGBIRD

As well as being a tuneful singer, the mockingbird is the best bird mimic in North America. It imitates a bewildering variety of sounds, from ringing telephones to barking dogs, and has been known to copy the songs and calls of up to 30 different birds. Mockingbirds are not spectacular to look at—their plumage is light and dark gray—but they are successful and adaptable. They live in cities as well as the countryside, feeding mainly on seeds, fruit, and small animals. Mockingbirds nest in trees and chase off any other birds that venture too close.

Adult mockingbird on a branch

SCIENTIFIC NAME *Mimus polyglottus*

DISTRIBUTION   North America

SIZE   Up to 10 in. (25cm) long

WINTER WREN

Wrens are small, highly active birds that often have upright tails. There are more than 60 species, but the winter wren is the only one that is found outside the Americas. This tiny bird can fly well, but it spends most of its time hopping and flitting over the ground or through bushes, probing for insects and spiders with its needle-sharp beak. During the breeding season, male winter wrens flutter onto treetops or telephone wires, where they sing suprisingly loudly. Winter wrens build domed nests in thick vegetation, and they raise up to two families a year.

SCIENTIFIC NAME *Troglodytes troglodytes*

DISTRIBUTION   North America, Europe, northern Africa, central Asia, Far East

SIZE   Up to 3 in. (8cm) long

BELOW LEFT *Because they are so small, winter wrens are vulnerable to the cold. This one has survived through to spring and is gathering food.*
BELOW *The songthrush starts singing in January— a sign that spring is not far away.*

Upright stance is typical of the songthrush

DIPPER

The dipper looks like a giant, white-breasted wren, but it has a remarkable lifestyle all its own. It feeds on insect grubs and other small animals in fast-flowing rivers, and it gets to its food by swimming and walking under water. It always walks against the current, with the force of the water pressing down on its back, which keeps it from bobbing back up to the surface. Dippers do not have webbed feet, but they have nictitating membranes, semitransparent eyelids that wipe water off their eyes.

SCIENTIFIC NAME   *Cinclus cinclus*

DISTRIBUTION   Europe, North Africa, parts of central Asia

SIZE   Up to 7 in. (18cm) long

BOHEMIAN WAXWING

This sleek, crested songbird normally lives in northern forests, where it feeds on insects in the summer and berries in the winter. Every few years, the berry crop fails, and the hungry waxwings fly south, turning up in places where they are rarely seen. Scientists call these sudden movements irruptions. Bohemian waxwings are gray-brown, with black and yellow tips to their wings and tails. They have large appetites and sometimes eat so much that they can hardly fly.

SCIENTIFIC NAME
Bombycilla garrulus

DISTRIBUTION   North America, Europe, northern Asia

SIZE   Up to 7 in. (18cm) long

SONGTHRUSH

Thrushes make up one of the largest families of songbirds, with more than 300 species. Many species, including the songthrush, are talented singers. Although they nest in trees, most of them feed on the ground, where they eat fruit and small animals such as earthworms. The songthrush is also an expert at eating snails. When it finds one, it hits it against a large stone, breaking open its shell. Thrush stones are easy to recognize because they are often littered with shattered shells.

SCIENTIFIC NAME   *Turdus philomelos*

DISTRIBUTION   Originally from Europe, northern Africa, Middle East, central Asia; introduced into Australia, New Zealand

SIZE   Up to 9 in. (23cm) long

Wings are strong and flexible

Streamlined body feathers

EUROPEAN BLACKBIRD

The European blackbird was originally a forest bird, but it often feeds and nests in backyards. It pulls up earthworms on lawns and turns over fallen leaves, snapping up insects and other small animals. Because they are ground-feeding birds, blackbirds must keep a constant lookout for danger. If a blackbird sees a predator, such as a cat, it follows it at a safe distance, noisily warning other birds. Only male European blackbirds are black; the females are dark brown. Males and females work together to make cup-shaped nests lined with mud and grass. They raise up to three families each year.

SCIENTIFIC NAME *Turdus merula*

DISTRIBUTION Originally from Europe, northern Africa, parts of Asia; introduced into Australia, New Zealand

SIZE Up to 9.5 in. (24cm) long

Flight feathers spread during takeoff

AMERICAN ROBIN

American and Eurasian robins both belong to the thrush family, and both have orange-red breasts. However, the American robin is a much larger bird, with a brown-gray back and a streaked, black and white throat. American robins often live in parks and gardens, where they pull earthworms from the ground. Like other large thrushes, they find worms by sight, but their habit of cocking their heads makes it look like they are listening for them instead. American robins are tuneful singers. They nest in trees and buildings and lay pale blue eggs.

SCIENTIFIC NAME *Turdus migratorius*

DISTRIBUTION North America

SIZE Up to 10 in. (25cm) long

ABOVE *A fast getaway helps the European blackbird survive in yards where cats are on the prowl. Its piercing alarm call warns other birds to be on guard.*

RIGHT *Like the European blackbird, the American robin is a woodland bird that has adapted to life in parks and gardens.*

EURASIAN ROBIN

This common bird is well known for its bright red breast and friendly behavior. These robins often follow gardeners to eat the worms they dig up, and they sometimes become so tame that they will take food from an open hand. They are not so neighborly with each other, however. Males vigorously defend their territories, chasing away any rival males, but allowing females to enter. After mating, the female builds a domed nest lined with moss and animal hair. The nest is usually hidden near the ground, but robins also nest in garages and garden sheds.

SCIENTIFIC NAME *Erithacus rubecula*

DISTRIBUTION Europe, northern Africa, Middle East, western Asia

SIZE Up to 5.5 in. (14cm) long

Both males and females have bright red breasts

Clawed feet can cling tightly to a perch

ABOVE *With an insect held tightly in its beak, a Eurasian robin comes in to land. Robins are very good at spotting the slightest movement, and they often swoop on worms or insect grubs from several yards away.*

NIGHTINGALE

The nightingale has a reputation for being one of the finest singers in the bird world. Its plain, brown plumage and secretive habits make it difficult to see, but its rich, fluty song is impossible to mistake. Nightingales are unusual because they sing at night as well as by day, which is how they got their name. They feed on insects and fruit, and nest low down in tangled vegetation.

SCIENTIFIC NAME *Luscinia megarhynchos*

DISTRIBUTION Breeds in Europe, central Asia; migrates mainly to Africa in the winter

SIZE Up to 6.75 in. (17cm) long

EASTERN BLUEBIRD

Bluebirds are not outstanding singers, but they are among the most colorful birds in the thrush family. There are three species in North America. The eastern bluebird has an orange-red chest and a deep blue head and back. Unlike most thrushes, bluebirds nest in holes; eastern bluebirds often use holes made by woodpeckers. During the last century, they have had to cope with stiff competition from introduced starlings, but birdhouses are now helping them survive.

SCIENTIFIC NAME *Sialia sialis*

DISTRIBUTION Eastern North America, Central America

SIZE Up to 7 in. (18cm) long

ABOVE LEFT *The nightingale lives mostly in woodlands.*

ABOVE RIGHT *Reed warblers are often tricked by cuckoos (page 203) into raising their young.*

REED WARBLER

Warblers are small, unobtrusive birds that feed largely on insects. There are more than 300 species scattered across Europe, Africa, Asia, and Australia, and although some look almost identical, their distinctive songs help in telling them apart. The reed warbler lives in reedbeds, where it usually stays well out of sight. It makes a cup-shaped nest slung between three or four reed stems and raises two families a year. Its song sounds like busy chatter, with many notes repeated three or four times in quick succession. Like most other warblers, it migrates to breed. American warblers (page 220) share similar lifestyles, but they belong to a separate family of birds.

SCIENTIFIC NAME *Acrocephalus scirpaceus*

DISTRIBUTION Breeds in Europe; migrates mainly to Africa in the winter

SIZE Up to 5 in. (12cm) long

GOLDCREST

The goldcrest, one of the tiniest warblers, has a green and white body and a bright yellow stripe on its head. It lives mainly in coniferous forests, where it flits along branches and twigs to eat small insects and their eggs. It makes a cup-shaped nest out of moss and spiders' webs, often hanging it near the end of a branch. The goldcrest has four equally small relatives in forests across the Northern Hemisphere. They are known collectively as kinglets.

SCIENTIFIC NAME
Regulus regulus

DISTRIBUTION Europe, northern Africa, central Asia, Far East

SIZE Up to 3.5 in. (9cm) long

Narrow beak for extracting insect grubs and eggs from bark

ABOVE *Weighing as little as 0.2 oz., the goldcrest is one of Europe's smallest birds. Despite its small size, this fearless fighter will peck at anything that comes near its nest.*

Short, slightly forked tail

Clawed feet well developed for perching

GREAT TIT

The great tit belongs to a family of small birds known as titmice. They are acrobatic, often hanging upside down in trees as they search for insects and seeds. Many of them store food for the winter, and they often visit birdfeeders in cold weather. The great tit, the largest species, lives over a wide area. Its color varies, but it usually has a black head and a bright yellow underside marked with a black stripe. Like other titmice, it nests in holes and often raises two families a year.

SCIENTIFIC NAME	*Parus major*
DISTRIBUTION	Europe, northern Africa, central and southern Asia
SIZE	Up to 5.5 in. (14cm) long

Open beak is used as a threat

Blue tits can fit through a hole just 1 in. across

BLACK-CAPPED CHICKADEE

The chickadee is one of about 12 titmice found in North America. It gets its name from its call, which sounds like "chickadee-dee-dee." The black-capped chickadee has a black head and a gray back, as do several other chickadees with slightly different songs. Chickadees live in tree-filled yards and woodlands. During the spring, they feed their young on caterpillars and other insects, but in the winter, they feed on small nuts and seeds.

Black-capped chickadee

Short, compact wings

SCIENTIFIC NAME	*Parus atricapillus*
DISTRIBUTION	North America
SIZE	Up to 5 in. (12cm) long

AFRICAN PARADISE FLYCATCHER

Paradise flycatchers are not much larger than sparrows, but the males have long tail feathers that more than double their total body length. These elegant, white or chestnut-colored birds feed on flying insects, fluttering from a perch to snatch them out of the air. There are several species of paradise flycatchers, found from Africa east to Japan. They all build well-constructed, cup-shaped nests held together with spiders' silk.

SCIENTIFIC NAME	*Tersiphone viridis*
DISTRIBUTION	Africa
SIZE	Males up to 16 in. (40cm) long, including tail feathers

SPLENDID WREN

The splendid wren is one of Australia's brightest birds. The females are brown, but in the breeding season, the males are often an intense light blue. Though splendid wrens share their long, upturned tails, they are not closely related to true wrens, which live in other parts of the world.

SCIENTIFIC NAME	*Malurus cyaneus*
DISTRIBUTION	Central and southern Australia
SIZE	Up to 5.5 in. (14cm) long

ABOVE *A great tit (top) and a blue tit (Parus caeruleus) (center) argue over a nest hole. For these birds, a good supply of nest holes is almost as important as a good supply of food.*

EURASIAN NUTHATCH

Nuthatches are small, short-tailed birds with surprisingly powerful beaks. They scuttle up and down trees by grasping the bark with their sharp claws. During the summer, they feed mainly on insects, but in the fall and winter, nuts make up a large part of their diet. Nuthatches jam large nuts into crevices in tree bark, then peck them open with hard blows that are easily heard from the ground. There are about 25 species of nuthatches, and most of them nest in holes. The Eurasian nuthatch often uses old woodpecker holes, making the entrances smaller by plastering mud around them.

SCIENTIFIC NAME *Sitta europaea*

DISTRIBUTION Europe, central Asia, Far East

SIZE Up to 5.5 in. (14cm) long

Powerful, chisellike beak

Dark streak across the head

Slender, curved beak

ABOVE *This nuthatch has wedged a nut firmly into a crevice in a tree trunk so that it can peck at it to feed.*
RIGHT *The wallcreeper (Tichodroma muraria) belongs to the same family of birds as nuthatches and treecreepers. It scampers up mountain rock faces, probing the crevices for insects.*

Wallcreepers in summer and paler winter plumage

TREECREEPER

This small, brown-backed bird feeds on insects and spiders it finds on trees, using its narrow, curved beak to pick them out of crevices in the bark. It starts looking for food at the base of a tree, then works its way up with a jerky movement, using its tail as a prop. When it reaches the top, it flies to the bottom of another tree and starts again. Treecreepers nest behind pieces of loose bark and lay up to six eggs at a time. In North America, the brown creeper (*Certhia americana*) lives in a very similar way.

SCIENTIFIC NAME *Certhia familiaris*

DISTRIBUTION Europe, central Asia, Far East

SIZE Up to 5 in. (12cm) long

SCARLET-CHESTED SUNBIRD

Sunbirds live in Africa, Asia, and Australia. Their lifestyle is like that of hummingbirds (pages 204–205), and so too are their brilliant, metallic colors. The African scarlet-chested sunbird is a typical species—the male has a scarlet chest and a shiny green head, while the female is mostly brown. Unlike hummingbirds, sunbirds cannot hover, so they perch on flowers to feed. Its long, slightly curved beak is ideal for reaching into flowers to feed on nectar. It also eats insects. Like most sunbirds, this species makes a purse-shaped nest that hangs from the end of a branch. The nest has an entrance hole near the top, covered by a roof.

SCIENTIFIC NAME *Nectarinia senegalensis*

DISTRIBUTION Tropical and southern Africa

SIZE Up to 6 in. (15cm) long

NOISY FRIARBIRD

This large, Australian bird is one of the few songbirds that have almost bald heads. Its beak is large and slightly curved, with a small knob on the top, just above the base. Apart from these physical oddities, its most noticeable feature is its voice. It sounds harsh and aggressive, particularly when it is squabbling over food. Noisy friarbirds feed mainly on nectar and fruit, although they also eat insects. They live in a wide range of habitats, including forests, gardens, and parks, and make their nests high in trees.

SCIENTIFIC NAME *Philemon corniculatus*

DISTRIBUTION Eastern Australia

SIZE Up to 14.5 in. (37cm) long

RIGHT *Treecreepers move in a spiral up tree trunks. They use their stiff tail feathers to brace themselves as they feed.*

BLUE-FACED HONEYEATER

The blue-faced honeyeater is a close relative of the noisy friarbird, but its head is partly feathered. It got its name from the patch of bright blue skin behind each eye. Blue-faced honeyeaters are bold, aggressive birds and are not afraid of people. As well as eating nectar and fruit, they raid banana plantations and eat syrup in fields of harvested sugar cane. They sometimes build their own nests, but they often take over nests made by other birds.

SCIENTIFIC NAME *Entomyzon cyanotis*

DISTRIBUTION Eastern and northern Australia, New Guinea

SIZE Up to 13 in. (33cm) long

ABOVE *Darwin's finch is one of the few birds that use tools to get their food. In captivity, some other Galapagos Island finches have been seen to copy its behavior.*

DARWIN'S FINCH

This bird is known for the way it uses tools to get its food. It normally picks insects and other small animals from wood or from crevices in bark. If an insect is hard to reach, however, the finch sometimes uses a cactus spine to pry out its prey. Darwin's finch is one of 13 species of finches on the remote Galapagos Islands in the eastern Pacific Ocean. Biologists believe that these finches all evolved from one original species that reached the islands from the South American mainland thousands of years ago.

SCIENTIFIC NAME *Camarhynchus pallidus*

DISTRIBUTION Galapagos Islands

SIZE Up to 6 in. (15cm) long

NORTHERN CARDINAL

With its spiky crest and crimson plumage, the male northern cardinal is one of the most colorful birds in North America. Unlike most songbirds, both the males and females sing, and they keep up their song for most of the year. Cardinals live in woodlands, thickets, and gardens. They eat insects and seeds and often visit birdfeeders during the winter. During the last century, cardinals have spread steadily northward—food provided by people during the winter may be helping them to thrive.

Adult male northern cardinal

SCIENTIFIC NAME *Cardinalis cardinalis*

DISTRIBUTION Originally from Eastern North America, Central America; introduced into Hawaii

SIZE Up to 8.5 in. (22cm) long

WESTERN TANAGER

Tanagers are brightly colored birds found only in the Americas. There are more than 200 species. Many live in the tropics year-round, but some, including the western tanager, migrate to breed. They feed mainly on insects and often hide in trees and bushes. Western tanagers nest in mountain forests. The female makes the nest and incubates the eggs. She is yellow-green, but during the breeding season, the male is yellow with black wings and a red head.

SCIENTIFIC NAME *Piranga ludoviciana*

DISTRIBUTION Breeds in western North America; migrates to Central America in the winter

SIZE Up to 8 in. (20cm) long

Extra-large claws cling to bark

Short, rounded wings

Tips of tail feathers are worn to sharp points

YELLOW WARBLER

This bright yellow insect-eater belongs to a family of birds called wood warblers, which contains about 100 species throughout the Americas. About half of them, including the yellow warbler, migrate north every spring to breed. Wood warblers often join other species to form mixed flocks when they migrate, and they travel in straggling waves containing millions of birds. The yellow warbler makes a small, cup-shaped nest near the water's edge and lays up to five eggs at a time.

SCIENTIFIC NAME *Dendroica petechia*

DISTRIBUTION Breeds in North America; migrates to Central America, northern South America in the winter

SIZE Up to 5 in. (12cm) long

FAR LEFT *Tucked up in its nest, a yellow warbler incubates its clutch of eggs.*
LEFT *An eastern meadowlark sings on a fencepost. Like many other birds that breed in grassy fields, meadowlarks are threatened by farm machinery, which often destroys their nests.*

Spotted flanks

Black, V-shaped band on breast

Strong feet for feeding on the ground

BLACK-AND-WHITE WARBLER

Though many North American wood warblers look very similar, this species is easy to recognize because it is entirely black and white. It scuttles up and down tree trunks and along branches, picking insects out of crevices in the bark. This warbler is among the earliest to fly north in the spring because the insects on which it relies feed on bark, not on leaves, and so are more plentiful before the trees' leaves return.

SCIENTIFIC NAME *Mniotilta varia*

DISTRIBUTION Breeds in North America, except the west; migrates to Central America, northern South America in the winter

SIZE Up to 5 in. (12cm) long

COMMON GRACKLE

Grackles look similar to crows (page 228), but they are smaller, with narrow beaks and slender legs, and often have a purple sheen. They belong to the American blackbird family, which also includes meadowlarks, bobolinks, orioles, cowbirds, and oropendolas. These birds live in a wide variety of habitats, and they are all good fliers, with long, pointed wings. Common grackles feed in farmland and cities, and although they eat many insect pests, they can

be a problem when they raid fields for grain. They breed in small groups, but in the winter they gather together in immense, noisy roosts that can contain more than one million birds.

SCIENTIFIC NAME *Quisqualus quiscula*

DISTRIBUTION Eastern North America

SIZE Up to 12.5 in. (32cm) long

EASTERN MEADOWLARK

Meadowlarks are birds of open, grassy places. They nest and feed on the ground, using their needle-sharp beaks to probe the grass for worms and other animals. The eastern meadowlark has a streaked, brown and white back, a yellow breast, and a whistlelike song. A similar species, called the western meadowlark (*Sturnella neglecta*), looks almost identical, and the two birds' ranges overlap. They sound very different, which helps ensure that they breed only with their own kind.

SCIENTIFIC NAME *Sturnella magna*

DISTRIBUTION Breeds in North, Central, and South America; northern birds migrate to southern North America, Central and South America in the winter

SIZE Up to 10 in. (25cm) long

Broad wings

Long, black and orange tail

BELOW *Northern orioles have two different plumage patterns. Male birds from the east of their range, like the one shown here, have all-black heads.*

White wing patch

NORTHERN ORIOLE

With their bright orange and black plumage, male northern orioles are easy to find throughout North America during the spring and summer months. The female's green-brown plumage is not as eyecatching as the male's. Northern orioles live in woodland and open ground with trees, and they feed on fruit and insects. They lay their eggs in pouch-shaped nests that hang from the outer branches of trees.

SCIENTIFIC NAME	*Icterus galbula*
DISTRIBUTION	Breeds in North America; migrates to Central America, northern South America in the winter
SIZE	Up to 8.5 in. (22cm) long

BROWN-HEADED COWBIRD

Cowbirds are the only birds in North America that always lay their eggs in other birds' nests. Unlike the common cuckoo (page 203), the brown-headed cowbird is not at all fussy when it chooses foster parents—more than 200 species are known to raise its eggs. The cowbird leaves a single egg in each nest. This egg usually hatches before the other bird's eggs, giving the cowbird chick a good chance of getting the most food. Some birds throw out the cowbird egg, but most raise the chick along with their own. Cowbirds eat insects. They got their name because they often feed among cattle in fields.

SCIENTIFIC NAME	*Molothrus ater*
DISTRIBUTION	North America
SIZE	Up to 7.5 in. (19cm) long

CRESTED OROPENDOLA

This tropical rain forest bird is one of the largest members of the American blackbird family. It is mainly black, with a yellow and black tail, and it has a flat forehead that seems to merge with its beak—a typical feature in this group of birds. Oropendolas make an amazing array of sounds, but their most interesting feature is the way they nest. They breed together in very tall trees, building hanging nests up to 3 ft. (1m) long. There can be over a hundred nests in a single tree, and from a distance, the hanging nests look like giant fruit dangling from the branches.

SCIENTIFIC NAME	*Psarocolius decumanus*
DISTRIBUTION	Central South America, tropical South America
SIZE	Up to 19 in. (48cm) long

ABOVE *This young, male northern oriole has a colored face, which shows that it comes from the western part of its range. As it matures, its plumage will turn more orange. Most northern orioles spend the winter in the tropics, but a few stay behind, particularly in areas where people put out food.*

BOBOLINK

The bobolink is named for the males' bubbling songs. Females have brown plumage, but during the breeding season, the males are mostly black and white. Bobolinks feed on insects and seeds, and they nest on the ground. Like many other ground-nesters, they have been affected by modern farming methods because grass is often cut before the spring is over. This makes it harder for them to raise their young.

SCIENTIFIC NAME	*Dolichonyx oryzivorus*
DISTRIBUTION	Breeds in North America; migrates to South America in the winter
SIZE	Up to 7 in. (18cm) long

AMERICAN GOLDFINCH

Finches are small songbirds with short, strong beaks. They feed mainly on seeds, cracking open the husks to get to the nutritious food inside. There are hundreds of species of finches, and they are found all over the world, particularly in woodlands, farmland, and grassy places. The American goldfinch is a typical farmland species that often feeds in weed-covered fields. It is most noticeable in late summer and fall, when large flocks gather to feed on thistle and sunflower seeds. The Eurasian goldfinch (*Carduelis carduelis*) is a close relative. It is about the same size, but has a bright red face.

SCIENTIFIC NAME	*Carduelis tristis*
DISTRIBUTION	North America, from Canada to Mexico
SIZE	Up to 5 in. (12cm) long

ABOVE *This male American goldfinch is in his breeding plumage. When the summer ends, he will lose his black cap, and his body will turn gray-brown.*

Broad wings help the bird take off quickly

CHAFFINCH

This lively little finch is one of Europe's most common birds. It feeds mainly on the ground in fields, gardens, and other open places, and it nests wherever there are bushes or trees. If it gets enough food, it can raise two families a year, and its young can fly just 12 days after they hatch. Chaffinches collect insects when they are feeding their young, but in the winter they live mainly on seeds. At this time of year, they often form mixed flocks with other small birds—a habit that helps them spot danger.

SCIENTIFIC NAME	*Fringilla coelebs*
DISTRIBUTION	Europe, northern Africa, western Asia
SIZE	Up to 6 in. (15cm) long

LEFT *Like all finches, the chaffinch has short, broad wings that are ideal for quick bursts of flight when searching for food. This bird is female. Males have brighter colors.*

Female

Male

Male

Legs held against the body during flight

GOULDIAN FINCH

Named after John Gould, a famous English ornithologist, this Australian bird is one of the most colorful finches in the world. It has a black, red, or yellow face, bright green wings, a lilac breast, yellow undersides, and a light blue base to its tail. Gouldian finches are found only in Australia's far north, and because changes in farming methods have made life harder for them, they are now rather rare. During the dry season, they feed on seeds, but during the wet season, when they nest and raise their young, they eat mainly flying insects.

SCIENTIFIC NAME	*Chloebia gouldiae*
DISTRIBUTION	Northern Australia
SIZE	Up to 5 in. (12cm) long

Female   Male

Male   Female

ABOVE LEFT *In Europe, greenfinches (Chloris chloris) often live on farms and in gardens.*
ABOVE *The hawfinch (Coccothraustes coccothraustes) has a heavy-duty beak that can crack open cherry pits.*

ABOVE *The serin (Serinus serinus) is a common finch in southern Europe. It lives in parks, farmland, and gardens.*

ABOVE *The bullfinch (Pyrrhula pyrrhula) is not popular with fruit growers because it eats fruit tree buds in winter.*

RED CROSSBILL

Crossbills are very unusual finches that live in coniferous forests. They feed on seeds from cones, and they get their food using their remarkable beaks, which have tips that cross over. This kind of beak is particularly useful for dealing with green, unripe cones. Crossbills hold the cones with their feet, then slice them open to reach the juicy seeds hidden inside. Each of the four species of crossbills specializes in tackling seeds from a different tree. The red crossbill, the most widespread, feeds mainly on spruce seeds. Only the male is red; the female is a drab olive-gray.

SCIENTIFIC NAME *Loxia curvirostra*

DISTRIBUTION Northern Hemisphere, particularly in the far north

SIZE Up to 6 in. (15cm) long

Parrot crossbill

HOUSE SPARROW

The house sparrow is one of the world's most successful birds. It originally lived only in southern Europe, northern Africa, and the Middle East, but because it thrives wherever people live, it has managed to spread to almost all the inhabited parts of the world. It swept across North America after arriving in 1852, and it did almost as well in Australia when it was introduced about ten years later. House sparrows eat seeds, insects, and leftover food. They rarely stray far from buildings, and they often make their domed nests in holes in walls, using dry grass. They lay up to six eggs at a time and raise up to three families a year.

SCIENTIFIC NAME *Passer domesticus*

DISTRIBUTION Worldwide

SIZE Up to 6 in. (15cm) long

VILLAGE WEAVER

Close relatives of the house sparrow, weaver birds live in Africa and southern Asia. They usually breed in groups and are known for their nest-building skills. The village weaver makes its nest from strips of grass and hangs it high in a tree. The male weaves the grass into a hollow ball. He finishes it by adding a hanging entrance, then flutters beneath it, enticing females to look inside. If a female likes the nest, she moves in and lays her eggs. Village weavers are the most common species of weaver bird in Africa, and a single tree can hold many nests.

SCIENTIFIC NAME *Ploceus cucullatus*

DISTRIBUTION Tropical and southern Africa

SIZE Up to 6.75 in. (17cm) long

RED-BILLED QUELEA

This small, pale brown African weaver is probably the most abundant bird in the world. Flocks of queleas sometimes contain more than one hundred thousand birds, and the total number of breeding adults may be as high as 1.5 billion. Queleas usually live in grassy places and scrub, but they can cause devastation when they settle in fields of crops.

SCIENTIFIC NAME *Quelea quelea*

DISTRIBUTION Tropical and southern Africa

SIZE Up to 5 in. (12cm) long

Male pine grosbeak

Female pine grosbeak

ABOVE *The red crossbill has an unusual beak. The top half almost always crosses over to the right.*

FAR LEFT *Parrot crossbills* (Loxia pytyopsittacus) *got their name from their habit of gripping cones with their feet as they feed, as parrots do.*

LEFT *The pine grosbeak* (Pinicola enucleator) *is a relative of the crossbills. At 8 in. long, it is Europe's largest finch.*

RIGHT *House sparrows are highly adaptable birds. They have been found living high inside skyscrapers and even down in coal mines.*

NESTS

Animals make nests to shelter their young and to protect themselves from predators or the weather. Birds are the best-known nest-builders, but other animals make nests too. The largest nests, made by termites (page 55), can be up to 20 ft. (6m) high.

Animals use a wide variety of building materials, including sticks, leaves, mud, and saliva, but when they build their nests, they always follow the same plan. This is because they work by instinct, following a pattern of behavior that is unique to each species. Although they do not need to learn how to build, they often improve with experience.

For male weaver birds, producing a good nest is essential because these birds often use their nests to attract mates. If a nest does not impress any females, the male bird will often abandon it and build a new one.

Weaver bird at its nest

EUROPEAN STARLING

This familiar flocking bird feeds on the ground, jabbing its beak into grass to find insects and worms. It also snaps up leftover food, so it thrives in cities.

Starlings normally nest in tree holes, but they often take over birdhouses meant for other birds. Outside the breeding season, starlings often gather together to roost. In some cities, thousands pour in from the countryside on winter afternoons to settle on trees or under bridges for the night.

SCIENTIFIC NAME
Sturnus vulgaris

DISTRIBUTION Originally from Europe, northern Africa, Middle East, western Asia; introduced into North America, South Africa, Australia

SIZE Up to 8 in. (20cm) long

Adult has staring, yellow eyes

LEFT *This European starling's spotted plumage shows that it is an adult. Young birds are gray-brown all over.*
BELOW LEFT *The superb starling is a noisy and sociable bird that feeds in small flocks.*

European starling

Wings with pointed tips

SUPERB STARLING

There are more than 100 species in the starling family, many of which are brightly colored. The African superb starling is one of the showiest, with a glossy green back, orange undersides, and pale yellow eyes. Superb starlings originally lived in wooded grassland, but today they often live in fields and gardens as well. Like most starlings, they are not afraid of people, and they gather at campsites to feed on leftover scraps of food. Superb starlings nest in holes in trees or in thorn bushes.

SCIENTIFIC NAME *Spreo superbus*

DISTRIBUTION Eastern Africa

SIZE Up to 7 in. (18cm) long

Glossy plumage without speckles

RED-BILLED OXPECKER

Oxpeckers have an unusual way of feeding. Using their strong feet and sharp claws, they scamper over rhinoceroses, giraffes, and other grazing mammals, picking off ticks and other parasites. The oxpeckers' hosts seem to realize that they are useful visitors and do not brush them away. If alarmed, an oxpecker may scuttle around its host until it is out of sight, like a squirrel hiding behind a tree trunk. There are two species of oxpeckers. The red-billed oxpecker is mainly brown, with a bright red beak.

SCIENTIFIC NAME *Buphagus erythrorhynchus*

DISTRIBUTION Eastern and southern Africa

SIZE Up to 7.5 in. (19cm) long

Red-billed oxpeckers looking for food on a rhinoceros

Superb starling

HILL MYNAH

Hill mynahs are popular cage birds because they are good at imitating human speech. They are more talkative than parrots—they can even become a nuisance because they make so much noise. Hill mynahs are mainly black, but they have yellow beaks and a conspicuous patch of bare, yellow skin around the sides and back of their heads. In the wild, they eat fruit and insects, getting their food from trees.

SCIENTIFIC NAME	*Gracula religiosa*
DISTRIBUTION	Southeast Asia
SIZE	Up to 12 in. (30cm) long

GREAT RACKET-TAILED DRONGO

Drongos are tree-dwelling birds found in Africa, southern Asia, and Australia. Most of them are black and glossy. They feed on insects, pouncing on them in midair and carrying them back to a perch. They are well known for their aggressive behavior and will launch furious attacks on anything that comes near their nests. The racket-tailed drongo is the largest and most flamboyant of these birds. It got its name from its two extra-long tail feathers, which have narrow shafts and rounded ends, like a pair of tennis rackets.

SCIENTIFIC NAME	*Dicrurus paradisaeus*
DISTRIBUTION	India, Southeast Asia
SIZE	Up to 25 in. (63cm) long, including tail feathers

SADDLEBACK

This rare bird from New Zealand belongs to a family called the wattlebirds, which are named for the fleshy wattles on either side of their beaks. The saddleback's wattles are red, and its body is black and brown. Saddlebacks feed in trees. They once lived all over New Zealand, but today they survive on only a handful of islands. The huia, a relative of the saddleback, died out in 1907. It was the only bird with a different beak shape for each sex—the male's was straight, and the female's was long and curved.

SCIENTIFIC NAME	*Creadion carunculatus*
DISTRIBUTION	Offshore islands of New Zealand
SIZE	Up to 10 in. (25cm) long

MAGPIE-LARK

The magpie-lark is neither a magpie nor a lark. It belongs to a small family of songbirds found only in Australia and New Guinea. Magpie-larks have long legs and black and white plumage. They live in a wide variety of habitats, including cities, but they usually stay near water, where they find most of their food. Pairs of magpie-larks often sing duets, taking turns to call. Both birds help make a nest out of mud and grass, often on a branch overhanging water.

SCIENTIFIC NAME	*Grallina cyanoleuca*
DISTRIBUTION	Australia
SIZE	Up to 12 in. (30cm) long

AUSTRALIAN MAGPIE

Australian magpies are larger than magpie-larks, and they are known for their musical calls. They feed on insects and other animals on the ground. Australian magpies nest in groups of up to six birds, headed by a single dominant male. Each group has its own territory and will fight off other magpies that come within range.

SCIENTIFIC NAME	*Gymnorhina tibicen*
DISTRIBUTION	Originally from Australia, New Guinea; introduced into New Zealand
SIZE	Up to 16 in. (40cm) long

TOP AND CENTER *Hill mynahs have strong beaks for collecting fruit and insects, and sturdy legs for perching as they reach out for food.*
ABOVE *A young magpie-lark stands on the edge of its nest. Magpie-larks often wade through shallow water searching for insects and snails to eat.*

COUNT RAGGI'S BIRD OF PARADISE

Male birds are often more colorful than their mates, but with birds of paradise the difference is astounding. The females are drab, but the males have flamboyant plumage that they show off during their courtship displays. When Europeans first saw the birds' feathers nearly 500 years ago, they thought they came from paradise, which is how the birds got their name. Like most of its relatives, Count Raggi's bird of paradise lives in the dense tropical forests of New Guinea. The male has a yellow head, a metallic green throat, and a bushy, crimson tail. During the breeding season, rival males show off their plumage in the treetops, trying to attract the attention of passing females. After mating, the females build nests and look after the nestlings on their own.

SCIENTIFIC NAME *Paradisaea raggiana*

DISTRIBUTION New Guinea

SIZE Up to 13 in. (33cm) long

BLUE BIRD OF PARADISE

The blue bird of paradise lives in forest-covered mountains and eats fruit and insects. Males of this species have blue-black heads, turquoise wings, and two long tail-streamers that look like pieces of wire. During their courtship displays, they hang upside down from branches, fluttering their open wings to show off their beautiful colors. They also make a variety of harsh noises that sound like machinery. Little is known about how this bird breeds, but as with other birds of paradise, the males probably take no part in caring for the young.

SCIENTIFIC NAME *Paradisaea rudolphi*

DISTRIBUTION New Guinea

SIZE Up to 12 in. (30cm) long, excluding tail-streamers

BELOW LEFT A male Count Raggi's bird of paradise shows off the lustrous plumage on his head and neck. Most male birds of paradise display to females on their own, but the males of this species gather in small groups, then compete to provide the best show. At the climax of the display, the male tips his body forward and spreads a ruff of red plumes over his back.

Strong beak for collecting fruit, buds, and insects

Contrasting feathers at the base of the beak

Male blue bird of paradise

Male Count Raggi's bird of paradise

Metallic feathers on the throat collar

KING OF SAXONY BIRD OF PARADISE

This is one of several birds named after royalty when European naturalists explored the forests of New Guinea over 100 years ago. Compared to some birds of paradise, the males look ordinary, but they have one remarkable feature—a pair of plumes on their heads that look like giant antennae. The plumes can be up to 20 in. (50cm) long, and they have a row of blue flaps along one side. The males usually keep their plumes close to their backs, but during courtship displays, they hold them almost upright.

SCIENTIFIC NAME	*Pteridophora alberti*
DISTRIBUTION	New Guinea
SIZE	Up to 8.5 in. (22cm) long

KING BIRD OF PARADISE

There are about 40 different birds of paradise, and this species is one of the smallest. The males are bright orange-red with white undersides, and they have two long tail-streamers with tips that are coiled like springs. Like other birds of paradise, they feed on insects and fruit and spend most of the time high above the ground.

SCIENTIFIC NAME	*Cicinnurus regius*
DISTRIBUTION	New Guinea
SIZE	Up to 6.75 in. (17cm) long

MAGNIFICENT RIFLEBIRD

This long-beaked bird of paradise got its name from its call, which sounds like the whine of a rifle bullet. The females are brown and white, but the males are much more spectacular, with shiny, blue-green caps and throats, and blue-black wings. Instead of hanging upside down when they display, the males perch on top of high branches with their wings held out like a pair of fans. During the display, they shake their bodies and flick their heads from side to side.

SCIENTIFIC NAME	*Ptiloris magnificus*
DISTRIBUTION	New Guinea, northern Australia
SIZE	Up to 13 in. (33cm) long

SATIN BOWERBIRD

Bowerbirds are close relatives of the birds of paradise, but instead of using bright plumage to attract their mates, the males make structures called bowers. They build their bowers out of sticks on the ground. Some bowers are shaped like miniature circus rings or thatched huts, but the satin bowerbird makes a long, narrow bower with two walls but no roof. When it is complete, the male bird daubs it with "paint" made from saliva and fruit and decorates it with blue objects

TOP *A female satin bowerbird peers into a bower built by a male. This is the signal for the male to begin his courtship display.*
ABOVE *Perched on a high branch, a male king bird of paradise shows off his remarkable tail-streamers, which hang in the air behind him.*

of all kinds, from feathers to bottle caps. If a female comes close to the bower, the male picks up these objects during his display, as he tries to entice her to mate.

SCIENTIFIC NAME	*Ptilonorhynchus violaceus*
DISTRIBUTION	Eastern Australia
SIZE	Up to 12.5 in. (32cm) long

GARDENER BOWERBIRD

Males of this species make the largest and most complicated bowers of all. They find a sturdy sapling and build up sticks around it, using the tree as a central support. The finished bower has a steeply sloping roof up to 6 ft. (2m) high, and it opens out into a "garden" area that the male bird decorates with flowers and shells. Bowers this large can take weeks to build, and instead of making a new one each year, gardener bowerbirds often repair ones that they have used in previous breeding seasons.

SCIENTIFIC NAME	*Amblyornis inornatus*
DISTRIBUTION	New Guinea
SIZE	Up to 10 in. (25cm) long

Common raven has a strong, thick beak

Red-billed chough has a long, curved beak

COMMON RAVEN

Common ravens are the largest birds in the crow family, with wings that can measure nearly 5 ft. (1.5m) from tip to tip. They have jet-black bodies, deep, croaking calls, and beaks strong enough to break a finger. They live on hillsides and in open country. Common ravens fly high up, like some birds of prey. They feed mainly on dead remains, but they are also effective predators, killing rabbits and other birds. They often travel in pairs, and during the breeding season, they carry out acrobatic display flights, rolling and tumbling toward the ground.

SCIENTIFIC NAME	*Corvus corax*
DISTRIBUTION	Northern and western North America, Europe, northern Asia
SIZE	Up to 25.5 in. (65cm) long

Powerful, all-purpose beak

CARRION CROW

There are about 100 species in the crow family, and they include some of the world's most intelligent and adaptable birds.

TOP *The common raven can be identified by its large size and by the shaggy feathers below its throat.*
ABOVE *Unlike many of its relatives, the red-billed chough is a shy bird that avoids people.*
RIGHT *Carrion crows usually have jet-black plumage, though a variety called the hooded crow is black and gray.*

Thickset neck

The carrion crow, one of the most widespread, lives across Europe and Asia. It is normally black all over, with a heavy beak and powerful wings. Carrion crows feed on a wide range of food, from seeds and baby birds to the remains of dead animals, called carrion. They often visit garbage dumps, where they eat leftovers of all kinds. Carrion crows nest in the tops of trees, and they make a loud, "cawing" sound if anything comes too close.

SCIENTIFIC NAME	*Corvus corone*
DISTRIBUTION	Europe, Middle East, central Asia, Far East
SIZE	Up to 19 in. (48cm) long

RED-BILLED CHOUGH

This bird is easy to tell apart from its all-black relatives, because it has a bright red beak and feet. Its beak is also an unusual shape—it is long and curved, with a sharp point. Choughs live in flocks on mountains and along seashore cliffs, and they use their beaks to probe for insects living in grass. They are famous for their aerobatic skill, swooping and diving over rocky crags, even in the strongest winds.

SCIENTIFIC NAME	*Pyrrhocorax pyrrhocorax*
DISTRIBUTION	Western Europe, parts of southern Asia
SIZE	Up to 16 in. (40cm) long

CLARK'S NUTCRACKER

This gray and black bird lives in the mountain pine forests of western North America, where winters are cold and long. It eats pine seeds and survives the winter by amassing a giant seed bank before the cold weather sets in. A nutcracker can collect up to 100 pine seeds at a time. It buries them individually, storing up to 30,000 a year. During the summer, nutcrackers often visit picnic sites, where they take food that people put out for them.

SCIENTIFIC NAME	*Nucifraga columbiana*
DISTRIBUTION	Western North America
SIZE	Up to 12 in. (30cm) long

Glossy, black plumage

BLUE JAY

This bright blue, North American bird is a frequent visitor to parks and gardens, where it feeds on insects, nuts, and seeds. Like other jays, it also eats eggs and nestlings, so it is not always welcome. Blue jays are noisy birds with bold habits. They feed in groups and often bury nuts and seeds to help them survive through the winter.

SCIENTIFIC NAME
Cyanocitta cristata

DISTRIBUTION Eastern North America

SIZE Up to 11 in. (28cm) long

Long tail spread out in flight

RIGHT *The black-billed magpie chatters loudly as it searches for food. Despite its size, it is often chased away by smaller birds.*

White flight feathers tipped with black

EURASIAN JAY

Jays are much more colorful than crows, and they spend more of their time in trees. The Eurasian jay has a pink-brown body, a black tail, and a striking patch of pale blue on each wing. Jays eat many things, including insects, eggs, and young birds, but in the winter they often survive on acorns. During the fall, they bury acorns in the ground, and several months later, when food is hard to find, they dig them up again. Although jays have good memories, some of the buried acorns are forgotten, which helps oak trees spread.

SCIENTIFIC NAME
Garrulus glandarius

DISTRIBUTION
Europe, Asia, Far East

SIZE Up to 13.5 in. (34cm) long

Pale blue patch on wing

Body colors may vary depending on where the bird comes from

ABOVE *The Eurasian jay's screeching call makes it easy to pinpoint, even when it is hidden high up in the trees. This common woodland bird is noisiest in the winter and early spring. It becomes quieter when raising its young, to avoid attracting predators to its nest.*

BLACK-BILLED MAGPIE

Magpies have rounded wings and long, straight tails. Compared to other members of the crow family, they are not powerful fliers, and they spend much of their time in trees and on the ground. The black-billed magpie is a striking, black and white bird with a harsh, noisy call. It originally lived in woodland but is now found on farmland and in towns. It usually eats insects, seeds, and dead remains, but it sometimes steals the eggs and chicks of smaller birds.

SCIENTIFIC NAME *Pica pica*

DISTRIBUTION Western North America, Europe, northern Asia, Far East

SIZE Up to 19 in. (48cm) long

AZURE-WINGED MAGPIE

This black, gray, and blue magpie has a puzzling distribution. It is found mainly in China and neighboring parts of the Far East, but some azure-winged magpies live in Spain and Portugal, thousands of miles to the west. Some ornithologists believe that the European birds were accidentally introduced by sailors returning from China centuries ago. Azure-winged magpies often hang from branches to feed.

SCIENTIFIC NAME
Cyanopica cyana

DISTRIBUTION Spain, Portugal, Far East

SIZE Up to 13 in. (33cm) long

Azure-winged magpie

MAMMALS

NUMBERING ABOUT 4,000 SPECIES, MAMMALS
ARE A VERY VARIED GROUP OF ANIMALS. THEY
ARE THE ONLY ANIMALS THAT HAVE HAIR
AND FEED THEIR YOUNG ON MILK.

Eyes and ears are set in grooves on the sides of the head

Beak has sensitive edges

TOP *The platypus closes its eyes under water and finds its food entirely by touch.*
ABOVE *The long-nosed spiny anteater feeds on earthworms as well as ants.*

The earliest mammals lived on land, but modern mammals also live in fresh water, sea water, and the air. Land mammals have four legs; swimming mammals often have flippers instead. Mammals that fly and glide, such as bats and flying squirrels, have flaps of stretchy skin that help them stay aloft. Many mammals have good eyesight and a keen sense of smell. Compared to other animals, their brains are highly developed. Because they are warm-blooded, they can remain active when it is cold. Most mammals give birth to live young, but a few lay eggs.

EGG-LAYING MAMMALS

Of all the mammals alive today, egg-laying mammals, or monotremes, are the most primitive. There are three species of monotremes, found only in New Guinea and Australia. Monotremes have other features that make them unusual. The adults have beaklike mouths without teeth, and the females produce milk, but do not have teats. The milk comes from mammary glands scattered over the skin.

PLATYPUS

When the first stuffed platypus reached Europe about two centuries ago, scientists were so amazed that they thought it was a hoax. This is hardly surprising, because the platypus looks like a cross between a mammal and a bird. It has soft, brown fur and four webbed feet, but it also has a rubbery beak. Platypuses live in lakes and rivers. They use their beaks to probe the mud on the bottom for insect grubs, crustaceans, and other small animals. During the breeding season, the female digs a long burrow, where she lays two or three eggs. She curls around the eggs until they hatch, then feeds her young on milk for up to five months. Male platypuses have poisonous spurs on their back legs that can inflict a painful wound.

SCIENTIFIC NAME
Ornithorhynchus anatinus

DISTRIBUTION Eastern Australia, Tasmania

SIZE Up to 23.5 in. (60cm) long, including tail

LONG-NOSED SPINY ANTEATER OR ECHIDNA

There are two species of spiny anteaters, and this one is the larger. It has a round body covered with fur and spines, and a remarkable curved snout that is little wider than a pencil. Its short legs end in feet with powerful claws that are good for digging. Spiny anteaters use their claws to break open the nests of ants and termites, before sweeping them up with their long tongues. During the breeding season, the females lay between one and three eggs, which they incubate inside a temporary pouch. When the young hatch, they stay in the pouch for up to eight weeks, when their spines begin to develop.

SCIENTIFIC NAME *Zaglossus bruijni*

DISTRIBUTION New Guinea

SIZE Up to 31.5 in. (80cm) long

MARSUPIALS

Marsupials are mammals that raise their young inside a pouch. They include kangaroos, wallabies, and koalas, as well as some lesser-known animals that look like mice. A marsupial's young are very poorly developed when they are born, and they usually stay in the pouch until their bodies are fully formed. There are teats in the pouch so the young can feed safely inside. Marsupials are found mainly in forests or on grasslands, and many of the smaller species are nocturnal. There are about 250 species in total. Most of them live in Australia or New Guinea, but more than 75, including the ones on this page, live in the Americas.

VIRGINIA OPOSSUM

This ratlike animal, the largest marsupial in the Americas, is the only one that lives north of Mexico. It has a pointed snout, untidy fur, and a long, bare tail. Virginia opossums are tree-dwelling animals. They feed after dark and will eat almost anything—alive or dead. If cornered, they protect themselves by "playing possum," or pretending to be dead. Females can give birth to more than 30 young at a time, but only a small number survive.

RIGHT *When young Virginia opossums grow too large for their mother's pouch, they ride on her back instead.*

SCIENTIFIC NAME	*Didelphis virginiana*
DISTRIBUTION	North and Central America
SIZE	Up to 3 ft. (1m) long, including tail

Ears can fold close to the head

MOUSE-OPOSSUM

This animal is one of nearly 50 species of mouselike opossums in the forests of Central and South America. It spends most of its time in trees, tracking down insects and other animals after dark with its keen eyesight and hearing. Female mouse-opossums have simple, flaplike pouches, and their young have to cling to their mother's fur as she scuttles around.

Large eyes for seeing in the dark

SCIENTIFIC NAME	*Marmosa murinum*
DISTRIBUTION	Northern South America
SIZE	Up to 20 in. (50cm) long, including tail

Small, sharply pointed teeth

WATER OPOSSUM OR YAPOK

This is the only marsupial that lives partly in water. It has a long body with a ratlike tail, water-repellent fur, and webbed back feet. Yapoks dive to catch fish and other water animals to eat. Females can shut their pouches with a ring of muscle when they dive, to prevent their young from drowning.

RIGHT *Unlike true mice, mouse-opossums live by hunting. Grasshoppers and crickets are among their favorite prey. They eat most of the insects' bodies, but throw away their legs.*

SCIENTIFIC NAME	*Chironectes minimus*
DISTRIBUTION	Central America, South America
SIZE	Up to 31.5 in. (80cm) long, including tail

ABOVE *Eastern quolls can give birth to about 25 young—many more than they can feed. About six of the young manage to fasten themselves to the mother's teats, but the rest do not survive.*

EASTERN QUOLL

Quolls are the marsupial equivalents of small cats. There are six species, all from Australia or New Guinea. Most have lithe and slender bodies, large eyes, and spotted fur, and they all climb well. Quolls live in forests and open country. They eat all kinds of small animals, including lizards and small birds, and are efficient hunters, although they are not good at defending themselves against the cats and dogs that have been introduced. The eastern quoll has almost disappeared from the Australian mainland, leaving Tasmania as its last stronghold.

SCIENTIFIC NAME *Dasyurus viverrinus*

DISTRIBUTION Southeastern Australia, Tasmania

SIZE Up to 31.5 in. (80cm) long, including tail

KOALA

The koala is one of Australia's most famous animals. Although it is often called a koala bear, koalas and bears are very different. The koala is a marsupial, and it feeds entirely on the leaves of the gum tree, or eucalyptus, getting all its water from its food. Koalas have sharp claws that allow them to grip even the smoothest bark and shinny up to reach their food. Female koalas have one offspring at a time. Their pouches open near the rear of their bodies, so when they are upright, the opening faces the ground. Although this sounds dangerous, the young koalas never fall out.

SCIENTIFIC NAME *Phascolarctos cinereus*

DISTRIBUTION Eastern Australia

SIZE Up to 33.5 in. (85cm) long

COMMON WOMBAT

Heavily-built wombats spend their lives on or under the ground. They are even more bearlike than koalas, with powerful front feet equipped with impressive claws. They use these claws to dig burrows up to 100 ft. (30m) long. During the day, wombats rest inside their burrows, but at night, they emerge to feed on grass and other plants. There are three species of wombats, found only in Australia and Tasmania. The common wombat is the heaviest, weighing up to 75 lb. (35kg).

SCIENTIFIC NAME	*Vombatus ursinus*
DISTRIBUTION	Southeastern Australia, Tasmania
SIZE	Up to 4 ft. (1.2m) long

MARSUPIAL MOLE

This animal is one of Australia's most elusive marsupials—partly because it lives in remote places, but mainly because it spends most of its life under ground. It has silky, golden-yellow fur, long claws, and a flat shield on its head with which it pushes sand aside as it burrows. It can dig to depths of 8 ft. (2.4m). Marsupial moles feed on insects, and the females have backward-opening pouches.

SCIENTIFIC NAME	*Notoryctes typhlops*
DISTRIBUTION	Northern and central Australia
SIZE	Up to 8 in. (20cm) long, including tail

BRUSH-TAILED POSSUM

This squirrellike animal is one of Australia's most common marsupials and one of the few that is at home in cities. Originally a tree-dweller, it often runs over roofs or into attics after dark, making so much noise that it keeps people awake. Brush-tailed possums feed on leaves, flowers, and fruit. They spend the day holed up out of sight, so they are heard more often than they are seen.

SCIENTIFIC NAME	*Trichosurus vulpecula*
DISTRIBUTION	Originally from Australia, Tasmania; introduced into New Zealand
SIZE	Up to 3 ft. (1m) long, including tail

GREATER GLIDER

There are no flying marsupials, but some species are experts at gliding from tree to tree. They launch themselves from the treetops and glide up to 300 ft. (100m) on flaps of tightly stretched skin. When they land on another tree trunk, the skin folds up, and they scamper away. The greater glider is the largest of these airborne marsupials, with a body about the size of a cat's. Its skin flaps reach from its elbows to its ankles, and it balances with its long, flattened tail.

Greater gliders feed on leaves and rarely come to the ground.

SCIENTIFIC NAME	*Schoinobates volans*
DISTRIBUTION	Eastern Australia
SIZE	Up to 3 ft. (1m) long, including tail

PYGMY GLIDER

This mouse-sized animal is the smallest gliding marsupial. Though it is nocturnal, it is easy to see with a flashlight because it is gray on top and white underneath. Pygmy gliders feed on insects, flowers, and eucalyptus gum. A female can hold up to four young in her pouch, and the young stay on board at all times— even when their mother launches into the air.

SCIENTIFIC NAME	*Acrobates pygmaeus*
DISTRIBUTION	Eastern Australia
SIZE	Up to 6 in. (15cm) long, including tail

The Tasmanian devil was once endangered

TASMANIAN DEVIL

The Tasmanian devil hunts slow-moving animals, including insects and snakes, but feeds mainly on dead animals such as birds, wombats, and sheep. It will eat the whole carcass, including the fur and feathers— it can even crush the bones with its teeth. Tasmanian devils usually search for food on their own, but they gather in groups where there is plenty to eat.

SCIENTIFIC NAME	*Sarcophilus harrisi*
DISTRIBUTION	Tasmania
SIZE	Up to 3.5 ft. (1.1m) long, including tail

TOP *A young common wombat stays with its mother for at least a year.* **ABOVE** *The marsupial mole has no eyes, so it finds its food by touch and smell. It has extra-long claws on two of its fingers for digging.* **BELOW** *Brush-tailed possums have become a problem where they have been introduced into New Zealand, because they damage young trees.*

EASTERN GRAY KANGAROO

Kangaroos are the world's largest marsupials and also the fastest. Eastern gray kangaroos are up to 5 ft. (1.5m) tall when they rest on their haunches, but they are even taller when they stand on their toes. They can run at up to 35 mph (55km/h) in short bursts, taking leaps the length of two cars. Kangaroos live in dry, open country. They feed mainly on grass and breed whenever the food supply is good enough.

RIGHT Long-footed potoroos use their front feet to dig for roots and insect grubs and to hold their food while they eat.

1

2

3

ABOVE A young gray kangaroo is helpless when it is born, and its first priority is to find its mother's pouch. **1** *Using its front legs, the newborn joey crawls through its mother's fur.* **2** *The joey enters the pouch and fastens itself to one of its mother's teats.* **3** *Within six months, the joey completely fills the pouch and is large enough to feed outside.*

LEFT While its mother watches for danger, a young gray kangaroo peers out from her pouch. Muscles in the wall of the pouch tighten when the mother hops, so the joey stays secure.

Female kangaroos give birth to one baby, or joey, at a time. A newborn joey is less than 2 in. (5cm) long, and only its front legs are fully formed. It crawls through its mother's fur to her pouch, where it spends the next six months. Then it leaves the pouch, but for several months it will climb back in if danger threatens.

SCIENTIFIC NAME *Macropus giganteus*

DISTRIBUTION Eastern Australia, Tasmania

SIZE Up to 8 ft. (2.4m) long, including tail

LONG-FOOTED POTOROO

Potoroos belong to the kangaroo family, but they look more like giant rodents. They have soft, silky fur and pointed muzzles, but they also have the kangaroo "trademark"—powerful back legs paired with much smaller front legs. Potoroos live in grassland and scrub. Compared to their larger relatives, they eat a wide range of food, including grass, insects, and fungi.

SCIENTIFIC NAME *Potorous longipes*

DISTRIBUTION Southeastern Australia

SIZE Up to 9 ft. (2.7m) long, including tail

MUSKY RAT-KANGAROO

This miniature kangaroo lives in Australia's rain forests, where it feeds on leaves, fruit, and small animals. It is unusual for several reasons. For example, it often darts around on all fours, trailing its ratlike tail. It is also the only kangaroo that gives birth to twins—all other kangaroos have just one joey at a time. Musky rat-kangaroos sleep in nests that they build on the ground. Most mammals carry nesting material in their mouths or paws, but these kangaroos use their tails instead.

SCIENTIFIC NAME *Hypsiprymnodon moschatus*

DISTRIBUTION Northern Queensland in Australia

SIZE Up to 20 in. (50cm) long, including tail

YELLOW-FOOTED ROCK WALLABY

Rock wallabies are similar to kangaroos, but they are much more agile. They live in mountains and other rocky places and have soft, nonslip pads on their feet. These give them such a good grip that they can climb vertical cliffs and bound across ravines up to 13 ft. (4m) wide. Unlike most kangaroos, their tails do not have a thickened base, and they use them for balance rather than as a prop. The yellow-footed rock wallaby is the largest of the six species of rock wallabies. It is also one of the most endangered because, until recently, it has been hunted for its fur.

SCIENTIFIC NAME *Petrogale xanthopus*

DISTRIBUTION Eastern Australia

SIZE Up to 5 ft. (1.5m) long, including tail

RUFOUS HARE-WALLABY OR MALA

This endangered marsupial is little larger than a hare. It lives on dry plains studded with clumps of drought-resistant spinifex grass, and it feeds on seeds and leaves. During the day, it rests in any shade that it can find, dashing off like a hare if it is disturbed. Two hundred years ago, rufous hare-wallabies were common across much of Australia. Today very few are left, and a program is underway to save the species from extinction.

SCIENTIFIC NAME
Lagorchestes hirsutus

DISTRIBUTION
Western Australia

SIZE Up to 3 ft. (1m) long, including tail

QUOKKA

The quokka was one of the first marsupials Europeans saw when they explored the coast of western Australia in the late 1600s. Thinking it was a kind of rat, they called one of its main breeding areas Rat's Nest Island. Quokkas are actually much larger than rats, but they do have rodentlike faces and long,

almost bare tails. They feed on plants, sometimes climbing into shrubs to get to leaves.

SCIENTIFIC NAME *Setonix brachyurus*

DISTRIBUTION Southwestern Australia

SIZE Up to 3 ft. (1m) long, including tail

BENNETT'S TREE KANGAROO

Tree kangaroos live in tropical rain forests and are very different from kangaroos that live on the ground. Their front and back legs are almost the same length, and their feet have soft pads and sharp, curved claws. Instead of tapering to a point, their tails are the same thickness all the way down, often with a fluffy tip. Tree kangaroos eat leaves and fruit, and they spend most of the time in the forest canopy. Bennett's tree kangaroo is one of two Australian species. Several others live in New Guinea—the most recently discovered was found in 1990.

SCIENTIFIC NAME *Dendrolagus bennettianus*

DISTRIBUTION Northern Queensland in Australia

SIZE Up to 5.5 ft. (1.7m) long, including tail

Keen hearing to listen for danger

Shaggy coat with soft underfur

BELOW *A female yellow-footed rock wallaby cannot climb with a large joey in her pouch. She will leave the joey in a safe place while she searches for food.*

BELOW *Balancing with its tail, a Bennett's tree kangaroo gets ready to jump from a branch. Like other tree kangaroos, it feeds at night and spends the day sleeping high in the treetops.*

LEFT *The rufous hare-wallaby has become extinct on the Australian mainland and is now found wild only on offshore islands.*

ANTEATERS, ARMADILLOS, SLOTHS, PANGOLINS, AND AARDVARKS

Anteaters, armadillos, and sloths are closely related. They all have small teeth or none at all, and they are the only living mammals to have specially reinforced backbones for digging. There are 30 species in total, all of which live in the Americas. Some of them feed on ants and termites; others eat leaves. Pangolins and aardvarks have no close relatives, so biologists classify them in groups of their own. They live in Asia and Africa and also eat ants and termites.

GIANT ANTEATER

Although ants and termites are tiny, they are often extremely numerous. Several mammals specialize in eating them, and the giant anteater is one of the largest. Weighing up to 90 lb. (40kg), it has a bushy tail and powerful front legs armed with long claws. It has no teeth, but its extraordinary snout contains a long, very sticky tongue. The giant anteater rips open ant and termite nests with its claws. While the insects rush for cover, the anteater sweeps them up into its mouth with its tongue. It eats up to 30,000 ants in a day. Female giant anteaters give birth to a single baby, which rides on its mother's back.

SCIENTIFIC NAME *Myrmecophaga tridactyla*

DISTRIBUTION Central America, South America

SIZE Up to 6 ft. (2m) long, including tail

TOP LEFT *Using its front claws, a nine-banded armadillo digs its way into an underground ant nest.*
TOP RIGHT *When an armadillo rolls up into a ball, its head and tail fit side-by-side to make the ball complete.*
ABOVE *Giant anteaters walk on the knuckles of their front feet to keep their long digging claws out of the way.*

COLLARED ANTEATER OR TAMANDUA

This animal is much smaller than the giant anteater, and it lives in trees rather than on the ground. It uses its slender, prehensile tail to hang on to branches as it feeds. If a collared anteater is threatened by a predator, it can prop itself up on its back legs and tail and defend itself with its front claws.

SCIENTIFIC NAME *Tamandua mexicana*

DISTRIBUTION Central America, tropical South America

SIZE Up to 3.5 ft. (1.1m) long, including tail

ABOVE AND RIGHT *The collared anteater is a picky eater, avoiding ants that have powerful bites or stings. A creature of habit, it often follows the same route night after night, looking for ant and termite nests to raid.*

GIANT ARMADILLO

Armadillos got their name from the armor-plating that covers most of their bodies. The armor is formed by hundreds of small, hard scales that work like a flexible shell. Some armadillos can roll up into a ball if they are attacked, but with a body weighing up to 130 lb. (60kg), the giant armadillo is too large to do this. Instead, it either runs for safety or digs into the ground, using its armored back for protection. Giant armadillos live in forests, feeding on termites and other small animals. They shelter in underground burrows, where the females give birth to one or two young each year.

SCIENTIFIC NAME *Priodontes maximus*

DISTRIBUTION South America

SIZE Up to 5 ft. (1.5m) long, including tail

NINE-BANDED ARMADILLO

There are 20 species of armadillos, but this is the only one that lives as far north as the United States. It usually has nine armored bands across its back, though the number can range between six and eleven. It is a good digger, and it can partly roll up, although given the chance, it more often runs away. Nine-banded armadillos always give birth to identical quadruplets. In each family, the young are either all male or all female.

SCIENTIFIC NAME *Dasypus novemcinctus*

DISTRIBUTION North, Central, and South America, from southeastern United States to Uruguay

SIZE Up to 3 ft. (1m) long, including tail

THREE-TOED SLOTH

The five species of sloths are the only mammals that spend almost their entire lives hanging upside down. They are well-suited to life in the trees, with long arms, hooked claws, and fur that hangs down to help the rain run off. Sloths feed on leaves and are famous for moving very slowly. During the day, they stay completely still, and even after sunset, they often move only a few yards in a night. Strangely, sloths clamber to the ground to bury their droppings—it is not known exactly why. The three-toed sloth has one baby a year, which the female carries on her chest for about five months.

SCIENTIFIC NAME	*Bradypus tridactylus*
DISTRIBUTION	Central America, South America
SIZE	Up to 26 in. (66cm) long

TREE PANGOLIN

With their overlapping, dark brown scales, pangolins look more like moving pine cones than mammals. Their scales cover most of their bodies, apart from their undersides and feet, and provide some protection from enemies. Pangolins feed on ants and termites, and like anteaters, they have long, sticky tongues but no teeth. The largest species live on the ground, but the tree pangolin has a long, prehensile tail and is a good climber.

SCIENTIFIC NAME	*Manis tricuspis*
DISTRIBUTION	Tropical Africa
SIZE	Up to 3.5 ft. (1.1m) long, including tail

AARDVARK

In Dutch, aardvark means "earth pig," which is a good description of this large, African mammal. It has a piglike snout and powerful claws. Aardvarks spend the day in underground burrows but surface at night, using their keen sense of smell to track down ants and termites. They also have very good hearing, thanks to their large, upright ears. When they go under ground into their burrows, their ears conveniently fold out of the way.

SCIENTIFIC NAME	*Orycteropus afer*
DISTRIBUTION	Tropical and southern Africa
SIZE	Up to 7.25 ft. (2.2m) long, including tail

ABOVE *The three-toed sloth gets its color from microscopic plants that grow in its damp fur.*
BELOW AND LEFT *The aardvark's sticky tongue is about a foot long.*

ABOVE AND LEFT
Pangolins sometimes protect themselves from attack by curling up. They can also raise their scales to expose their sharp edges.

Pangolins walk on the sides of their front feet

Overlapping scales have ridges and sharp edges

MOLES, HEDGEHOGS, AND SHREWS

The mammals in this group are known as insectivores because they feed mainly on insects and other small animals. Most of them are small and nocturnal and live on their own. Though they have poor eyesight, they have a good sense of smell and small, very effective teeth. There are nearly 400 species living in habitats ranging from deserts to fresh water. Moles and shrews are found across most of the world except Australia and New Zealand, but hedgehogs live only in Europe, Africa, and Asia.

EUROPEAN MOLE

This black, furry animal spends most of its life under ground, so it has very poor eyesight. Its movements are easy to track because it pushes piles of excavated soil, called molehills, onto the surface. With their spadelike front paws, European moles dig networks of tunnels for catching food. The moles patrol the tunnels at frequent intervals, eating any earthworms that have fallen in. They bite the worms' heads off and store the bodies for later.

SCIENTIFIC NAME	*Talpa europaea*
DISTRIBUTION	Western and central Europe, parts of Asia
SIZE	Up to 8 in. (20cm) long, including tail

STAR-NOSED MOLE

Unlike the European mole, the star-nosed mole likes wet ground, and it feeds in ponds and streams. Its nose has a ring of 22 pink, fleshy tentacles, which it uses to feel for insect grubs and other animals under water. Its large front feet work like paddles when it swims, and like shovels when it tunnels through the ground.

SCIENTIFIC NAME	*Condylura cristata*
DISTRIBUTION	Northeastern North America
SIZE	Up to 8 in. (20cm) long, including tail

PYRENEAN DESMAN

Desmans are strange, molelike animals that hunt in rivers and streams. Their feet are webbed, their fur is waterproof, and their long, flattened tail works like a cross between a rudder and a propeller. They are almost as blind as moles and find their prey by touch, feeling among underwater stones with their long,

Pyrenean desman at water's edge

Strong claws for digging

ABOVE *Holding an earthworm in its paws, a European mole starts to feed.*

quivering snouts. There are only two species of desmans. The Pyrenean desman has been affected by pollution, while the larger Russian desman has been hunted for its fur.

SCIENTIFIC NAME	*Galemys pyrenaicus*
DISTRIBUTION	Pyrenees Mountains in France and Spain
SIZE	Up to 12 in. (30cm) long, including tail

WESTERN HEDGEHOG

Many insectivores run away at the first sign of danger, but the hedgehog reacts very differently. Its back is covered with about 6,000 sharp spines, and if it is threatened, it rolls up into a ball and makes its spines stand on end. This behavior protects

it against most predators. Hedgehogs live in many habitats, from sand dunes to suburban backyards, hibernating for six months every year. They eat a wide range of small animals, including insects, spiders, slugs, and earthworms.

SCIENTIFIC NAME	*Erinaceus europaeus*
DISTRIBUTION	Originally from Europe; introduced into New Zealand
SIZE	Up to 10.5 in. (27cm) long

ETRUSCAN SHREW
The Etruscan shrew is the world's smallest land mammal. Even when fully grown, it could sit in a teaspoon. It has a short life span, reaching old age within a year. Shrews need to eat around the clock because their tiny bodies are difficult to keep warm. Unless they have a constant supply of food, they run out of energy and die. They find their food by smell and touch, then overpower it with the help of a poisonous bite. Etruscan shrews are extremely aggressive, but they are also highly strung—they sometimes die simply because they are picked up.

SCIENTIFIC NAME	*Suncus etruscus*
DISTRIBUTION	Europe, Africa, Asia
SIZE	Up to 3 in. (8cm) long, including tail

Etruscan shrew

Pygmy shrew
(*Sorex minutus*)

Water shrew
(*Neomys fodiens*)

FLYING LEMURS AND TREE SHREWS
Flying lemurs, also known as colugos, are the world's largest gliding mammals. They glide on flaps of skin that stretch down either side of their bodies, from their necks all the way down to their tails. There are two species. Both are nocturnal and live in the forests of Southeast Asia. Tree shrews come from the same part of the world, but they are climbers instead of gliders. There are 16 species, and unlike flying lemurs, most of them are active during the day.

PHILIPPINE FLYING LEMUR
When clinging to a branch, a flying lemur looks as if its body is covered by a spotted cloak. The cloak is actually the animal's flight membrane, an elastic sheet of skin that it uses to sail through the air. Its flight membrane is so large that it can glide through the air for more than 400 ft. (125m), a record for any mammal. Flying lemurs use gliding as a quick way to travel between the trees in search of leaves, flowers, and fruit to eat. Females give birth to a single baby each time they breed, and they carry it until its weight makes it hard for them to glide.

SCIENTIFIC NAME	*Cynocephalus volans*
DISTRIBUTION	Philippines
SIZE	Up to 28 in. (71cm) long, including tail

COMMON TREE SHREW
Despite its name, this animal looks more like a squirrel than a shrew. It has large claws and a bushy tail, and it feeds on almost any edible thing it can find, in trees or on the ground. Tree shrews are of particular interest to biologists because they strongly resemble fossils of the world's earliest mammals. They give us an idea of what the first mammals looked like and how they behaved.

SCIENTIFIC NAME	*Tupaia glis*
DISTRIBUTION	Southern and Southeast Asia
SIZE	Up to 16 in. (40cm) long, including tail

ABOVE LEFT *Shrews live all over the world, except in Australia, New Zealand, and parts of South America. These three species are all found in Europe.*

LEFT *Hedgehogs are useful animals in gardens because they eat slugs and insect pests. Despite having short legs, they can roam as much as a mile in their nightly search for food.*

TOP *This flying lemur is getting ready to jump from a branch high above the forest floor. Flying lemurs are superb gliders, but they are almost helpless if they accidentally land on the ground.*

ABOVE *With its long snout, keen sense of smell, and good eyesight, a common tree shrew can quickly track down food on the forest floor.*

BATS

There are nearly 1,000 species of bats, and they are found worldwide, except in very cold places. Bats are the only mammals that can truly fly instead of gliding. Their wings are made of skin stretched between long, slender fingers. Bats are nocturnal animals, and most of them feed either on fruit and flowers or on flying insects. The fruit-eating species have large eyes and can see in the dark, but the insect-eaters have poor eyesight. They find their prey using a technique called echolocation.

Fruit bat in flight

GIANT FRUIT BAT OR FLYING FOX

With a wingspan of up to 5 ft. (1.5m), this is the world's largest bat. It has a long muzzle and a keen sense of smell, and it roosts upside down in treetops with its wings wrapped around its body. At dusk, flocks of fruit bats set off to feed. They squash the fruit in their jaws, drinking the juice but dropping the seeds and flesh to the ground. Female fruit bats give birth to one baby each time they breed, carrying it around with them for two months.

SCIENTIFIC NAME	*Pteropus giganteus*
DISTRIBUTION	Southern and Southeast Asia
SIZE	Up to 16 in. (40cm) long

PIPISTRELLE

This common, European bat's body would fit inside a matchbox. It hunts by echolocation, using its large ears to pick up echoes from insects in the air. During the day, pipistrelles often roost in buildings. In the winter, they crowd together to hibernate in lofts and caves. Female pipistrelles normally have just one baby a year, which they leave in a nursery roost when they set off to feed.

SCIENTIFIC NAME	*Pipistrellus pipistrellus*
DISTRIBUTION	Europe, parts of Asia
SIZE	Up to 3 in. (8cm) long, including tail

GREATER HORSESHOE BAT

The 70 species of horseshoe bats got their name from their strangely shaped noses, which have complicated folds of bare skin. They use these

TOP RIGHT *The Eastern horseshoe bat (Rhinolophus megaphyllus) lives in New Guinea and eastern Australia.* **ABOVE LEFT** *The pipistrelle is the smallest European bat.* **LEFT** *The greater horseshoe bat is guided by its sensitive hearing.*

folds to focus bursts of sound when they hunt by echolocation. Unlike most insect-eating bats, the greater horseshoe bat collects some of its food on the ground. It swoops down on insects and carries them to a perch to feed.

SCIENTIFIC NAME	*Rhinolophus ferrumequinum*
DISTRIBUTION	Europe, northern Africa, Asia
SIZE	Up to 6.7 in. (17cm) long, including tail

KITTI'S HOG-NOSED BAT

This minute, insect-eating bat is probably the world's smallest mammal. It weighs about 0.07 oz. (2g), and its body is only about 1 in. (2.5cm) long. It has a tiny, piglike snout and well-developed ears, but no tail. Kitti's hog-nosed bat was first seen by scientists in 1973. It lives in tropical forests, roosting in caves by day.

SCIENTIFIC NAME	*Craseonycteris thonglongyai*
DISTRIBUTION	Thailand
SIZE	Up to 1 in. (2.5cm) long

Kitti's hog-nosed bat on a finger

Wings used as legs when the bat is on the ground

Blunt muzzle helps bat bite

Upper front teeth pierce the victim's skin

ABOVE *To survive, an adult vampire bat has to drink about half a fluid ounce of blood every day. This is enough to fill two teaspoons.*
RIGHT *Swooping low over a pond, a fisherman bat snatches a fish from the water with its claws.*

FISHERMAN BAT

Several species of bats eat frogs, but the fisherman bat is one of the few that catch fish. It hunts over rivers and ponds and along the shore, probably finding its prey by sensing ripples on the surface of the water. The bat will snatch up a fish in its claws and eat it either on the wing or once it has landed at a roost. Fisherman bats usually hunt at night, but they have been seen during the day catching fish that have been disturbed by birds.

SCIENTIFIC NAME	*Noctilio leporinus*
DISTRIBUTION	Central America, South America
SIZE	Up to 5.5 in. (14cm) long, including tail

VAMPIRE BAT

The vampire bat is notorious for its eating habits because it feeds on fresh blood—usually from horses and cattle, but sometimes from human beings. To feed, the bat lands close to its victim, then scuttles nearer, using its wings as legs. After biting away any fur or feathers, it makes an incision in the skin and patiently sucks up its meal. Vampire bats do not drink much blood when they feed, but they are harmful because they can spread rabies, a potentially fatal disease that can infect humans.

SCIENTIFIC NAME	*Desmodus rotundus*
DISTRIBUTION	Central America, South America
SIZE	Up to 3.5 in. (9cm) long

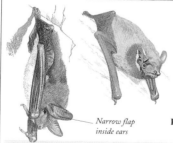

Narrow flap inside ears

ABOVE *The common long-eared bat (Plecotus auritus) has ears as long as its body.*
LEFT *The noctule bat (Nyctalus noctula) roosts in trees.*
FAR LEFT *The greater mouse-eared bat (Myotis myotis) hibernates in caves.*

ECHOLOCATION

Echolocation allows some animals to hunt in total darkness by sending out bursts of high-pitched sound. If another animal is nearby, some of the sound bounces back from its body, and the hunter can then home in on its prey. Echoes also bounce back from other objects, helping the hunter build up a picture of its surroundings. Insect-eating bats are the most adept in the use of echolocation, but other echolocating animals include dolphins, some whales, and tiny shrews.

Long-eared bat homing in on a moth

PRIMATES

Primates are mammals that are adapted for life in trees. They have long arms and legs, with flexible fingers and toes that they curl around branches to get a good grip. Most of them have flat nails instead of claws. Primates also have forward-pointing eyes, a feature that helps them judge distances as they jump and climb high above the ground. There are about 230 species of these mammals, found mainly in warm parts of the world. Because the world's tropical forests are fast disappearing, many primates are in serious danger of becoming extinct.

Ring-tailed lemurs run on all fours

RING-TAILED LEMUR

Like most of the animals on these two pages, lemurs are primitive primates, or prosimians. They live on the island of Madagascar, which has more prosimians than anywhere else. The ring-tailed lemur has a catlike face and a gray and white body. Its most eyecatching feature is its bushy, upright tail, which has bold gray and black rings. Ring-tailed lemurs are unusual because they are active during the day and feed on the ground. They eat leaves, fruit, and sugary sap, which they get by biting through bark. They live in troops of up to 20 animals.

SCIENTIFIC NAME	*Lemur catta*
DISTRIBUTION	Madagascar
SIZE	Up to 3 ft. (1m) long, including tail

GRAY MOUSE LEMUR

Mouse lemurs are among the world's smallest primates. They look very much like mice, but they have forward-facing eyes, tiny fingers and toes, and long tails with fluffy tips. They often weigh less than 2 oz. (50g)—about 6,000 times less than the largest primate, the gorilla (page 248). Like many prosimians, mouse lemurs are active at night. They eat a wide range of food, including insects, fruit, and leaves. They give birth to two or three young after a gestation period of about eight months, a long time for animals of their size.

SCIENTIFIC NAME	*Microcebus murinus*
DISTRIBUTION	Madagascar
SIZE	Up to 12 in. (30cm) long, including tail

TOP *Ring-tailed lemurs use the position of their tails to indicate their rank in the troop. These two are showing they are dominant males.*

ABOVE *A gray mouse lemur wraps its fingers and toes around a twig as it sits in a tree.*

Indri in typical pose

INDRI

The indri looks like a gray and black teddy bear, with a very small tail and large, rounded ears. As well as being Madagascar's largest primate, it is the loudest, with an extraordinary song that can be heard more than 1.25 mi. (2km) away. Indris sing to claim a territory in the treetops for their family groups. They feed during the day, eating leaves, buds, and fruit.

SCIENTIFIC NAME	*Indri indri*
DISTRIBUTION	Madagascar
SIZE	Up to 32 in. (81cm) long, including tail

AYE-AYE

The aye-aye is about the size of a cat. It lives in Madagascan rain forests, feeding on fruit, bird eggs, and insects. The aye-aye's middle fingers are much longer than the others. It uses these extra-long fingers to tap against trees. If it hears movement beneath the bark it probes inside with a finger and pulls out its prey.

SCIENTIFIC NAME	*Daubentonia madagascarensis*
DISTRIBUTION	Madagascar
SIZE	Up to 3 ft. (1m) long, including tail

GREATER BUSHBABY

The bushbaby is one of 11 primitive primates that live on the mainland of Africa. It got its name from its bushy tail and childlike cry. The bushbaby resembles a large squirrel. It feeds at night, using its keen senses to find fruit, insects, and sweet tree sap. Like most primates, bushbabies climb well because they have opposable thumbs. This means their thumbs close around branches opposite their fingers, increasing their grip.

Greater bushbaby gripping a branch

SCIENTIFIC NAME	*Otolemur crassicaudatus*
DISTRIBUTION	Eastern and southern Africa
SIZE	Up to 3 ft. (1m) long, including tail

SLENDER LORIS

Most primates are fast-moving animals, but the slender loris is not. It creeps along branches on its spindly legs, rarely coming to the ground. The slender loris has a flat face with large eyes, and hardly any tail. It spends the day asleep. At night, it ambushes insects and other small animals to eat. Instead of using its teeth to catch prey, the slender loris lunges forward and grabs its victims with its hands.

SCIENTIFIC NAME	*Loris tardigradus*
DISTRIBUTION	Southern India, Sri Lanka
SIZE	Up to 10 in. (25cm) long

ANGWANTIBO OR GOLDEN POTTO

This small, African primate has soft, woolly fur, slender arms and legs, and almost no tail. It has five toes on each foot, but its hands are unusual, with two long fingers and two much shorter fingers, one of which is little more than a fleshy pad. Despite this, the angwantibo is a good climber, moving slowly and stealthily through trees and bushes. It feeds mainly on insects, either picking them off twigs and leaves or, occasionally, grabbing them as they fly past.

SCIENTIFIC NAME *Arctocebus calabarensis*

DISTRIBUTION Tropical Africa

SIZE Up to 12 in. (30cm) long

WESTERN TARSIER

Tarsiers are insect-eating primates from the forests of Southeast Asia. Although they are small enough to fit into a pocket, they have long tails, large fingers and toes, and enormous eyes—characteristics that suit their unusual way of life. Instead of climbing along branches to find insects, tarsiers look and listen for them in the dark. Once they have spotted a likely meal, they leap through the air to catch their prey. They can jump distances of up to 17 ft. (5m), and they feed sitting up, chewing with their tiny teeth. Tarsiers give birth to a single baby each year, after a gestation period of about six months.

SCIENTIFIC NAME *Tarsius bancanus*

DISTRIBUTION Indonesia

SIZE Up to 17 in. (43cm) long, including tail

RIGHT *The woolly monkey's thick coat is made up of long outer hairs with much denser underfur close to the body. When it rains, the outer coat gets wet, but the underfur stays dry.*

Flat face with short muzzle

ABOVE *Pygmy marmosets weigh up to 5 oz.—about the same as a well-fed hamster. These tiny but highly active primates have sharp teeth, and they bite holes in tree bark to feed on the sticky sap.*

BELOW *The golden lion tamarin's fur glints in the sun like gold.*

PYGMY MARMOSET

Marmosets and tamarins are found only in Central and South America. Many of them look like small monkeys with extra-long tails, but unlike true monkeys, they do not have grasping hands and feet. Instead of clinging to branches, they scamper along the top. The pygmy marmoset, the smallest species, is the tiniest primate anywhere in the Americas. It has gray-brown fur that camouflages it among the branches, and yellowish hands and feet. Like other marmosets, it feeds during the day, eating insects, fruit, sugary nectar, and sap.

SCIENTIFIC NAME *Cebuella pygmaea*

DISTRIBUTION Northern South America

SIZE Up to 14 in. (35cm) long, including tail

GOLDEN LION TAMARIN

This rare animal is one of the world's most beautiful and endangered primates. It has a luxurious coat of orange-yellow fur, with a flowing mane and a long, silky tail. Golden lion tamarins come from forests on the Atlantic coast of Brazil—a habitat that has almost vanished in the last 25 years. To make matters worse, many

golden lion tamarins have been caught and sold as pets. It is now illegal to catch or buy golden lion tamarins, and an international breeding program is working to save the species.

SCIENTIFIC NAME *Leontopithecus rosalia*

DISTRIBUTION Eastern Brazil

SIZE Up to 22 in. (55cm) long, including tail

WOOLLY MONKEY

This black-furred monkey is one of more than 40 species that live in Central and South America. Unlike monkeys from Africa and Asia, these New World monkeys all have nostrils that open sideways. Many of them, including the woolly monkey, also have prehensile tails. Their tails work like an extra leg, helping them hang on to branches as they feed. Woolly monkeys live in large troops and feed mainly on fruit and seeds. They have one baby each time they breed, and the mother carries her newborn infant on her chest or back.

SCIENTIFIC NAME *Lagothrix lagothricha*

DISTRIBUTION Northern South America

SIZE Up to 4.5 ft. (1.4m) long, including tail

BLACK SPIDER MONKEY

No other monkey can rival this species for sheer acrobatic skill. It can swing arm-over-arm through the treetops faster than a person can run, and it can hang from branches by its tail, leaving its arms and legs dangling in the air. Like the woolly monkey, its tail has a bare patch near the tip, which gives it a good grip. Spider monkeys feed mainly on fruit and nuts, and they live in troops up to 30 strong.

Prehensile tail works as an extra hand

Black spider monkey balanced on a branch

SCIENTIFIC NAME *Ateles paniscus*

DISTRIBUTION Northern South America

SIZE Up to 4.5 ft. (1.4m) long, including tail

RED HOWLER MONKEY

Howler monkeys are named for their loud calls, which ring out over the treetops at dawn and late in the day. To produce the calls, they use a resonating chamber in their throats. It acts like a built-in amplifier, allowing the sound to be heard up to 2 mi. (3km) away. There are six species of howlers. They are the largest New World monkeys and also the most sluggish. They survive almost entirely on leaves, so they never have to travel far to find their food. The red howler is a deep rusty color, but other howlers are black, brown, or gray.

Red howler monkeys howling

SCIENTIFIC NAME *Alouatta seniculus*

DISTRIBUTION Northern South America

SIZE Up to 5 ft. (1.5m) long, including tail

SQUIRREL MONKEY

This is one of the smallest New World monkeys, measuring as little as 12 in. (30cm) from the top of its head to the base of its tail. However, its total length more than doubles if its tail is included. Squirrel monkeys' tails are not prehensile, so they cannot grasp things with them. Instead, they use them for balance when they sit or climb. In undisturbed forests, squirrel monkeys form large troops, numbering up to 500 animals.

SCIENTIFIC NAME *Saimiri sciureus*

DISTRIBUTION Northern South America

SIZE Up to 27.5 in. (70cm) long, including tail

UAKARI

This South American monkey is instantly recognizable by its bald, bright red head and face. It is also the only monkey in the Americas that does not have a long tail. Uakaris live in parts of the Amazon rain forest that are flooded during the wet season. They are shy, unaggressive monkeys, and they feed mainly on seeds and nuts. They stay in the treetops, hardly ever coming to the ground.

SCIENTIFIC NAME *Cacajao calvus*

DISTRIBUTION Northern South America

SIZE Up to 25.5 in. (65cm) long, including tail

DOUROUCOULI

Also known as the night monkey, this is one of the few nocturnal monkeys. It has a small body, a long tail, and a round head with large eyes. Its eyesight is so good that it can run along branches and jump between trees even on dark, moonless nights. Douroucoulis eat a wide range of food, including insects and fruit. They have stretchy pouches under their throats, which they inflate when they call.

SCIENTIFIC NAME *Aotus trivirgatus*

DISTRIBUTION Central and northern South America

SIZE Up to 30 in. (76cm) long, including tail

BELOW *Uakaris have white or red fur and extra-strong jaws for cracking open nuts.*

Scarlet skin looks sunburned

JAPANESE MACAQUE

Nearly 100 species of monkeys live
in the Old World, which includes
Europe, Africa, and Asia. Unlike
New World monkeys, which live
in the Americas, these animals have
nostrils that are close together, and
their tails are never prehensile. The
Japanese macaque is a typical Old
World monkey in many ways, but
its fur is unusually thick. It needs
this warm coat because it lives in a
cold climate, farther north than any
other primate in the world. Japanese
macaques feed on the ground and
in trees. During the winter, they
sometimes lounge in hot springs
to avoid the worst of the cold.

SCIENTIFIC NAME *Macaca fuscata*

DISTRIBUTION Japan

SIZE Up to 3.5 ft. (1.1m) long,
including tail

BARBARY MACAQUE

This macaque is the only monkey
that lives in Europe. It is similar
to the Japanese macaque, but it
has no tail. In prehistoric times,
Barbary macaques were common in
southwestern Europe, but today their
only European home is Gibraltar,
where they are specially protected.
Females give birth to one baby at
a time. At first, the young macaque
clings to its mother's underside,
but it later rides on her back.

SCIENTIFIC NAME *Macaca sylvanus*

DISTRIBUTION Gibraltar, northern
Africa

SIZE Up to 30 in. (76cm) long

VERVET MONKEY OR GREEN GUENON

This lively and agile animal
is one of about 25 closely
related species that live
in Africa. Most of these
monkeys have slender
bodies and long tails,
and the easiest way to
tell them apart is by the
colors and patterns on
their faces. The vervet
usually has a black face
surrounded by white fur,
and a green-gray body. It lives
mainly on plants and is just as

*ABOVE Cradling its baby
to keep it warm, a Japanese
macaque braves the cold.
Its fur insulates it from the
snow and ice. During the
winter, these monkeys have
to survive on a meager diet
of bark, buds, and roots.*
*LEFT This female vervet
monkey is grooming her
baby's fur. Grooming is
important for monkeys
that live in groups. They
do it to keep clean and
also to show friendship
or submission to each other.*

good at running as it is at climbing trees. Vervets
breed all year round. The mothers suckle their
young until they are about six months old.

SCIENTIFIC NAME *Cercopithecus aethiops*

DISTRIBUTION Eastern and southern Africa

SIZE Up to 5 ft. (1.5m) long, including tail

OLIVE BABOON

Baboons are powerfully built African monkeys
that spend most of their time on the ground.
They have doglike muzzles and sloping backs,
and the males, which are about twice as large as
the females, have fearsome teeth. Baboons will
eat almost anything, including young antelope

and other mammals. To protect themselves, they forage and sleep in large troops. If a predator threatens them, the males go on the attack while the females and young run up trees for safety.

SCIENTIFIC NAME *Papio anubis*

DISTRIBUTION Tropical Africa

SIZE Up to 5.5 ft. (1.7m) long, including tail

MANDRILL

Mandrills are closely related to baboons. They are the heaviest monkeys in the world, weighing up to 120 lb. (55kg). Male mandrills are much larger than females, and they have brilliantly colored faces, with red and blue muzzles. These monkeys live on the ground in dense rain forests and form troops of up to 20 animals, led by an adult male. Although they mostly eat plants, they will also kill anything they can overpower.

SCIENTIFIC NAME *Mandrillus sphinx*

DISTRIBUTION Tropical western Africa

SIZE Up to 3 ft. (1m) long

LANGUR

In southern Asia, this black-faced monkey often lives near houses, where it is always on the lookout for food. It is a good runner and an agile climber, so it can escape quickly if it manages to snatch a meal. In the wild, langurs live in forests and rocky places, but they find most of their food on the ground. Langurs are regarded as sacred animals in India, and this has helped them thrive.

SCIENTIFIC NAME *Presbytis entellus*

DISTRIBUTION India, Sri Lanka

SIZE Up to 6 ft. (2m) long, including tail

PROBOSCIS MONKEY

The male proboscis monkey is impossible to mistake because it has a pink face and a long, swollen nose. Its nose normally hangs down in front of its mouth, but it straightens out when the monkey calls. Proboscis monkeys live in mangrove swamps and feed on shoots and leaves. They normally climb among the mangroves, but they are also good swimmers and will cross deep channels to reach food or to escape from danger.

SCIENTIFIC NAME *Nasalis larvatus*

DISTRIBUTION Borneo

SIZE Up to 5 ft. (1.5m) long, including tail

Thick mane of gray fur

LEFT *There are five species of baboons. This is a Hamadryas baboon (Papio hamadryas). Males of this species are twice as large as the females.*

Long, fleshy nose of a mature male

Back feet are partly webbed

ABOVE *The male proboscis monkey's remarkable nose develops as the monkey grows older. It probably helps the male attract females. In females and young males, the nose is small and upturned.*

EASTERN BLACK AND WHITE COLOBUS

Colobus monkeys live in African forests, and they hardly ever go down to the ground. The eastern black and white colobus has a remarkably luxurious coat, with black fur over most of its body, apart from two long, white fringes along its sides. Its tail is like a giant tassel, with an enormous tuft of white fur at the tip. Although they do not have thumbs, colobuses are superb climbers. They cling on with their fingers as they run or leap through the trees.

SCIENTIFIC NAME *Colobus guerzera*

DISTRIBUTION Tropical Africa

SIZE Up to 5 ft. (1.5m) long, including tail

ABOVE AND LEFT *The male mandrill has deep grooves down either side of its brightly colored muzzle. The color changes with age.*

Colobus monkey sitting on a branch

MAKING TOOLS

For humans, using tools is part of everyday life, but in the animal world, it is much rarer. Some animals pick up objects and use them as tools, but very few shape tools for particular tasks. The chimpanzee is one animal that does this. Chimpanzees often feed on ants and termites, but their fingers are too large to reach into the nests. Instead, they pick up sticks and chew them or strip off the bark. Then they poke the sticks into the nests and eat the insects that swarm over them. Chimpanzees also use stones to crack open nuts and even use leaves to pick up water so that they can drink or wash.

A young chimpanzee learns how to use a stick by watching its mother

LAR GIBBON

Most primates are good climbers, but gibbons are the unrivaled experts at speeding through the treetops. They have short legs and long arms, and they use their hands like hooks as they swing from branch to branch. This way of moving is called brachiation. Gibbons are so good at it that they can reach a speed of about 10 mph (15km/h), flinging themselves across gaps between the trees. There are eleven species of gibbons, all of which live in the dense forests of the Far East and Southeast Asia. Like all its relatives, the lar gibbon has no tail.

Lar gibbon swinging through the forest canopy

SCIENTIFIC NAME	*Hylobates concolor*
DISTRIBUTION	Asia, from southeastern China to Cambodia
SIZE	Up to 26 in. (66cm) long

LEFT A female gorilla holds her baby. Gorillas usually have just one baby at a time, and their young are born about three or four years apart. This baby is about two years old.

SIAMANG

The siamang is the largest gibbon, weighing up to 30 lb. (14kg). It has long, black fur and eats mainly fruit, as well as some flowers, buds, and insects. Gibbons live in small family groups. They have loud, hooting calls, and the siamang has one of the loudest. The males and females perform a duet that can be heard over half a mile (1km) away. Siamangs usually pair for life and have one baby at a time.

SCIENTIFIC NAME	*Hylobates syndactylus*
DISTRIBUTION	Malaysia, Sumatra
SIZE	Up to 3 ft. (1m) long

GORILLA

Weighing up to 650 lb. (300kg), gorillas are the largest primates in the world. They belong to a group of primates called the great apes. There are only four species of great apes—the gorilla, two kinds of chimpanzees, and the orangutan. They have large brains and are good at picking up and holding things with their hands and feet. Unlike monkeys, great apes sometimes stand upright, and they do not have tails. Gorillas live in forests in groups of up to 20 animals, led by a large male. They feed on the ground and in trees, snapping off leaves and stems with their hands. The group moves on slowly during the day. In the late afternoon, each gorilla makes itself a nest of branches and leaves and settles down to sleep. Recently, the number of gorillas has fallen fast, as a result of hunting and deforestation.

SCIENTIFIC NAME	*Gorilla gorilla*
DISTRIBUTION	Western and central Africa
SIZE	Up to 6 ft. (2m) high

CHIMPANZEE

Chimpanzees are our closest living relatives and, after humans, probably the most intelligent animals. They live in large groups in grassland and open woodland, communicating with facial expressions and more than 30 different calls. They feed mainly on plants, insects, and other small animals, but they have been known to hunt much larger animals, including monkeys. In the wild, chimpanzees begin to breed between the ages of 13 and 16, and they can live to be about 60 years old.

SCIENTIFIC NAME	*Pan troglodytes*
DISTRIBUTION	Western and eastern Africa
SIZE	Up to 5 ft. (1.5m) high

LEFT *Clinging to its mother with its hands and feet, a young bonobo is safe from attack.*

BONOBO OR PYGMY CHIMPANZEE

Bonobos are rarely seen outside their natural home, so they are not as well known as chimpanzees. From a distance, they look very similar to chimpanzees, but their faces are often black, and they have smaller ears and longer legs. They also live in a different habitat—dense rain forest, instead of open woodland. Bonobos feed mainly on fruit and leaves, which they collect in trees.

SCIENTIFIC NAME	*Pan paniscus*
DISTRIBUTION	Central Africa
SIZE	Up to 3 ft. (1m) high

ORANGUTAN

The orangutan is the second-largest great ape after the gorilla, as well as the only one with red fur. The males can weigh up to 200 lb. (90kg), and as they get older they develop fleshy pads on either side of their faces. Unlike gorillas, they spend most of their time in the trees and often live alone. Because orangutans depend on forests for their survival, they are very vulnerable to habitat change. Over the last ten years, their natural home has shrunk dramatically, because large areas of forest have been burned or cut down. Young orangutans are also sometimes taken from their mothers and sold as performing pets—a sad fate for such intelligent animals.

SCIENTIFIC NAME	*Pongo pygmaeus*
DISTRIBUTION	Sumatra, Borneo
SIZE	Up to 5 ft. (1.5m) high

RIGHT *Orangutans move slowly, but they are good climbers. They have slender legs, and their fingers and toes can keep a tight grip for a long time.*

RABBITS, HARES, AND PIKAS

This group of plant-eating mammals contains about 65 species, scattered across many parts of the world. All of them live on the ground, where they nibble food with their sharp front teeth. They escape danger by running, and most of them have keen eyesight and hearing—adaptations that give them a head start on any predators. Rabbits and hares live in open country of all kinds, from grassland to desert, but pikas often live on rocky mountain slopes.

Mountain hare in winter coat

Mountain hare in summer coat

TOP *European hare leverets are ready to breed when they are six months old.* **ABOVE** *Several species of hares turn white in the winter. The mountain hare (Lepus timidus) lives in northern Europe and Asia.*

EUROPEAN RABBIT

With its long ears and fluffy, gray fur, the European rabbit is an appealing animal, but it is also a farmland pest. It eats grass and crops, and because it breeds quickly, it can cause a lot of damage. European rabbits usually live in burrows. They come out to feed in the evening and stay above ground all night. If a rabbit senses danger, it strikes the ground with its back feet. When other rabbits hear this, they run for safety. Rabbits have been bred for food and for their fur for over a thousand years. Today there are more than 60 varieties of domestic rabbits, many of which are kept as pets.

SCIENTIFIC NAME *Oryctolagus cuniculus*

DISTRIBUTION Originally from Europe, northern Africa; introduced into Australia and New Zealand

SIZE Up to 16 in. (40cm) long

EUROPEAN HARE

Hares look like large rabbits with extra-long ears. Unlike rabbits, they are usually solitary animals, and they spend all of their lives above ground. Because they do not have burrows, hares depend on speed for safety, and they can run at up to 30 mph (50km/h). Female European hares have several families a year, giving birth in a shallow hideaway called a form. Compared to baby rabbits, young hares, called leverets, are well developed when they are born, and they can run within a few hours.

SCIENTIFIC NAME *Lepus europaeus*

DISTRIBUTION Originally from Africa, Europe, Asia; introduced into North and South America, Australia, New Zealand

SIZE Up to 28 in. (71cm) long

LEFT *This snowshoe hare is alert to danger at all times. Its predators include the arctic fox (page 266).*

SNOWSHOE HARE

Snowshoe hares live in the Arctic, and they change color with the seasons. During the summer, they are brown, but in winter, they turn white to match the snow, except for a patch of black on the tips of their ears. Using fur-trappers' records, scientists have found that the number of snowshoe hares rises and falls in a ten-year cycle. Their population rises dramatically when there is plenty of food, but as soon as the food supply begins to run out, their numbers slump.

SCIENTIFIC NAME *Lepus americanus*

DISTRIBUTION Northern North America

SIZE Up to 22 in. (55cm) long

AMERICAN PIKA

Pikas are close relatives of rabbits and hares, but they do not have long ears. Some species live in woodlands, but the American pika lives on rock-strewn mountain slopes, where there are plenty of places to hide. During the summer, pikas gather grass and pile it up in heaps. When snow covers the ground in winter, they use this stored grass for food.

SCIENTIFIC NAME *Ochotona princeps*

DISTRIBUTION North America

SIZE Up to 9 in. (23cm) long

Eurasian red squirrel   Gray squirrel

LEFT *Squirrels use their bushy tails for balance as they scamper along branches.*

RODENTS

With more than 1,800 species, rodents make up the largest group of mammals. They include squirrels, rats, porcupines, and many other animals from all over the world. Rodents got their name from the Latin word *rodere*, meaning "to gnaw." They have sharp front teeth, or incisors, which never stop growing and always stay sharp. Many rodents use them to gnaw through obstacles or to burrow, and beavers use them to cut down trees. Compared to other mammals, rodents have a short life span, but they reproduce rapidly.

ABOVE *Chipmunks store any surplus food in their underground burrows.*
BELOW *Alpine marmots have keen eyesight, which helps them spot predators, such as birds of prey.*
BOTTOM *A young black-tailed prairie dog samples a piece of grass.*

EASTERN GRAY SQUIRREL

Squirrels are bushy-tailed rodents that are normally active by day. Some live on the ground, but many, including the gray squirrel, live in trees. The gray squirrel is a familiar inhabitant of the countryside, towns, and cities, foraging for nuts, seeds, and bulbs to eat. It has been introduced into other parts of the world, including Europe, where it has displaced the native Eurasian red squirrel (*Sciurus vulgaris*). The American red squirrel (*Tamiasciurus hudsonicus*) is similar to its European relative but lacks the distinctive tufts of fur on its ears.

SCIENTIFIC NAME *Sciurus carolinensis*

DISTRIBUTION Eastern North America; introduced into Europe

SIZE Up to 20 in. (50cm), including tail

EASTERN CHIPMUNK

Rodents are not always popular animals, but the chipmunk is regarded with affection. This small, striped animal lives in forests, spending most of its time on the ground. Chipmunks are bold and inquisitive, and they show little fear of people. They normally forage for seeds and berries but will also help themselves to picnic leftovers. Chipmunks raise about eight young each year.

SCIENTIFIC NAME *Tamias striatus*

DISTRIBUTION Eastern North America

SIZE Up to 12 in. (30cm) long, including tail

BLACK-TAILED PRAIRIE DOG

This animal is not a dog at all, but a large, ground-dwelling squirrel with a doglike bark. It lives on grassy plains, digging burrows beneath the surface. A network of prairie dog burrows, called a township, has a ventilation system and sleeping quarters. One township can house thousands of animals. Before the prairies were plowed up, more than 100 years ago, prairie dogs were extremely common. Today, with little prairie left, some species are rare.

SCIENTIFIC NAME *Cynomys ludovicianus*

DISTRIBUTION Central United States

SIZE Up to 16 in. (40cm) long, including tail

ALPINE MARMOT

Marmots live in mountain pastures. During the long winters, they hibernate in deep burrows for up to nine months a year. Before hibernating, they build up their body fat, which acts as a food supply, keeping them alive while they "sleep." There are at least ten species of marmots scattered across the Northern Hemisphere.

SCIENTIFIC NAME *Marmota marmota*

DISTRIBUTION Europe

SIZE Up to 28 in. (71cm) long, including tail

DESERT KANGAROO RAT

Kangaroo rats live in dry areas of North America and have large eyes, long tails, and extra-long legs. They move by jumping like kangaroos—up to 6 ft. (2m) in one jump. They get most of their water from the plants they eat, and they also save water by coming out only at night, when the air is cooler and moister than during the day. There are more than 20 species of these animals. The desert kangaroo rat is one of ten species that live in the southwestern United States.

SCIENTIFIC NAME	*Dipodomys deserti*
DISTRIBUTION	Southwestern United States, northern Mexico
SIZE	Up to 15 in. (38cm) long, including tail

AMERICAN BEAVER

Mammals are not great builders, but beavers are an exception to this rule. They cut down trees to dam streams, making lakes where they are safe from attack. Beaver dams can be more than 1,600 ft. (500m) long, and they are so strong that they can easily bear a person's weight. Beavers are shaped for life in water, with webbed feet and paddle-shaped tails. They feed on bark and leaves, storing branches under water for winter food. Their home is a mound of branches called a lodge, which they build in the middle of the lake. The entrances are under water, so the beavers can come and go without being seen.

SCIENTIFIC NAME	*Castor canadensis*
DISTRIBUTION	North America
SIZE	Up to 5 ft. (1.5m) long, including tail

SPRING HARE

Despite its name, this curious African rodent looks less like a hare and more like a squirrel with giant back legs. It normally moves on all fours, but when threatened, it can hop more than 12 ft. (4m) in a single bound—a feat that helps it escape leopards, lions, and other predators. Spring hares spend the day in large burrows and come out at night. They eat plants and roots, digging them up with their front feet.

SCIENTIFIC NAME	*Pedetes capensis*
DISTRIBUTION	Eastern and southern Africa
SIZE	Up to 3 ft. (1m) long, including tail

GOLDEN HAMSTER

Hamsters are burrowing rodents that live in dry parts of Europe and central Asia. The golden hamster is just one of more than 12 species, but it is the best-known by far because it is often kept as a pet. Hamsters feed on seeds and insects. To survive when food is scarce, they collect seeds in their cheek-pouches and store them in their burrows. At the end of the summer, a golden hamster's store may contain more than 20 lb. (10kg) of food, enough to see it through the winter.

SCIENTIFIC NAME	*Mesocricetus auratus*
DISTRIBUTION	Syria
SIZE	Up to 8 in. (20cm) long, including tail

LEMMING

The lemming's fame is based on the myth that large numbers of lemmings commit mass suicide by throwing themselves into the sea. In fact, this Arctic rodent is a very successful animal.

When there is plenty to eat, lemmings have many young, and their numbers rise sharply. As the population expands, food starts to run out, and hungry lemmings move away to find more. Many starve or accidentally drown, reducing the population to its original level. Lemmings live above ground, but they tunnel beneath the snow in winter.

SCIENTIFIC NAME	*Lemmus lemmus*
DISTRIBUTION	Scandinavia
SIZE	Up to 7 in. (18cm) long, including tail

BANK VOLE

Voles look similar to mice, but they have blunt noses and short tails. Though active through the day and night, they are not often seen as they stay under cover, often in long grass. However, this does not protect them from foxes and owls, which hunt by sound as much as by sight. Bank voles nest on the ground and raise up to four families a year.

SCIENTIFIC NAME	*Clethrionomys glareosus*
DISTRIBUTION	Europe, central Asia
SIZE	Up to 7 in. (18cm) long, including tail

MUSKRAT

The muskrat is a giant relative of voles and lemmings, sometimes weighing more than 4 lb. (2kg). It is a good swimmer, with webbed back feet and a flat tail that it uses as a rudder. It also has a thick, waterproof coat. Muskrats eat waterside plants, and occasionally small animals. They normally burrow into riverbanks, but if the ground is flat, they make a home by piling plants into a heap up to 3 ft. (1m) high.

SCIENTIFIC NAME	*Ondatra zibethicus*
DISTRIBUTION	Originally from United States; introduced into Europe
SIZE	Up to 24 in. (61cm) long, including tail

GERBIL

Gerbils specialize in living in dry places. Like kangaroo rats, they obtain nearly all their water from food, and they avoid the worst of the heat by staying under ground during the day. Gerbils also have furry feet, another adaptation that helps keep them cool. There are many species of gerbils. The ones most often kept as pets are Mongolian gerbils, or jirds (*Meriones unguiculatus*).

SCIENTIFIC NAME	*Meriones* and other genera
DISTRIBUTION	Southern Europe, Africa, Middle East, Asia
SIZE	Typical length 8 in. (20cm), including tail

ABOVE *A bank vole feeds on some seeds.*

ABOVE *Field voles* (Microtus agrestis) *live in grassland and meadows. They eat leaves, sometimes causing damage to crops.*

ABOVE *The northern water vole* (Arvicola terrestris) *swims well and often lives on riverbanks.*

BELOW *Like most rodents, muskrats can use their front feet to hold their food. Their back feet are webbed to help them swim.*
BOTTOM *A female Egyptian gerbil* (Gerbillus *species*) *watches over her family.*

Fur can be brown, brown-gray, or black

Newborn mice do not have fur

TOP *Carrying a baby in her mouth, a female house mouse moves to a new nest.* **ABOVE** *Mice are naturally inquisitive, which helps them to find food.*

Since then, it has taken up life in houses and farms, and spread all over the world. In the wild, house mice feed mainly on seeds. When they live indoors, they eat all kinds of starchy food, from grain to breakfast cereals. Female house mice can give birth to more than 12 young at a time, and they can have more than ten families a year.

SCIENTIFIC NAME	*Mus musculus*
DISTRIBUTION	Worldwide
SIZE	Up to 7.5 in. (19cm) long, including tail

Long whiskers help the rat judge the size of openings

NORWAY RAT

This intelligent and adaptable rodent is one of the world's least-loved mammals. One reason is that it eats almost anything, from other animals to leftover food; another is that it spreads disease. Norway rats originated in the Far East, but they have followed people all over the world. Compared to mice, they are large and aggressive, and they will attack if they are cornered. Getting rid of rats is not easy because they learn to steer clear of traps and are wary of poisoned food.

SCIENTIFIC NAME	*Rattus norvegicus*
DISTRIBUTION	Worldwide
SIZE	Up to 24 in. (61cm) long, including tail

TOP AND ABOVE *The Norway rat can find its way in complete darkness using its nose and sensitive whiskers.*

HOUSE MOUSE

This familiar rodent is one of the most successful mammals in the world. It originally comes from central Asia, where it lives in open grasslands.

HARVEST MOUSE

Unlike the house mouse, this tiny, light brown rodent never ventures indoors. It lives in hedgerows and fields, where it feeds on seeds and small insects. Harvest mice build round nests woven from strips of grass. Each nest, about the size of a tennis ball, is slung between several grass stems about 4 in. (10cm) above the ground. The nest keeps the young mice warm and protects them from predators. Harvest mice have up to eight young each time they breed, and when there is a plentiful food supply, they may have up to six or seven families in a year.

SCIENTIFIC NAME	*Micromys minutus*
DISTRIBUTION	Europe, Asia, Far East
SIZE	Up to 6 in. (15cm) long, including tail

WHITE-FOOTED MOUSE

This mouse is one of the most common rodents in eastern North America. It lives in forests and woodlands of all kinds, from Canada to the steamy jungle of southeastern Mexico. It feeds mainly on seeds and insects, and like the house mouse, it is not often seen indoors. One of its closest relatives, the deer mouse (*Peromyscus maniculatus*) is found throughout North America, right up to the Arctic.

SCIENTIFIC NAME	*Peromyscus leucopus*
DISTRIBUTION	Eastern and central United States, southeastern Mexico
SIZE	Up to 8 in. (20cm) long, including tail

FAT DORMOUSE

Dormice have gray fur and large, fluffy tails, which makes them look like squirrels. They get their name from the Latin word *dormire*, meaning "to sleep," because they hibernate for several months each year. There are about 20 species of dormice, and they are found in Africa, Europe, and Asia. The fat dormouse is one of the largest species. Like most of its relatives, it lives in woodlands and is a good climber. It comes out after dark to feed on fruit and nuts.

SCIENTIFIC NAME	*Glis glis*
DISTRIBUTION	Europe, Asia
SIZE	Up to 12.5 in. (32cm) long, including tail

ROUGH-LEGGED JERBOA

Jerboas live in dry places in Africa and Asia. Like desert kangaroo rats (page 252), they bounce along on their back legs instead of running on all fours. A jerboa's back legs are more than four times larger than its front legs, allowing it to cover 10 ft. (3m) or more in a single jump. Jerboas live in burrows, and they come out after dark. During the day, the rough-legged jerboa seals off the entrance to its burrow, helping it stay cool inside during hot weather.

SCIENTIFIC NAME	*Dipus sagitta*
DISTRIBUTION	Central Asia, Far East
SIZE	Up to 14 in. (35cm) long, including tail

NAKED MOLE-RAT

These African animals are the strangest rodents in the world. They have pink, almost bald bodies, tiny eyes, and large, gnawing teeth. They feed on roots and spend their lives in burrows under ground. Naked mole-rats live in colonies of up to 100 animals, controlled by a single female, or queen. The queen gives birth to all the colony's young, while the other adults burrow for food. If the queen dies, one of the female workers takes her place and begins to produce young of her own.

SCIENTIFIC NAME	*Heterocephalus glaber*
DISTRIBUTION	Eastern Africa
SIZE	Up to 5 in. (12cm) long, including tail

LEFT TOP *The number of harvest mice has fallen due to changes in farming practices. Modern machinery can destroy their nests.*
LEFT BELOW *A white-footed mouse searches for food.*

TOP *The fat dormouse gains weight in the fall before it hibernates.*
ABOVE *Naked mole-rats from neighboring nests confront each other in an underground fight for space.*

HIBERNATION

Many mammals, reptiles, amphibians, and insects survive cold winters by hibernating. A hibernating animal looks as if it is asleep, but sleep and hibernation are very different. When an animal sleeps, its body stays warm and its heart beats normally. When it hibernates, its temperature drops until it is just a few degrees above its surroundings, and its heart beats so slowly that it sometimes seems to have stopped. Some hibernating animals can move if they are touched, but others stay so still that they look dead. Animals in hibernation cannot eat, and they survive on stores of body fat. When the weather warms up in spring, their temperature rises, their hearts speed up, and they gradually wake up and become active.

A hibernating common dormouse (*Muscardinus avellanarius*)

CRESTED PORCUPINE

Crested porcupine with its quills half raised

As well as being Africa's largest rodent, this animal is by far the best armed. Its back and sides are covered with hollow spines, called quills, which can be up to 14 in. (35cm) long. Shorter quills on its tail rattle when they are shaken. If it is threatened, the porcupine raises its quills and rattles its tail before charging backward at its enemy. Its quills are easily dislodged, and they can stick in skin, with very painful results. Crested porcupines feed on the ground at night, eating roots and fallen fruit.

SCIENTIFIC NAME	*Hystrix cristata*
DISTRIBUTION	Northern and tropical Africa, parts of southern Europe
SIZE	Up to 32 in. (81cm) long, including tail

ABOVE *An American porcupine climbs down a tree. Although these porcupines spend most of their lives above ground, they are short-sighted, and they clamber around instead of jumping. Surprisingly, they are good swimmers because their air-filled quills work like floats.*

AMERICAN PORCUPINE

Unlike porcupines in other parts of the world, American porcupines are good at climbing trees. They often climb high above the ground to find buds and bark to eat. Their quills are only 3 in. (8cm) long, but they have over 30,000 of them mixed among long hairs. The spines have barbed tips to make them stick in skin. If these porcupines are threatened, they use their tails as weapons, lashing them from side to side.

SCIENTIFIC NAME	*Erithizon dorsatum*
DISTRIBUTION	North America
SIZE	Up to 3 ft. (1m) long, including tail

CAVY

This small, South American rodent is the original ancestor of the guinea pig, one of the world's most popular pets. It lives on grasslands and mountain slopes, feeding on grass and leaves and sheltering in burrows and rocky crevices. Compared to other small rodents, newborn cavies are well developed and can fend for themselves when they are only a few days old. Cavies were first domesticated more than 3,000 years ago. They were originally kept for food, a practice that continues in South America.

SCIENTIFIC NAME	*Cavia tschudii*
DISTRIBUTION	Central Andes Mountains in South America
SIZE	Up to 16 in. (40cm) long

MARA

The mara looks like a cross between a hare and a deer, with a long head and neck, and feet that end in hooflike claws. It usually rests like a hare, sitting on its haunches, but at the first sign of trouble, it races off in a peculiar, bounding run, reaching speeds of up to 30 mph (50km/h). Maras are vegetarians that feed during the day. They have just two young each time they breed—a tiny number compared to many other rodents.

SCIENTIFIC NAME	*Dolichotis patagona*
DISTRIBUTION	Argentina
SIZE	Up to 30 in. (76cm) long

LEFT *A female mara watches for danger as she suckles her young. Maras can have two or three families a year.*

CHINCHILLA

Many rodents have soft fur, but the chinchilla is in a class of its own. It is so luxurious that some people will pay almost anything to wear it. This gray, rabbit-sized animal lives high in the Andes Mountains, where its coat protects it from the nighttime cold. It has large ears and a bushy tail, and lives in crevices among rocks, emerging during the day to feed on plants. Millions of chinchillas are now raised in captivity, but after years of hunting, the species is rare in the wild.

SCIENTIFIC NAME
Chinchilla laniger

DISTRIBUTION Central Andes Mountains in South America

SIZE Up to 21 in. (53cm) long, including tail

Large, rabbitlike ears

Fur grows in densely packed clusters

AGOUTI

Like many South American rodents, the agouti has few defenses apart from its speed. It reacts to danger by first freezing, then running for safety. Its back legs are about twice as long as its front legs, which helps it run fast. There are 11 species of agoutis. They are common throughout the American tropics. Many live in forests, where they follow troops of monkeys, picking up fruit and seeds that the monkeys have dropped.

SCIENTIFIC NAME *Dasyprocta* species

DISTRIBUTION Central America, South America

SIZE Up to 24 in. (61cm) long, including tail

CAPYBARA

The capybara is the world's largest rodent, weighing up to 165 lb. (75kg). It looks like a giant guinea pig, with a large head, a blunt nose, and hardly any tail. Capybaras feed in herds in grassy places by rivers and lakes, never straying far from the water. If one of them senses danger, it gives a short bark, and all the others around it gallop into the water for safety. Capybaras are good swimmers and have partly webbed feet.

They can dive and stay under water for up to five minutes. They can also swim with only their ears, eyes, and nostrils showing above the surface.

SCIENTIFIC NAME *Hydrochoerus hydrochaeris*

DISTRIBUTION Tropical South America

SIZE Up to 4 ft. (1.2m) long

PLAINS VISCACHA

South American rodents are famous for their curious shapes, and the plains viscacha is no exception. It has a large, striped head, a heavy body, large legs, and a stumpy tail. Plains viscachas live in burrows in groups of up to 50 animals. They inherit their burrows from their parents. As a result, the burrows can cover a large area and may be many centuries old. Viscachas feed on plants, but they pick up all kinds of objects, from stones to camping equipment, and take them under ground.

SCIENTIFIC NAME *Lagostomus maximus*

DISTRIBUTION Paraguay, Argentina

SIZE Up to 34 in. (86cm) long, including tail

ABOVE *This family of chinchillas have grown up in captivity. Captive chinchillas can live for more than 20 years.*

ABOVE *Capybaras live in herds of up to 20 animals. Each herd is headed by a large, powerful male.*

WHALES, DOLPHINS, AND PORPOISES

Whales, dolphins, and porpoises belong to a group of animals called cetaceans. While they look like giant fish, they are really mammals that spend their entire lives in water. Unlike fish, they breathe air, and their tails consist of a pair of horizontal, rubbery flukes, or lobes, instead of a vertical fin. There are about 80 species of these animals. They feed in two distinct ways. Baleen whales, shown on these two pages, do not have teeth. They eat by filtering fish or plankton through baleen plates. The whales on pages 260-261, together with dolphins and porpoises, have teeth, and they feed by chasing their underwater prey. Apart from some dolphins, all the species in this group live in the sea.

BLUE WHALE

The blue whale is the largest animal that has ever lived. Some weigh more than 150 tons—twice as much as the heaviest dinosaurs. Blue whales have huge mouths, with several hundred baleen plates hanging from their upper jaws. When they take in water and close their mouths, the plates filter krill and other small animals from the water. Females begin to breed when they are about ten years old, giving birth once every two or three years. In the early 1900s, there were about 200,000 blue whales. There are now only about 12,000 left.

SCIENTIFIC NAME *Balaenoptera musculus*

DISTRIBUTION Worldwide, mainly in cold seas

SIZE Up to 100 ft. (30m) long

TOP *The blue whale and its relatives are known as rorquals. These whales have deep grooves running down their throats. When they feed, the grooves open out to let their mouths expand. Rorquals feed only during the summer and may swallow up to four tons of krill or fish every day.*

ABOVE *After the blue whale, the fin whale (Balaenoptera physalus) is the second largest animal on earth, growing more than 80 ft. long. It can dive to more than 650 ft. and often swims on its right side to feed.*

RIGHT *Bursting through the water's surface, a humpback whale shows its baleen plates. The plates are hard but have frayed edges that trap the whale's food.*

MINKE WHALE

The minke whale belongs to the same family as the blue whale, but it is much smaller and more common. It has a gray back and a white or pale gray underside. When in cold seas, minke whales feed on krill and other small animals that abound there, but they eat fish in warmer waters. Minkes are the only baleen whales still hunted commercially. Like other whales, minkes sometimes leap headfirst out of the water, hitting the surface again with a huge splash. The reasons for this behavior, called breaching, are not yet known.

SCIENTIFIC NAME *Balaenoptera acutorostrata*

DISTRIBUTION Worldwide

SIZE Up to 33 ft. (10m) long

HUMPBACK WHALE

The humpback's enormous front flippers distinguish it from other baleen whales. The flippers are up to 17 ft. (5m) long, and the whale beats them like a pair of wings. Humpbacks have notched tails with black and white markings that are unique to each individual. Like blue whales, humpbacks migrate great distances, often following the coast, between the tropical waters where they breed and the cold waters where they feed.

SCIENTIFIC NAME *Megaptera novaeangliae*

DISTRIBUTION Worldwide

SIZE Up to 65 ft. (20m) long

GRAY WHALE

This whale is famous for its long migrations. It breeds off the coast of Mexico, but it spends the summer on the edge of the Arctic Ocean, about 6,000 mi. away. It has mottled gray skin, and its head is encrusted with barnacles (page 39). Unlike most large whales, gray whales feed on the seabed, stirring up the surface with their mouths. After sucking up the muddy water, they filter out any crustaceans and worms.

SCIENTIFIC NAME *Eschrichtius robustus*

DISTRIBUTION Northern Pacific Ocean; extinct in Atlantic Ocean

SIZE Up to 50 ft. (15m) long

Humpback whale swimming (above) and breaching (top)

SOUTHERN RIGHT WHALE

Right whales got their name because they swim slowly and they float when they are dead. Because they were easy prey, whalers considered them to be the "right" whales to hunt. There are two species, one in the Northern Hemisphere and one in the Southern. Over the centuries, so many have been killed that the northern right whale (*Eubalaena glacialis*) is almost extinct. Both species have blunt heads with enormous rows of baleen plates, and fat, blue-black bodies with white markings on their undersides. They feed on plankton and give birth once every three or four years.

SCIENTIFIC NAME *Eubalaena australis*

DISTRIBUTION Temperate and polar waters in the Southern Hemisphere

SIZE Up to 60 ft. (18m) long

TOP *A southern right whale feeds off the coast of South America. The white growths on its head are areas of hard skin covered with barnacles and parasitic lice. All right whales have these, but no one knows why.*

ABOVE *Right whales have steeply arched mouths, and their eyes are set low, nearer their undersides than their backs.*

Pale ring close to tail flukes

BOWHEAD WHALE

The bowhead is a close relative of right whales and has a similar shape and the same enormous head. Like right whales, it was hunted to the verge of extinction. After several decades of being protected, there are still only about 10,000 bowheads. They live all year round in the cold waters around the Arctic, usually near the edge of floating sea ice.

SCIENTIFIC NAME *Balaena mystaceus*

DISTRIBUTION Arctic Ocean

SIZE Up to 65 ft. (20m) long

ABOVE *The bowhead whale is kept warm by a layer of insulating fat, or blubber, which can be more than 2 ft. thick. Unlike right whales, it has no growths on its head.*

SPERM WHALE

With an enormous head and formidable teeth, the 50-ton sperm whale is the largest hunting animal in the sea. Instead of straining plankton out of the water, as baleen whales do, it dives after giant squid, sometimes reaching depths of over a mile (2km). It can hold its breath for nearly two hours. The sperm whale often hunts in total darkness, finding its prey by echolocation (page 241). Its head contains a waxy substance, called spermaceti, which probably helps focus beams of sound, as well as controlling the whale's buoyancy. Sperm whales usually live in deep parts of the oceans, away from shallow coasts. They are easy to recognize when they surface by the single nostril, or blowhole, on the left side of their heads. When they breathe out, it produces a slanting cloud of vapor, or "spout."

SCIENTIFIC NAME	*Physeter macrocephalus*
DISTRIBUTION	Worldwide
SIZE	Up to 60 ft. (18m) long

warbles, and clicks. Female belugas begin to breed at about seven years old and have one calf every three years.

SCIENTIFIC NAME	*Delphinapterus leucas*
DISTRIBUTION	Arctic Ocean, northern Pacific Ocean, northern Atlantic Ocean
SIZE	Up to 17 ft. (5m) long

NARWHAL

The male narwhal is the only whale that is armed with a tusk. The tusk, which can be up to 10 ft. (3m) long, is a modified tooth that grows forward through the animal's upper jaw. At one time, scientists thought that narwhals used their tusks to feed or to deter predators, but it seems more likely that they use them to fight rival males. Very occasionally, female narwhals develop

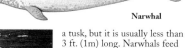

Narwhal

a tusk, but it is usually less than 3 ft. (1m) long. Narwhals feed on fish and squid. They are close relatives of belugas, but they live farther north than any other whale and often swim underneath the sea ice.

SCIENTIFIC NAME	*Monodon monoceros*
DISTRIBUTION	Arctic Ocean
SIZE	Up to 17 ft. (5m) long

TRUE'S BEAKED WHALE

Compared to other marine mammals, beaked whales are mysterious animals. There are nearly 20 species, but some are known only from dead remains washed up on the shore. True's beaked whale is a medium-sized species, with a gray and cream body, small flippers, and a narrow, protruding "beak." Its two teeth stick out when its mouth is closed, but they are too small to be used for eating. Like its many relatives, this whale is a good diver and feeds mainly on squid.

SCIENTIFIC NAME	*Mesoplodon mirus*
DISTRIBUTION	Worldwide
SIZE	Up to 17 ft. (5m) long

BELUGA OR WHITE WHALE

This small whale is the only species in the world with creamy white skin. It has small flippers, a rounded head, and a beaklike mouth packed with up to 40 teeth. It lives in the cold seas of the far north, where it feeds on crustaceans and fish. Belugas find their prey partly by echolocation and partly by sight. They spend much of their time at the surface or in shallow water, and they are sociable and very noisy animals. They use sound to keep in touch with each other, producing a range of squeaks,

Beluga whale

ABOVE LEFT *The beluga's rounded forehead changes shape when it makes sounds, bulging outward, then shrinking.*

LONG-FINNED PILOT WHALE

Pilot whales belong to the dolphin family. They got their name from their habit of swimming in front of ships as if they were guiding them. They are mostly black, with curved flippers and bulbous heads. They live in groups, or pods, of up to 40 animals, feeding mainly after dark on fish and squid. Like other toothed whales, pilot whales navigate and find food by using sound. This system works well in deep water, but pilot whale pods sometimes lose their way in shallow water and become stranded on the shore. Mass strandings can also occur with other whales. The exact reason for this is not known.

SCIENTIFIC NAME *Globicephala melas*

DISTRIBUTION Northern Atlantic Ocean, cold seas in Southern Hemisphere

SIZE Up to 20 ft. (6m) long

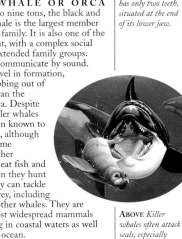

TOP *The long-finned pilot whale has unusually long and slender front flippers, with a backswept curve.*
ABOVE *True's beaked whale has only two teeth, situated at the end of its lower jaw.*

KILLER WHALE OR ORCA

Weighing up to nine tons, the black and white killer whale is the largest member of the dolphin family. It is also one of the most intelligent, with a complex social life based on extended family groups. Killer whales communicate by sound. They often travel in formation, sometimes bobbing out of the water to scan the surrounding sea. Despite their name, killer whales have never been known to attack humans, although they are fearsome predators of other animals. They eat fish and squid, but when they hunt as a group, they can tackle much larger prey, including walruses and other whales. They are among the most widespread mammals on earth, living in coastal waters as well as in the open ocean.

SCIENTIFIC NAME *Orcinus orca*

DISTRIBUTION Worldwide

SIZE Up to 33 ft. (10m) long

LEFT *With its head pointing down, a sperm whale sets off on a dive. This whale is surrounded by fish, which are hitching a ride and grazing food off the whale's skin.*

ABOVE *Killer whales often attack seals, especially pups, because they are easier to catch than adults. The whales sometimes throw themselves onto beaches to catch pups near the water's edge.*

TOP *The Atlantic white-sided dolphin (Lagenorhynchus acutus) lives in large schools that may be up to 1,000 strong.* **ABOVE** *The rough-toothed dolphin (Steno bredanensis) lives in warm waters worldwide.* **BELOW** *Common dolphins can dive for more than five minutes, but spend most of their time near the surface.*

COMMON DOLPHIN

Dolphins belong to the same group of mammals as whales, but their smaller size and streamlined shape makes them look even more like fish. They are fast-moving, acrobatic, playful animals, capable of swimming at up to 25 mph (40km/h), sometimes bursting right out of the water. The common dolphin, one of the most widespread species, is marked with a complicated pattern of white, yellow, black, and gray. Like most other ocean-going dolphins, it feeds on fish and has beaklike jaws containing more than 200 small teeth. Dolphins are famous for their intelligence and their close family life. When a dolphin gives birth, other females gather around to help the baby dolphin swim to the surface to breathe.

SCIENTIFIC NAME *Delphinus delphis*

DISTRIBUTION Warm waters worldwide
SIZE Up to 8 ft. (2.4m) long

ABOVE *Boutos are slow swimmers, but they are experts at finding fish to eat in the murky water of the Amazon River.*

BOTTLENOSE DOLPHIN

Of the more than 30 species of dolphins, this all-gray species is by far the best-known. This is because it is sometimes kept in captivity, where its sociable nature and intelligence make it a star performer. In the wild, bottlenose dolphins live in schools of up to 12 animals. Like other dolphins, they use echolocation to find fish, often cooperating to round up their prey. They frequently ride the bow-waves of boats and will sometimes approach swimmers, allowing themselves to be patted or stroked.

SCIENTIFIC NAME *Tursiops truncatus*

DISTRIBUTION Worldwide, except in polar waters
SIZE Up to 13 ft. (4m) long

INDUS RIVER DOLPHIN

This rare, gray-brown animal is one of a handful of dolphins that live in fresh water. It has very slender jaws armed with needle-sharp teeth, and broad flippers that look like paddles. Its eyes are so small that it is almost blind, so it finds its food entirely by echolocation. At one time, these dolphins were found throughout the Indus River, but several dams have been built on the river, preventing the dolphins from swimming up and down. In total, there are probably fewer than 500 of these endangered animals left. A closely related species lives in the Ganges River in India.

SCIENTIFIC NAME *Platanista minor*

DISTRIBUTION River Indus in Pakistan
SIZE Up to 8 ft. (2.4m) long

BOUTO

The bouto is the world's largest river dolphin and one of the few that is still fairly common. It lives in the Amazon and Orinoco rivers, a vast network of waterways in the heart of South America. Like the Indus river dolphin, it has very narrow jaws, but its color varies from gray to bright pink. Boutos feed on fish, crayfish, and other small animals, finding their prey by sight and touch as well as by echolocation. During the dry season, they gather in schools of up to 12 animals, but during the rest of the year, they usually live in pairs.

SCIENTIFIC NAME *Inia geoffrensis*

DISTRIBUTION Amazon and Orinoco rivers in South America
SIZE Up to 8 ft. (2.4m) long

DALL'S PORPOISE

Unlike dolphins, porpoises have short snouts and barrel-shaped bodies. There are six species, and Dall's porpoise is the largest, weighing up to 450 lb. (200kg). Although it is not much longer than an adult human, this black and white porpoise is one of the world's fastest sea-going mammals, reaching speeds of up to 35 mph (55km/h). Dall's porpoises live in schools of up to 20 animals, but many more may gather where

ABOVE *Harbor porpoises start to breed when they are about five years old and usually have one calf a year. Unlike the teeth of true dolphins, which are pointed, porpoises' teeth have two flat sides and a sharp edge.*

there is plenty of food. They can dive to at least 1,600 ft. (500m) to hunt fish and squid. Although their eyesight is good, they probably use echolocation to help them when they hunt.

SCIENTIFIC NAME	*Phocoenoides dalli*
DISTRIBUTION	Northern Pacific Ocean
SIZE	Up to 7.5 ft. (2.3m) long

HARBOR PORPOISE OR COMMON PORPOISE

This gray and white animal spends most of its life close to the coast or in shallow seas offshore. It sometimes swims into estuaries and harbors, which is how it got its name. Although harbor porpoises are widespread, they are not often seen because they rarely jump out of the water and they avoid moving boats. Like dolphins, porpoises have been harmed by modern fishing techniques. When they become tangled up in nets, they cannot swim to the surface to breathe, and eventually die.

SCIENTIFIC NAME	*Phocoena phocoena*
DISTRIBUTION	Northern waters worldwide
SIZE	Up to 6 ft. (2m) long

VAQUITA

This highly endangered animal is one of the smallest cetaceans—the group of mammals that also includes dolphins and whales. A newborn vaquita is only about 2 ft. (60cm) long, and when fully grown, it rarely exceeds 5 ft. (1.5m). It lives close to the shore in the Gulf of California, a long arm of the Pacific Ocean off northwestern Mexico. Vaquitas are gray with stumpy bodies, and they feed mainly on fish. At present, only a few hundred of these porpoises survive. Without careful protection, they will almost certainly become extinct.

SCIENTIFIC NAME	*Phocoena sinus*
DISTRIBUTION	Gulf of California
SIZE	Up to 5 ft. (1.5m) long

LEFT *This bottlenose dolphin is swimming over a coral reef in the Caribbean Sea. In some parts of the world, bottlenose dolphins are so tame that they approach the shore to beg people for fish.*

DOGS AND FOXES

With their keen senses, long legs, and sharp teeth, dogs and foxes are well equipped for hunting. They belong to a group of meat-eating mammals called carnivores (page 266) that feed mostly on living prey. Wild dogs and their relatives usually catch their prey by chasing it down, but foxes often hunt by stealth, pouncing before their target can escape. Most of these animals hunt alone, but some, notably the gray wolf, hunt in packs. There are about 36 species of wild dogs and foxes. The best-known member of the family is the domestic dog, which is descended from the wolf.

GRAY WOLF

This is the largest member of the dog family. It once lived in most of the Northern Hemisphere, but after centuries of persecution, it is now found mainly in remote areas, particularly in dense forests. Gray wolves live in packs consisting of a pair of adults with several generations of their young. They cooperate when they hunt, which allows them to kill animals several times their own size. Although they share their food, wolves have a strict hierarchy, and junior wolves must to give way to larger, older animals.

SCIENTIFIC NAME *Canis lupus*

DISTRIBUTION Eastern Europe, Asia, parts of North America

SIZE Up to 6 ft. (2m) long, including tail

Ready to attack   **Friendly expression**

LEFT *Gray wolves use facial expressions to communicate with members of their pack.*

COYOTE

The coyote usually finds food on its own. It eats all kinds of food, including snakes, insects, fruit, and dead remains, but it also has a reputation for attacking farm animals. Although hundreds of thousands of coyotes have been poisoned or shot over the years, the species has managed to survive. In the spring, females give birth to litters of about six pups in a burrow. The father brings them food while they stay safely under ground.

SCIENTIFIC NAME *Canis latrans*

DISTRIBUTION North America

SIZE Up to 4.5 ft. (1.4m) long, including tail

GOLDEN JACKAL

Jackals look similar to coyotes. Like most members of the dog family, they survive by a combination of hunting and scavenging, using their keen hearing and sense of smell to track down food after dark. Golden jackals live in dry places, sometimes close to farms and villages. Although they attack livestock, they also perform a useful service for farmers by killing poisonous snakes.

SCIENTIFIC NAME
Canis aureus

DISTRIBUTION Southeastern Europe, northern Africa, Middle East, southern Asia

SIZE Up to 4.5 ft. (1.4m) long, including tail

Golden jackal

DINGO

Australia has no native dogs of its own, but it does have the dingo, which was brought to the continent by people thousands of years ago. Some dingos escaped and established themselves in the wild, and today their descendants roam across the outback. Unlike domesticated dogs, dingos cannot bark. They have extra-large paws, and ears that are always upright. Dingos can be a problem because they often attack sheep. To prevent this, the farming area of southeastern Australia is cordoned off by a dingo-proof fence more than 3,000 mi. (5,000km) long.

SCIENTIFIC NAME *Canis familiaris dingo*

DISTRIBUTION Australia

SIZE Up to 6 ft. (2m) long, including tail

AFRICAN WILD DOG

With its blotchy fur and rounded ears, this animal is one of the most distinctive members of the dog family. It is small and lightly built, but because it hunts in packs, it can kill animals as large as wildebeest (page 299). African wild dogs hunt in open grassland, literally dragging their prey to its knees. Once the animal has collapsed, there is no escape, and the pack immediately starts to feed.

LEFT *Gray wolves use speed and endurance to outpace their prey. They can run at over 30 mph (50km/h) for half an hour—long enough to exhaust large animals such as moose.*

ABOVE *African wild dogs are messy killers, but they are not aggressive toward each other. When these pups are old enough, the adults will give them the first turn at feeding after a successful hunt.*

ABOVE AND BELOW *A raccoon dog's diet includes seeds and insects, as well as frogs, birds, and small mammals.*

African wild dogs were once common, but their numbers have fallen, probably due to disease and change in habitat. Today, only about 2,000 survive.

SCIENTIFIC NAME *Lycaon pictus*

DISTRIBUTION Tropical Africa

SIZE Up to 4 ft. (1.2m) long, including tail

BUSH DOG

This rare, brown dog lives in forests and grassland. Its legs and tail are short and stumpy, and it is a good swimmer. Unlike most dogs, it is active during the day, feeding on large rodents. Bush dogs live in packs of up to ten animals.

SCIENTIFIC NAME *Speothos venaticus*

DISTRIBUTION Northern South America

SIZE Up to 3 ft. (1m) long, including tail

RACCOON DOG

With its small ears and black eye patches, this dog looks very like a raccoon (page 270). It has smaller teeth than other dogs, and it is the only dog that hibernates. Though native to the Far East, it was taken to Russia over 50 years ago for its fur. It has since spread across Europe as far as France.

SCIENTIFIC NAME *Nyctereutes procyonoides*

DISTRIBUTION Originally from the Far East, including Japan; introduced into Europe

SIZE Up to 30 in. (76cm) long, including tail

Pups will be ready to breed when they are one year old

TOP AND ABOVE *The arctic fox's winter coat is the warmest in the animal world. In summer, the fox loses its long fur, which makes it look much slimmer.*
RIGHT *By playing at fighting, these two red fox cubs are learning skills that will help them hunt as adults.*

Short, blunt claws

Front legs are used for pouncing on prey

Coat stays the same color all year

Tail usually has a white tip

ARCTIC FOX

There are ten species of foxes. They belong to the same family as dogs, but they are more lightly built, and instead of chasing animals, they often pounce on them like a cat. The arctic fox can survive temperatures of -60°F (-50°C), thanks to its thick coat and warm fur on the undersides of its paws. Its brown summer coat turns white in the fall and winter for camouflage. Arctic foxes eat live animals and dead remains, sometimes crossing the frozen Arctic Sea to find food left by polar bears. They make dens on the tundra, but if caught in a blizzard, they dig burrows in the snow.

SCIENTIFIC NAME	*Alopex lagopus*
DISTRIBUTION	Arctic regions
SIZE	Up to 3 ft. (1m) long, including tail

RED FOX

The red fox is both the largest and the most widespread fox. It is nocturnal, and it hunts alone or in family groups rather than in packs.

CARNIVORES

A carnivore is any meat-eating animal. But the same word is also used in a narrower way to mean mammals that specialize in eating flesh. Mammalian carnivores include dogs, foxes, bears, and cats, as well as many smaller hunters such as raccoons, badgers, otters, and skunks. Despite their differences, mammalian carnivores have many features in common. They all have keen senses and teeth that are designed to deal with meat. At the front of their mouths, they have pointed canine teeth, which are shaped to stab and grip. Toward

Carnivore skull

the back, many of them have long carnassial teeth, which work like scissors to slice through the toughest flesh. Because these animals can eat their food in pieces instead of swallowing it whole, they can sometimes tackle prey that is larger than they are. Some mammalian carnivores hunt by day, but most are active at night, when their victims find it harder to escape. There are about 240 species of these mammals living all over the world, from the tropics to the Arctic ice.

Red foxes raise their cubs in underground dens. Their natural habitat includes forests and open grassland, but in some places they have successfully established themselves in suburban gardens and even in busy urban areas.

SCIENTIFIC NAME *Vulpes vulpes*

DISTRIBUTION Originally from North America, Europe, Asia; introduced into Australia

SIZE Up to 4.5 ft. (1.4m) long, including tail

SWIFT FOX OR PRAIRIE FOX

This small, sandy-colored, American fox feeds mainly on rodents. Like other foxes, it sometimes kills more than it can eat in a single meal, so it buries the surplus food to eat later. Swift foxes are harmless to livestock, but in recent years, they have been harmed by poisoned food left for coyotes.

SCIENTIFIC NAME *Vulpes velox*

DISTRIBUTION Southern Canada, midwestern United States

SIZE Up to 32 in. (81cm) long, including tail

FENNEC

This nocturnal desert animal is the smallest member of the wild dog family, and its ears are enormous compared to the size of its body. They give the fennec the keen hearing it needs to track down rodents and other small animals to eat. They also help the fennec keep cool—with their large surface area, they give off a lot of body heat. Fennecs are sandy colored, an adaptation that helps camouflage them if they venture out during the day.

SCIENTIFIC NAME *Fennecus zerda*

DISTRIBUTION Northern Africa, Middle East

SIZE Up to 24 in. (61cm) long, including tail

GRAY FOX

Gray foxes live in forests and desert scrub, as well as on the outskirts of cities. They usually raise their cubs in a den, either on or underneath the ground, though in some places they breed in trees. If threatened, gray foxes sometimes hide under boulders, but more often they climb trees to escape danger. They grip the tree trunks with the strong claws on their back feet, clinging on with their front legs. To climb down to the ground again, they have to move tailfirst.

SCIENTIFIC NAME *Urocyon cinereoargenteus*

DISTRIBUTION North and Central America, northern South America

SIZE Up to 4 ft. (1.2m) long, including tail

CRAB-EATING FOX

Despite its name, this fox eats much more than just crabs. Rodents and insects make up part of its diet, as do bird eggs and freshwater turtles. The crab-eating fox has even been known to raid plantations for bananas and other fruit, making it unpopular with farmers. These bushy-tailed, gray-brown animals live in grassland and open woodland. Because their habitat is warm, they can breed at any time of year.

SCIENTIFIC NAME *Cerdocyon thous*

DISTRIBUTION South America

SIZE Up to 3 ft. (1m) long, including tail

TOP *The fennec's huge ears give it extremely sensitive hearing.*

ABOVE *Gray foxes are sometimes attacked and eaten by coyotes, especially in the winter, when other food is scarce.*

LEFT *A crab-eating fox hunts in grassland in Brazil.*

BEARS

With their heavy bodies and powerful jaws, bears include the largest meat-eating animals that live on land. A male polar bear can weigh more than 1,300 lb. (600kg) and can be as tall as 5.5 ft. (1.7m) at the shoulder when standing on all fours. Bears lumber along on their massive paws, but are capable of sudden bursts of speed. They have a varied diet, and despite their fearsome teeth, many of them eat fruit, roots, and insects as well as meat. There are seven species of bears. Some scientists also classify the giant panda (page 270) as a bear, bringing the total to eight.

POLAR BEAR

This well-known animal is the world's largest bear. Females can weigh over 650 lb. (300kg), but the males may be double this weight and more. During the summer, polar bears often eat berries and rodents. In the winter, they wander over the frozen sea, attacking seals as they surface to breathe. Polar bears are superb swimmers that have been seen in open water hundreds of miles from land. Their dense fur keeps their skin dry, and their furry paws give them a nonslip grip on ice. The males are usually active year round, but the females hibernate in ice dens during the winter. They give birth to their cubs there and emerge with their youngsters in spring.

SCIENTIFIC NAME	*Thalarctos maritimus*
DISTRIBUTION	Arctic regions
SIZE	Up to 8 ft. (2.4m) long

GRIZZLY BEAR

The fearsome and unpredictable grizzly is one of a group of brown bears that includes the Alaskan brown bear, also called the Kodiak, and the brown bears of Europe and Asia. It can stand more than 10 ft. (3m) high on its hind legs and is strong enough to drag away a horse. Grizzly bears live mainly in forests. They are not good climbers, but over short distances they can run at high speed. They eat almost anything, including fruit, deer, and fish, and they can catch and kill other bears. In places with cold winters, grizzly bears hibernate in underground dens. In late winter, the females give birth to two to four cubs, which stay with their mother for at least a year.

ABOVE *The brown bear (Ursus arctos) stands up on its hind legs when it feels threatened or when it is trying to catch a scent in the air.*

SCIENTIFIC NAME	*Ursus horribilis*
DISTRIBUTION	Western North America
SIZE	Up to 9 ft. (2.7m) long

ABOVE *Female polar bears have to guard their cubs carefully because adult males may attack them.*
BELOW *For a polar bear, winter is the best time for hunting.* **1** *It waits by a seal's breathing hole for a seal to surface.* **2** *Then it drags the seal from the water onto the ice.*

ASIATIC BLACK BEAR

This animal resembles the American black bear, but it has a broader face and a V-shaped patch of white fur on its chest. A good climber, it clambers up trees to reach fruit and honey from the nests of wild bees. It also eats insects and other small animals, and sometimes attacks farm livestock. In some parts of Asia, black bears are at risk of dying out because their natural habitat is being destroyed by deforestation. Hunters, who can sell bears' body parts for use in traditional medicines, pose a further threat to this species.

SCIENTIFIC NAME	*Ursus thibetanus*
DISTRIBUTION	Central and Southeast Asia, Far East
SIZE	Up to 6 ft. (2m) long

lives in trees, sleeping during the day in nests made of leafy branches.

SCIENTIFIC NAME
Helarctos malayanus

DISTRIBUTION
Southeast Asia

SIZE Up to 4.5 ft. (1.4m) long

ABOVE *The spectacled bear is named for the white rings around its eyes.*

SPECTACLED BEAR

This is the only bear that lives in South America. Apart from its white "spectacles," its fur is mostly black or brown. Though they weigh 225 lb. (100kg) or more, spectacled bears are good climbers. They build platforms in trees from which they forage for fruit and young leaves to eat. Because they live in a warm climate, they do not need to hibernate.

SCIENTIFIC NAME *Tremarctos ornatus*

DISTRIBUTION Tropical South America

SIZE Up to 6 ft. (2m) long

SLOTH BEAR

For a bear, this shaggy Asian animal has a very unusual diet. It feeds mainly on termites, which it sucks up like a vacuum cleaner. Closing its nostrils while it feeds ensures that it does not breathe in the termites and choke. This method of eating is very noisy, and a feeding sloth bear can be heard over 500 ft. (150m) away. Sloth bears have powerful feet and long claws. They are not normally dangerous to people, but like all bears, they have bad eyesight and poor hearing, and may attack if they are caught by surprise.

SCIENTIFIC NAME *Ursus ursinus*

DISTRIBUTION Southern Asia, from Nepal to Sri Lanka

SIZE Up to 6 ft. (2m) long

ABOVE *This American black bear cub will stay with its mother for about a year. It will be able to breed by the age of four.*

AMERICAN BLACK BEAR

The American black bear is much smaller than the grizzly bear and much more widespread. It is often found in national parks, where it raids campsites for food. It usually hunts at night, using its keen sense of smell. The American black bear hibernates during the winter, but like the brown bear, its winter sleep is light, and its body temperature drops only a few degrees. If disturbed, it can wake up quickly. These bears tend to steer clear of people, but can be dangerous if they are disturbed while protecting their cubs.

SCIENTIFIC NAME *Ursus americanus*

DISTRIBUTION North America, including northern Mexico

SIZE Up to 6 ft. (2m) long

SUN BEAR

This is both the smallest bear and one of the most intelligent. Its fur is black and short. Sun bears live in tropical forests, feeding on fruit and a variety of animals. They spend much of their

PANDAS AND RACCOONS

Compared to other carnivores, pandas and raccoons do not show a special liking for meat. Many of them catch birds, insects, and other small animals, but they are just as fond of eggs, seeds, and fruit. The giant panda is highly unusual because it rarely eats meat at all. Pandas and raccoons are good climbers, and most of them become active at night, using their eyes and keen sense of smell to find food. There are 20 species in this family of mammals. Apart from pandas, which live in Asia, they all live in the Americas.

ABOVE AND LEFT *Raccoons remain active throughout the year, but they hole up in a den if the weather turns very cold. Females give birth to three or four young in early spring.*

GIANT PANDA

Few endangered animals are as well-known as the giant panda. It is almost entirely vegetarian, feeding on the shoots of bamboo plants, whereas all its relatives are carnivorous. It eats sitting down, gripping its food in its front paws with the help of special pads that work like thumbs. Giant pandas have become rare, partly through hunting, but mainly because their natural habitat, the bamboo forests of central China, is slowly being destroyed. Giant pandas survive well in captivity, but it is very difficult to encourage them to breed. Baby pandas are about 3 in. (8cm) long when they are born. They feed on their mother's milk for at least nine months.

ABOVE *The giant panda is one of the world's most remarkable mammals. Some scientists classify it as a relative of the red panda and raccoon, but others think that it is an unusual kind of bear.*

SCIENTIFIC NAME	*Ailuropoda melanoleuca*
DISTRIBUTION	Central China
SIZE	Up to 5.5 ft. (1.7m) long, including tail

LESSER PANDA OR RED PANDA

This animal looks very unlike its larger and more famous relative, the giant panda. It has bright, rusty-red fur, slender legs, and a long, bushy tail. Red pandas are nocturnal, and they live in mountain forests. Although they are good climbers, they feed mainly on the ground, eating shoots, roots, and small animals.

BELOW *The lesser panda lives in areas up to 2.5 mi. high, so it must cope with cold temperatures. When it is asleep, it curls its tail around its body to keep itself warm.*

SCIENTIFIC NAME	*Ailurus fulgens*
DISTRIBUTION	Southern Asia, China
SIZE	Up to 3.5 ft. (1.1m) long, including tail

RACCOON

Like the red fox (page 266), the raccoon is a woodland animal, though it has learned how to live in built-up areas. In its natural habitat, it eats all kinds of food, from frogs to fruit. In cities and suburbs, however, it raids garbage cans and eats the remains of animals that have been run over by cars. Raccoons are nocturnal, with a keen sense of smell, and are good climbers. They have long fur and black patches around their eyes, which makes them look as if they are wearing a mask. Compared to most mammalian carnivores, they are very adept with their paws, which they use to pick up and hold their food.

SCIENTIFIC NAME	*Procyon lotor*
DISTRIBUTION	North and Central America
SIZE	Up to 3 ft. (1m) long, including tail

COATI

Coatis belong to the same family as raccoons and red pandas, but they are active by day instead of by night. They are also sociable, living in groups of up to 20 animals. Coatis have long snouts and long, banded tails that they hold upright when on the ground. They snuffle among low-growing plants and fallen leaves in woods and forests, searching for small animals, fruits, and seeds. Adult coatis have few enemies, but the young are attacked by jaguars and snakes.

SCIENTIFIC NAME	*Nasua nasua*
DISTRIBUTION	North, Central, and South America, from Arizona to Argentina
SIZE	Up to 4 ft. (1.2m) long, including tail

MUSTELIDS

The mustelid family contains nearly 70 species of carnivorous mammals, including martens, weasels, badgers, and skunks. Most mustelids are long-bodied animals with short legs. They hunt using the senses of sight and smell. Although they are not large, they can be ferocious and remarkably strong, killing larger animals and sometimes chasing other predators away from their kills. Mustelids live across most of the world, except in Australia, New Zealand, and Antarctica.

ABOVE *Like many mustelids, the American marten has thick fur that keeps it warm in winter.*
BELOW *The least weasel is the smallest carnivorous mammal in the world.*

AMERICAN MARTEN

Martens are skillful climbers with red-brown fur and short, stocky legs. Although they find some of their food on the ground, they also hunt in trees. The American marten lives in coniferous forests and is an expert at catching squirrels, which it chases through the treetops.

SCIENTIFIC NAME	*Martes americana*
DISTRIBUTION	Canada, Alaska, western United States
SIZE	Up to 26 in. (66cm) long, including tail

SABLE

Many mustelids have thick, soft fur, but the sable's is the most luxurious of all. The sable lives in the coniferous forests of northern Asia, where its extra-long winter coat helps it survive the penetrating cold. It lives on the ground, feeding on nuts and berries, as well as small animals. For hundreds of years, sable fur has commanded very high prices, and hundreds of thousands of these animals have been trapped in the wild. Today, sables are also farmed commercially for their fur.

SCIENTIFIC NAME	*Martes zibellina*
DISTRIBUTION	Siberia, Korea, Japan
SIZE	Up to 25 in. (63cm) long, including tail

LEAST WEASEL

This tiny hunter's slender body is not much thicker than a finger. It lives in a variety of habitats, hunting day and night for animals such as mice. Because it is so small, it can chase mice into their burrows, which few other predators can do. Its young grow quickly and can kill prey when they are eight weeks old, using their small, but very sharp, canine teeth.

SCIENTIFIC NAME	*Mustela nivalis*
DISTRIBUTION	Originally from North America, Europe, northern Africa, Asia; introduced into New Zealand
SIZE	Up to 12 in. (30cm) long, including tail

ERMINE

The ermine looks like a larger version of the least weasel. In summer it is mainly brown, but in northern regions, its fur often turns white in the winter. Ermine live wherever there is cover, breeding in hollow trees and burrows. They feed on rodents and birds, and can kill fully grown rabbits several times their own size.

SCIENTIFIC NAME	*Mustela erminea*
DISTRIBUTION	Originally from North America, Europe, Asia; introduced into New Zealand
SIZE	Up to 16 in. (40cm) long, including tail

Long, slender body with a flexible spine

ABOVE AND RIGHT *In winter, the ermine is all white, except for a black tip on its tail. In summer, only its underparts are white.*

TOP AND ABOVE
Eurasian badgers often follow the same route each night when they are hunting for food. They also collect leaves and dry grass to line their underground chambers.
RIGHT *Ratels are good climbers, clinging to trees with their sharp claws. This ratel is foraging for insects on a dead tree.*

EURASIAN BADGER

With its striped face and pointed nose, the badger is a familiar animal throughout Europe, but because it is nocturnal, few people get a chance to see one. Eurasian badger burrows, called setts, are usually in woodland and often have many entrances. Setts are handed down from one generation to another, and large ones may be more than a century old. Badgers emerge after dusk to forage along well-worn paths. They eat anything they can find, but earthworms and insects often feature in their diet. Although they do not hibernate, they become dormant, or sleepy, in the winter. The females give birth to up to five cubs before spring. Their relative, the American badger (*Taxidea taxus*), is found from southwestern Canada to central Mexico.

SCIENTIFIC NAME *Meles meles*

DISTRIBUTION Europe, northern Asia, Far East

SIZE Up to 3 ft. (1m) long, including tail

Ratels can produce a foul-smelling fluid from their undertail glands

ABOVE *Looking like a cross between a dog and a bear, the wolverine is the largest mustelid that hunts on land. It is so ferocious that it can even drive bears away from their kills.*

WOLVERINE OR GLUTTON

This formidable hunter is known for its strength and its large appetite. It lives in northern forests and tundra, and its legs are so powerful that it can chase reindeer across the snow. During the summer, when the ground is boggy, it feeds mainly on fruit and dead remains, wandering up to 25 mi. (40km) a day to find food.

SCIENTIFIC NAME *Gulo gulo*

DISTRIBUTION Scandinavia, Siberia, North America

SIZE Up to 3.5 ft. (1.1m) long, including tail

RATEL OR HONEY BADGER

This low-slung animal has unusual coloring, with black sides and underparts and white fur along its head and back. Its eating habits are stranger still, because it specializes in breaking open bees' nests to reach the honey inside. In Africa, ratels are often led to bees' nests by a bird called the honeyguide. In return for showing the ratel where to get a meal, the honeyguide eats the leftovers of the nest, including the wax. Ratels have long claws on their front feet, and their thick fur protects them from being stung. Their tough skin is unusually loose. This allows them to twist around and bite anything that attacks them.

SCIENTIFIC NAME *Mellivora capensis*

DISTRIBUTION Africa, Middle East, southern Asia

SIZE Up to 3 ft. (1m) long, including tail

SPOTTED SKUNK

Many carnivores have glands that produce strong scents, but in skunks the scent is so powerful that it makes a very effective weapon. When a spotted skunk is threatened by another animal, it raises its bushy tail, turns around, and produces a jet of spray from glands just beneath its tail. The spray makes it difficult for the attacker to breathe, and it is so strong that it can be smelled almost a mile (1.5 km) downwind. Like its more common relative, the striped skunk (*Mephitis mephitis*), the spotted skunk eats both plants and small animals.

Spotted skunks fending off a lynx

SCIENTIFIC NAME *Spilogale putorius*

DISTRIBUTION United States, Mexico

SIZE Up to 22 in. (55cm) long, including tail

BELOW *This giant otter is feeding on a piranha. Its sharp front claws give it a good grip.*

EURASIAN OTTER

Otters are carnivores that hunt in water. There are more than 12 species, all of which have lithe bodies, thick, waterproof underfur, tapering tails, and webbed feet. The Eurasian otter lives in rivers and lakes, as well as on rocky coasts. It feeds mainly on fish and frogs, but it also catches land animals such as rabbits. It is largely nocturnal, hiding away to rear its young in a riverbank den called a holt. During the last one hundred years, otters in Europe have been badly affected by water pollution, but where rivers have been cleaned up, they are making a comeback.

Eurasian otter trying to pick up a scent

SCIENTIFIC NAME *Lutra lutra*

DISTRIBUTION Europe, northern Africa, Asia, Far East

SIZE Up to 4.5 in. (1.3m) long, including tail

GIANT OTTER

This South American animal is the world's longest otter, although it is not as heavy as the sea otter. It lives in rivers and swamps in thick forest and feeds mainly on fish. Unlike smaller freshwater otters, which have cylindrical tails, its tail is flattened toward the tip. Giant otters have become rare because they are hunted for their fur. They are easily tracked by hunters because they feed by day and make loud calls.

SCIENTIFIC NAME *Pteronura brasiliensis*

DISTRIBUTION Tropical South America

SIZE Up to 8 ft. (2.4m) long, including tail

SEA OTTER

Otters often feed on the shore, but this species is the only one that spends its entire life at sea. It stays close to the coast, usually in beds of giant kelp, the world's fastest-growing seaweed. Sea otters feed on fish and crabs, but they specialize in eating mollusks. To eat clams, they float on their backs and smash open the shells with a stone. Unlike most sea mammals, sea otters do not have blubber to keep them warm. Instead, their fine, dense fur traps a layer of air so their skin never gets wet. Female sea otters have just one pup at time. The mother floats on her back, nursing her pup on her chest.

SCIENTIFIC NAME *Enhydra lutra*

DISTRIBUTION Northeastern Pacific Ocean, inshore from Aleutian Islands to California

SIZE Up to 5 ft. (1.5m) long, including tail

GENETS, CIVETS, AND MONGOOSES

This family of mammals contains about 70 species of carnivores, all from Europe, Africa, or Asia. They are slender-bodied predators with short legs and long tails, and their thick fur is often boldly marked. They live in forests or grassland, and many of them are graceful and agile climbers, pouncing on other animals in trees or among rocks. Mongooses will hunt by day, but genets and civets are nocturnal, and although they live near people, they are rarely seen. All of these animals are good at defending themselves. They have scent glands at the base of their tails, and some use these to squirt a foul-smelling liquid at anything that comes too close.

BELOW *A small bird makes a tasty snack for a common genet. Genets can creep stealthily through trees and bushes to catch their prey unawares.*

Large ears pick up faint sounds

COMMON GENET

Common genet on a branch

With its long tail and spotted coat, the common genet looks very much like a cat (pages 276-279), it has a pointed muzzle, and its claws only partly retract when they are not being used. Common genets live in woodland, scrub, and rocky ground, and they hunt during the night. They feed mainly on rodents, particularly mice, but they also specialize in hunting roosting birds. Most birds are reluctant to fly after dark, making this a good time for the genets to attack them.

SCIENTIFIC NAME *Genetta genetta*

DISTRIBUTION Southwestern Europe, Africa, Middle East

SIZE Up to 3.5 ft. (1.1m) long, including tail

AFRICAN CIVET

This gray and black animal has a doglike muzzle and a long, bushy tail. It lives in forests and grassland. Hunting after dark, it can catch and kill young antelope, but its usual foods are fruit and small lizards and rodents. Like all its relatives, the civet has a keen sense of smell, and it marks its territory with scent.

SCIENTIFIC NAME *Viverra civetta*

DISTRIBUTION Africa, south of the Sahara Desert

SIZE Up to 4.5 ft. (1.4m) long, including tail

BANDED MONGOOSE

Mongooses eat a variety of foods, but they are famed for their ability to attack snakes. They rely on speed to catch a snake before it strikes, gripping it just behind the head. Mongooses' thick fur gives them some protection, and they also have partial immunity to venom. There are more than 25 species of mongooses. The banded mongoose from Africa has light and dark bands running across its back. It lives in family groups of up to 30 animals and feeds during the day.

SCIENTIFIC NAME *Mungos mungo*

DISTRIBUTION Africa, south of the Sahara Desert

SIZE Up to 30 in. (76cm) long, including tail

Banded mongoose attacking a cobra

BINTURONG

This black, shaggy-furred animal is one of the few carnivorous mammals that has a prehensile tail. It uses its tail to climb through Asia's tropical forests to find food. Compared to most carnivores it moves slowly, though it still manages to catch insects and roosting birds. Binturongs swim well, despite their long fur.

SCIENTIFIC NAME *Arctitis binturong*

DISTRIBUTION Southeast Asia

SIZE Up to 6 ft. (2m) long, including tail

MEERKAT

For meerkats, living together is the key to survival. These African animals feed during the day in dry, open country, where they are vulnerable to attack. To protect themselves, while some of the group look for insects and other small animals to eat, others act as lookouts, propping themselves up on their hind legs and tails. At other times, meerkats shelter in underground burrows. A typical community contains between 20 and 30 animals belonging to several separate families.

Meerkats looking for food

SCIENTIFIC NAME *Suricata suricatta*

DISTRIBUTION Southern Africa

SIZE Up to 24 in. (61m) long, including tail

FOSSA

The fossa is Madagascar's largest carnivore. It has a sleek, red-brown body and a very long, slender tail. Fossas are nocturnal. They live in forests, hunting on the ground and in trees. Like many mammals in Madagascar, they have been badly affected by deforestation.

SCIENTIFIC NAME *Cryptoprocta ferox*

DISTRIBUTION Madagascar

SIZE Up to 5.5 ft. (1.7m) long, including tail

LEFT *Fossas look very much like cats. They are superb climbers and sometimes chase lemurs through the trees.*

HYENAS AND AARDWOLVES

Hyenas look like dogs, but they belong to a different family of mammals. There are four species, and three of them are among the most versatile carnivores in the world. Hyenas often hunt live prey, but they also specialize in eating dead remains. They have amazingly strong jaws and teeth, and can tear apart and eat every scrap of a carcass, including the bones. The fourth member of this family, called the aardwolf, follows a very different way of life, feeding entirely on insects. Hyenas and aardwolves are found in Africa and warm parts of Asia, and they are mainly nocturnal.

Short hind legs

ABOVE RIGHT *Spotted hyenas can swallow pieces of bone up to 3.5 in. long, and they can even digest their prey's teeth. They eat all kinds of dead remains, including those that are several months old.*

BELOW *Aardwolves are easy to tell from meat-eating hyenas because they have long manes down their backs, and they live alone instead of in packs.*

SPOTTED HYENA

Weighing up to 175 lb. (80kg), this is the largest, most powerful hyena. It lives on Africa's open plains in packs up to 100 strong, preying on animals such as zebras. A spotted hyena can eat nearly 35 lb. (15kg) of food at one meal. Spotted hyenas have shaggy fur and sloping backs, and can run at up to 35 mph (55km/h). They breed in underground dens, and the females give birth and suckle their cubs in a central nursery area.

SCIENTIFIC NAME *Crocuta crocuta*

DISTRIBUTION Africa, south of the Sahara Desert

SIZE Up to 6 ft. (2m) long, including tail

AARDWOLF

Instead of eating meat, the aardwolf feeds mainly on termites, which it laps up with its sticky tongue. Compared to hyenas, it has weak jaws and small teeth, but its hearing is very good, which helps it track down food. Aardwolves feed after dark, using their paws to dig insects out of the ground. During the day, they hide in underground burrows, often those that have been abandoned by aardvarks (page 237).

SCIENTIFIC NAME *Proteles cristatus*

DISTRIBUTION Eastern and southern Africa

SIZE Up to 3.5 ft. (1.1m) long, including tail

CATS

With their lithe bodies, keen hearing, and superb eyesight, cats are the stealthiest hunting mammals. Compared to other carnivores, most cats are dedicated meat-eaters, ignoring all other foods in favor of living prey. They usually kill with a single bite, though they catch their prey with their sharp claws. All cats except the cheetah can retract their claws inside a protective sheath when they are not in use. There are about 38 species in the cat family. Many are now rare, either because they are killed for their fur and body parts, or because their habitat is being destroyed.

TOP RIGHT *As well as using their paws to catch fish, fishing cats sometimes wade into the water to catch fish in their mouths.*
TOP LEFT *A Eurasian wildcat flattens its ears and exposes its teeth as a warning to enemies.*
ABOVE *The serval is sometimes hunted by people, but one of its most dangerous enemies is a larger member of the cat family—the leopard (page 279).*

EURASIAN WILDCAT

Though the world's largest cats are heavyweight predators, other species, like this one, are not much larger than a domestic cat. The Eurasian wildcat is solidly built, with thick fur and a bushy tail. It lives in rocky places and forests, and feeds on rodents, rabbits, and occasionally young deer. Because it hunts mainly by night and is wary of people, it is seldom seen. The African wildcat (*Felis libyca*) is similar, but less shy. It is thought to be the ancestor of all domestic cats.

SCIENTIFIC NAME	*Felis sylvestris*
DISTRIBUTION	Europe, Middle East, central and southern Asia
SIZE	Up to 3.5 ft. (1.1m) long, including tail

AFRICAN GOLDEN CAT

This cat lives in the dense forests of tropical Africa. It is twice the size of a domestic cat and has golden-brown fur. Some golden cats are spotted all over, but others have hardly any spots at all. Like most cats, it is solitary and nocturnal, and hunts in trees and on the ground.

SCIENTIFIC NAME	*Felis aurata*
DISTRIBUTION	Western and central Africa
SIZE	Up to 4.5 ft. (1.4m) long, including tail

FISHING CAT

Apart from the jaguar (page 278), most cats avoid water and try not to get wet. But the fishing cat spends most of its life along rivers and streams, and it often wades or swims. Fishing cats eat frogs and snakes, but fish make up most of their diet. They wait at the water's edge for a fish to swim near, then flick the fish onto land with their partly webbed front paws.

SCIENTIFIC NAME	*Felis viverrina*
DISTRIBUTION	India, Sri Lanka, Southeast Asia
SIZE	Up to 3.5 ft. (1.1m) long, including tail

SERVAL

With its long legs, large ears, and short tail, the serval is one of Africa's most distinctive cats. It lives in scrub and grassland, where it uses its keen hearing to pinpoint prey in the undergrowth before pouncing to catch animals with its front paws. The serval has such sensitive hearing that it is able to find mole-rats by listening for the faint sounds they make as they tunnel under ground.

SCIENTIFIC NAME	*Felis serval*
DISTRIBUTION	Africa
SIZE	Up to 4.5 ft. (1.4m) long, including tail

CARACAL

The caracal has long legs, an unspotted coat, and tufts of black fur at the tips of its ears. It lives in dry, open country and hunts mainly at night. An expert at catching birds, the caracal has such quick reactions that it can knock low-flying birds out of the air.

Caracal leaping after a flying bird

SCIENTIFIC NAME	*Lynx caracal*
DISTRIBUTION	Africa, Middle East, southwestern Asia
SIZE	Up to 4 ft. (1.2m) long, including tail

LYNX

Lynx look very different from other cats, with very short tails and tufted ears. Experts disagree about how many species there are. Some think there is only one, but many believe that there are three—one in North America, another in Europe and Asia, and a third in Spain and Portugal. Wherever they are found, lynx live mainly in forests and other places where there is cover. They eat a wide variety of birds and small mammals, but in North America they particularly depend on snowshoe hares (page 250). North American lynx have large, round paws, which help them walk on snow.

SCIENTIFIC NAME *Lynx lynx*

DISTRIBUTION North America, Europe, northern and central Asia

SIZE Up to 5 ft. (1.5m) long, including tail

BOBCAT

Though this North American cat looks like a lynx, it is smaller and lives farther south. Its ear-tufts are also shorter and can be difficult to spot. Bobcats live in a wide range of habitats. They feed mainly on rodents, rabbits, and hares, and in the winter they sometimes attack deer. They also eat animal remains, but only if the remains are fresh. Bobcats make dens in rocky crevices and hollow trees, where females produce a litter of up to six kittens every year.

Bobcat on a rock

SCIENTIFIC NAME *Lynx rufus*

DISTRIBUTION North America, from southern Canada to Mexico

SIZE Up to 4 ft. (1.2m) long, including tail

OCELOT

Ocelots live in a wide variety of habitats and find their prey mainly on the ground, including deer, monkeys, rodents, and sometimes snakes. Female ocelots usually give birth to two kittens at a time. The male helps his partner by bringing food to the den. Spotted cats are often hunted for their fur, but few have suffered as much as the ocelot. Its markings are so attractive that its fur fetches an extremely high price, and at one time more than 10,000 ocelot skins were sold every year. The trade is now banned, but hunting still continues.

SCIENTIFIC NAME *Felis pardalis*

DISTRIBUTION North, Central, and South America, from Arizona to Argentina

SIZE Up to 5.5 ft. (1.7m) long, including tail

TOP *Despite its cuddly looks, the ocelot is an effective killer. Like other cats, it sharpens its claws on trees and retracts them when they are not needed.*
RIGHT *Lynx have disappeared from many parts of Europe, though they have been reintroduced into some countries, including France.*

The dominant male watches over the pride

PUMA OR COUGAR

This widespread American predator has many alternative names. It is also known as a mountain lion, although it has little in common with a true lion. Unlike a lion, the puma screams instead of roaring, and it hunts on its own. Deer are among its favorite prey. If a puma catches more than it can eat, it often hides the remains under branches, returning later to finish feeding. Female pumas have up to six kittens a year. The kittens are spotted when they are born, but lose their spots during their first few months.

SCIENTIFIC NAME *Felis concolor*

DISTRIBUTION Western North America, Central and South America

SIZE Up to 7.5 ft. (2.3m) long, including tail

CHEETAH

Instead of hunting by stealth, the cheetah relies on speed. The fastest land animal, it can reach 60 mph (95km/h) in just four seconds. Cheetahs are built for speed, with slender bodies, long legs, and flexible spines. Unlike other cats, they do not have retractable claws on their front feet, so they bring down their prey by knocking it to the ground. Cheetahs feed mainly on antelope and other grazing mammals. They live in grassland and semidesert.

SCIENTIFIC NAME *Acinonyx jubatus*

DISTRIBUTION Africa, south of the Sahara Desert, parts of Middle East

SIZE Up to 7.5 ft. (2.3m) long, including tail

ABOVE *The lions in a pride often relax together. The females form the core of the pride, although the males are in charge. When a male lion grows old and weak, he is driven away by a younger male, which takes his place.*

Puma about to pounce on its prey

RIGHT *This tiger lives in India, where there are more tigers than anywhere else. Its stripes break up its outline in the dappled forest shade, camouflaging it from its prey.*

A cheetah chasing a young antelope

LION

Although it is often called the king of the jungle, the lion lives on plains and in woodlands, not in dense forest. It is the world's second largest cat, after the tiger, and one of the few that hunts in groups. A typical lion group, or pride, consists of about 15 animals. Two or three are adult males; the rest are females and their young. The females carry out most of the hunting, but after a successful kill, the males soon arrive to take their share. Lions can bring down animals as large as buffalo. When food is short, however, they will eat anything they can find, including tortoises, lizards, and dead remains. Thousands of years ago, lions roamed across Africa, southern Europe, and Asia. Today, most lions live in Africa, with just a few hundred in northwestern India.

SCIENTIFIC NAME *Panthera leo*

DISTRIBUTION Africa, Gir Forest in northwestern India

SIZE Up to 10 ft. (3m) long, including tail

JAGUAR

Although it is slightly shorter than the leopard, the jaguar is more heavily built and can weigh up to 325 lb. (150kg). During the 1950s and 1960s, huge numbers of jaguars were hunted for their beautiful fur. Jaguars live mainly in forests and swamps. Unlike most cats, they are good swimmers and seem to enjoy going into water. They often hunt along riverbanks, attacking otters, turtles, and even large snakes. Jaguars are capable of killing people, but attacks are rare, and the cats normally avoid humans.

SCIENTIFIC NAME *Panthera onca*

DISTRIBUTION North, Central, and South America, from Mexico to Argentina

SIZE Up to 8.5 ft. (2.6m) long, including tail

LEOPARD

This lithe and beautiful animal lives in a remarkable variety of habitats, from grasslands and deserts to mountain slopes. Most leopards are spotted, but the black leopard's coat is so dark that the spots cannot be seen. Leopards feed mainly at night, attacking from close quarters instead of chasing their prey. They are good climbers and are strong enough to lift animals heavier than themselves. They often haul their kills into trees to thwart hungry scavengers.

Female leopard carrying a cub

SCIENTIFIC NAME *Panthera pardus*

DISTRIBUTION Africa, Middle East, central and southern Asia

SIZE Up to 10 ft. (3m) long, including tail

SNOW LEOPARD

Less is known about the snow leopard than about most big cats because it lives in remote mountains at altitudes of up to 20,000 ft. (6,000m). Its soft, gray fur is exceptionally thick, and it has an extra-long tail that it wraps around its body to keep warm. During the day, snow leopards attack all kinds of wild animals, as well as farmed livestock. They are sometimes killed by farmers, and they are hunted for their fur. No one knows exactly how many of these magnificent cats live in the wild, but the number may be as few as 5,000.

SCIENTIFIC NAME *Panthera uncia*

DISTRIBUTION Central Asia

SIZE Up to 7.5 ft. (2.3m) long, including tail

TIGER

The cat family includes many fearsome hunters, but the tiger is the largest and most powerful of them all. The record weight for an adult male is more than one third of a ton. Despite their enormous size, they can stalk their prey in almost total silence before pouncing at close range. They grip their victims with their front claws and kill them with a bite to the throat. Tigers have killed many people, too, especially where humans have moved into the tiger's natural habitat. In recent years, the world's tiger population has collapsed, mainly because of illegal hunting. Today, fewer than 7,000 tigers are left in the wild.

SCIENTIFIC NAME *Panthera tigris*

DISTRIBUTION Southern and Southeast Asia, eastern Siberia

SIZE Up to 12 ft. (3.6m) long, including tail

SEALS, SEA LIONS, AND MANATEES

Seals and sea lions are carnivorous mammals that spend most of their lives in water. They can stay at sea for weeks at a time, though they give birth on land. They have flippers instead of legs and are expert swimmers and divers. They feed mainly on fish. Manatees belong to a group of mammals called sirenians. They eat plants, and they spend their entire lives in water. There are about 34 species of seals, sea lions, and their relatives, and four kinds of sirenians. Seals can live in polar waters, but sirenians are found only in warm places.

ABOVE *The leopard seal's unusually long muzzle is well suited to grabbing adult penguins in its jaws.*

The winner gathers together a band of females and fathers all their pups. Elephant seals got their name from their size and from the male's bulbous, trunklike nose.

SCIENTIFIC NAME	*Mirounga leonina*
DISTRIBUTION	Cold water regions in and near the Southern Ocean
	SIZE Up to 16 ft. (4.9m) long

GRAY SEAL

On land, the gray seal is a cumbersome animal that lumbers along with its body on the ground. In water, it is very different, a fast and graceful swimmer that can dive to more than 250 ft. (75m). Like all true seals, it uses only its hind flippers to swim, spreading them out and then closing them together in a clapping motion. Gray seals usually give birth to their pups on isolated rocks and beaches between September and March. The pups have soft, white fur when they are born, but they soon grow a new coat of gray fur and follow their mothers into the sea.

Adult gray seal with spotted coat

Young gray seal with silky, white coat

SCIENTIFIC NAME	*Halichoerus grypus*
DISTRIBUTION	Northern Atlantic Ocean
SIZE	Up to 12 ft. (3.6m) long

LEOPARD SEAL

This slender seal is one of the Southern Ocean's largest and most ferocious predators, with sharp teeth and powerful jaws. It will feed on fish, krill, and even other seals, but it specializes in preying on penguins. It lurks in the sea near penguin colonies and grabs the penguins as they enter the water. The seal shakes the bird from side to side to kill it, then either eats it piece by piece or swallows it whole.

SCIENTIFIC NAME	*Hydrurga leptonyx*
DISTRIBUTION	Southern Ocean
	SIZE Up to 12 ft. (3.6m) long

SOUTHERN ELEPHANT SEAL

Male seals are often much larger than females, but in the southern elephant seal, the difference is greater than in any other species. The males can weigh a colossal 8,000 lb. (3,500kg)—more than four times as much as the females. Male elephant seals use their tremendous bulk to battle with their rivals for a mate during the breeding season. Facing each other head on, they rear up and strike with their teeth.

BELOW *With his nose inflated, a male southern elephant seal roars at his rivals on a breeding beach.*

Nose expands when the seal roars

CALIFORNIA SEA LION

Sea lions look much like seals, but they are more adept at moving on land. Their front flippers are strong enough to hold their bodies off the ground, and their back flippers can turn forward to work like feet. Instead of shuffling along like true seals, they can almost gallop. There are five species of sea lions. The shiny, black California sea lion is the best known because it is easy to tame and train. In the wild, California sea lions live on rocky coasts, feeding on fish and squid.

SCIENTIFIC NAME	*Zalophus californianus*
DISTRIBUTION	California, Galapagos Islands
SIZE	Up to 8 ft. (2.4m) long

ANTARCTIC FUR SEAL

Most seals have a coat of short, rough fur. Fur seals, however, have a thick layer of soft underfur as well. Their underfur is waterproof, and it helps to keep them warm. There are nine species of fur seals, found mainly in the Southern Hemisphere. The Antarctic fur seal, which is one of the most common, lives farthest south of all, breeding on islands at the very edge of Antarctica. At one time, these seals were hunted for their fur, almost to the point of extinction. They are now protected and have made a spectacular recovery.

SCIENTIFIC NAME *Arctocephalus gazella*

DISTRIBUTION Southern Ocean

SIZE Up to 6 ft. (2m) long

WALRUS

After the elephant seal, the walrus is the second largest sea mammal that comes ashore to breed. It feeds in the cold waters of the northern polar regions. The males have two large, downward-pointing tusks. At one time, it was thought that male walruses used their tusks to

Male walrus showing fanglike tusks

TOP *A female harbor seal (Phoca vitulina) lies beside her pup on the shore of the northern Atlantic Ocean.*
ABOVE *Mediterranean monk seals (Monachus monachus) are among the world's rarest sea mammals.*

BELOW *A Caribbean manatee playfully bites at one of its partner's flippers. Manatees have large mouths and can weigh as much as half a ton. They are harmless vegetarians.*

feed, but most experts now think that the tusks act as status symbols when the walruses compete for the chance to mate. Walruses feed mainly on mollusks, sucking them up whole, then spitting out the empty shells.

SCIENTIFIC NAME *Odobenus rosmarus*

DISTRIBUTION Arctic Ocean and surrounding seas

SIZE Up to 12 ft. (3.6m) long

CARIBBEAN MANATEE

Although this endangered animal looks like a giant seal from a distance, it differs from seals in several ways. It has a paddlelike tail instead of hind flippers, and its mouth and jaws are designed for grazing on underwater plants, not for catching fish. Manatees live in rivers and coastal lagoons, and they never venture onto land. They feed at night, often spending the day dozing near the surface of the water. They are difficult to see, and in heavily traveled waters, sleeping manatees are often injured when they collide with boats.

SCIENTIFIC NAME *Trichecus manatus*

DISTRIBUTION Gulf of Mexico, Caribbean Sea, from Florida to Guyana

SIZE Up to 13 ft. (4m) long

Elephants

Both species of elephants—Indian and African—are instantly recognizable by their gigantic size and their trunks. A trunk is a long, flexible nose with nostrils right at the tip. An elephant uses it for breathing and for other tasks, such as sucking up water to clean itself, stripping leaves off branches, or gently nudging a calf out of harm's way. Elephants eat plants of all kinds, and even smash down trees to reach the topmost foliage. They chew their food with a small number of large, flat-topped teeth at the back of their jaws. Intelligent and sociable, elephants are among the longest-living animals in the wild, often surviving 70 years or more.

Tusks

One third of tusk is in skull

Tusks are specialized teeth. They grow out of an animal's mouth and can point up, down, or occasionally straight ahead. Tusks grow throughout the animal's life, often developing a curved or spiral shape. Elephants have the largest and most versatile tusks in the animal world. They use them to dig for water, to strip bark from trees, and to fend off rivals and predators. Some other tusk-bearing animals, such as male walruses and narwhals, use their tusks during contests in the breeding season, just as elephants do. The contestants rarely hurt each other, but when tusks are turned on other animals, the results can be deadly.

Cross-section of an elephant head showing tusk formation

number of Indian elephants living in the wild has fallen in recent years.

Scientific name
Elephas maximus

Distribution India, Sri Lanka, Southeast Asia

Size Up to 13 ft. (4m) long, excluding trunk

African elephant

Standing up to 12 ft. (3.6m) high at the shoulder, the African elephant is the world's largest land animal. Adult males, or bulls, can weigh up to six tons. They eat up to 650 lb. (300kg) of food and drink more than 25 gallons (100 liters) of water a day. African elephants have sloping backs and rounded ears. Their trunks have two tips, which they use like fingers to pick things up. Both males and females have tusks, but the males' are much larger, often growing to 10 ft. (3m) long. African elephants live in herds that include several adult females and their young. Calves feed on milk for at least 18 months, and they do not breed until they are at least 11 years old. Elephants were once common in Africa, but ivory hunting has destroyed many herds.

Scientific name
Loxodonta africana

Distribution Africa, south of the Sahara Desert

Size Up to 15 ft. (4.6m) long, excluding trunk

Above *This Indian elephant is giving itself a shower in a river. Elephants are good swimmers, and they bathe regularly when they have the chance. In shallow water, they often roll over onto their sides.*

Indian elephant

The Indian elephant is the smaller of the two species of elephants. It has a slightly different shape from the African elephant, with an arched back, smaller ears, and just one fingerlike tip on its trunk. Indian elephants live mainly in forests, feeding on grass and leaves. Like African elephants, they use their trunks to pull up plants or rip branches off trees. Males sometimes have large tusks, but the females have small tusks, or none at all. Indian elephants have been tamed and used as working animals for at least 4,000 years. They are still caught and trained, and the

HYRAXES

With their compact bodies and stubby legs, hyraxes look rather like rodents. However, they differ from rodents in many ways, and strange though it may seem, biologists think that their closest living relatives may be either hoofed mammals or elephants. Hyraxes live in rocky places or in forests and are good climbers. Instead of claws, their stubby toes end in flattened nails, and their bare soles give them a good grip. They are vegetarians, feeding either by day or night, depending on where they live. There are seven species of hyraxes, which are found in Africa and southwestern Asia.

ROCK HYRAX

This agile, inquisitive animal is common on Africa's plains, where it lives among piles of boulders called kopjes. It feeds during the day on grass and the leaves of shrubs, sometimes climbing along the branches to get to the newest growth. It lives in groups of about 50 animals, which often huddle together at night for warmth. The rock hyrax's many enemies include eagles, leopards, and snakes. Some hyraxes are tame enough to take food scraps from people.

ABOVE
Rock hyraxes need shelter to survive because they cannot cope with extremes of either heat or cold. This rock hyrax is warming itself by sunbathing on a ledge.

SCIENTIFIC NAME *Procavia capensis*

DISTRIBUTION Arabian Peninsula, eastern and southern Africa

SIZE Up to 18 in. (46cm) long

TREE HYRAX

The tree hyrax is heard much more often than it is seen—its bloodcurdling call echoes through African forests after dark. It feeds in trees, often several feet above the ground, tearing off leaves with its back teeth. Like rock hyraxes, tree hyraxes are mainly brown, but they have a tuft of white hair on their backs that stands erect when they are alarmed.

SCIENTIFIC NAME *Dendrohyrax arboreus*

DISTRIBUTION Eastern and southern Africa

SIZE Up to 24 in. (61cm) long

RIGHT *Tree hyraxes can eat one third of their body weight a day.*

Tusks can be used as dangerous weapons

LEFT *With its ears spread wide, a bull African elephant strides across the ground. This behavior shows that the elephant has sensed danger and may be about to charge.*

HORSES, RHINOCEROSES, AND TAPIRS

There are four species in the horse family, five species of rhinoceroses, and four species of tapirs. They are all solidly built grazing or browsing animals, with long legs ending in hoofed toes. Horses live in open country; tapirs live in forests. The largest rhinoceroses live in open grasslands, but the smallest ones are forest animals. While some species in the horse family are still common, rhinoceroses and tapirs have been badly affected by hunting and deforestation.

PRZEWALSKI'S WILD HORSE

Many "wild" horses are descendants of horses that have escaped from captivity. Przewalski's wild horse, however, is a completely wild animal. It has brown fur, an upright, black mane, and a black tail. The future of this species looks uncertain. It is endangered by hunting and is also threatened by domesticated horses, which have taken over most of its habitat. Almost all Przewalski's wild horses are now kept in zoos, but some are being released into the wild.

SCIENTIFIC NAME	*Equus ferus*
DISTRIBUTION	Mongolia, China
SIZE	Up to 6 ft. (2m) long, excluding tail

ABOVE *African asses use their oversized ears to listen for signs of danger.*

BELOW *There are only about 1,000 Przewalski's wild horses in the world.*

AFRICAN ASS

This gray-brown animal is the ancestor of the domestic donkey. Though it resembles a donkey, it has stripes on its legs and a lighter build. African asses live in hot, dry places, in herds of up to 50 animals. They rely on speed for self-defense, although they can also give a powerful kick. Wild African asses are now rare, but domestic donkeys, or burros, have escaped into the wild in many parts of the world.

SCIENTIFIC NAME	*Equus africanus*
DISTRIBUTION	Northern Africa
SIZE	Up to 6 ft. (2m) long, excluding tail

COMMON ZEBRA OR PLAINS ZEBRA

Bold black and white stripes make this one of Africa's most recognizable mammals. It lives in open grassland in scattered herds that contain hundreds of animals. Like other wild horses, it depends on speed for survival, running at up to 25 mph (40km/h). There are three species of zebras. The common zebra is the only one with a striped underside.

SCIENTIFIC NAME	*Equus burchelli*
DISTRIBUTION	Eastern and southern Africa
SIZE	Up to 8 ft. (2.4m) long, excluding tail

LEFT *Common zebras move in herds. Their stripes may act as markers, helping the zebras recognize each other and stay together as they travel.*

White rhinoceros
(Ceratotherium simum)

Sumatran rhinoceros
(Dicerorhinus sumatrensis)

Black rhinoceros
(Diceros bicornis)

Javan rhinoceros
(Rhinoceros sondaicus)

ABOVE *Different species of rhinoceroses are distinguished by their size, the number of horns they have, and the shape and texture of their skin.*

WHITE RHINOCEROS

After elephants, white rhinoceroses are the largest land animals—males can weigh up to 3.5 tons. They eat grass with their broad mouths and sport a pair of horns. They have bad eyesight, but good hearing and a keen sense of smell. These peaceful animals usually run away from people instead of launching an attack. This is not enough to save them from poachers, who hunt rhinoceroses to sell their horns. Today, there are probably fewer than 7,000 white rhinoceroses left.

SCIENTIFIC NAME	*Ceratotherium simum*
DISTRIBUTION	Tropical and southern Africa
SIZE	Up to 15 ft. (4.6m) long, excluding tail

BLACK RHINOCEROS

The black rhinoceros feeds on trees and shrubs, which it collects with its flexible, pointed upper lip. It is more aggressive than the white rhinoceros, and instead of running away from danger, it often charges toward it. In the early 1960s, there were about 100,000 black rhinoceroses, but after four decades of poaching, their numbers have dropped to about 2,000. It is probably the world's fastest-disappearing large mammal. Anti-poaching patrols have been established to protect the black rhinoceros. Without them, the species would almost certainly become extinct.

SCIENTIFIC NAME	*Diceros bicornis*
DISTRIBUTION	Tropical and southern Africa
SIZE	Up to 12 ft. (3.6m) long, excluding tail

INDIAN RHINOCEROS

This rhinoceros's thick, gray skin looks like armor plating. It hangs down in heavy folds and is studded with small bumps. The Indian rhinoceros has a single, stubby horn. It lives in grassy swamps, feeding on leaves, branches, and fruit. Like its African relatives, it is targeted by poachers and must be protected by armed guards in national parks.

SCIENTIFIC NAME	*Rhinoceros unicornis*
DISTRIBUTION	Nepal, northern India
SIZE	Up to 12.5 ft. (3.8m) long, excluding tail

MALAYAN OR ASIATIC TAPIR

Tapirs are found in two widely separated parts of the world—Southeast Asia and South America. They all have piglike bodies, long heads, and fleshy snouts. The Malayan tapir is the only black and white species. Its snout is so long that the tapir can use it to feel for food, as an elephant uses its trunk. Malayan tapirs feed after dark and usually stay close to water. Their young have white stripes and spots to camouflage them on the forest floor.

SCIENTIFIC NAME	*Tapirus indicus*
DISTRIBUTION	Southeast Asia
SIZE	Up to 8 ft. (2.4m) long, excluding tail

ABOVE *Indian rhinoceroses can weigh two tons and are dangerous if they charge.*

ABOVE *Malayan tapirs live in dense rain forest, a habitat that is fast disappearing.*

HOOFED MAMMALS

A hoof is a toe designed for carrying an animal's weight. Its reinforced tip is made of keratin, the same substance found in claws and fingernails. Hooves are compact but tough, providing a good grip on the ground and allowing an animal to run fast. Biologists divide hoofed mammals into two groups. The larger group includes pigs, camels, deer, giraffes, and antelope (pages 286–303). These animals are sometimes called "cloven-hoofed" because their hooves are split in two down the middle. The other group includes horses, rhinoceroses, and tapirs. These animals have an uneven number of toes, from as few as one to as many as five.

Horse's hoof is a single toe

PIGS, PECCARIES, AND HIPPOPOTAMUSES

Pigs and peccaries are intelligent, adaptable animals. Wild pigs
are found in Europe, Africa, and Asia, while peccaries live in
the Americas. They both live in forests or open grassland,
digging up the ground with their flattened snouts to feed.
Unlike other hoofed mammals, they are not strict vegetarians,
and they often eat small animals and dead remains. There are
11 species in total. There are two species of hippopotamuses,
both found in Africa. They eat plants and spend most
of the day lounging in water or mud.

WILD BOAR

This forest animal is the ancestor of the
domestic pig, but it looks very different
from the pigs that are now raised on
farms. It has bristly fur, small ears, and
powerful legs. The males have two pairs
of short tusks, which they use to fight
off attackers. Wild boars live alone or
in small herds, and they usually feed at
night. The females give birth to litters of up to
ten striped piglets inside nests made of leaves.

**Wild boar in
winter coat**

SCIENTIFIC NAME	*Sus scrofa*
DISTRIBUTION	Europe, northern Africa, Asia
SIZE	Up to 5.5 ft. (1.7m) long, excluding tail

BUSH PIG

Most wild pigs are gray, but this species is
brightly colored. It has a black and white head,
red fur over its sides and legs, and a white mane
running along its back. Bush pigs live in forests
and swampy places, and they feed both by day
and by night. In some parts of Africa, they
cause serious problems by raiding crops.

SCIENTIFIC NAME	*Potamochoerus porcus*
DISTRIBUTION	Africa, south of the Sahara Desert, Madagascar
SIZE	Up to 5 ft. (1.5m) long, excluding tail

WARTHOG

With its straggly fur and knobbly
face, the warthog is probably
the most unusual member
of the pig family. It is,
however, one of
the toughest.

RIGHT *The babirusa
sharpens its lower tusks
by rubbing them
against trees. Its
upper tusks can
be over 10 in.
long but are
usually blunt.*

BELOW
*Warthogs
wallow in
mud to cool
off. This keeps
their skin in
good condition.*

Its strength and alertness help it survive in open grassland, even though it is easily spotted by predators. Warthogs feed mainly on grass, and they often drop down onto their knees to eat. If they spot danger, they run to shelter in burrows or among rocks, although if they have to, they will stand and fight with their tusks. During the breeding season, male warthogs use their tusks in head-on battle. These battles are not as dangerous as they look, because the animals' thick, warty skin protects them from serious injury.

SCIENTIFIC NAME	*Phacochoerus aethiopicus*
DISTRIBUTION	Tropical and southern Africa
SIZE	Up to 4.5 ft. (1.4m) long, excluding tail

BABIRUSA
This rare wild pig from Southeast Asia has highly unusual tusks. The male's bottom pair grows up from the corners of the mouth, but the top pair grows through the animal's snout. As the tusks get longer, they curve back toward its eyes. The babirusa lives near rivers in forests and feeds during the day.

SCIENTIFIC NAME	*Babyrousa babyrussa*
DISTRIBUTION	The Philippines
SIZE	Up to 3.5 ft. (1.1m) long, excluding tail

COLLARED PECCARY
Peccaries are small, piglike animals with bristly fur and slender legs. They live in large, roving herds and eat a wide range of food, from insects and seeds to the stems of prickly pears. Compared to some pigs, their tusks are short, but they are still good at fighting off attack. Collared peccaries got their name from the band of white fur around their necks. They are the most widespread species and the only peccaries that live in the United States. Despite being hunted for food, they manage to thrive in the wild.

SCIENTIFIC NAME	*Tayassu tajacu*
DISTRIBUTION	North, Central, and South America, from Arizona to Argentina
SIZE	Up to 3 ft. (1m) long, excluding tail

RIVER HIPPOPOTAMUS
The river hippopotamus is one of Africa's largest mammals, with a barrel-shaped body that can weigh more than three tons. Its huge jaws hold a pair of tusks up to 20 in. (50cm) long. These are strong enough to smash through the side of a boat. Despite this weaponry, the hippopotamus is a vegetarian. It lounges in water or mud by day and

ABOVE Hippopotamuses float well but swim slowly. When they dive, they often walk along the riverbed.

Hippopotamus foot with four webbed toes

Hippopotamus has large tusks in lower jaw

BELOW A pygmy hippopotamus's skin is covered by a slippery fluid to keep it moist.

emerges at night to feed. It will wander as far as 3 mi. (5km) to feed and eats an average of 90 lb. (40kg) of food each night. Hippopotamuses have webbed feet and nostrils that they can close. They can stay under water for more than 15 minutes. Their skin is unusually thin, but it is protected by an oily, red fluid that acts as a natural sunscreen. Females give birth on land, usually bearing one calf each year.

SCIENTIFIC NAME	*Hippopotamus amphibius*
DISTRIBUTION	Africa, south of the Sahara Desert
SIZE	Up to 13 ft. (4m) long, excluding tail

PYGMY HIPPOPOTAMUS
Unlike the common hippopotamus, this rare animal lives in Africa's tropical forests. It looks like a miniature version of its larger relative, but its mouth is narrower and its body sleeker. Pygmy hippopotamuses feed on leaves and fallen fruit. They run into water to escape danger, but otherwise spend most of their lives on land.

SCIENTIFIC NAME	*Hexaprotodon liberiensis*
DISTRIBUTION	Tropical western Africa
SIZE	Up to 5.5 ft. (1.7m) long, excluding tail

CAMELS AND THEIR RELATIVES

The animals in this family live in two different parts of the world. Camels themselves live in Africa and Asia, while guanacos and vicuñas live in South America. They all have long necks, divided upper lips, and only two toes on each foot. Camels live in places that can be dry and hot by day, but often chillingly cold at night. Guanacos and vicuñas live in high mountains, where the air is very thin. There were originally four wild species in this family, but all of them have been domesticated.

BELOW *Like all camels, dromedaries walk by moving both left feet together, then both right feet. When they lie down, they tuck their legs underneath their bodies.*

Hump stores fat, not water

Dense fur keeps skin cool in the sun

Long legs with rounded feet

Long eyelashes keep sand out of eyes

Slit-shaped nostrils to keep out sand

DROMEDARY

In northern Africa and the Middle East, this one-humped camel is used to carry people and their belongings. It was domesticated more than 5,000 years ago, and the original wild species has since died out. Dromedaries are well equipped for life in dry places. They have cushioned feet that spread their weight over the ground, and they are able to close their nostrils when sand is blowing in the wind. They can drink more than 13 gallons (50 liters) of water at a time, and their humps contain fat reserves for times when food is scarce.

SCIENTIFIC NAME *Camelus dromedarius*

DISTRIBUTION Originally from northern Africa, Middle East; introduced into Australia

SIZE Up to 11 ft. (3.4m) long, excluding tail

BACTRIAN CAMEL

Unlike the dromedary, the Bactrian camel is brown rather than yellow, and it has two humps. It lives in the deserts of central Asia, where winter temperatures fall far below freezing. To survive these conditions, it grows an extra-thick coat in the fall, then sheds it the following spring. A few hundred of these camels still survive in the wild, mainly in Mongolia and China, but most Bactrian camels are domesticated. The gap between their two humps makes a comfortable seat for riding.

SCIENTIFIC NAME	*Camelus bactrianus*
DISTRIBUTION	Central Asia
SIZE	Up to 10 ft. (3m) long, excluding tail

ABOVE *This Bactrian camel has its winter coat. In spring, the winter fur peels away in long patches.*

VICUÑA

Compared to camels, the vicuña is a dainty animal. It has a slender body and a deerlike head, but it is much tougher than it looks. It manages to survive on barren mountain slopes up to 16,500 ft. (5,000m) high. At this altitude, the air contains much less oxygen than in lower areas, but the vicuña can still run as fast as 30 mph (50km/h). Vicuñas live in small herds, and they feed on grass and other plants. In the past, they were extensively hunted, so they are now rare in the wild.

SCIENTIFIC NAME	*Vicugna vicugna*
DISTRIBUTION	Central Andes Mountains in South America
SIZE	Up to 5.5 ft. (1.7m) long, excluding tail

GUANACO

The guanaco looks similar to the vicuña, but it is larger and has darker fur. It lives in the Andes Mountains and on South America's grassy plains in family groups of up to 12 animals. It is a fast runner and a good swimmer. It shares an unusual characteristic with camels—when it lies down, it drops onto its front knees and tucks its legs under its body. Female guanacos usually have one calf a year. Within hours of being born, the calf can run almost as fast as its mother.

SCIENTIFIC NAME	*Lama guanicoe*
DISTRIBUTION	South America, from Peru to Tierra del Fuego
SIZE	Up to 5.5 ft. (1.7m) long, excluding tail

LLAMA

The llama is a domesticated form of the guanaco, with a larger body and more powerful legs. Its thick fur can be brown, black, or white. Like the guanaco, the llama is sure-footed, which makes it ideal for journeys along narrow mountain paths. Before horses and donkeys were introduced into South America, it was the only animal that could be used to carry food and goods. It was also used as a source of food, leather, and fur, which could be made into rope.

SCIENTIFIC NAME	*Lama glama*
DISTRIBUTION	Andes Mountains in South America
SIZE	Up to 7.5 ft. (2.3m) long, excluding tail

Llamas in the Andes

Alpacas grazing in high-altitude pasture

ALPACA

Like the llama, the alpaca is a domesticated descendant of the guanaco. Instead of being used as a pack animal, however, it is raised for its fine wool. Some alpacas' wool is so long it almost touches the ground. Though llamas can survive by browsing shrubs, alpacas need grass, so they are kept in pastures.

SCIENTIFIC NAME	*Lama pacos*
DISTRIBUTION	Andes Mountains in South America
SIZE	Up to 4.5 ft. (1.4m) long, excluding tail

RIGHT *The guanaco is the tallest wild mammal in South America, standing up to 6 ft. high.*

DEER

With their slender legs and long necks, deer are among the most graceful plant-eating mammals. They have plain or spotted coats and two-toed hooves, and are the only mammals that grow antlers. Antlers are made of bone and, in most species, develop only in adult males, called stags. They are used during the breeding season, when the stags compete for a chance to breed. There are about 45 species of true deer and four species of mouse deer. They live in most parts of the world, except Australia.

Male Chinese muntjac

1   **2**   **3**   **4**

LESSER MOUSE DEER OR CHEVROTAIN

Mouse deer are secretive animals that live in tropical forests and swamps. They have slender, humpbacked bodies with pencil-thin legs, and they are not much larger than a hare (page 250). Mouse deer do not have antlers, but they have tiny, downward-pointing tusks. Despite their name, they are probably more closely related to wild pigs than to other deer. The lesser mouse deer is both the smallest deer and the tiniest hoofed mammal. The females, or does, though larger than the males, are still only knee-high.

SCIENTIFIC NAME	*Tragulus javanicus*
DISTRIBUTION	Southeast Asia
SIZE	Up to 20 in. (50cm) long, excluding tail

FOREST MUSK DEER

Musk deer are unusual in several ways. The males have long, downward-pointing tusks instead of antlers. They also have a pouch on their undersides that produces a strong-smelling substance called musk. They use this to scent-mark the boundaries of their territories. People use musk to make perfume, and because it is difficult to collect, it can be very expensive. The forest musk deer lives in mountains and usually feeds alone, eating grass, moss, and buds. All five species of musk deer are threatened by the demand for musk.

SCIENTIFIC NAME	*Moschus chrysogaster*
DISTRIBUTION	Central Asia, from Afghanistan to China
SIZE	Up to 3 ft. (1m) long, excluding tail

RIGHT Two male fallow deer lock antlers as they fight for a female. Although these fights look dangerous, they rarely result in injury because the loser usually runs away.

ABOVE Like most male deer, an elk stag grows a new set of antlers every year. 1 The antlers start to form from two bumps on the top of the skull. 2 At first, the antlers are covered with "velvet," a soft, furry skin. 3 As the antlers grow, they begin to form branches. 4 Finally, the velvet becomes loose, and the deer rubs it away.

CHINESE MUNTJAC

This small, Far Eastern deer lives in woodland and forests. The male's antlers, among the smallest of any deer's, are only about 6 in. (15cm) long. Chinese muntjacs often feed at night, when they are safer from attack. They make a loud, barking sound when alarmed, sometimes barking for more than an hour.

SCIENTIFIC NAME	*Muntiacus reevesi*
DISTRIBUTION	Originally from China, Taiwan; introduced into northwestern Europe
SIZE	Up to 3 ft. (1m) long, excluding tail

FALLOW DEER

With its spotted coat and broad, flat-tipped antlers, this is the most handsome deer in Europe. It lives wild in woodland, forests, and farmland. It is normally shy, though where it is kept in parks, it feeds out in the open. Female fallow deer live in scattered herds, but adult males usually live alone. At the start of the fall breeding season, rival males battle for supremacy, locking antlers in a test of strength. Each female gives birth to one fawn in early summer. Though the fawn can stand soon after it is born, it spends most of the time safely out of sight until it is several weeks old.

SCIENTIFIC NAME	*Dama dama*
DISTRIBUTION	Western and central Europe
SIZE	Up to 5.5 ft. (1.7m) long, excluding tail

CHITAL

The chital is India's most widespread deer. It has a red-brown coat dappled with white spots, and the males have long, branching antlers. Chitals live in open woodland and grassy plains in herds of up to 200 animals. Thousands of chitals were once killed by tigers each year, but because tigers are now rare, few chitals die in this way today.

SCIENTIFIC NAME *Axis axis*

DISTRIBUTION Originally from Southern Asia, from Nepal to Sri Lanka; introduced into other parts of the world

SIZE Up to 5.5 ft. (1.7m) long, excluding tail

ELK OR WAPITI

The elk, known as the red deer in Europe, is one of the world's most widespread deer. It lives in forests, woodland, and open hillsides, feeding on leaves, buds, and bark. Elk stags are larger than the females, called hinds. In prime breeding condition, they have shaggy manes and antlers up to 5 ft. (1.5m) long. In the fall mating season, they roar at their rivals, then lock antlers, pushing and twisting to throw each other off balance. Calves are born in late spring and have dappled fur for camouflage.

SCIENTIFIC NAME *Cervus elaphus*

DISTRIBUTION Originally from North America, Europe, northern Africa, northern Asia, Far East; introduced into New Zealand

SIZE Up to 9.5 ft. (2.9m) long, excluding tail

ABOVE *A herd of chitals drinks at a lake. Their spots help camouflage them on a sunlit forest floor.*

Male elk, or stag

SAMBAR

A close relative of the elk, this species lives in woodland, often on mountain slopes. It has a dark brown coat and unusually thick antlers with two or three branches. Male sambars can weigh as much as one fourth of a ton, and their antlers grow up to 3 ft. (1m) long.

SCIENTIFIC NAME *Cervus unicolor*

DISTRIBUTION Originally from southern and Southeast Asia; introduced into the United States, Australia, New Zealand

SIZE Up to 8 ft. (2.4m) long, excluding tail

RIGHT *While her fawn nudges her for attention, a female sambar listens intently for signs of nearby predators.*

MOOSE

Male moose

This is the world's largest deer. Males can weigh more than half a ton and have flattened antlers with a spread of up to 6 ft. (2m). Moose have long heads, drooping upper lips, and a flap of skin hanging beneath their throats. They live in woodland and open country. In winter, they eat twigs and bark; in summer, they wade into rivers and lakes to eat water plants. Adults live alone, but the calves stay with their mothers for a year.

SCIENTIFIC NAME *Alces alces*

DISTRIBUTION
Far north worldwide

SIZE Up to
10 ft. (3m) long,
excluding tail

RIGHT *A female roe deer sets off to find food.* **BELOW** *Père David's deer (Elaphurus davidianus) lives in China but is also kept in parks and zoos.*

Widely spaced branches

Antlers are larger in males

Velvet falls away in strips

RIGHT *This reindeer's antlers have finished growing, and their velvet is falling off. This happens in late summer—a difficult time for reindeer, because the peeling skin attracts flies.*

ROE DEER

Although it is a shy animal, this small, European deer has been remarkably successful at surviving alongside people. It normally lives in woodland, but also feeds in fields, leaping over walls and fences to find its food. It usually lives alone and feeds at night, a habit that allows it to avoid being seen by people. Male roe deer have short, spiky antlers. In the summer, males and females are plain, sandy brown, but their coloring darkens when they grow their winter coats.

SCIENTIFIC NAME
Capreolus capreolus

DISTRIBUTION Europe

SIZE Up to 4.5 ft. (1.4m) long,
excluding tail

REINDEER OR CARIBOU

This deer is the only species in which both males and females have antlers. Its hooves work like snowshoes, preventing it from sinking into the snow. This helps it survive in the far north, where snow can lie for up to six months a year. In Scandinavia, reindeer herds can be several hundred animals strong, but in North America, they can number more than 500,000. During the summer, these herds wander over the open tundra; in the fall, they trek to southern forests, traveling up to 65 mi. (100km) a day. Reindeer feed on leaves, twigs, and lichen, a mosslike plant that grows on trees and rocks. In Europe and Siberia, they were tamed more than 3,000 years ago, and they are still kept for meat and milk.

SCIENTIFIC NAME *Rangifer tarandus*

DISTRIBUTION Far north worldwide

SIZE Up to 7.5 ft. (2.3m) long,
excluding tail

PAMPAS DEER

Before farming began on the grassy plains, or pampas, of South America, this deer was a very common animal. Today, with most of its original habitat grazed by cattle, it is struggling to survive. The pampas deer has spotted fawns, but it is brown or gray when it is fully grown. The males have narrow antlers with two or three branches. Like other deer, this animal has a good sense of smell, and males mark their territory by scent. They have scent glands on their hooves, which leave a "signature" wherever they go.

SCIENTIFIC NAME	*Ozotoceros bezoarcticus*
DISTRIBUTION	South America, from Brazil to central Argentina
SIZE	Up to 4.5 ft. (1.4m) long, excluding tail

WHITETAIL DEER

No other deer can match this species, also known as the Virginia deer, in coping with different habitats. The whitetail deer can survive in forests in the cold Canadian subarctic, on dry mountainsides in Mexico, and in the steamy heat of Central and South America. One reason for this wide range is that it feeds on many different kinds of food, including leaves, bark, and fallen fruit. The whitetail deer's coat is reddish in the summer and gray in the winter. The deer got its name from a patch of white fur on the underside of its tail. When it is threatened, it runs for cover, holding up its tail. The flash of white acts as an alarm signal for other deer.

SCIENTIFIC NAME	*Odocoileus virginianus*
DISTRIBUTION	Originally from North, Central, and South America, from Canada to Brazil; introduced into Finland
SIZE	Up to 7 ft. (2.1m) long, excluding tail

SOUTHERN PUDU

Pudus are the smallest true deer in the world. There are only two kinds, both found in the forested foothills of the Andes Mountains. The southern pudu, the smaller species, weighs just 15 lb. (7kg) when fully grown. It has a sleek, rodentlike body, short legs, a tiny tail, and miniature antlers that look like a pair of spikes. Southern pudus have been endangered by hunting and the destruction of their forest home.

SCIENTIFIC NAME	*Pudu puda*
DISTRIBUTION	Chile, Argentina
SIZE	Up to 28 in. (71cm) long

Whitetail deer stag and doe with fawn

BELOW *Like most of its relatives, the pampas deer has scent glands just in front of its eyes and on its hooves.*

ANTLERS AND HORNS

Antlers and horns can look similar, but they are made from different substances and grow in different ways. Antlers are made of solid bone and are shed and regrown each year. They develop from two knobs on the top of a deer's skull and grow at their tips, like a plant sprouting from the ground. Antlers usually branch, and the number of branches often increases each time a new set grows. Horns are made of keratin, as are claws, nails, and hair. They grow from the bottom up and usually last throughout an animal's life. Horns are hollow and less heavy than they look. They are often curved, but never branch.

A moose with huge, flattened antlers

GIRAFFES AND OKAPIS

This family of mammals contains just two species, both found in Africa. Despite their different shapes, the giraffe and okapi share many features, including long legs, a long neck, and an extremely long, flexible tongue. Their front legs are longer than their back ones, which helps them reach the leaves they eat. Giraffes and okapis have short, stubby, skin-covered horns.

GIRAFFE

This is the world's tallest living animal. The average male is about 17 ft. (5m) tall, but the tallest giraffes on record have measured nearly 20 ft. (6m). Giraffes live in open woodland and gather food with their tongues. Their necks, which make up about half their height, allow them to reach leaves far above the ground. Their height helps them watch for danger, but if attacked, they fight back with a deadly kick.

Tough lips protect against thorns

SCIENTIFIC NAME	*Giraffa camelopardalis*
DISTRIBUTION	Africa, south of the Sahara Desert
SIZE	Up to 18 ft. (5.5m) high

Neck is lowered when the giraffe is drinking or sleeping standing up

Front legs are used for kicking enemies

ABOVE *The okapi is a daytime feeder. Its stripes break up its outline, making it harder to see.*

OKAPI

Until 1901, the okapi was unknown outside central Africa. It remained undiscovered for so long because it lives in dense rain forest and is seldom seen. From the shoulders down, it looks like a long-legged horse, with a brown coat and horizontal white stripes on its back legs and flanks. It has an extra-long neck, and its black tongue is long enough to lick its eyes. Okapis live alone, except when caring for their calves.

SCIENTIFIC NAME	*Okapia johnstoni*
DISTRIBUTION	Central Africa
SIZE	Up to 6 ft. (2m) long

PRONGHORNS

The pronghorn is a grazing mammal that is classified in a family of its own. With its hooves and short, hooked horns, it looks like a cross between a deer and an antelope. Unlike antelope and their relatives, it sheds and regrows its horns every year.

PRONGHORN

Pronghorns live in open prairie and scrub, where speed is essential for survival. It is the fastest hoofed mammal in the world, cruising at 30 mph (50km/h), but reaching over 50 mph (80km/h) in short bursts. It takes long bounds on its slender legs, and it has an unusual habit of shaking itself when it comes to a halt. Pronghorns have distinctive brown and white markings, and their horns are almost black. The horns curve backward at the tip, and in males, they also have a forward-pointing prong. Before Europeans arrived in North America, more than 30 million pronghorns roamed the prairies. By the 1920s, hunting and farming had reduced their numbers to about 20,000. Today, the pronghorn is protected, and the total population is nearly one million.

Male pronghorn with curving horns

LEFT *Giraffes have a number of different coat patterns, which vary from place to place. This is a reticulated giraffe, which has a netlike pattern of fairly straight, pale lines.*

SCIENTIFIC NAME	*Antilocapra americana*
DISTRIBUTION	Western United States, adjoining parts of Canada and Mexico
SIZE	Up to 5 ft. (1.5m) long, excluding tail

ANTELOPE, CATTLE, AND THEIR RELATIVES

With about 140 species, these animals make up the largest family of hoofed mammals. In the wild, their natural range covers most of the world, except for South America, Australia, and New Zealand. Their domesticated relatives, including cattle, sheep, and goats, are found almost everywhere. Many species are grazers, which means that they feed on grass, but others are browsers, eating the leaves of shrubs and trees. They have complicated digestive systems that enable them to break down the plants they eat. These animals often live in herds, which increases their chances of spotting danger and avoiding attack.

ABOVE For mammals like this nilgai, keen senses and quick reactions are essential for survival. Nilgais feed mostly at dawn and in the late afternoon, and are always ready to run if danger strikes. They can reach speeds of 30 mph—fast enough to escape predators as swift as the leopard, but only if they have a head start.

COMMON ELAND

This African animal is the world's largest antelope, with a maximum weight of just under a ton. From a distance, it looks like a pale brown cow or bull, but it has longer legs than farm cattle, and a longer neck with a narrower head. It also has straight horns with a spiral twist—a feature that is shared by many smaller antelope. Elands are browsers, feeding in open country scattered with trees. As well as eating leaves, they dig up roots with their hooves. Common elands are easy to tame and are sometimes farmed for their meat and milk.

SCIENTIFIC NAME	*Taurotragus oryx*
DISTRIBUTION	Tropical Africa
SIZE	Up to 11.5 ft. (3.5m) long, excluding tail

NILGAI OR BLUEBUCK

This is the largest antelope in Asia. The males can weigh more than 550 lb. (250kg), but as with most antelope, the females are smaller. Nilgai have sloping shoulders and small heads, and only the male has horns. They live in thorny scrub and rocky places, moving in small herds. They feed by grazing and browsing, and sometimes cause problems for farmers by raiding crops, especially sugar cane. Female nilgais usually give birth to twins at the beginning of the monsoon season, when food is easy to find.

SCIENTIFIC NAME	*Boselaphus tragocamelus*
DISTRIBUTION	India, Pakistan
SIZE	Up to 7 ft. (2.1m) long, excluding tail

GREATER KUDU

Of all Africa's antelope, the greater kudu has the most magnificent horns. They measure up to 3 ft. (1m) from base to tip, but because they are spiral-shaped, they are actually much longer than this. They are a mixed blessing because hunters kill kudus to take their horns as trophies. Greater kudus live in woodland and feed both day and night.

SCIENTIFIC NAME	*Tragelaphus strepsiceros*
DISTRIBUTION	Eastern, central, and southern Africa
SIZE	Up to 8 ft. (2.4m) long, excluding tail

CAPE BUFFALO

This buffalo is one of Africa's heaviest and most dangerous hoofed animals. Both sexes have large, curved horns; the bulls' horns meet at the base to form a shield called a boss. A bull buffalo can wound or even kill an adult lion with its horns. Cape buffalo live in grassland and forests. Grassland buffalo are gray; forest animals are smaller and reddish. Cape buffalo feed at dusk and at night, using their keen senses to detect danger.

SCIENTIFIC NAME	*Synceros caffer*
DISTRIBUTION	Tropical and southern Africa
SIZE	Up to 11 ft. (3.4m) long, excluding tail

WATER BUFFALO

This black-gray, Asian buffalo has the largest horns of any living animal—the longest pair on record measured more than 13 ft. (4m) from tip to tip. Water buffalo live in swamps and grassy places. These fairly peaceful animals were first domesticated about 5,000 years ago, and few of those alive today are truly wild.

SCIENTIFIC NAME	*Bubalus arnee*
DISTRIBUTION	Originally from southern and Southeast Asia; introduced into other parts of the world, including Australia, South America
SIZE	Up to 10 ft. (3m) long, excluding tail

ABOVE
Cape buffalo often play host to oxpeckers (page 224), birds that feed on parasites on the buffalo's skin.

RUMINANTS

Grass and leaves are easy to find, but they are hard to digest. To cope with this kind of food, some mammals have a four-chambered stomach and chew their food twice. These animals, called ruminants, include antelope, cattle, and their relatives, as well as deer, giraffes, okapis, and pronghorns. When ruminants swallow, the food travels into two stomach chambers, where it is mixed with saliva. Microorganisms feed on substances in the food, breaking it down and making it much easier for the animal to digest. The animal then regurgitates the food and chews it again, a process called chewing the cud. Once it has been swallowed for a second time, the food travels through the other two stomach chambers and is digested.

LOWLAND ANOA OR DWARF BUFFALO

This is the smallest buffalo in the world and one of the most endangered. Even when fully grown, the lowland anoa is often less than 3 ft. (1m) high at the shoulder, which makes it shorter than many species of deer. Lowland anoas live in tropical forests and lowland swamps. They have black coats and conical, backswept horns.

SCIENTIFIC NAME	*Bubalus depressicornis*
DISTRIBUTION	Island of Sulawesi in Indonesia
SIZE	Up to 6 ft. (2m) long, excluding tail

BELOW *Wallowing in a pool of mud, a water buffalo shows off its spectacular horns. Horns of this size appear heavy and cumbersome, but because they are hollow they are less heavy than they look. Like all horns, they keep growing throughout the buffalo's lifetime.*

Small intestine | Esophagus, or gullet

Four stomachs

ape buffalo showing -chambered stomach

VU QUANG OX OR SAO LA

This secretive forest animal was unknown to science as recently as 1992, when it was discovered in a remote part of Vietnam. It has dagger-shaped horns, like those of the gemsbok (page 299), and a dark brown coat. The Vu Quang ox almost certainly lives in herds and may be quite widespread. Because so few have been seen, little else is known about it.

SCIENTIFIC NAME *Pseudoryx nghetinhensis*
DISTRIBUTION Vietnam, possibly Laos
SIZE Up to 5 ft. (1.5m) long, excluding tail

YAK

With its long, shaggy coat and short, sturdy legs, the yak is well equipped for mountain life. It lives in the Himalayan Mountains and can survive above 20,000 ft. (6,000m)—higher than any other large mammal. Although it looks clumsy, it is a good climber, even at altitudes that would leave most animals gasping for lack of oxygen. Yaks were first domesticated more than 2,000 years ago, and tame animals now far outnumber those in the wild. They are smaller than wild yaks and are kept for meat, milk, and wool.

SCIENTIFIC NAME *Bos mutus*
DISTRIBUTION Tibet
SIZE Up to 10.5 ft. (3.2m) long, excluding tail

Domesticated yak carrying goods

AMERICAN BISON

Until the mid-1800s, when European settlers arrived on America's Great Plains, this was one of the world's most numerous grazing mammals. But in the 50 years that followed, so many bison were shot that the species came close to extinction. Compared to other wild cattle, the American bison looks front-heavy, with massive humped shoulders and an oversized head. Its head and forequarters are covered in shaggy, dark brown fur, which makes it look larger than it really is. American bison, often called buffalo, are highly sociable animals, and in the past, they formed vast herds more than 100,000 strong. Today's wild population totals only about 15,000 animals, confined mainly to national parks.

SCIENTIFIC NAME *Bison bison*
DISTRIBUTION North America
SIZE Up to 11.5 ft. (3.5m) long, excluding tail

American bison fighting during the breeding season

RIGHT *The European bison has a blunt, heavily built head, like its American relative. The European species nearly died out a century ago, but it survived because some animals were kept in zoos. Today, there are about 3,000 European bison and they are carefully protected.*

EUROPEAN BISON

The European bison is a forest animal, with a slightly smaller build and shorter fur than its American relative. It eats leaves in summer and bark and twigs in winter. Bison were once found throughout Europe, but today, herds survive only in Eastern Europe, where their original forest habitat is still intact.

SCIENTIFIC NAME *Bison bonasus*
DISTRIBUTION Poland, Belarus
SIZE Up to 11.5 ft. (3.5m) long, excluding tail

COMMON REEDBUCK

Reedbucks are African antelope that live in swamps and wet grassland. They have sandy-colored coats, and the males have short, ridged horns that point forward at the tips. There are three species of these animals. The common reedbuck is the largest, standing up to 3 ft. (1m) tall at the shoulder. Like its two relatives, it is a graceful animal and runs with high, bounding leaps. When reedbucks are alarmed, they make a whistling sound through their noses to warn the herd. If they catch the scent of a leopard or lion after dark, they can sustain this sound for more than half an hour.

SCIENTIFIC NAME	*Redunca arundinum*
DISTRIBUTION	Central and southern Africa
SIZE	Up to 4.5 ft. (1.4m) long, excluding tail

WATERBUCK

This sturdily built African antelope stands up to 4.5 ft. (1.4m) high at the shoulder and can weigh more than 450 lb. (200kg). It has a coarse, gray or red-brown coat, smeared with an oily substance that gives it a musky smell. The males have long, curved horns, with a slight bend that makes them look like a pair of tweezers. Waterbucks live up to their name by staying near water all the time. They feed mainly on grass. In the breeding season, the males defend their territories against rivals, sometimes injuring each other with their horns.

SCIENTIFIC NAME	*Kobus ellipsiprymnus*
DISTRIBUTION	Africa, south of the Sahara Desert
SIZE	Up to 7.5 ft. (2.3m) long, excluding tail

KOB

A close relative of the waterbuck, the kob is smaller, with shorter fur. It is usually light brown, with pale undersides and white rings around its eyes. The males have graceful, backswept horns. Kobs live on grassland close to rivers and waterholes, and they feed by grazing. Like many antelope, they bounce high into the air if they are threatened. This behavior, called stotting, may be a way of making predators believe that they can move quickly and are not worth chasing.

SCIENTIFIC NAME	*Kobus kob*
DISTRIBUTION	Tropical Africa
SIZE	Up to 6 ft. (2m) long, excluding tail

RIGHT *Sword-shaped horns and bold markings make the gemsbok easy to recognize. Compared to most other antelope, this handsome animal is good at defending itself—it has even been known to kill lions with its horns.*

BELOW *Waterbucks are usually safe in the open, but their liking for water brings danger. They are often caught by crocodiles, which lurk near the water's edge.*

Horns have sharp tips

Muscular neck

Herd of common wildebeest on the move

COMMON WILDEBEEST OR GNU

The common wildebeest is an ungainly-looking animal, with close-set eyes, an untidy beard and mane, and spindly legs. Despite its clumsy appearance, it is one of Africa's most successful grazers, forming some of the largest herds on earth. In Tanzania's Serengeti National Park, more than a million wildebeest migrate with the seasons, moving to find fresh grass. The females give birth at the start of the rainy season, and their calves can run soon after being born.

SCIENTIFIC NAME	*Connochaetes taurinus*
DISTRIBUTION	Eastern and southern Africa
SIZE	Up to 8 ft. (2.4m) long, excluding tail

GEMSBOK

The gemsbok belongs to a group of mammals called horse antelope, which get their name from their sturdy, horselike build. There are six species, and they all have long horns. Some have curved horns, but the gemsbok's are almost straight. They can be more than 3 ft. (1m) long with pointed tips, and are deadly weapons. Gemsboks survive well in dry places where water is hard to find. Instead of drinking, they get water from their food. They live in herds of up to 50 animals and breed throughout the year.

SCIENTIFIC NAME	*Oryx gazella*
DISTRIBUTION	Eastern and southwestern Africa
SIZE	Up to 5.5 ft. (1.7m) long, excluding tail

IMPALA

This sleek, graceful animal is one of Africa's most agile antelopes, capable of leaping more than 33 ft. (10m) in a single bound. It eats grass, leaves, and seeds it finds in open woodland and tree-studded savanna. Instead of staying in the open like most grazing antelope, impalas run for cover if they are threatened. Only male impalas have horns, but both sexes have a dark vertical stripe on their hindquarters and a tuft of black hair on their back legs.

SCIENTIFIC NAME	*Aepyceros melampus*
DISTRIBUTION	Eastern and southern Africa
SIZE	Up to 5 ft. (1.5m) long, including tail

HARTEBEEST

The hartebeest is a medium-sized antelope that lives on open grassland. It has sloping shoulders and short fur, and the males and females both have small, sharply bent horns, which grow from a bulge on the top of their heads. During the breeding season, the males use their horns to fight, but instead of standing up, rivals get down on their knees and push against each other in a test of strength. A century ago, the hartebeest was the most widespread African antelope, living as far north as Morocco and Egypt. After decades of hunting, it is now found only farther south.

SCIENTIFIC NAME	*Alcelaphus buselaphus*
DISTRIBUTION	Africa, south of the Sahara Desert
SIZE	Up to 8 ft. (2.4m) long, excluding tail

LEFT *This group of hartebeest is resting in the midday heat. They can survive without water by eating fruit and digging up roots.*

BELOW *Kirk's dik-diks got their name from the alarm call they make when they run from danger. The call warns other dik-diks to be alert and also lets other animals know that predators may be nearby.*
BOTTOM *These two klipspringers are using their scent glands to mark a bush. The scent will linger for several days to tell other klipspringers that they live in the area.*

ROYAL ANTELOPE

After the lesser mouse deer (page 290), the royal antelope is one of the smallest hoofed mammals in the world. When fully grown, it measures only about 10 in. (25cm) high at the shoulder and weighs roughly as much as a large chicken. The males' horns, the tiniest of any hoofed mammal, are only about 1 in. (2.5cm) long. Royal antelope live in dense forest, where they feed on leaves, flowers, and fruit. Solitary animals, they spend most of their time on their own, and they bound away like rabbits if they are disturbed.

SCIENTIFIC NAME	*Neotragus pygmaeus*
DISTRIBUTION	Tropical western Africa
SIZE	Up to 20 in. (50cm) long, excluding tail

KIRK'S DIK-DIK

This miniature antelope lives in dry African scrub—a habitat that teems with predators. Although it looks very vulnerable, it is able to look after itself. Its large eyes and ears are always alert for danger, and if it is alarmed, it runs away with zigzagging leaps, making it harder to catch. Dik-diks have furry crests on their heads and unusual noses that look like short snouts. The females normally give birth to one young at a time, but they can breed twice a year.

SCIENTIFIC NAME	*Madoqua kirki*
DISTRIBUTION	Kenya, Tanzania, Namibia, Angola
SIZE	Up to 28 in. (71cm) long, excluding tail

ORIBI

This long-necked animal is the largest of the dwarf antelope, a group that includes royal antelope, dik-diks, and klipspringers. It is the only one of these antelope that feeds mainly on grass, and it lives in places where the grass is short, so that it can keep watch for danger. The oribi feeds in groups of up to six animals. It is red-brown, with white underparts and a black tail. It also has a bare, black spot beneath each ear. This spot contains glands that release scent into the air.

SCIENTIFIC NAME	*Ourebia ourebi*
DISTRIBUTION	Africa, south of the Sahara Desert
SIZE	Up to 4.5 ft. (1.4m) long, excluding tail

KLIPSPRINGER

For an antelope, the klipspringer lives in a very unusual habitat—rocky outcrops and cliffs. It stands on the tips of its small, rubbery hooves, which give it extremely good grip. It jumps from rock to rock and can

Scent gland in front of eye

Small, pointed hooves

stand on ledges just a few inches wide. Klipspringers live in small groups, feeding on shrubs that grow among the rocks. They have rough, gray-brown fur, and the males have short, spiky horns.

SCIENTIFIC NAME
Oreotragus oreotragus

DISTRIBUTION Eastern and southwestern Africa, isolated groups in northern Nigeria

SIZE Up to 3 ft. (1m) long, excluding tail

THOMSON'S GAZELLE

Gazelles are medium-sized antelope with sleek, lithe bodies and slender legs. Most of them, including Thomson's gazelle, have golden-brown upper parts, white undersides, and curved horns ringed with ridges along their length. Both the females and the males grow horns. Thomson's gazelles feed in open grassland, and they live in straggling herds that can contain several thousand animals. To survive in the open, they must be vigilant at all times. Although they often lie down, they sleep for no more than an hour a day, in short bursts of five minutes or less. Thomson's gazelles begin to breed when they are two years old. The females usually have two young each year, roughly six months apart.

SCIENTIFIC NAME *Gazella thomsoni*

DISTRIBUTION Eastern Africa

SIZE Up to 3.5 ft. (1.1m) long, excluding tail

SPRINGBOK

During the 1800s, springboks formed some of the largest herds on earth. Some herds contained at least 10 million animals and were over 90 mi. (150km) long. Today, this brightly colored antelope is not as common as it was, but it has been reintroduced into many parks and game reserves. Springboks get their name from their amazing jumping ability. They can leap up to 11.5 ft. (3.5m) and seem to bounce up again when they hit the ground. Their most unusual feature is a fold of skin running along their backs. When they are excited or alarmed, the fold turns out to show a crest of white hairs.

SCIENTIFIC NAME *Antidorcas marsupialis*

DISTRIBUTION Southern and southwestern Africa

SIZE Up to 4.5 ft. (1.4m) long, excluding tail

BELOW Thomson's gazelles live in open grassland, where they have the best chance of spotting predators before they attack. In some parts of eastern Africa, these antelope form herds thousands of animals strong.

GERENUK

This African gazelle has an exceptionally long neck, and it stands on its back legs to feed on the leaves of trees and shrubs. It uses its front legs to keep itself steady and to pull branches within reach. Although the gerenuk measures only 3 ft. (1m) tall at the shoulder, it can reach 6 ft. (2m) high for food.

SCIENTIFIC NAME *Litocranius walleri*

DISTRIBUTION Eastern Africa

SIZE Up to 5.5 ft. (1.7m) long, excluding tail

Springbok leaping high into the air, or stotting, before fleeing from danger

BLACKBUCK

This Asian antelope is one of the few species in which the males and females look very different. Female and young blackbucks are yellow-brown with white undersides, but adult males have dark brown or black backs and white undersides. The males have spiral-shaped horns that can grow up to 24 in. (61cm) long. Blackbucks are grazers, and they live on open, grassy ground.

SCIENTIFIC NAME *Antilope cervicapra*

DISTRIBUTION India, Pakistan

SIZE Up to 4 ft. (1.2m) long, excluding tail

SAIGA

Like all the animals on these two pages, the saiga belongs to a group of hoofed mammals called goat-antelope. These animals are all very hardy, and many of them live in places where winters can be very cold. The saiga comes from the open plains of central Asia. It is a strange-looking animal with sandy-colored fur, downward-pointing nostrils, and a swollen muzzle. This may help the saiga in winter, by warming frosty air before it reaches the lungs.

SCIENTIFIC NAME	*Saiga tatarica*
DISTRIBUTION	Central Asia
SIZE	Up to 5.5 ft. (1.7m) long, excluding tail

Cretan wild goat

Appenine wild goat

CHAMOIS

Chamois on rocky ledge

As a mountaineer, the chamois is in a class of its own. It can run up almost sheer rock faces on its nonslip hooves, jumping from ledge to ledge. It runs downhill with equal skill, dropping up to 20 ft. (6m) in a single leap. Even chamois just a few days old can make these death-defying leaps. Chamois are compact, elegant animals with short horns that bend back to form a hook. They live high above the treeline during the summer, but during the winter, they come lower down to feed in forests.

SCIENTIFIC NAME	*Rupicapra rupicapra*
DISTRIBUTION	Originally from southern and central Europe, western Asia; introduced into New Zealand
SIZE	Up to 4.5 ft. (1.4m) long, excluding tail

American mountain goat

ABOVE *There are eight species of wild goats, mostly in mountains and rocky places. The Cretan and Appenine wild goats (Capra aegagrus) are both closely related to the domesticated goats kept on farms. The American mountain goat lives at high altitudes and has a thick coat.*

AMERICAN MOUNTAIN GOAT

Compared to the chamois, this goat is slow-moving, but it is an expert at surviving in difficult conditions. It lives on rocks near the snowline, feeding on grasses and low-growing plants. American mountain goats have long coats of white hair that extend down their legs like pants. This long hair shrugs off rain and snow, and a layer of wool underneath keeps the animal warm. American mountain goats have small horns and live in herds of up to ten animals.

SCIENTIFIC NAME	*Oreamnos americanus*
DISTRIBUTION	North America, from Alaska to the Pacific Northwest
SIZE	Up to 5.5 ft. (1.7m) long, excluding tail

MUSK OX

Although it looks like a buffalo, the musk ox is much more closely related to the chamois and the mountain goat. It lives in the Arctic tundra, kept warm by a shaggy coat of long, brown hair that reaches almost to the ground during the winter months. Its hooves are extra-large, which keeps it from sinking into the snow. Both sexes have large, downcurved horns that meet in the middle of their heads. Musk oxen live in herds of up to 100 animals and keep on the move constantly. If they are threatened—by wolves, for example—the adults group together to form a ring, with their calves hidden inside.

SCIENTIFIC NAME	*Ovibos moschatus*
DISTRIBUTION	Northern Canada, Greenland
SIZE	Up to 7.5 ft. (2.3m) long, excluding tail

ALPINE IBEX

This sure-footed wild goat lives high in the European Alps. It spends most of its life far above the treeline, where it eats mainly grass. Both sexes have large, backswept horns, but the males' are particularly impressive, reaching up to 4.5 ft. (1.4m) long. Alpine ibexes have long been hunted, and they also face danger from avalanches during the spring thaw. Over a century ago, the species was reduced to just one herd, containing about 60 animals. Since then, Alpine ibexes have been given protection, and their numbers have recovered to about 10,000.

SCIENTIFIC NAME	*Capra ibex*
DISTRIBUTION	Italy, France, Middle East, central Asia
SIZE	Up to 5 ft. (1.5m) long, excluding tail

RIGHT *This bighorn sheep is calling to rival males. If one is close, fighting will break out.*

LEFT *An Alpine ibex prepares to jump from a ledge. This exceptionally hardy animal lives at altitudes of up to 6,500 ft.*

*Impressive
horns spiral
around as
they grow*

*Short,
thick
summer
coat*

MOUFLON

Most experts think that this wild sheep,
originally from southwestern Asia, is either the
direct ancestor of today's domesticated sheep or
one of their closest living relatives. Compared to
farmed sheep, mouflons are sturdy animals. They
have coarse, black-brown hair, but in the winter
they also grow a layer of softer wool underneath.
The males have large horns that curve back
toward their shoulders, and they fight fiercely
during the breeding season, clashing head on.
Mouflons live in mountains in herds of up to
20 animals. They feed on a wide range of
plant food.

SCIENTIFIC NAME	*Ovis orientalis*
DISTRIBUTION	Southwestern Asia, Europe
SIZE	Up to 4.5 ft. (1.4m) long, excluding tail

*Curved
horns*

Male mouflon, or ram   **Female mouflon, or ewe**

BIGHORN SHEEP

Only two kinds of wild sheep live in North
America, and this species is easily the most
widespread. It lives on rocky
hillsides from southwestern
Canada to Baja California
in Mexico—a range of about
2,000 mi. (3,000km). Bighorn
sheep are gray-brown with
white hindquarters. The
females' small horns are
almost straight, but the males'
horns are curved and much
larger. For males, horns are
both weapons and status symbols.
In old males, they often curve
around so far that they form
a full circle.

**Male bighorn
sheep clashing
head on**

SCIENTIFIC NAME	*Ovis canadensis*
DISTRIBUTION	Western North America, from Canada to northern Mexico
SIZE	Up to 5.5 ft. (1.7m) long, excluding tail

GLOSSARY

The glossary explains most of the technical terms that are used in this book. Here you can find words that refer to animal body parts, life cycles, and behavior, as well as some of the processes that affect animals as a whole. Where a definition includes words in CAPITAL LETTERS, it means that these words have entries of their own. If you want to find out about particular animals or animal groups, refer to the index on pages 308–319.

Red fox *(Vulpes vulpes)*

ABDOMEN
The part of an animal's body that contains ORGANS used for DIGESTION, the elimination of waste, and reproduction. In arachnids, crustaceans, and insects, the abdomen is at the rear of the body.

ALGA (plural: ALGAE)
Plantlike ORGANISMS that often live in water. Most algae are microscopic, but seaweeds, which are the largest algae, can be several yards long.

AMPHIBIOUS
Describes an ORGANISM that lives both on land and in water.

ANTENNA (plural: ANTENNAE)
A long, slender structure on an animal's head that is used to gather information by touching or smelling. Antennae are sometimes called feelers.

ARTHROPOD
An animal that has a hard EXOSKELETON and legs that bend at joints. Arthropods include insects, spiders, and crustaceans.

BALEEN
The fibrous substance that large whales use to filter food from the water. Baleen hangs down like a curtain from the whale's upper jaw.

BARBEL
A fleshy feeler on the head of a fish. Barbels sense things by touch and taste.

BIOLUMINESCENCE
The production of light by living things. It is common in insects, fish, and simple animals that live in the ocean.

BLOWHOLE
A hole on the head of a dolphin or a whale that is used for breathing. It closes when the animal dives, to prevent water from getting into the lungs.

BLUBBER
A thick layer of fat that helps some sea animals keep warm. Whales, seals, polar bears, and penguins have blubber.

BROWSER
A plant-eating animal that feeds on leaves and shoots from trees and bushes, rather than on grass. Deer are typical browsers.

BYSSUS
A collection of tough threads that some bivalve mollusks use to fasten themselves in place.

CAMOUFLAGE
A pattern or coloration that helps an animal blend in with its surroundings. Animals use camouflage to ambush their PREY or to hide from enemies.

CANINE TEETH
Long, pointed teeth that meat-eating mammals have at the front of their mouths. The animals use their canine teeth to stab and grip food.

CARAPACE
A hard case or shield on an animal's back that protects its body. Crabs, tortoises, and turtles are examples of animals with a carapace.

CARNASSIAL TEETH
Long, sharp-edged teeth that meat-eating mammals have near the back of their jaws. Animals use their carnassial teeth to slice through food.

CARNIVORE
Any animal that eats meat. Also used to refer to a mammal that specializes in hunting other animals.

CARTILAGE
A rubbery substance found in the skeletons of VERTEBRATES. Cartilage helps cushion bones where they meet at joints. It also forms some parts of the body, such as the nose and ears. In cartilaginous fish, the whole skeleton is made of cartilage, instead of bone.

CASQUE
A hard "helmet" on a bird's head or on the top of its beak.

CELL
A microscopic unit of living matter. Cells carry out the basic processes that keep an animal or plant alive, although they often specialize in particular tasks. Most animals have millions of cells in their bodies, but the simplest living things have only one cell.

CHRYSALIS
A hard case that protects a caterpillar during its METAMORPHOSIS into a butterfly or moth.

CILIUM (plural: CILIA)
A microscopic, hairlike thread on the surface of a CELL. Living things use cilia to move themselves or other objects.

CLUTCH
A group of eggs laid at one time by a female animal, such as a bird or a reptile.

COCOON
A silk case spun by an insect or a spider, which it uses to protect itself or its eggs.

COLD-BLOODED
Describes an animal whose body stays at the same temperature as its surroundings. Cold-blooded animals are active when it is warm, but when the temperature drops, they slow down or stop altogether.

COLONY
A group of animals living together as a single unit. Some colony-forming animals are permanently joined together.

COMPOUND EYE
An eye that is divided into many separate compartments, which work together to produce a picture. Crustaceans and insects have compound eyes.

COURTSHIP
The behavior an animal uses to attract a partner to mate. Male animals use courtship behavior to show that they are fit and healthy and will make suitable partners.

DEFORESTATION
The deliberate destruction of forests by people, either to supply timber or to create open ground that can be farmed.

DIGESTION
The breaking down of food so that it can be absorbed and used by the body. Animals chew or grind up their food before powerful chemicals inside their bodies turn it into simpler substances.

DISTRIBUTION
All the places in the world where a species lives.

DOMESTICATED ANIMAL
An animal that is kept by people, instead of living wild. Some domesticated animals are kept as pets; others are used for food or for work.

DOWN FEATHERS
The fluffy feathers that a bird has next to its skin. Down feathers trap a layer of air, which keeps the bird warm.

ECHOLOCATION
A method some animals use to navigate and to find food. The animal produces bursts of high-pitched sound. The echoes from the sounds bounce back to the animal, which can then tell what is nearby. Animals that use echolocation include bats, whales, and dolphins.

EGG
A CELL that can develop into a new animal. Nearly all animals reproduce by making eggs, but their eggs develop differently. In most animals, the eggs are laid, and they develop outside the mother. In mammals and some other animals, they develop inside the mother's body.

ELYTRON (plural: **ELYTRA**)
The hardened forewing of a beetle. Beetles have two elytra. They fit over the ABDOMEN like a case, protecting the hind wings when not in use.

EVOLUTION
A very slow process of change that enables living things to adapt to the world around them. Instead of happening in a single lifetime, evolution takes place over many generations. During evolution, new SPECIES develop, replacing those that have become extinct.

EXOSKELETON
A skeleton that is around the outside of an animal's body, instead of inside it. Exoskeletons provide both protection and a solid structure for an animal's muscles to pull against.

EXTINCTION
The permanent disappearance of a SPECIES. Extinction can be caused by a number of things, including competition from other species, natural disasters, and hunting by people.

EYESPOT
A very simple eye, or a patch of color that looks like an eye.

FANG
A tooth or other mouthpart that is designed to stab. Some fangs inject poison, helping animals to overpower their PREY.

FERAL ANIMAL
A domesticated animal that has escaped from human control and taken up life in the wild.

FERTILIZATION
The process that enables a male cell and a female cell to join together, to form a single EGG.

FILTER FEEDER
An animal that gets its food by straining it from water.

FLIGHT FEATHERS
The large feathers that form the surface of a bird's wing and tail, enabling it to fly.

FLUKE
A whale or dolphin's tail. Unlike a fish's tail, it beats up and down, rather than from side to side.

GESTATION PERIOD
In mammals, the time it takes a young animal to develop inside its mother's body, from the moment of FERTILIZATION to the time it is born.

GILL
A body part that water-dwelling animals use to collect OXYGEN from the water. Gills may stick out from the body, or they may be hidden inside.

GLAND
A body part that produces particular substances, such as venom or MUCUS.

GRAZER
A plant-eating animal that feeds mainly on grass, rather than on the leaves and shoots of trees and bushes.

GRUB
A young insect that has either very short legs or no legs at all. (See LARVA)

HABITAT
The surroundings that a particular SPECIES needs to survive. Habitats include forests, grasslands, deserts, and coral reefs. Most species live in just one habitat, but some can survive in several.

HEMOGLOBIN
A red substance that carries OXYGEN in an animal's blood.

HALTERE
In flies, a small, drumstick-shaped ORGAN that replaces the hind wings. Halteres help flies balance in the air.

HIBERNATION
A deep winter sleep. Animals hibernate to survive through a time of year when food is hard to find.

HOST
An animal that a PARASITE uses as its home and food.

INCUBATION
The act of sitting on eggs to keep them warm. Birds must incubate their eggs, which do not develop properly if they are cold.

Holly blue (male)

Holly blue (female)
(*Celastrina argiolus*)

Clouded yellow
(*Colia crocea*)

Painted lady
(*Cynthia cardui*)

Peacock
(*Inachis io*)

Red admiral
(*Vanessa atalanta*)

Fulmar
(*Fulmarus glacialis*)

Great shearwater
(*Puffinus gravis*)

Little gull
(*Larus minutus*)

Cory's shearwater
(*Calonectris diomedea*)

Alpine swift
(*Apus melba*)

INSTINCT
The natural impulse that enables animals to follow a pattern of behavior without having to learn it first.

INSULATION
Something that slows down the flow of heat. Animals use fur, feathers, and fat as insulation to help them keep warm. (See BLUBBER, DOWN FEATHERS)

INTRODUCED SPECIES
A SPECIES that people have taken from one part of the world and released into another. In some areas, introduced animals have had a bad effect on local wildlife.

INVERTEBRATE
Any animal that does not have a backbone.

KERATIN
A strong but flexible substance in body parts that are often exposed to rubbing and pressure. These body parts include hair, fur, hooves, horns, and beaks.

LARVA (plural: LARVAE)
A young animal that looks completely different from its parents and changes shape as it matures. In many animals, the larva concentrates on feeding, while the adult concentrates on reproduction.

LEK
A place where male animals gather during the breeding season to attract females. The males often fight to be in the center of the lek.

LIFE CYCLE
All the stages in the life of an animal, including the way it starts life, the way it develops, and the way it breeds.

MANTLE
A fold of skin around the body of a mollusk. In most mollusks, it produces substances that harden to form a shell.

MEMBRANE
A thin film or a sheet of skin.

METAMORPHOSIS
The change in body shape that takes place as an animal grows. It can occur in many stages, as when a tadpole turns into a frog, or in just one, as when a caterpillar turns into a butterfly.

MIGRATION
A long journey that animals make to breed or to find food. Most animals migrate along set routes, guided by INSTINCT.

MIMIC
An animal, especially among insects, that imitates something else, often to avoid being eaten. Some mimics look like twigs or stones, but others imitate poisonous animals.

MOLAR TEETH
Teeth that mammals have at the back of their jaws, where their bite is strongest. Molar teeth are used to crush and chew food.

MOLTING
The shedding of an outer covering, such as fur, feathers, or skin. Animals that have EXOSKELETONS have to molt as they grow, because the skeletons do not grow with them.

MUCUS
A frothy or slimy liquid produced by an animal. Animals use mucus in many different ways. Slugs and snails use it to slide along, some insects use it to hide from predators, and treefrogs often use it to make their nests.

MUSCLE
A body part that makes an animal move. Muscles often work in pairs—one contracts while one relaxes—to move parts of an animal's body.

MUSK
An oily, strong-smelling substance produced by some mammals, such as deer.

NACRE
The smooth, shiny substance that makes up the inner surface of a mollusk's shell. Also known as "mother of pearl."

NECTAR
A sugary liquid produced by flowers. Plants make nectar to attract animals. In return for nectar, animal visitors spread the plants' POLLEN.

NEMATOCYST
In cnidarians, a specialized CELL that can shoot out a poison-tipped thread.

NOCTURNAL
An animal that is active mainly or entirely at night.

NOMADIC
An animal that does not have a fixed home. Nomadic animals usually stay on the move, traveling wherever there is food.

NOTOCHORD
In chordates, a reinforcing rod that runs down the body.

NYMPH
A young insect that resembles its parents but does not have fully formed wings or reproductive ORGANS.

OPERCULUM
A movable flap that seals an opening in an animal's body.

ORGAN
A part of the body that carries out particular tasks, such as DIGESTION, hearing, or breathing.

ORGANISM
Any living thing.

OXYGEN
An element that all animals need in order to get energy from the air, and dissolved oxygen is in fresh and salt water.

PARASITE
An animal that feeds on or inside another living animal, called the HOST. Unlike a PREDATOR, a parasite is usually much smaller than the animal it attacks.

PECTORAL FINS
A pair of fins on the underside of a fish, usually close to its head.

PELVIC FINS
A pair of fins on the underside of a fish, usually close to its tail.

PLANKTON
Microscopic plant and animal life that drifts near the surface of lakes and oceans. Plankton contains ALGAE, which collect energy from sunlight, and tiny animals, which eat algae or each other.

POLLEN
A dustlike substance that flowers make to produce seeds. Many plants use animals to spread their pollen from one flower to another.

POLYP
An animal that has a tube-shaped body, with a ring of TENTACLES around its mouth.

PREDATOR
Any animal that lives by hunting others.

PREHENSILE
Describes something that can wrap around objects to hold on to them or to pick them up. Elephants have prehensile trunks, and some monkeys have prehensile tails.

PREY
The animals that a PREDATOR hunts for food.

PROBOSCIS
A nose or a collection of long mouthparts. An elephant's trunk is a proboscis, as is a butterfly's tongue.

PROTOZOAN
A simple, animal-like ORGANISM that is made up of a single CELL. Protozoans live mainly in water or in damp HABITATS, such as soil.

PSEUDOPOD
An outgrowth from a CELL that works as a temporary foot. Many protozoans use pseudopods to move, as do some cells in an animal's body.

PUPA (plural: PUPAE)
A resting stage during the LIFE CYCLE of an insect. Inside the pupa, the young insect's body is broken down, and an adult one is assembled in its place. A pupa usually has a hard outer case and is often hidden inside a COCOON.

RUMEN
The large stomach chamber that many plant-eating mammals use to break down their food.

RUMINANT
A plant-eating mammal that has hooves and a four-chambered stomach. Deer, antelope, and cattle are all ruminants.

SCALES
Hard flaps that cover an animal's body. Scales usually help protect animals from attack, but in some butterflies and moths, they help keep the body warm.

SCAVENGER
An animal that lives on leftovers, including dead remains that have been left by PREDATORS.

SEGMENTS
Similar body parts that are arranged in a line. Segments are easy to see in earthworms and in the ABDOMENS of many insects.

SILK
Stretchy, natural fibers that insects and spiders make from a special liquid. These animals use silk to catch food, to help them move, or to protect themselves or their eggs.

SIPHON
An open-ended tube in an animal's body that sucks in or squirts out water.

SOARING
Gliding by rising on currents of warm air.

SPECIES
A single type of living thing. The members of a species can all breed with each other, but they normally do not breed with other species.

SPERM
CELLS produced by male animals for reproduction. Sperm cells usually have tiny "tails" that are used to swim toward female cells to fertilize them.

SPINNERET
In insects and spiders, a nozzle that produces silk.

SWIM BLADDER
A gas-filled bag inside a fish that works as an adjustable float to keep the fish from sinking through the water or rising to the surface.

SYMBIOSIS
A partnership that involves two different SPECIES of animals living together. By teaming up, each partner has a better chance of survival. Both partners may be animals, or one may be an animal and one a plant.

TALONS
The sharp claws that birds of prey use to attack other animals.

TENTACLES
Long, fleshy "feelers" that some animals use to catch their food.

TERRITORY
A space that is claimed by an animal, usually so it can breed. Most territories are set up by males. Females can enter, but rival males are chased away.

THORAX
The middle part of an animal's body. In insects, the thorax is the part that has legs and wings attached to it.

TRACHEA
A tube that allows air to flow into the body. In mammals, it is also known as a windpipe.

VENOMOUS
Describes an animal that is able to produce venom, or poison.

VERTEBRA (plural: VERTEBRAE)
One of several bones that link together to form the backbone. Vertebrae fit together at joints, allowing the backbone to bend.

VERTEBRATE
Any animal that has a backbone.

VOCAL SAC
An inflatable pouch of skin that helps an animal produce sound.

WARM-BLOODED
Describes an animal whose body stays at a steady, warm temperature. Warm-blooded animals are well insulated and can stay active even in the cold.

WARNING COLORS
Bright colors that warn that an animal is poisonous or dangerous in some way. Yellow and red are common warning colors.

Leopard
(Panthera pardus)

INDEX

ACKNOWLEDGMENTS

The publishers would like to thank the following for their contributions to this book:

Photographs

(*t* = top; *c* = center; *b* = bottom; *l* = left; *r* = right)

Front cover: Color library images. Page 1 *c* Warren Photographic; 3 *c* OSF; 4 *cl* Warren Photographic, *cl* Warren Photographic; 5 *cl* Warren Photographic, *br* NHPA, *tr* Kingfisher; 6 *tr* Warren Photographic, *c* Warren Photographic; 7 *cr* Warren Photographic, *br* Warren Photographic; 12 *c* NHPA, *cl* Warren Photographic; 13 *cr* Warren Photographic, *tl* Warren Photographic; 14 *cl* NHPA; 14–15 t Warren Photographic; 15 *cr* OSF, *crb* Warren Photographic; 16 *tl* OSF, *br* Warren Photographic; 17 *tr* OSF, *cr* OSF, *br* Warren Photographic; 18 *bl* Warren Photographic, *tr* Warren Photographic; 18–19 *t* Warren Photographic; 19 *b* Warren Photographic; 20 *br* Warren Photographic; 20–21 *t* Warren Photographic; 21 *bl* Warren Photographic, *tc* Warren Photographic; 22 *b* OSF, *cl* Warren Photographic; 23 *bc* NHPA, *tr* Warren Photographic; 24 *tl* NHPA; 25 *b* NHPA, *cl* Warren Photographic; 26–27 *c* OSF; 27 *tr* OSF, *c* Warren Photographic; 28 *tl* Warren Photographic; 29 *l* NHPA; 30–31 *c* NHPA; 31 *br* NHPA; 32 *bl* Warren Photographic, *cl* Warren Photographic; 32–33 *t* NHPA; 34 *cl* NHPA, *tl* Warren Photographic; 35 *bc* Warren Photographic, *tl* Warren Photographic; 36 *cl* OSF, *bl* Warren Photographic; 36–37 *t* Warren Photographic; 37 *cr* OSF; 38 *bc* Warren Photographic, *bl* Warren Photographic; 38–39 *t* OSF; 39 *br* Warren Photographic; 40 *c* Warren Photographic; 40–41 *b* Warren Photographic; 41 *trt* Warren Photographic, 41 *trb* Warren Photographic; 42 *t* NHPA; 43 *br* Warren Photographic; 44 *tl* Warren Photographic, *cl* Warren Photographic; 44–45 *b* OSF; 45 *cr* Warren Photographic; 46 *cl* Warren Photographic; 47 *rt* NHPA; 48 *cl* Warren Photographic; 49 *cr* Warren Photographic, *b* OSF; 50 *bl* Warren Photographic, *tr* Warren Photographic; 51 *br* Warren Photographic; 52 *bc* Warren Photographic, *bl* Warren Photographic, *tr* Warren Photographic; 53 *c* Warren Photographic; 54 *cl* Warren Photographic; 55 *tr* Warren Photographic; 56 *bl* Warren Photographic, *cl* Warren Photographic; 57 *t* Warren Photographic; 58 *cl* Warren Photographic, *tr* Warren Photographic; 59 *bc* Warren Photographic, *c* Warren Photographic; 60 *cl* Warren Photographic; 60–61 *t* Warren Photographic; 61 *tr* Warren Photographic; 62 *b* Warren Photographic; 63 *t* Warren Photographic; 64 *tl* Warren Photographic, *tr* OSF; 65 *br* Warren Photographic; 66 *tl* Warren Photographic; 67 *c* Warren Photographic, *tr* Warren Photographic; 68 *cr* Warren Photographic; 69 *tl* Warren Photographic; *b* Warren Photographic; 70 *cl* Warren Photographic, *t* Warren Photographic; 71 *b* Warren Photographic, *cl* Warren Photographic; 72 *cl* Warren Photographic; 73 *tr* Warren Photographic; 74 *t* Warren Photographic; 75 *t* Warren Photographic; 76 *bl* Warren Photographic; 76–77 *c* Warren Photographic; 78 *tl* Warren Photographic; 79 *tr* Warren Photographic; 80 *b* Warren Photographic; 81 *bl* Warren Photographic, *tl* Warren Photographic; 82 *r* Warren Photographic; 83 *l* Warren Photographic; 84 *b* Warren Photographic; 85 *tc* Warren Photographic; 86 *bl* Warren Photographic, *l* NHPA; 86–87 *t* Warren Photographic; 87 *cr* Warren Photographic; 88 *tl* Warren Photographic; 89 *bl* Warren Photographic, *t* Warren Photographic; 91 *bc* Warren Photographic, *l* NHPA; 92–93 *t* Warren Photographic; 93 *c* Warren Photographic; 94 *cr* STILL Pictures; 94–95 *t* STILL Pictures; 95 *bl* OSF, *br* OSF; 96 *t* NHPA; 97 *b* STILL Pictures; 98 *br* STILL Pictures; 98–99 *t* NHPA; 100 *cl* OSF; 101 *tr* STILL Pictures, *cl* OSF; 102–103 *t* Warren Photographic, *c* NHPA; 103 *b* NHPA; 104 *b* NHPA; 105 *t* NHPA; 106 *t* Warren Photographic; 107 *b* Warren Photographic, *bc* Warren Photographic; 108 *c* STILL Pictures; 109 *br* Warren Photographic; 110 *bl* Warren Photographic; 110–111 *t* Warren Photographic; 111 *tr* Warren Photographic; 112 *cr* OSF, *cl* OSF; 113 *b* Warren Photographic; 114 *r* Warren Photographic; 115 *b* Warren Photographic, *cr* Warren Photographic; 116 *cl* Warren Photographic, *b* Warren Photographic; 118 *bl* NHPA; 118–119 *c* NHPA; 119 *tr* NHPA; 120 *cl* OSF, *bc* NHPA; 121 *t* Warren Photographic; 122 *bl* OSF; 123 *t* Warren Photographic; 124 *b* OSF; 125 *tr* STILL Pictures, *cl* NHPA; 127 *cr* Warren Photographic; 128 *cl* Warren Photographic, *tc* Warren Photographic; 129 *t* Warren Photographic; 130 *bl* NHPA; *r* STILL Pictures; 132 *t* OSF; 133 *cr* Warren Photographic, *br* NHPA; 134–135 *b* Warren Photographic; 135 *t* Warren Photographic, *c* Warren Photographic; 136 *c* Warren Photographic, *b* Warren Photographic; 137 *tr* Warren Photographic; 138 *bc* OSF; 138–139 *t* Warren Photographic; 139 *br* Warren Photographic; 140 *cr* Warren Photographic, *t* Warren Photographic; 141 *br* Warren Photographic; 142 *cl* Warren Photographic; 142–143 *b* Warren Photographic; 143 *tr* Warren Photographic; 144–145 *t* Warren Photographic, *b* Warren Photographic; 146 *b* Warren Photographic; 147 *tr* Warren Photographic, *br* NHPA; 148–149 *t* Warren Photographic; 149 *br* Warren Photographic, *cr* NHPA; 150 *b* Warren Photographic; 151 *tr* OSF; 152 *tl* OSF, *br* OSF; 153 *br* Warren Photographic, *b* NHPA; 154 *c* Warren Photographic, *tr* Warren Photographic; 155 *t* Warren Photographic, *bl* Warren Photographic, *cl* Warren Photographic; 156 *bc* OSF; 156–157 *t* NHPA; 157 *cr* Warren Photographic; 158 *tr* Warren Photographic, *cl* Warren Photographic; 159 *l* Warren Photographic; 160 *br* Warren Photographic; 161 *b* Warren Photographic; 162 *bl* OSF; 163 *c* OSF, *cr* OSF; 164 *bl* NHPA; 165 *tr* Warren Photographic; *b* Warren Photographic; 166 *tr* Warren Photographic, *bl* NHPA; 167 *bc* Warren Photographic, *tr* STILL Pictures; 168 *bc* Warren Photographic; 168–169 *c* Warren Photographic; 169 *tc* Warren Photographic; 170 *l* Warren Photographic; 171 *bl* OSF; 172 *tl* Warren Photographic; 173 *b* OSF; 174 *b* Warren Photographic; 175 *tr* STILL Pictures, *cl* NHPA; 176 *tl* Warren Photographic; 177 *l* Warren Photographic; 178 *cl* NHPA; 179 *b* Warren Photographic, *tc* NHPA; 180 *cr* NHPA, *l* OSF; 181 *tr* STILL Pictures; 182 *l* OSF, 183 *tl* OSF; 184–185 *b* Warren Photographic; 185 *t* Warren Photographic; 186 *bl* NHPA; 187 *br* NHPA, *t* OSF; 188 *cl* Warren Photographic; 188–189 *b* Warren Photographic; 189 *tr* NHPA; 190 *bl* Warren Photographic, *tr* Warren Photographic; 191 *c* Warren Photographic; 191 *tr* Warren Photographic; 192 *bl* Warren Photographic, *b* Warren Photographic; 192–193 *b* Warren Photographic; 194 *cr* Warren Photographic, *t* Warren Photographic; 195 *br* Warren Photographic; 196 *l* Warren Photographic, *br* Warren Photographic; 197 *tc* Warren Photographic; 198 *l* Warren Photographic; 199 *tl* Warren Photographic; 200 *b* Warren Photographic; 201 *cr* Warren Photographic; 202 *bl* NHPA; 203 *tc* Warren Photographic; 204 *c* Warren Photographic; 205 *cr* STILL Pictures; 206 *t* Warren Photographic; 207 *br* OSF; 208 *t* Warren Photographic; 209 *tr* Warren Photographic; 210 *cl* OSF, *bl* OSF; 211 *l* NHPA, *tr* OSF; 212 *cl* Warren Photographic, *br* Warren Photographic; 213 *cr* Warren Photographic; 214 *c* Warren Photographic, *cl* Warren Photographic; 215 *br* Warren Photographic, *tl* Warren Photographic; 216 *b* Warren Photographic; 217 *r* Warren Photographic; 218 *l* Warren Photographic; 219 *bl* Warren Photographic; 220 *tr* NHPA, *cl* NHPA; 221 *l* OSF; 222 *c* Warren Photographic; 223 *cr* Warren Photographic; 224 *tc* Warren Photographic, *bl* Warren Photographic; 225 *tr* Warren Photographic; *br* NHPA; 226 *bl* NHPA; 227 *t* Warren Photographic; 228 *bl* Warren Photographic; 229 *cr* Warren Photographic; 230 *cl* NHPA; 231 *tr* OSF, *br* Warren Photographic; 232 *t* Floyd Sayers, *cl* NHPA; 233 *cr* NHPA, *br* NHPA; 234 *tr* NHPA, *l* Ardea; 235 *bc* OSF, *tr* NHPA; 236 *br* OSF; 237 *b* OSF; 238 *tr* Warren Photographic; 239 *bl* Warren Photographic, *cr* Warren Photographic, *tr* NHPA; 240 *t* Warren Photographic; 241 *c* NHPA, *t* NHPA; 242 *cl* OSF; 243 *br* OSF, *tl* OSF, *tr* NHPA; 244 *bl* Warren Photographic, *tr* NHPA, *cl* NHPA; 245 *br* NHPA; 246 *tr* STILL Pictures, *br* Warren Photographic; 247 *tc* Floyd Sayers, *c* NHPA; 248 *bl* Planet Earth Pictures; 249 *tl* Planet Earth Pictures, *r* Planet Earth Pictures; 250 *cr* Warren Photographic, *tl* Warren Photographic; 251 *br* OSF; 252 *t* Warren Photographic; 253 *cr* OSF, *tc* Warren Photographic, *br* Warren Photographic, *tr* Warren Photographic; 255 *cr* OSF, *br* Warren Photographic; *cl* Warren Photographic, *tl* Warren Photographic; 256 *br* OSF, *cl* OSF; 257 *tr* OSF, *t* Warren Photographic; 258–259 *b* Planet Earth Pictures; 259 *t* Planet Earth Pictures; 260 *cl* OSF; 260–261 *c* OSF; 262 *cl* Planet Earth Pictures, *bl* Ardea; 263 *l* Planet Earth Pictures; 264 *r* Ardea; 265 *tc* OSF, *br* NHPA; 266 *tr* Warren Photographic; 267 *tr* Warren Photographic, *cr* NHPA, *br* NHPA; 268 *cl* Ardea; 268–269 *t* Ardea; 269 *tr* NHPA; 270 *tl* OSF, *tr* Warren Photographic; 271 *cl* OSF, *br* Warren Photographic; 272 *tl* Warren Photographic, *tr* NHPA; 273 *tl* OSF; 274 *l* Warren Photographic; 275 *br* OSF, *tr* OSF; 276 *tr* STILL Pictures, *t* Warren Photographic, *cl* NHPA; 277 *tl* OSF, *br* Warren Photographic; 278 *t* Gallo Images (SA); 279 *l* OSF; 280 *tr* STILL Pictures, *bl* OSF; 281 *b* STILL Pictures; 282 *bl* NHPA; 282–283 *c* Ardea; 283 *c* Warren Photographic, *br* Warren Photographic; 284 *tr* Warren Photographic; 285 *tr* STILL Pictures, *cl* OSF; 286 *bl* Warren Photographic, *r* NHPA; 287 *tr* Warren Photographic, *br* Warren Photographic; 288 *c* OSF; 289 *br* Warren Photographic, *t* NHPA; 290–291 *b* Warren Photographic; 291 *tr* NHPA, *c* NHPA; 292 *bl* Warren Photographic; 293 *cr* NHPA; 294 *bl* Warren Photographic, *tr* NHPA; 295 *t* NHPA; 296 *b* STILL Pictures; 297 *r* Warren Photographic, *cl* NHPA; 297 *tl* OSF; 298 *c* Warren Photographic; 298–299 *t* Warren Photographic, *b* Warren Photographic; 300 *cl* Warren Photographic, *b* NHPA; 301 *cr* Warren Photographic; 302 *bl* Warren Photographic; 303 *l* NHPA; 304 *tl* Warren Photographic; 307 *br* Warren Photographic.